We Need to Talk About . . .
Kevin Bridges

Kevin Bridges, Scotland's 'young comedy prodigy' (*Guardian*), has followed a meteoric path, from his first five-minute set in The Stand comedy club in Glasgow to selling out the SECC to a record-breaking 100,000 fans. He was born in Clydebank, and still lives in Glasgow. Now, at the tender age of just twenty-seven, Kevin puts pen to paper to tell his story so far in his brilliant memoir, *We Need to Talk About . . . Kevin Bridges*.

'Kevin Bridges might just become the best
stand-up in the land' *The Times*

'The Best Scottish Stand-up of his Generation' *Scotsman*

'One of the most exciting talents to have emerged from
Scotland since Billy Connolly' *Guardian*

We Need to Talk About . . .
Kevin Bridges

KEVIN BRIDGES

MICHAEL JOSEPH
an imprint of
PENGUIN BOOKS

MICHAEL JOSEPH

Published by the Penguin Group
Penguin Books Ltd, 80 Strand, London WC2R 0RL, England
Penguin Group (USA) Inc., 375 Hudson Street, New York, New York 10014, USA
Penguin Group (Canada), 90 Eglinton Avenue East, Suite 700, Toronto, Ontario, Canada M4P 2Y3
(a division of Pearson Penguin Canada Inc.)
Penguin Ireland, 25 St Stephen's Green, Dublin 2, Ireland (a division of Penguin Books Ltd)
Penguin Group (Australia), 707 Collins Street, Melbourne, Victoria 3008, Australia
(a division of Pearson Australia Group Pty Ltd)
Penguin Books India Pvt Ltd, 11 Community Centre, Panchsheel Park, New Delhi – 110 017, India
Penguin Group (NZ), 67 Apollo Drive, Rosedale, Auckland 0632, New Zealand
(a division of Pearson New Zealand Ltd)
Penguin Books (South Africa) (Pty) Ltd, Block D, Rosebank Office Park,
181 Jan Smuts Avenue, Parktown North, Gauteng 2193, South Africa

Penguin Books Ltd, Registered Offices: 80 Strand, London WC2R 0RL, England

www.penguin.com

First published 2014
002

Copyright © Kevin Bridges, 2014

The moral right of the author has been asserted

Set in 13.5/16pt Garamond MT Std
Typeset by Jouve (UK), Milton Keynes
Printed in Great Britain by Clays Ltd, St Ives plc

A CIP catalogue record for this book is available from the British Library

HARDBACK ISBN: 978–0–718–17845–1
TRADE PAPERBACK ISBN: 978–0–718–18013–3

www.greenpenguin.co.uk

Dedicated to Addison

We Need to Talk About . . .
Kevin Bridges

I

It's nearly 10 p.m. on a Friday night. The seat belt sign has just been turned off on my plane from Heathrow to Buenos Aires. I've opened up my bag, which had previously been safely stowed away in the overhead locker, switched on my laptop, opened a new Word document and here we are, another comedian writes an autobiography.

I didn't intend to have started writing on this flight but after a failed attempt at conversing in Spanish with a fellow passenger, I need to look busy and pretend not to be out of my depth in 'Club World Plus'.

I am evidently out of my depth, though. The guy has probably paid thousands for his ticket; I paid hundreds and would be sat at the opposite end of the cabin, but for a senior figure at British Airways introducing herself as a fan of my stand-up and offering a complimentary upgrade.

Extra legroom, a seat that reclines into a bed, a higher standard of food – all complimentary, no four-figure sums of money required and no working-class guilt that naturally accompanies any extravagant purchase – complimentary alcohol as well, and flight socks.

The socks, that's how the problem started, the fucking socks.

The guy had a Hispanic look, and he was putting on a pair of flight socks. I'd taken Spanish lessons prior to this trip, so I know the Spanish for 'Where are the socks?' I practised it a few times in my head, making sure of the correct tenses and all the specifics that make first-time foreign language

3

learners think, 'Close enough, for fuck's sake' when they're corrected.

I went in with full confidence, knowing fine well where the socks we located, but it wasn't about that. I didn't need this guy's help finding them. I had a long flight ahead, I was on my own and feeling a strange sensation of panic.

I was looking for a friendly conversation and wishing to proudly showcase my new language skills. '*Mi amigo, dónde están los calcetines?*' I asked, in a throwaway tone. It felt natural. 'Where did you get the socks, mate?' is how I'd hoped to sound.

I hoped to sound cool; it was a warning shot, a show of strength, fuelled by my own uncertainties, flying to Argentina on my own, a country where I know absolutely no one. 'It doesn't faze me, I speak the language, and I'll blend in. It'll be good. My only immediate concern is finding the flight socks.'

The guy turned and looked at me; he looked at me far too long without speaking. It wasn't the atmosphere I'd intended to create – the question had to be answered, fast.

I didn't even want a spoken answer, a pointed finger would have sufficed. The reassurance and the feeling of self-satisfaction that I'd conversed in Spanish was all that I'd been looking for.

I wish I'd hurried up with, '*Es tranquilo, tranquilo, mi amigo,*' and grabbed the socks out myself, but I'd asked the question, I'd committed.

'*Cal-seh-teen-es,*' he replied, correcting my pronunciation.

For the first time in years I felt myself blushing, a proper red face. I'd 'hit a riddy', as it's known in Glasgow. 'Riddy' means red in Glasgow, and I have no idea why, like 'dug' means dog. One change of a vowel and anyone not from the area is left baffled. It got worse, though. 'In that bottom drawer, just pull the little handle,' he'd gone on, in a Birmingham accent.

4

He'd corrected the Spanish in my question and then, in a show of zero confidence in my ability to understand the answer in a second language, he'd replied in English.

I'd been done, totally done.

I'd had him down as Argentinian, South American at least, but he was just a well-tanned businessman from the Midlands, who spoke fluent Spanish. I tried to laugh, the small-talk department of my brain anxiously rifling through the 'Birmingham' file: 'Who's your team, then, Villa? City? West Brom?'

He just went back to his iPad, back to looking at Excel documents or spreadsheets or whatever else people in suits who work on the way to work look at on their iPads; they never just chill out and play Angry Gran.

I haven't dressed with a potential upgrade in mind; I have a hooded jumper on, jeans and a pair of exhausted-looking Puma trainers. I'd have bought new holiday trainers, as is the tradition, but my last day in the UK was spent trying to locate Argentinian Pesos. I never imagined it being so difficult, but it seems it's a dying currency.

I haven't followed the global economic downturn as closely as I should. As a stand-up comedian it's important to know what's going on; you're a social commentator and you should know these things.

But I've never fully understood the complexities of the financial crisis. I see it as being like one of those Sky Atlantic, HBO shows that everyone else is talking about; you put it on one night, but it's season four, episode ten and you don't have a clue what is going on or who is who.

If you weren't in it from the start, you've been left behind, so you just ignore it. This guy knows his economics, I'd say. Definitely.

'*Cal-seh-teen-es.*'

I'm all for being educated, but it was his condescending tone, speaking to me as though I was sat in first class wearing a hooded jumper, jeans and a pair of exhausted-looking Puma trainers.

Flying to South America, solo.

He maybe thinks I've got about twenty condoms full of heroin in my stomach or a couple of suitcases full of cocaine checked in. He doesn't want a conversation; he wants to keep his distance. He can't be seen with me when we land, in case I get pounced on by armed cops, a fist in my arse and an Alsatian in my face.

I begin to think in my claustrophobic, beginning-of-a-long-haul-flight mindset, 'Why am I sitting here?' If this was a bus I could get up and move. I could get off at the next stop.

It is as if this could have been 'The Guy', the omnipresent guy who's feared by everyone who makes a living from trying to make strangers laugh, the guy who appears in your head before every gig, during every sound check, when the venue is empty, venues where you once watched Oasis and the Red Hot Chili Peppers.

You're on that stage tonight . . .

It is far-fetched, too far-fetched, but I'm terrified of that guy, the guy who will see through it all, the poster boy for all your anxieties. The guy who will finally say, 'Wow, wow, everybody, he's been getting away with this and nobody said anything?'

The guy who knows that you don't speak Spanish, that you shouldn't be sat next to these moneymen, these corporate whores, that you shouldn't be on a long-haul flight. He's the guy who reminds you that you have no place in such exalted company.

Alicante or Palma should have been the pinnacle of my worldly exploration, drinking room-temperature 330 ml cans

6

of Amstel and annoying the cabin crew. But I'm here now, and for the next fourteen hours The Guy and I are equals. And if he has any objections, he can take them up with the senior figure at BA who created this mess in the first place.

I hadn't planned on drinking much on this trip but I bought a packet of Kalms from Boots in Heathrow airport and the packet 'warns' that taken with alcohol, they cause drowsiness. You can't be bothered thinking when you're drowsy. It sounds an ideal state to be in.

They have a selection of whiskies; I ask for an Oban 14 or any other single malt. They don't have the Oban 14 but at least I sound like I know what I'm talking about, restoring some personal pride after the sock incident.

They have Glenlivet, Tony Soprano's favourite. I instantly feel better before it's even poured.

One Kalm and a Glenlivet 12.

I recline my seat and start to laugh into myself. I imagine the Brummie businessman's reaction if I were to place both flight socks on my hands and put on an impromptu sock-puppet show for him.

'*Cal-seh-teens*,' says the confused voice.

'*CAL-SEH-TEEN-ES!*' replies the angry voice.

The End.

A quick tools and word-count check shows we're at the 1408 stage.

I've given up reading books long before 1408 words, so if you've got here we can both begin to relax.

As I write this, I'm picturing you standing there, considering the purchase.

A comedian's autobiography?

I wonder if he ever used humour to deflect from his insecurities. To avoid being bullied.

Is there heartache behind the humour?

I wonder if he's a manic-depressive.

Tears of a clown?

Yes, all of that.

Some other stuff as well, but mainly that.

To paraphrase 1990s Nickelodeon stars Kenan and Kel (as I don't think anyone has ever done in the opening of their autobiography):

'Ahhh, here goes!'

First of all, I have never written a book before, and you probably haven't either, so there we have it; a connection is established between reader and writer.

Hopefully now you'll take this over to the till and I can accompany you for the next wee while. That's the benefit of book shops, reading the little bit and then deciding if the author deserves to be part of your carefully selected three-for-two deal, or part of your plane journey, train journey, your next bath, your next shite.

We're losing this luxury with online book shopping. That's far more of a gamble; all you can do is read the most critical review, read the most positive review, read the positive reviewer's other reviews – you need to see what the person's all about before going on their recommendation.

He might have loved the book you're considering buying, but he also loves books about Steve Jobs, the film *Drive*, he preferred *Prison Break* to *The Sopranos* and gave a three-star review to a toaster.

With online book shopping you can only read the first few lines when it's purchased and delivered to your door. By that time it's too late, it's yours.

It sits in the cabinet with the rest of them. *The Great Gatsby* – when were you ever going to read that? High school or never . . .

Thinking Fast and Slow? The Rules of Life? You didn't need a self-help book; you were just bored in WH Smith.

Next time buy a £1 Galaxy Cookie Crumble and relax.

A lesson learned, a vital lesson in self-improvement.

However you obtained this book, thank you and a very warm welcome.

I'm currently trying to fix up a music playlist that will help me unlock the memories and the characters who've shaped my life thus far. Music has always helped me to switch off, daydream and think a little deeper about things, big and small. As I begin to write this book, I realize that I haven't added a new song to my iTunes in years. I don't think I've downloaded a song since back in the Napster days.

Other than a few other wildcard tunes from the Napster era my music collection is made up entirely of CDs I've uploaded, most of which are from the mid-90s and stolen from my brother, John.

'Neighbourhood' by Space is the only song that tempts me to hit Play, but I know it won't be as good a song as I remembered. From the Napster time in my life I also have Limp Bizkit's 'Chocolate Starfish and the Hot Dog Flavored Water'.

What kind of title is that? Cruising about in his convertible, singing about 'keepin rollin'. SHUT IT, MATE!

It's easy to laugh now, but at the time I thought Fred Durst was the man. I think I even had the red New York Yankees hat, like everyone else in school at the time.

I remember having to refute allegations that my hat was a fake. 'A fake' was such a hurtful accusation to have levelled at an item of clothing or an accessory at school.

A lesson in parenting: they might look like Adidas trainers but that extra stripe could be catastrophic to your child's reputation. Four-stripe 'Adidas' trainers should be listed alongside violent films, computer games like *Grand Theft Auto* and Marilyn Manson as a tabloid media explanation for high-school gun massacres.

> It's understood he'd just had enough of it all following weeks of relentless mockery regarding his new trainers, which were said to have four stripes, tragically one more than the famous logo of sportswear giant Adidas.
>
> Sniggering was heard in the courtroom following the witness's testimony, with the judge also aiming a stern look of bemused outrage at the defendant's parents, whose eye for a bargain proved costly.
>
> The trial continues.

School could be a brutally harsh place. I'll get to all this later.

Right now British Airways Club World Plus is proving to be a brutally harsh place, especially now that I need to disturb the sleeping CEO or hedge-fund manager beside me as I stumble my way to the bathroom, situated at the front of the cabin, on this Airbus A340–800.

I'm twenty-seven years old; I turn twenty-eight this year so I think it is about time that I write my autobiography.

Being asked to write your life story induces quite a surreal feeling and one that taps into every insecurity in the human conscience. Who wants to read this? Who gives a fuck? Etc., etc. . . . All the nice, down-to-earth, modest disclaimers needed before convincing yourself to get on with it.

Maybe if I'd waited a few years I wouldn't have those thoughts, if I'd given it time to complete the necessary ascent up my own arsehole to become a real celebrity, paying someone to write this for me, boring the batteries flat on a tabloid journalist's Dictaphone, regaling it with exaggerated stories of hedonistic nights out and my showbiz friends, all the early stuff forgotten . . .

I have the advantage of still remembering the wee guy I was before you knew of me, the anxiety-ridden wee guy who worried about anything and everything, the wee guy who I think of every single night in the few meditational minutes I take before walking on stage in front of hundreds and sometimes thousands of people.

Convincing myself to write this took a while and I do realize it is a ridiculously young age for reflection, but seventeen years old is also a ridiculously young age to start out in stand-up comedy, traditionally a middle-aged, post-mental breakdown, post-battle with drugs and alcoholism, mid-divorce sport.

Over the following chapters I will be reminiscing about the good old days.

Back in the day, back when it was only the PlayStation 2, back when mobile phones had only 2 megapixel cameras, when iPods could hold only 1000 songs.

I've never felt my age, nor looked it.

'You've had a tough paper round, mate,' I just said to myself in my internal middle-England accent, the accent I also use when reading negative reviews on Trip Advisor.

I've never understood 'tough paper round' as a metaphor for a harsh upbringing; if you grow up in a shit hole, you've got a straightforward paper round.

Where I grew up, people read the *Sun* and the *Daily Record*, two light tabloids, easy to carry, easy to fold and fit through a letterbox. In an affluent suburb, people read the *Telegraph*, *The Sunday Times*, the *Guardian*, with all the supplements and pull-outs: Sophie Dahl's top-ten dinner party recipes, a free Frisbee.

Difficult to fold without causing damage, going round to collect paper money a few nights later and the quantity surveyor/estate agent/middle-management wanker refuses to pay, complaining that his paper was ripped and his Frisbee was missing.

That's a tough paper round.

I had a piss-easy paper round.

The working class also tip far more generously.

We're an hour into this flight; two other corporate-whore, business-type travellers behind me are talking about their respective air mile totals. My friend from Birmingham is fast asleep.

It's a fourteen-hour journey, a high scorer for the avid air-mile collector, and it's set to send the guy on the aisle seat over the thirty thousand mark, the elusive target for a free flight, from what I hear.

I've never bothered with air miles. I turn positives into negatives too easily for that. I wouldn't see thirty thousand air miles as being due a free flight; I'd see thirty thousand air miles as being due a plane crash. I wonder how they'd react if I joined in their conversation and volunteered my own views on collecting air miles. I decide not to, though. They don't seem the sort of guys who laugh at much. I picture them in the clubhouse of a prestigious golf course with more guys like them, drinking red wine, making self-deprecating jokes about their putting abilities and talking about their favourite episodes of *Top Gear*.

This makes me smile, before I put on my headphones and get back to my music: 'Female of the Species' and 'Mr. Psycho'. Space had some pretty catchy tunes. I wonder what they're up to these days. The same with kids Kenan and Kel. I'd rather not know and just preserve the fond recollections.

Before Sky, Nickelodeon and Kenan and Kel, *The Hurricanes* was a children's TV favourite of mine, a cartoon about a football team of good guys. They were a team of total underdogs, but they and their Scottish manager, Jock Stone, and his female assistant (a ground-breaking show) would always come off best in the face of adversity, up against dirty tactics and cheating opponents.

I seem to remember them winning every game 2–1 after conceding a controversial early goal. Great show. I'd buy the box set if it were available. Maybe they could bring it back, or at least a spin-off, a far more cynical spin-off: sports governing bodies investigating irregular betting activity prompted by the frequently repeating 2–1 score line, which threatens to taint the team's achievements in their mid-90s heyday.

'Neighbourhood' by Space has finished playing. Writing about mid-90s children's television means I now have the *Wizadora* theme tune in my head. 'Wizadora, we adore her, she's the one with the something, something, something . . .'

I only remember the edgier playground version: 'Wizadora, we ignore her, she's the one with her finger up her bum.' She joined the likes of 'Margaret Thatcher (the bare-bum scratcher)' in the repertoire of slanderous primary school cover ballads.

The Hurricanes, Kenan and Kel, Wizadora – all of these shows were probably total shite. It's a shame to admit it, but any midweek kids' TV show in that 3–5 p.m. slot will only evoke good memories and be synonymous with the hyperactive feeling of having finished school for another day.

It's also a shame when it emerges that the presenters were paedos.

I can only imagine what those of you who grew up in the 1980s must be feeling.

I think I'll go for a font change here. By the time this

comes to print, the good people at Penguin will have decided on all that but for now I'm in charge.

When I write out a stand-up routine on a computer I always use Comic Sans font, to make it funny, obviously.

Who's going to laugh at a joke that was initially written in Times New Roman? An amateur mistake.

There's also Wingdings, the font with all the pictures instead of letters. I'd go for that, but you'd need to be Rain Man to understand it.

I've browsed a few fonts and decided upon Lucida Sans, mainly because it sounds like a woman, and she sounds like a ride.

I'm not sure if you care which font I'm writing in, but that's where we're at. I feel it's important to keep the reader in the loop.

I've always been a fairly easily distracted person, a bit of a daydreamer, and I definitely struggle to follow instructions.

How's that for a character description?

Thankfully I am writing a book based on a story of relative success as opposed to a CV.

How many job interviews would that opening 'about me' section deny me?

3

I always try to resist the view that stand-up comedy is a job. I don't mean that in a condescending 'I can't believe I get paid to do something I love so much' sense. The people who say those things tend to be the most ruthless, career-minded, dead-behind-the-eyes robots in entertainment.

To me, stand-up comedy is a thing of extremes too disparate to be dismissed simply as a 'job'.

It comes in cycles, in my opinion.

There are times it means much more than a job and requires so much more from you. Times it becomes your life and to call it a job would be ridiculous.

These are the times when it is most exhilarating and rewarding, when you're struggling to sleep because of the ideas that keep appearing in your head, forcing you out of bed to find a pen.

You're waking up beside scrap pieces of paper with these ideas scribbled down, sometimes just a few words.

A few words there to work with all day, to build on and add to and try out in front of an audience that same night and then decide whether to bin the idea, go home and rework it again, or keep it and add and add to it until you feel it turn into a whole new stand-up routine.

The latter is the greatest thing in comedy, for me.

One of the most satisfying feelings I've experienced in life, and the times when everything else is forgotten, is when it's just you and your stupid, daft thoughts that have created something you can be proud of, something which makes a crowd of people laugh and applaud.

There are times when it feels like a job, though, and that can be as miserable as the aforementioned can be euphoric. When you slip into a bit of a rut and a show is just another night at work. You're not taking risks any more and nothing excites you about performing.

It's important to recognize these ruts and rectify them, by doing something different. Maybe something that frightens you, like dropping the best joke from your set or telling a story a different way. It's your story, your jokes; you don't want it to become a script.

You're a comedian, not an actor.

Throw in a brand-new joke right at the start of your set, see what happens. Or even walk away for a while, cancel everything you have booked in your diary until you rediscover what that initial attraction was.

I begin to write this not long after finishing a tour, a tour that broke box-office records and all that stuff that doesn't really matter.

Nobody remembers Richard Pryor for how many tickets he sold.

I've never been concerned with numbers but, obviously, when thousands of people come out to see you for so many nights it does leave you a little taken aback.

It is what most people strive for.

The fame and the popularity are key components in how you view yourself and how you believe you are viewed by others, especially today, in a world where status, style, image and money seem to count for everything, a world that would have definitely left me behind if it hadn't been for stand-up comedy.

I don't resent fame or celebrity or anything like that but I definitely see through it; there is something really tragic about those who don't.

Reaching the 'household name' level makes it easy to forget the road up and you feel yourself becoming driven, more career-minded and more protective of what you have, probably because of the novelty of having something for the first time.

I'd planned to take a year away from comedy, taking advice from my dad, who told me I should step back, get off the 'treadmill' (an expression he must have heard elsewhere as he's never been near a gym).

I lasted only a month of my year off before I decided to book myself in for a few spots at the Stand comedy club in Glasgow, where it all started for me.

The gigs were therapeutic and it brought everything back to the beginning.

I felt like myself, standing up there, in jeans, a T-shirt and a pair of trainers, like for my very first gig, when I knew nothing of stand-up, when I just spoke about my life at the time.

It was Jerry Seinfeld who said that a good crowd will help you write and a bad crowd will help you edit; I totally agree.

When a gig is going well it's pretty self-indulgent to bask in it all. I feel you need to keep building on these ideas of yours that the audience have clearly bought into, adding on an extra few lines, rinsing the joke dry – even stuff you thought of only on the way to the venue or backstage but didn't think funny enough to find a pen to give it a life, throw it in there.

Recognizing and acting on these moments when they come is what can make a great comic.

When an audience are in raptures at a part of the show,

the fear of the next bit not being as funny or causing a dip will set in but you can navigate that. I used to have times when I felt a warm satisfaction during this sort of storming show, when I'd take a moment to think, 'This is great!' Part of your brain is saying, 'Job done,' but you need to avoid feeling complacent and see how far you can take it.

Experiment before something happens, something that needs to be reacted to in an instant. A glass will smash, a drunk will unleash a barrage of futile shite, a fight will break out, someone will get up to go to the toilet, a phone will ring. Anything as big or as subtle as that can totally change the flow.

There are so many gear changes to make and then there's the part of making it look easy. That's the real skill.

No one wants to see a self-conscious, nervous wreck, even if you may feel like one.

Relax the audience into thinking you're just a guy up there shooting the shit; convince everyone watching that it could be them or their funny pal on the stage.

At the bar after one of the shows (a fatal time and place for a comic to hang around; it's where many egos have been destroyed), a guy who looked in his forties came over to me and said, 'Well done.' I thanked him before he followed up with, 'Anybody can do what you do, though, mate.'

It had been meant as a dig, an archetypal 'Made in Scotland' dig, but, after thinking about it, I decided that it was one of greatest compliments I've ever received.

Anybody can do what I do and do what I've done. I wholeheartedly agree with that.

The point is that there are people who actually go and do it, and then there are the people at the bar who just tell how they could have done it.

A few weeks after my somewhat therapeutic gigs at the

Stand and a few months into my year away from everything, an offer came in, this offer, to tell you my story.

It's been almost ten years now since I lay awake in my bedroom thinking about where my life would go and what I wanted to do with myself and now I'm on a plane to Argentina, heading over to watch Boca Juniors versus River Plate.

That may mean nothing to you but it's something I've wanted to do since watching Channel 5 on a Friday night as a child and seeing clips of a chubby Diego Maradona, cigar in his mouth, both hands in the air, leading the crowds singing in 'La Bombonera', as part of the global football round-up on a programme called *Trans World Sport*.

To me, this trip is one I've thought about since childhood, something I told myself I'd love to do, safe in the knowledge that it was unrealistic, but now I've run out of reasons not to go for it, and here I am. I wasn't such a cultured world football enthusiast as a child that I'd stay awake purposely to watch *Trans World Sport*. It was more that I found it difficult to sleep following the adrenalin rush that came with watching an erotic thriller, the erotic thrillers that made Channel 5 on a Friday night the must-watch channel.

A channel that went on to face a struggle against the rise of home Internet, gradually losing its stranglehold on the market of pubescent young male viewers and never really recovering.

I think I'll hit File and Save now and I'll be back in a couple of weeks, well, in a page.

When I return I'll share my story.

There's no real tragedy, no heroin, no hookers and very little violence.

If that's what you're looking for in an autobiography, then I'd highly recommend those of Anthony Kiedis, and Slash from Guns N' Roses; maybe with these you can complete your three-for-two deal. (I'm guessing you have bought this book by now; if you've made it this far without making a purchase then the staff at your local bookshop are extremely tolerant.)

'Columbia' by Oasis has just come on my playlist.

I'll have a listen to that and try to get some sleep before we begin our descent to Buenos Aires.

There we were, now here we are!

Hasta luego, mi amigos.

4

My earliest memories consist mainly of me crying, my mum crying and my occasional acts of rage-fuelled vandalism.

My old bedroom in my parents' house has had the same wallpaper since I was a child; despite a few paint jobs over the years, the aftermath of one of my first temper tantrums is still proudly on show.

In protest at being put to bed for a display of petulance in front of a house full of my mum and dad's friends and family, I'd shown my disapproval by digging my nails into the soft, spongy, patterned wallpaper, the wallpaper that every council house had by the mid-1990s. I'd done as much scraping as I could until I felt my point had been made.

My dad came up to check on me and maybe even apologize for what I felt was a harsh early dismissal from the living-room festivities. He was always the first to take my side, no doubt feeling some sort of responsibility when I showcased my short fuse.

My short fuse that I'd definitely inherited from him.

He probably walked in to show solidarity with my cause, but when he saw the baldy patches on the wall and the wallpaper on the carpet, he went absolutely mental.

He was working whilst my mum stayed at home to look after me, having quit her job in a whisky distillery shortly before I was born. We'd recently swapped houses with my grandparents from my mum's side – Annie and Tommy.

Annie and Tommy had still been living in the same house where my mum and her two young brothers, George and

Kevin, grew up, in the Hardgate area of the town of Clyde-bank, on the outskirts of Glasgow.

My mum, dad and my older brother, John, all lived in a two-bedroom, second-floor flat around the corner from Annie and Tommy. But when I came on the scene, Annie and Tommy suggested their house would be more suited for us, with the extra bedroom and a garden area.

The new house had only just been decorated. My dad was the only one out working to pay the rent for his wife and two sons and I was at his back causing destruction.

He calmed down pretty quickly after the wallpaper-ripping incident, and a short while later a wardrobe was moved, strategically placed to cover the bare patches on the wall. Everything was harmonious again thanks to a little bit of working-class feng shui.

Thursday, 13 November 1986 was the day I was born, and also, according to Wikipedia, the day a French comedian named Thierry Le Luron died. I haven't managed to find much of his work, but I used to perform a routine which ended in me attempting the French for 'Do you mind if I shite in your kettle?'

That can be my own personal tribute to the man.

Thursday, 13 November, almost exactly nine months after Valentine's Day, so I was maybe conceived after a blissfully romantic evening. But the ten-year age gap between me and my older brother and also the fact we had to move house not long after I was born means I was more likely to have been an accident.

'An apology letter from Durex' was the school insult for these situations, I think. However I got here, I was causing mayhem right from the beginning, before the beginning, even.

Twenty-six hours of labour I put my mum through. My

dad claims this stubbornness and refusal to do things on anyone else's terms have stayed with me my whole life, which is a kind of compliment, I suppose. I like a long lie; I still do to this day.

Every time I'm with my dad and we pass through the Partick area of Glasgow, near where the Queen Mother Hospital where I was born used to be, my dad still points at 'Lena's' fish and chip shop and tells me how he had one of the best fish suppers of his life the night I was born.

He'd been following my mum's instructions to 'fuck off' after having the audacity to complain about being hungry during her twenty-six-hour struggle.

He quickly ran down to the chippy and was back up to see the birth of his second child. His burst of pace was definitely a result of fearing the ramifications if he hadn't been back in time.

I realize that I'm doing little here to shatter the stereotypes of a West of Scotland upbringing, but being born with the smell of grease, deep-fried chips and battered haddock hanging in the air didn't take away from the occasion; it was my grand entrance to the world, my debut as a person.

I wouldn't have been named Kevin if it wasn't for the traumatic childbirth experience my mum went through. At the start of it all, the doctor who was to deliver me, Dr Kevin Hanretty, had been jokingly hinting to my mum how he'd never had a child named after him despite years of working in the maternity ward of the Queen Mother Hospital.

My mum explained that she had two brothers, one named George and one named Kevin, and that it wouldn't be fair on George to name me Kevin, and she certainly wasn't planning to go through an ordeal like this again just to christen a child George (or Georgina).

But after twenty-six hours of excruciating pain, I think

she was past caring; she'd have named me after the doctor even if his name had been Adolf.

So there I was, Kevin Andrew Bridges.

I still reckon my dad should have relinquished his hold on the middle name, but I'm sure after all these years my Uncle George has gotten over the snub.

I've asked my mum what my name would have been if the doctor hadn't got involved and she told me she'd always liked the name Brian.

Brian Bridges – far more showbiz.

I imagine there's a Brian Bridges out there tonight, hosting a 1980s pop quiz at an all-inclusive holiday resort or playfully flirting with pensioners in a bingo hall somewhere in Fife.

5

By all accounts I wasn't born at a very happy time. Months before I was born, Annie, my 'Nana' (she'd never wanted to be known as Gran or Granny as she felt it'd make her sound old) had been diagnosed with cancer. Being pregnant, together with looking after her mum, who was facing the prospect of dying before her sixtieth birthday, meant my mum was going through a pretty difficult time.

My dad's dad, my Granddad John, after whom my older brother was named (obviously a much more straightforward birth hence my mum sticking to the plan) died when I was just three months old. He was an old school, hard-working guy – my only reference point to what he was like is my dad telling me Sir Alex Ferguson reminds him a lot of his dad.

He'd served with the Royal Navy during the Second World War and then spent the rest of his days working in the Singer sewing machine factory, where my dad would go on to work, and where the majority of men in Clydebank worked before it closed in 1980, leaving huge unemployment in the area.

From what I gather from talking to my dad about his dad, their relationship wasn't as close as the one my dad has with my brother and me. Only towards the end of his dad's life did he really begin to appreciate what a good man he was.

My mum speaks very highly of her father-in-law, who made her feel welcome into his family and who really thanked her for helping my dad to grow up, settle down, and stop drinking and being a general loose cannon.

A taxi driver once told me: 'When Andy Bridges was drinking, you stayed out of Duntocher.' He meant this in a complimentary sense and was proud to be congratulating me on being the son of a local hard man.

I found it funny in its ridiculousness and still quote the 'When Andy Bridges . . .' line to my dad. I've never seen him have even one can of beer, nor could I imagine him in any sort of fight.

I think the taxi driver was affectionately letting me know that my dad was, like so many other working guys from the small towns in Glasgow and surrounding areas, an 'arsehole with a drink in him'. My dad himself has since confirmed this.

An arsehole. A good arsehole, but an arsehole all the same.

He's now a reformed arsehole, thanks to my mum.

One thing a lot of people find strange to hear is that I've never had a pint with my dad, be it on a birthday, on holiday, going to the football, or even for the landmark 'first pint with your old man on your eighteenth birthday' custom.

He stopped drinking after waking up in a police cell, about six years before I was born and when John was only four years old. He'd finished his work at Singer's on a Friday afternoon and headed straight to the pub to put a sizeable dent in his wages, as was the weekly tradition amongst himself and the majority of his colleagues.

The workers at the time were paid cash in hand, which was great news to local landlords and bookmakers, but could often be devastating to the workers' families.

At the time my mum, dad and John lived in a top-floor flat in an area of Clydebank called Dalmuir. It was a basic one-bedroom council flat, which didn't offer much other than being on the same street as a shit load of takeaway food shops.

Chinese, Indian, Turkish and, of course, a few chippies and those takeaways that don't have an identity – no prejudice, they'll deep fry food from any country and serve it with chips, in a polystyrene tray.

It was a culinary multicultural melting pot where you could significantly increase your chances of a heart attack.

The street hasn't changed much nowadays really. Some more takeaways have opened (a few cunning entrepreneurs taking advantage of the clear gap in the market!), a pawnshop, several off-licences, a bookie's and, rather ironically, a shop called 'Walter's Trophy Shop'. Some prick called Walter looked at the takeaways, the bookie's, the pawnshop, the off-licences and thought, 'This looks like a place where people achieve.'

On the walk home from the pub, being drunk and carrying a bag of pakoras, my dad was overcome with fatigue and his legs decided they couldn't take him any further. But convincing anyone else that 'fatigue' was to blame seemed a big ask; it's like one of the excuses drunk people make for the state they've been in when they're refusing to hear a bad word about alcohol.

A few years later he was diagnosed with rheumatoid arthritis, so it's maybe fair to blame the feelings of tiredness, at least partly.

In a drunk (and exhausted) state, he'd used a parked car to prop himself up. But being propped up wasn't offering the respite he needed, so he'd grabbed the car handle and opened the door, which was unlocked (everyone was a lot more trusting 'back in the day', he'll always tell me, missing the irony that it was actions like his that contributed to this changing) and sat in the driver's seat before passing out.

A woman who'd witnessed this immediately phoned the police and reported an attempted car theft; an attempted car theft by a man who was in no fit state to successfully execute a car theft. Anyway, the police soon arrived to find my dad asleep at the wheel. He was arrested and taken to the police station to be charged.

He woke up mortified and with no recollection of the night before. Fortunately the owner of the car knew him and took to his defence and the charges were dropped.

My mum, who'd been at home with her young son, not knowing where her husband had been all night, packed all of her and John's things and moved back in with her mum and dad.

It took my dad weeks of apologies, to my mum, to my Nana and my Granddad Tommy. Eventually my mum, not wanting to live the tragic life of being stuck at home looking after a child whilst her husband worked all week and then drank all the proceeds, issued an ultimatum: it was his family or being the life and soul of the party in the pubs and running wild with his mates.

I don't think she ever told him never to drink again, but he took it upon himself to stop completely.

In place likes Clydebank, the pubs are full of funny guys, cheery guys; people who everyone loves, but who tend to be bastards to those who love them. He decided against being that guy and it is something I'll always be proud of him for.

I've never heard any fighting stories from my dad or fighting stories from others about him. But there is at least that one taxi driver out there who is doing his bit to perpetuate the myth that he was a real tough bastard, who had an aura only seen in lead characters of western movies, a man who could clear a whole village just by ordering up a shot of whisky.

My dad tells me, though, that my Granddad John, known as 'Dixie' throughout the village of Duntocher, was a no-nonsense type of guy, a man of principles, a man who was well respected. Well respected by most in the area with the exception, in one instance, of my other granddad, Tommy.

Years before my mum and dad had met, John and Tommy were involved in a punch-up outside a pub following a 'debate' about Ireland's role in the First World War. I say 'debate' as I imagine it started out as a debate, but with alcohol's assistance it was promptly fast-tracked to argument status before moving to full-on physical combat.

There was never any tension between them and they went on to become good friends, confessing to my mum and dad about the fight not long after it became clear they were going to be the father-in-law of each other's child.

My mum told me the incident became known simply as 'The Fight' and was often brought up and discussed in great, undoubtedly exaggerated, detail at Christmas, birthdays and any other family event, with the two of my granddads showing modesty seldom associated with the ancient art of pugilism, the two of them claiming the other had won the fight.

Both men would sit in the corner drinking cans of Export and whisky and complimenting their opponent's performance. Neither could have been more fulsome in his praise of the other's key attributes, the talk of great strength, speed and technique.

The way my dad describes it, every family occasion became like an episode of ESPN Classics, with the two sat on the couch talking as though it were Muhammad Ali and Joe Frazier reminiscing about the 'Thrilla in Manila'.

Although the fight itself was a subject of thorough in-depth analysis, the cause of it was never really brought up. The fact that the fight stemmed from a heated conversation on Ireland probably summed up the differences in the two of them. John was an ex-Royal Navy man whilst Tommy had refused to serve in the Second World War; he was a 'conscientious objector', I'm told, choosing instead to go down the mines. However misguided Tommy may have been as a young guy, his family were Irish and he was immensely proud of these roots.

A television show I'd love to do is *Who Do You Think You Are?* I think it would be worthwhile tracing the Scottish and Irish history of my grandparents. I know only that my Granny Jane's family were from Mayo, Tommy's people were from Sligo and my Nana's family came from Dublin, with some of them moving to Glasgow during the famine and some to Liverpool.

I don't mean to bore you here with all this family tree shite, but it is something I'm interested in and that I think about a lot. I recently read a book entitled *The Fight* by a writer called Norman Mailer. The book, surprisingly not about my two granddads' Friday night bar brawl, focused on another fight which took place in the 1970s: 'The Rumble in the Jungle', Muhammad Ali versus George Foreman.

For any younger readers, George Foreman was a World Champion boxer; Ali wasn't a hot-headed technophobe going to extreme lengths to take out some anger on a kitchen appliance.

The book tells you a lot about African culture and beliefs, owing to the writer being based in the Congolese capital, Kinshasa, for weeks prior to the fight. He mentions a thing called 'Bantu' philosophy, which he roughly explains is the belief that every man is the combined force of those who have been before him.

I seek some solace in that when I feel under pressure or before I go on stage, when I'm getting myself motivated, when the nervous energy is building, when the reality of preparing to stand in front of strangers with nothing but your thoughts hits you.

I take ten minutes away on my own to think everything through, my jokes, my reasons for doing this, positive thoughts, funny thoughts, thoughts about the people who inspire me and also, every night, my grandparents, who I never really knew and who never got to see me perform and go on to be the first person in our family to truly do something they loved for a living.

I don't know if I fully understand Bantu philosophy, and from what I gather after further reading it has been largely discredited, like most belief systems. Whatever, though, it's a nice thing to think of.

My Nana died when I was eighteen months old. I think about her and imagine what she'd have been like. I know my mum maybe never really got over the shock of losing her, and losing her at what should have been a happy time.

As sad as it is, I'm sure she'd be delighted at how everyone turned out, and I am constantly stopped and told by elderly people in my home town how she was a generous, kind and caring person and how much of her they see in my mum.

Before Annie died, she said to my mum that she was sad she'd never see me grow up, but that she was convinced I was born for a reason. I don't think this was meant in a 'he'll go on to make a bit of cash and buy your house for you' kind of way, but that having me around would stop my mum spiralling into a grieving depression with not much else to think about and focus her days on. John was at school, had loads of pals and was happy, whilst my dad would be out working, but now she had someone who was utterly dependent on her.

Consequently, I grew up with a very close bond with my mum. Coupled with the big age gap between my older brother and me, and the fact we'd spend every single day together, just the two of us, I became a proper mummy's boy.

Rappers and R 'n' B artists can say that and make it sound cool, but I was a mummy's boy in the most tragically uncool way imaginable, panicking if we were separated for even a few minutes.

6

My first day at nursery was when my mum knew she had a problem.

I would have been three years old when she enrolled me into St Mary's nursery in Duntocher.

I was allocated a place in the afternoon group, which would mean I'd be in from around 1 p.m. until 4 p.m., five days a week. They hardly sound the most gruelling hours, but I would make sure that for everyone around me, they were.

My mum would soon be starting her new job with West Dunbartonshire Council, working part time as a home help, and the plan was that she would have all morning to look after me. We'd go to the shops, she'd clean the house, do some cooking and all the usual domestic stuff. Then she'd take me to nursery and head off to do her shifts locally, finishing in time to pick me up, go home and cook dinner. By this time my dad would be home from work, and she'd go back out for a few more hours, working teatime and early evening shifts.

The mornings I'd spend watching cartoons and a show called *Playbus* and then a show called *Mr Boom*. Mr Boom was supposed to be a spaceman; he lived on the moon and played a whole selection of musical instruments, at the same time.

He had a mouth organ attached to his jaw, easily accessed for his instrumental solos in between lyrics. He had a cymbal on his head, a drum on his back and a keyboard at his fingers, and he'd sing these wee songs every day to entertain the children before a hard day at nursery. He didn't entertain me, though. The man was clearly a multi-talented musician, but I always remember him being a bit of a creepy fucker.

He scared me a little bit at that age, but I was petrified of everything. As well as Mr Boom, I had an irrational fear of Lion Bars. This fear stemmed from a throwaway comment from my brother, who was trying to talk me out of putting a crippling dent in our budget during a routine Sunday night trip to the ice-cream van.

John would be given money by Mum and told to get himself what he wanted and a little thing for me. I'd usually accompany him on the journey and he'd teach me how to cross the road properly and attempt to answer as many of my rapid-fire questions as he could.

The ice-cream van used to intrigue me, the sheer selection, with just this one man driving around amongst all these crisps, chocolate and ice cream.

The guy in the van was pretty friendly and he'd sense my fascination; one day he even let me climb in the van and have a look around. It kind of shattered the illusion but, still, it was considerate of him.

John has always been a fair guy, so rather than indulge in any excessive spending on high-end confectionery like Munchies or Mintolas and fob me off with a ten-pence mixture, he'd settle for more modest purchases to allow me a Milky Way or a packet of Chocolate Buttons and a ten-pence mixture. He was under strict instructions not to buy me a cone on account of a previous carpet-threatening incident.

I was starting to sense John was a soft touch and, with my built-in resistance to being treated second to him, I decided that I'd have whatever he was having. John had asked for a Lion Bar, so I asked for a Lion Bar as well. Not a luxury purchase, but by no means a bargain.

John tried to explain that this would make me sick and how a Lion Bar was a more sophisticated, grown-up chocolate bar. I wasn't for lowering my demands, though. I had a sense of my own rights, particularly when it came to sibling rivalry.

If I was told to go to bed, I'd ask why John wasn't being told to go to bed as well, never taking into account that John was ten years older than me. We were brothers, we had the same mum and dad, therefore I believed we should have been treated the same.

I only ever remember John as a grown-up; even when he was fourteen or fifteen and I was four or five, he still seemed like a man.

Our relationship wasn't a traditional older-and-younger-brother one, at least until later on in life anyway, when the gap seemed to close.

I'd ask him why he didn't beat me up and do things that other people's big brothers did. Mark would beat up Gary, his little brother, and Stephen would beat up Mark, his little brother.

John was there when it mattered, though, and he was kind to me, even if I drove him a bit nuts at times.

John is laid-back and the total opposite of me, much calmer, more content and consistent, and during his childhood and teenage years I don't think he gave my mum and dad anywhere near the problems I did during mine.

I've always found John funny, and making him laugh would give me a sense of approval, like I was his mate and not a burden to him, which is a reflection of my own inferiority complex and nothing to do with anything he ever said or did.

I think I looked up to John a lot and I'd talk about him, proudly, in a 'my big brother' sense.

I can't picture John ever doing anyone a bad turn, even if he was tempted, on several occasions, to accept my invitations and give me a good hiding.

My dad's auntie Lilly, who was well known for her kindness, once saw us at chapel and came over to talk to my mum and dad. Before she left, she gave money to both John and me in a 'get yourself something nice, son' old auntie kind of way. These spontaneous acts of generosity are usually followed by parents protesting, 'Don't be daft, that's too much,' with the children thinking, 'Fucking stay out of this, Mum, we're getting weighed in here.'

Lilly had given John a £10 note and me a £5 note, which was pretty fair since I was ten years younger, although I had no hesitation in speaking out in protest at the inequalities in her payment structure. 'How come John got a brown one and I got a blue one?' I asked.

They all laughed. I was deadly serious, though.

Anyway, John was good at keeping me in line. But the Lion Bar debacle was reaching a stand-off and John, looking to keep the peace and not just point-blank refuse me the Lion Bar (I was still at the age when I could use tears and a tantrum as a bargaining tool), decided to tell me a Lion Bar would be too frightening for me as some of the wrappers contained an actual lion.

At three years old I was gobsmacked, speechless, utterly silenced.

An actual lion – wow! I realized I was in far too deep.

John could have spent the lot on himself and it wouldn't even have registered. I was stunned. An actual lion . . .

I don't think John was aware of my mentally unstable state; he didn't know that this would stay with me.

He'd probably totally forgotten about the comment and that trip to the ice-cream van until Christmas Day, a few months later. My dad was unwrapping a selection box for me. He went to open a Lion Bar, and I jumped up and flew behind my mum screaming, 'Don't open that! Do not open that! John said there could be a lion in there!'

I was calmed down and reassured by my dad, who opened it with me looking at him as if he was Steve Irwin. 'It's fine,' he said, as he jokingly inspected the inside before taking a bite.

I think John got a telling-off, a row for feeding a naive, impressionable youngster with this sort of fear-mongering.

I've never been a fan of Lion Bars since. Maybe it's the taste or Nestlé's trade practices, or maybe there's still that little bit of fear in my head that I could pick the wrong one and be mauled and severed to death.

The morning of my first day at nursery I remember watching television, playing with my toy cars and having a great time, except, of course, for Mr Boom frightening the shit out of me. In the afternoon my mum and I walked from the house round to the nursery, about a ten-minute walk. A ten-minute walk during which I probably bombarded her with questions and spoke all sorts of inane drivel.

I was a bit of a motor mouth and quite chirpy and excited when I was in my comfort zone, my comfort zone being when I wasn't far from my mum.

We walked into the classroom and I was introduced to the Nursery Nurse, Mrs Parkinson, who gave us the tour, showed us all the toys and a fridge full of milk and biscuits. She introduced us to the other children and mums as they began arriving. It was a perfectly friendly, peaceful and happy wee place.

I wandered off, my curiosity taking me into the Wendy house, where a few of my new classmates had assembled. I crawled in to see what we were going to be dealing with.

My mum must have thought it was a breakthrough moment: the timid, nervous wreck of a child who'd hide behind her when anyone she knew said hello to me in Asda was now off exploring, not a worry in the world. Somebody could have brought in a multipack of Lion Bars and I'd still have been too besotted by my new surroundings to care.

Then came the turning point, the game changer. My mum, thinking I was settled, had said goodbye to Mrs Parkinson and was walking out of the nursery door, her mind probably turning to her afternoon off and having the house to herself for a few hours. But, seeing her leave, I let out a panicked, piercing, hysterical scream: 'MUMMMM!'

'This wasn't what I signed up for,' I was thinking. 'You're coming to nursery as well.'

My mum turned back to reassure me, but by this point I was struggling to get out of the Wendy house, too overcome with emotion to calmly kneel down and crawl out the door. I stood up but I was taller than the Wendy house, so as I stood up the Wendy house came off the floor, ripped from its foundations.

I was trying to run but I couldn't see, owing to my head being stuck in the highest point of the Wendy house roof. The back wall was banging off the heads of the other residents, who had by now also started crying, terrified at the mayhem that was spreading throughout the nursery.

Mrs Parkinson rushed over to try to restore order. The other parents had no idea what was going on, and all they could see were my feet and a moving Wendy house. In my fear, I managed to find the strength to throw the Wendy house off my head, toppling it to the floor and leaving it in pieces, destroyed.

I ran towards my mum, absolutely distraught and crying inconsolably. She was utterly stunned as she surveyed the aftermath of my destruction. Wendy house debris and hysterical toddlers everywhere. There had probably been smoother entrances.

It was pretty evident she was going to have problems.

My mum stayed in the class and helped Mrs Parkinson with the recovery operation, whilst I sat in the corner, crying and keeping a look-out for any sudden movements towards the door. At around 4 p.m. we headed home, the rest of the class, my mum and me all traumatized.

I'd established myself as being a bit mental, which is probably a smart move on your first day in prison, but I'd say nursery is a little different.

My dad came home from work just after 5 p.m. to see me still sat on the couch, staring at the wall and doing the heavy, staggered breaths that children do after they've been crying hysterically. My mum explained all. I don't think he fully believed her, but this wasn't to be a one-off.

I don't reckon any of them thought this chaotic day would set the tone for the next few years, all through my stint at nursery and on through primary school. But sadly it did . . .

7

It was fair to say nursery was a struggle, from what I can remember. After the summer holidays, my first day at primary school was almost an identical re-make of the emotionally charged drama of my first outing at nursery.

My first day at primary school was the first day I remember meeting Gary Docherty. Gary would become one of my best friends and have his name shortened to 'Doc' and then 'Big Doc' as he gradually grew to the point where he was taller than some of the teachers.

My mum and his dad are first cousins and my mum had been stood talking with Gary's mum at the school gates, waiting to meet the teachers, taking photographs of us in our new uniforms and making a fuss about us, saying all the usual 'can't believe how fast they're growing up' shite that parents talk.

Sending your child to school for the first time is a monumental milestone for a parent, I'd say. Our mums stood there, trying to get us to talk. Gary made an effort and drove the basic conversation, whilst I anxiously sought refuge behind my mum.

The teachers came out to collect us and file us into lines; they told us to find a 'partner', someone to walk hand in hand with into the assembly hall to see what classes we'd be in.

My mum and Gary's mum encouraged us to be partners, probably my mum more so as she'd had a year of trying to get me into nursery without a scene and thought it'd be better if I'd met a 'wee pal' and a potential ally.

Understandably apprehensive, my mum began to relax and stood with the other parents, waving us off. As soon as I entered the assembly hall, I panicked. I looked around at the size of the place and at how many of us there were. My year hadn't looked as strong in numbers when we were lined up, with our partners, in an orderly procession.

The assembly hall was also the dinner hall and the PE hall. There were huge climbing frames against the walls and gym mats rolled up in the corner.

Everyone was talking and I didn't know what to do.

I broke free from the hand of my partner and quickly looked around, assessing my escape options, then I sprinted back through the main door and out of the school. The fresh air hit me. The freedom. I was out, but they'd be after me; it was a chase. I began running, for my life, down the hill outside the school, and the momentum of running downhill meant my legs were almost giving way; I couldn't stop, even to try to figure out a route. I knew my mum couldn't be that far away.

One of the straps of my school bag began to slide down my shoulders so I pulled the arm free. The bag was slowing me down so I let it fall to the ground, duly abandoned, along with my lunch box.

I had to keep running and not turn back until I found my mum.

She had been standing at the bus stop, relieved that my first morning at school had passed without incident, that nursery was consigned to history and I'd settle down and enjoy my seven years at St Mary's.

She had some time to herself now; she had the day off and was probably planning out her day, thinking about what we needed from the shops, looking forward to getting a seat on the bus and a glance through her magazine to pass the short journey.

I let out a scream, on sight: 'MUM!'

She turned round to see who this distressed-sounding child was.

Her calm and content mood changed dramatically when she saw it was me, hurtling towards her at pace and shouting again, 'MUM!'

This time louder and echoing off all the houses, disrupting the early morning tranquillity.

The peace in the immediate aftermath of rush hour, shattered.

She looked at me as if to say, 'What's wrong?' and I looked at her as if to reply: 'What the fuck do you mean, what's wrong? You just ditched me, again.'

I ran right to her, grabbed her in a bear hug and began sobbing.

'Kevin, Kevin.' She was calmly trying to get me to release my grip, but my face was buried inside her unzipped jacket.

'What happened?' she kept asking. 'It's all right, you're okay,' she reassured me, trying to get some information out of me. It was only school, it wasn't this bad, surely?

I eventually pulled back and looked her, my hands still round her waist. I'd nearly dehydrated myself crying and my only words were: 'I love you and I like you but please don't leave me here.'

I had no idea this line would go down in family history, yet I'm still reminded of it just now, over twenty years later. Pretty embarrassing, but I was dependent on total desperation tactics; either that or face school.

It was like nursery, but bigger, more strangers, longer days, a uniform and not even a Wendy house to take out some frustration on.

My mum had to slowly walk back to school with me, stopping to pick up my school bag and then, further up the hill, my Teenage Mutant Ninja Turtle lunch box. I may have been a cry baby or a mummy's boy, but no one was disputing that I had a cool-as-fuck lunch box.

My mum tried to explain that I'd make friends and that she'd be there waiting for me at the end of the day. She'd always try the sympathetic approach at first, but I gradually wore her down to the point where she resorted to more direct reasoning: 'If you don't go to school, I'll go to jail.'

I'd imagine lots of children would cry when leaving their mum at nursery, or for the first few days, weeks or even months of primary school. But I continued for years.

The first date on record of me showing up at primary school in an emotionally stable condition was sometime during Primary 4 – a full four years into my schooldays. Ridiculous.

Teachers had tried everything, from being overly nice and taking extra time to help me settle, asking if anything was wrong, asking if I was being bullied, to tough love, where they'd just shout and go nuts at me.

A couple of years into my tumultuous start at school, in my anxiety I'd managed to develop a nervous twitch which made me really overemphasize my blinking. It was like the way a child actor in a comedy film would blink when accidentally catching a look at a pair of boobs.

One teacher had lost patience trying to figure me out. When questioning me about why I was so quiet and so uneasy, she just snapped: 'And would you stop that stupid blinking!' It didn't stop me blinking frantically. The rest of my class all laughed, so it maybe even made it worse.

I'm pretty sure there's a scene in one of the *Home Alone* films where Macaulay Culkin does the exact blink I'm talking about. The teacher could at least have made her outburst funny and quoted the line from the film: 'Kevin, you're such a disease.' I could have accepted all my classmates laughing at me if it had been a good line.

Another teacher even incorporated my situation into her in-class reward-points system. Points were awarded for neat handwriting, passing spelling tests, reciting the times tables and so on.

She announced that I'd now be awarded points for not running away from the school gates every morning and having my mum chase me and drag me back whilst I was kicking out, screaming, shouting and holding on to railings.

Having a teacher announce that to the class pretty much finished off any hope I had of gaining any popularity. Looking back now, as an adult, it was probably a pretty humiliating thing to do to a child. It drew more attention to me and it also created division.

If I acquired enough points to land the big end-of-term prize, then my achievements would be tainted, given that I'd be winning points for something that was taken for granted from the rest of the class. If I didn't win, it would be pretty embarrassing, given how easy she'd made it for me.

At the end of each term, the prize for the top points scorer was usually a selection box, an Easter egg or whatever chocolate suited the time of year. With my clear advantage, I should have romped it.

I won fuck all.

To be honest, it must have been pretty frustrating for the teachers. I was often referred to the school auxiliary nurse, who'd gently try to talk to me about why I was so unhappy. 'I want to go home,' is all I'd give her. Some days they'd just give up and let me go home.

I do feel sorry for the nurse now. She was really there only to help put plasters on skinned knees and maybe check for head lice now and then. She wasn't qualified to offer any psychoanalysis or act as a therapist to a seemingly troubled child.

I feel sorrier for my mum, however. It must have been horrible watching your child in such a state and not knowing why. If you're trying to picture me as a child, then imagine a chubbier, curly haired version of Hayley Joel Osment's character in *The Sixth Sense*, a permanently concerned, worried expression on his face, and prone to freaking out now and then. At least he had an excuse, though; the poor little prick could see dead people. I just didn't like school.

I've never really figured out why I had these emotional, abandonment-type issues throughout my early life. I had everything there for a happy childhood, but I just don't remember being all that happy, not outside the house anyway.

When I think of the early years at primary school all I think of is my incessant worrying, worrying about absolutely everything, big and small. The idea that a lot of sad stuff had gone on during my early childhood is maybe something to explore when trying to figure out why I was such a temperamental, anxiety-ridden, neurotic wee guy.

To add to my Granddad John's and my Nana's deaths, shortly after I started primary school, my Granddad Tommy passed away as well, dying of a heart attack. I am aware that the death toll in this book now stands at three and that we're entering *X Factor* audition territory, but that's all of the casualties for now.

Out of the three, Tommy is the only one I have memories of, and one of the last of these is watching him leaving our house in an ambulance and me being reassured by my mum that he was just going to the doctor's and that he'd be back soon.

I remember being very upset the day he died. It didn't take much to upset me – i.e. being left temporarily unattended in a Wendy house – but it was a genuine feeling of sadness this time.

I was just five years old, old enough to sense how much he was loved, and some of my first memories were of the summer holidays when he'd look after me and my cousins, Mark and Gary.

He'd take us up the hills behind where we lived. We'd help him hunt for twigs, branches and anything that he'd decide could go up in flames. He was a total pyromaniac who'd often leave a trail of destruction in his wake.

Thankfully, he lived in Scotland, a land of greenery and constant rain. If he'd lived somewhere like Australia then I'm sure he'd be serving some serious time for his woodland fire-starting hobby.

I missed out on spending a lot of time with him, and I can rely only on a few of my vague recollections and on what I've heard about him from the rest of my family.

When my Nana died he'd be down at our house every day. My mum would make him dinner, and he'd sit and have a whisky and watch football with my dad. He'd always play with me and have a carry-on even though my mum and dad would tell him to sit back down in case he injured himself. He'd be getting on a bit by then, but to me he was my big pal.

The only times he wouldn't carry on with me would be when Celtic were playing on TV or the radio. Desperate for attention during one Old Firm game, when my dad and he were absorbed in it, I grew frustrated at Tommy not chasing me or telling me any stupid stories or answering my questions. 'Grandda, Grandda, GRANNNDDAAAA!' I shouted, before he snapped and answered, 'What is it?'

I paused and glared at him for a few seconds, I sheepishly

looked down at my feet and then back up at him and said, 'Come on the Rangers!' I then ran out of the living room, as he and my dad immediately burst into hysterics. I'd managed to defuse such a heated, volatile occasion as an Old Firm game, and at such a young age.

Like I said, in the house I was hyperactive and bursting with confidence. So it was totally unfathomable why I became such a different, introverted, reclusive child as soon as we got to the school gates.

Football dominates my few memories of Tommy. He was a Celtic fan and went to see them all his life, from childhood until he was no longer fit enough to travel to the games.

He used to tell me about a guy called Charlie Tully, his hero when he was a young guy in the late 1940s and 1950s. Charlie Tully was a showman, a George Best-style winger from Belfast who had once scored directly from a corner kick, which apparently confused everyone on the pitch; they had never seen that happen before. So the referee ordered the corner to be retaken. Tully scored again, the exact same way, and this time the goal stood.

I have no idea if that is one of those stories that people got away with before the days of regular televised football and YouTube. But I've heard it from a lot of other older folk since. So unless they all used to meet after the games and say, 'What bullshit can we make up to tell our grandchildren in forty years about that game?' it's fair to say there's truth in it.

Even though I was only four or five years old and had no idea what a corner kick was, any time I ran around with a ball doing a running commentary, Charlie Tully was the name I'd give myself.

When John and I, and our cousins, were in the house with our Celtic strips on, all the aunties and uncles would ask us playfully who our favourite Celtic player was. Celtic had a pretty poor team at the time, and Paul McStay would dominate the vote, with an honourable mention for John Collins.

It would get to me, and I'd answer 'Charlie Tully', and the house would erupt into laughter. I didn't know why they were laughing, but it felt great that my answer had provoked such a reaction.

'Cha-lay Tully, Cha-lay Tully,' I'd begin to chant, the 'r' in his first name getting lost in my excitement.

'He's spending too much time with Tommy,' they'd laugh, and Tommy would give a denying shrug of the shoulders, pretending to refute the allegations that he'd influenced my choice.

8

The spare room in Tommy's flat had a snooker table, one of those Argos fold-away ones that my mum and dad had bought for John one Christmas. Our house wasn't big enough for it, so Tommy's spare room became the place to be in the evenings and during school holidays for John, Paul, Stephen and their pals.

As always, I wasn't allowed to play with them. They were teenagers, and I'd only just started school, but my mum would demand that they at least let me sit in the room with them whilst she visited Tommy.

Being allowed to sit in the room kept me content for only so long. They'd begin to ignore me, worn down by my relentless questions. To them I was just this little chubby, curly haired pest who, despite his young age, had mastered the art of utterly exasperating people with his interrogation skills.

My dad used to joke that I'd be a great addition to the law enforcement field and that through my sheer persistence even the most hardened criminals would crumble, break down and confess the lot.

As soon as John or one of his friends would tell me to piss off from the snooker room, I'd run straight downstairs to my mum and tell her. She'd sometimes tell me to piss off as well, but usually she'd take a break from cooking for Tommy or cleaning his house and accompany me upstairs to insist they let me join in.

I'd hide behind her, acting innocent and upset, trying to fully play the victim in a calculated bid to maximize the telling-off she'd give John. As soon as she left the room, I'd be back to being hyperactive and pestering them all. I was a little bell-end, to be honest, almost a parody of a 'pal's little brother'. My mum definitely sensed this, and she'd turn on me some nights when she'd decided that John and his pals deserved some peace.

One night it came to a head, and my mum came up to drag me out of the room and bring me downstairs to help her with the washing-up. I was fucking livid and refused to leave without a fight. In the midst of all the kicking and screaming, I managed to grab one of the snooker balls and break free from my mum's grip. I ran down the stairs at top speed, straight into the living room and threw the ball on to Tommy's coal fire.

I knew I was in big trouble. My mum went berserk and marched me down the street to our house. My feet hardly touched the ground between Tommy's house and my bed. The neighbours were at their windows to see what the drama was, watching my mum pulling me by the hand as I was trying to dig my heels into the pavement to make myself a dead weight, crying and screaming, 'Sorry!'

I was pretty used to my mum shouting at me, but this time I knew it would be my dad as well. He'd reserve his temper for serious offences. Throwing a snooker ball on to the fire was definitely a serious offence. For my dad, it was maybe not the incident itself that annoyed him, more that his evening peace and quiet was being interrupted by my mum demanding he spoke to me. 'He's out of control' she said.

My mum was beaten down, worn out and just wanted to unwind. So it was left to my dad to walk me back up to Tommy's so I could apologize to John and his mates and, of course, to Tommy himself.

I was probably facing being sent to bed early again, but

Tommy defused the tension. He was the only one who seemed to take a positive from the situation, as he pointed out, 'At least it was the blue ball.'

Everyone started laughing, but I didn't get why it was funny. There were definitely no footballing motives for my actions, the blue ball being grabbed at random, an innocent caught up in it all.

But whatever, I was just relieved that I was off the hook.

John, my older cousins Paul and Stephen and their mates from the time have loads of great stories about Tommy, and every Christmas Day there will be people in hysterics laughing at stories of Tommy and the stuff he'd get up to. The same stories every Christmas that are probably only funny to those who knew him. But I suppose it's in the spirit of Christmas to be nostalgic and keep the memory of lost family and friends alive.

Tommy worked his whole life; he did loads of odd jobs but was primarily a foundry worker. As was the case with most working men in Clydebank at the time, a substantial chunk of his wages was set aside to generate a healthy income for local publicans.

He brought home enough money; his family were definitely secure, but not much more. It was maybe a little difficult for his wife and three children, but working long hours in such a harsh and unhealthy environment as a foundry meant you deserved a drink on a Friday, I'd say.

Tommy was well known in the pubs. He had the charm that could get him out of any sort of trouble. He was renowned for being the joker, the singer, the life and soul of it all. Nobody wants you to leave and everybody wants to buy you a drink. Being a 'character' can be addictive and an easy way to descend into alcoholism. Tommy didn't go that far, fortunately.

He was definitely not a bad husband or father, but he had all the attributes to make an excellent granddad, where the responsibilities are less about providing and more focused on having a carry-on and being a child again yourself.

He was viewed as an authority figure to parents who had no idea what he was like, so as long as they were told by their sons that 'John and Paul's granddad is taking us' they'd trust him to be the designated responsible adult and agree to let their children disappear for the afternoon.

It was testament to everyone's loyalty to him that the parents never got to hear details of what a typical day out under Tommy's watch would involve: lighting fires, making swings, climbing trees and just being allowed to run wild in the hills that were miles away from home. It was either loyalty or the knowledge that they'd never get to go on one of his mad adventures again if their parents knew he was the biggest child of them all.

Mark and Gary and their older brothers, Paul and Stephen, grew up in the flat behind our house, the block just opposite Tommy's flat. Our family had a strong contingent in the Hardgate area at the time, and it was great.

Given the age gap between John and myself, we didn't share friends, and it was always a chore if Mark and Gary weren't about and John had to take me out to hang around with him and his pals. They'd usually play football, and I'd always demand to be allowed to play. I don't think I was too arsed about playing, but as soon as I sensed that I wasn't being allowed to, I'd protest.

I'd love to claim to have had a rebellious nature, but I think it was more that I was a pain in the hole and really enjoyed annoying them. They'd try all sorts of tactics to get rid of me for a while, booting a spare ball into the bushes and telling me to go and find it whilst the game continued using another one. By the time I'd found the ball, I'd be covered in nettle stings and their game would be in full swing, so other ways of distracting me would have to be devised.

I think the closest I got to a game was being told I was a substitute. I'd constantly seek reassurance that the substitute's role was important. There were never any injuries, nor did they operate any sort of squad rotation system, but I'd spend the whole day behind the goals patiently 'warming up', doing jumping jacks and holding my ankle in my hand behind my arse, any sort of stretch I'd seen football players doing on TV.

It kept me distracted and entertained, though. They played football as I stood on the sidelines taking the title of first and youngest person in Clydebank to practise yoga.

9

A few months after Tommy died, my Uncle George and my Auntie Maureen moved away, along with Paul, Stephen, Mark and Gary. They moved to an area called Mountblow (feel free to say that out loud, fully enunciating both syllables and having a childish laugh to yourself, it still gets me, anyway . . . I hate brackets) on the outskirts of Clydebank and far enough away that I would no longer have Mark and Gary to hang around with every day.

A lot had changed, and very quickly. No Tommy, no Mark, no Gary and hardly anyone my age living in the streets near our house in Hardgate. Playing snooker at Tommy's was also sadly no longer an option, as his flat was back in the hands of the council and a new family had moved in.

John and his mates were far too old for me, and they were starting to move on from hanging around the streets kicking a ball about. They were discovering computer games. A whole crowd of them had grown up in the same streets, all roughly the same age as each other, which must have been great, but it was probably the end of an era for them.

The children a little younger than John and his pals were still between four and six years older than me. I'd try to hang around with them and play on the grassy banking right in front of our house, thinking they were my pals, that I had my crowd, in the same way John had his.

Since I was the youngest, and being so shy and timid, naturally they'd take the piss out of me. I'd be sent to get the ball, a role that suited me, given my past experience. On the odd occasion I'd even be promoted from ball boy to goal-keeper, having shots blasted at me for hours.

I didn't save many and, when I did, it was usually with my face. I'd walk home crying, and my mum would tell me that they were too old for me and that I was to just play in the garden.

That would last for only a few days. I'd watch them all playing from the garden, where I'd be digging holes in the grass, or booting a ball off the wall of our house, and I'd eventually wander over, looking to join in again.

I had a ball, so that meant I could play with them as soon as theirs had been kicked into the bushes. Within a few minutes I'd be back in goal, and the cycle of sore face, tears and the short walk back home would continue.

One day the entire grassy banking was mobbed, far busier than usual. Everyone had bikes, and a ramp had been built using an old plank of wood and some piled-up bricks.

The object was to accumulate some speed by cycling from the top of the downhill slope at the far end of the banking and then hit the ramp, with the momentum taking you up into the air whilst the crowd watched to see how far you could fly. The distance of how far you could fly was measured in people. People would lie down on their backs behind the ramp, and the more bodies you jumped, the more you impressed everyone else.

I explain this as though I was part of it. I was part of it, but again, like being the ball boy or the goalkeeper at football, I was landed with another undesirable role. This time I was to lie down at the end of the line of three or four or – for one (and only) time – five others.

Fifth place, the furthest-away body and the most likely to serve as a human landing pad for an over-ambitious stunt-man and his BMX.

It wasn't the greatest qualifying position, but then

qualifying was determined by age. I was the youngest and just delighted to be involved.

Jumping three bodies was fairly standard and the level most of them seemed to be working at. Four had been done and, although impressive, the crowd wanted more.

Stuart Gravil, the middle of the three Gravil brothers, had expressed his willingness to attempt the jumping of five bodies. Five! To be fair to the brothers, they were fairly mental and often put on a show, so it was never in any doubt that Stuart would stick to his word.

The Gravil brothers were adrenalin junkies who got off on mayhem, and they certainly didn't rest on their reputation as the local family of nutcases. They were always looking to push themselves into outdoing their previous escapades.

They didn't do things to impress anyone, though. They lived in their own world and any patronizing, 'go on, you'll be a legend' kind of encouragement was never required.

They weren't into football or anything like that. Their passion lay more in blowing up telephone boxes, spray-painting, smashing windows and throwing wheelie-bins on top of bonfires. They could all confidently drive a car from about the age of nine onwards, and whatever they did, they did on their terms.

I should point out that Stuart was actually known as Stuarty, his cousin Scott (equally as mental) was known as Scotty and so on.

Having a 'y' added to the end of your name is a coming-of-age moment, a rite of passage, an honour bestowed upon any adolescent who has proven himself to be a bit of a crackpot.

It's a proud day for a Craig when he becomes a Craigy. The 'y' is never to be removed except when being addressed by parents or teachers and, later in life, by a partner or, in some cases, the law.

Anticipation was beginning to build and preparations were in place for Stuarty's ambitious five-man jump. I'd been standing at the back with my ball, watching and paying attention to what was going on. I'd gone unnoticed until the seniors in the crowd had encountered the problem of trying to recruit bodies willing to be used as hurdles.

One or two older ones had agreed, but only providing they were closest to the bricks. Third and fourth from the bricks proved a difficult sell as always, but they were filled without too many dead arms, chicken noises and choruses of 'Shitebag, shitebag, shitebag'.

Fifth place, though, was dangerously unknown territory. That's when I was noticed. I was back in the gang, one of the lads again. 'Go on, Kev,' came the faux-friendly encouragement. With 'you can hang about with us all the time' being the only terms I was offered, the lure was too much, and I agreed.

I took my place at the end; five of us were lying there, me at the very end. We were all pretty nervous, but there definitely wasn't any camaraderie between us, no togetherness. Everyone had their own individual safety fears, me most of all.

Stuarty cycled up the slope in the banking, and the shouts of encouragement grew louder as he began the return journey back down. I was petrified and hoping my mum or dad was watching from the window of our house and would come out and put a halt to it. I began desperately trying to budge up. Tempers were flaring: 'Stop fucking pushing. There's no room, you fat bastard!'

I was too scared to look up to see how close Stuarty was, but it seemed like he was taking ages. There was more pushing and attempts to budge up towards the bricks, mainly by me and the person in fourth place. But this time there was an excess of pushing. The pressure from us all was too much for the bricks, and just as Stuarty was about to commence his ascent, the ramp gave way.

The bricks collapsed but Stuarty hadn't noticed in time to try to swerve to the side or clutch his brakes.

I closed my eyes and braced myself for impact. The bike collided with the bricks and I heard a scream from the person closest to them, one of Stuarty's mates, who'd only agreed to be an obstacle as long as he was in the supposed safest spot.

The bike hit him and then landed on the next two people.

I opened my eyes. I didn't want to get up and run away because I didn't know what else was flying through the air. It was like a slow-motion scene from a slapstick comedy, or the outtakes of a show like MTV's *Jackass*, with a stern 'do not try this at home' warning appearing across the screen.

Stuarty landed.

I remember the initial shocked silence of it all, the noise of the thud as his whole body weight fell from a great height on to the grass, and then his howl of pain.

He'd cleared the five of us, and by some distance, and the judges could only fault him on the technicality that, whilst he'd made the jump, his bike hadn't.

It was difficult not to sympathize as he lay there in a swastika-like shape. He'd dislocated both his shoulders and, after a few seconds, he stood up and walked away in a trance.

If this had happened today, someone would have it recorded on a smart phone and Stuarty would be a YouTube smash. 'Epic BMX ramp jump fail. Ouch!'

I stood up as well, then ran across the banking and up the steps to the safety of the house. I wasn't hanging around for the crash-scene investigation, as it would no doubt end in the culpability being laid on the furthest one away, the one who'd done the most pushing. Everyone else had been pushing too, but I was the youngest and rules are rules.

In fairness, though, Stuarty saw the funny side, as did his brothers. He was fully recovered and back on the scene in no time.

I was promised I'd be allowed to hang around with them, but I decided I'd wait a while before cashing in that chip. Although they'd laughed it off, I wasn't so naive as to think they wouldn't be looking for some form of revenge.

My next run-in with the Gravils was on a day I was playing alone in the garden. I was slowly beginning to resign myself to being a loner. So I'd spend most weekends, holidays and evenings after school just booting my ball off the wall of the house and trying to see if I could do any tricks with it.

I was pretty committed to the solitary side of football training, which is probably why today I'm useless in a game of football, but I can comfortably do a few hundred 'keepy-ups'.

If comedy goes to shit for me, then maybe I can fall back on being a half-time entertainer at lower league games, walking about the pitch, keeping the ball in the air, waving at the couple of thousand fans whilst decked out in shorts and a T-shirt emblazoned with the name of a local scaffolding firm who've kindly sponsored me for the day, to earn myself a coin.

A tragic thought, but a man needs to have a back-up plan.

This time the Gravils came carrying weapons; they were tooled up, tooled up with cream cakes, custard pies, chocolate gateau, the lot. It was as though Mr Kipling was backing their latest armed campaign.

I'm presuming they were out-of-date cakes stolen from behind a nearby bakery, as I could never picture them as patisserie enthusiasts who'd spend a morning beating and whisking eggs and butter, mixing in flour, etc., just as a means to terrorize the neighbourhood. Ways to terrorize the neighbourhood wasn't something they tended to struggle coming up with.

They even had proper cream cakes like the ones you've never seen anyone eat, the ones you used to see on light-hearted game shows being comically shoved in someone's face.

I was in the wrong place at the wrong time, and the Gravils had obviously been watching a lot of light-hearted game shows. They saw me as the ideal person to assume the role of the contestant who'd just answered a question incorrectly or failed a challenge.

It was all over in seconds.

I'd gone from innocently kicking my ball, alone in my own wee world, to standing, stunned and frozen still, utterly emulsioned in mousse, chocolate, raspberry jam and any other produce that helps form a cake, whilst the three or four of them ran away, giggling hysterically and shouting insults at me. 'Enjoy your dessert, fat boy!'

My mum had been in the house going about her housework when I walked in. Initially, I was too shocked to cry. She just looked at me, in total bemusement, trying to process what was being presented before her.

I managed an outraged 'Look what the Gravils have done to me!' before the tears began leaking out from my foam-encrusted eyes, navigating their way through the whipped cream and down my cheeks. It was the worst kind of attack: embarrassing, but too comical for anyone to be angry on your behalf.

Although sympathetic, my mum found it difficult not to laugh. She also faced a dilemma. She could walk round to the Gravils' house and show their parents what they'd done to me, but making the situation even more farcical by parading me through the streets, or she could help me clean myself up, in turn burying the evidence, and then go round. It was a tough call.

She helped me wash my face and looked out a change of clothes for me. I tried to play up the trauma a little, but it was fairly half-hearted. I think, inside, I knew it was pretty funny.

When my dad came home from work, my mum told him what had happened. I stood by her side trying to look innocent and vulnerable, but she struggled to keep a straight face when regaling him with the details.

I'd been hoping my dad would march round to their house via a bakery and execute a revenge attack. But I later found out that the owner of the car my dad had been arrested in and accused of breaking into whilst drunk on his way home from work years ago was the Gravils' dad. The guy who'd defended him and ensured charges were dropped. I suppose my dad owed it to him to let it slide.

I don't think this crossed his mind, though. I think he just thought it was funny. He knew also that the Gravils weren't bullies. They'd just sourced a shit load of cakes on this day and chosen not to eat them. They'd used them instead as weapons against anything and anyone they passed and deemed to be a legitimate target. I was one of those legitimate targets, and that's fair enough. I think I've almost gotten over it, and I'm ready to move on.

I still bump into the Gravils from time to time when I'm back at my mum and dad's. They're all genuinely nice guys.

Stuarty was telling me how he was working on a railway and had managed to source some dynamite. If I was ever interested in purchasing some . . . Which is always good to know.

I last saw Stuarty when I went fishing for the first and only time in my life, up in the Kilpatrick Hills, not too far from my mum and dad's house in Hardgate, at a place known as 'The Jaw'.

Stuarty was there with his brothers and a few of their mates. Even though we were all adults now, the sight of them still brought back the childhood feelings of trepidation.

In my head I'll always be one of River Phoenix's character's crowd from *Stand by Me* and the Gravils will always be one of Kiefer Sutherland's. Stuarty being Ace and me being Vern, if you're looking for specifics.

Our companies gradually merged and Stuarty proved himself to be a valuable addition to a fishing trip, especially as neither my mates nor I knew how to fish properly. My mate somehow managed to catch a perch, and, excited and not entirely sure what to do next, he hurriedly requested Stuarty's assistance.

He strolled over, carefully placed his can of Tennent's lager on the grass, unhooked the fish and calmly asked if we had a mallet. We didn't have a mallet, but that wasn't a problem, as he took a long final draw of his cigarette, flicked it away and then put the fish, which was still frantically wriggling about, into his mouth and bit its head clean off.

It was done in such a blasé way that I wasn't really shocked at the time, unable to fully process what I'd just watched, or perhaps sort of convincing myself that I hadn't just been witness to a man biting a live fish's head clean off.

It's only just now, recalling the incident and telling you about it, that I shake my head in delayed disbelief and laugh in a 'What can you do? He's a mate', *Trainspotting*-type summary of the man.

A profound moment and, although disturbing, it was good to see that the Gravils were still alive, well and patrolling their native Hardgate and the surrounding areas.

10

I didn't have much choice with regards to children my age to hang around with in Hardgate at the time, but it didn't really bother me too much. I'd sometimes play with my next-door neighbour, Stephen Howie, who was only a year older than me. In the block of flats opposite our house lived Ryan Evans, who was the same age as Stephen.

Both Ryan and Stephen had brothers three or four years older than them, so they had the option of hanging around with the older crowd and not having the piss ripped out of them to the same extent as I had on my few failed attempts at getting involved. I was developing a 'fuck them' sort of attitude and beginning to be content in my own company.

But my Uncle George and my Auntie Maureen came up to our house about once or twice a week. So I'd have Mark and Gary there, someone to carry on with, kick the ball around, have an argument and a fight with, shake hands, make up and then repeat the next time.

Sometimes their older brother Stephen would be with them and that always meant we could venture further than the front garden and the grassy banking, as he was older and deemed responsible enough to look after us. I'd always feel a sense of security when he was there. I wouldn't be under attack from cream-cake-carrying youths when I was with 'my big cousin'.

Stephen was the biggest child of us all. He was hyper-active, rough, and always taking a 'dummy' fight too far. 'You don't know your own strength,' he'd be told, whilst Mark or Gary lay crying in agony.

He was cheeky and swore constantly, even in front of adults. 'You're impressing nobody, Stephen,' was another one of my Uncle George or Auntie Maureen's staple lines when he was talking back or doing something he shouldn't be. He was older and always showing off to Mark, Gary and me.

I'd always be impressed, though, and I admired his anarchic ways.

At school, I'd begun to make a couple of pals. It still didn't mean that I enjoyed it or looked forward to going but once the day got underway I'd settle down a bit and get on with it.

My age group at St Mary's had sixty pupils, divided into two classes, Primary 1a, Primary 1b, and then 2a and 2b and so on. I was in Primary 1a, and my first teacher was Mrs McInnes. I remember her being very friendly and always trying to calm me down and reassure me that school wasn't all that bad. I'd usually calm down as the days went on and I think she definitely helped.

My friendship with Doc, my second cousin or whatever you'd call the son of your Mum's cousin, would have to wait a while because he wasn't in my class for the first three years, and he didn't live in Hardgate.

On our first day at school, at the morning break or 'playtime', whilst everyone else was running around the playground, hyper and screaming, I sat on the bottom step of the fire escape, on my own and sobbing away.

Doc came over to talk to me and asked if I was okay. I was just mumbling answers. The only way I'd have cheered up was if my mum had come over and taken me home, away from the place, but nevertheless it was a nice touch from the big fella.

Mrs McInnes arranged her class into groups, maybe five or six groups from the class of thirty, and the groups she determined by alphabetical order. Off the top of my head my group was Stephanie Aitken, Stephen Boag, John Boyd, Kevin Bridges, Anthony Clark and Kerry Clark.

I remember this mainly because it was thanks to the alphabet that I first met Anthony Clark – again his name would soon change and he'd be known as Tony, Big T, T-Bomb, Bomber, and shit loads of other nicknames as we grew older.

At St Mary's, Tony was the total opposite of me, always laughing, smiling, cracking jokes; he was the first to gel his hair, the first to get his ear pierced, the first to address your mum and dad by their real names and not Mr or Mrs, but never in an obnoxious way. He had a natural charm about him. He was only five years old, but carried himself like a Mafia boss, oozing confidence. He definitely helped bring me out of my shell a bit.

I'd forget the trauma of the morning and we'd even start to get told off by Mrs McInnes for talking and giggling in class. Mrs McInnes maybe never knew at the time that she was to be the first of many authority figures to reprimand us and that her early telling-offs set the precedent for my friendship with Tony.

Despite being told off for talking in class a lot, teachers would compliment me on my work, my reading, my spelling, my grasp of times tables and all the basic elementary stuff. I picked things up pretty quickly and worked hard but, still, even being considered one of the brighter pupils in the class and having made a friend, I was becoming infatuated with trying to find ways of avoiding school.

Mrs Fallon, a deputy head teacher, had begun to monitor me after having caught me, on a few occasions, trying to leave the school grounds at playtime and go out on to the streets of Duntocher.

She was only concerned about the dangers of a child being

left to roam the area and cross busy roads unattended. I saw it as being forced to stay in school against my will, which I was, but it was only school and not a concentration camp was their point, I suppose.

She'd call my mum and bring her in for meetings to discuss my progress on the psychological front, which was never that great, except for one week when she'd promised me a certificate if I managed a whole week showing up at school without crying or making an escape bid.

I managed it and she handed me the certificate, which simply said: 'For a whole week.' She'd spared me the embarrassment of adding any further details.

The following week the tears were back.

My mum had now gone full-time in her home-help job, which she'd started a few months into my turbulent nursery campaign.

Up until then, it had been only my dad out earning. They weren't struggling, but they had hopes of getting a mortgage and buying our house from the council. Also, my dad had always wanted us to go on a family holiday, the four of us, before John was too old and wouldn't want to go abroad with his mum and dad and pain-in-the-arse little brother.

At the time my dad was working as a social worker for people with disabilities. He'd not long been diagnosed with rheumatoid arthritis himself, which was rapidly beginning to worsen to the point when the doctor told him he might not be able to continue working at the same rate.

I think my dad took it pretty bad; he'd been used to working, and he was from a generation where the husband was the main source of income. So he dismissed the doctor's advice and kept on as normal.

My mum, always thinking of the worst-case scenario, was keen to get some sort of back-up plan in place. So she put herself forward for more hours as a home help, working early mornings, evenings and then weekends.

She'd be out around 7 a.m. and carefully work it so she'd have time to nip back home, take me to school and then go and visit her houses in Duntocher. She began working constantly, but I never remember her not being there to take me to school or to pick me up at home time, except on one occasion when John had been off on exam leave from school and my class was going on a school trip for the morning to Hunterston Power Station in Ayrshire, on the west coast of Scotland, south of Glasgow.

I have no idea why anyone would want to take a class of primary school children to a Nuclear Power Station, but anyway, that was my first school trip. My mum signed my permission slip and packed me some lunch for the day and reassured me that a school trip would be good fun.

My mum didn't want John lying in his bed all day when he was supposed be up and studying for his exams. So she asked him to take me to school for the morning. That would also allow her a slight bit of respite from her daily rushing around.

John reluctantly agreed and we left the house at the usual time. I'd always spoken about him in class; I was proud that he was ten years older than me and I looked up to him a lot, copying everything he did. On the way to school I pretended we were just out for a walk together, managing to forget where we were headed and overlooking the fact that he'd had to be almost physically dragged out of his bed and more or less forced to take me to school.

John walked much faster than my mum and was only concerned with how quickly he could drop me off and get back to bed. My mum and dad were at work so he'd have the house to himself. We arrived at the school. As always, my heart had started racing, and I'd got a sick feeling in my stomach when we'd turned on to the school's street.

I looked up to see teachers standing with their registers, ticking names off and checking permission slips, and everyone being lined up with their partner and ready to get on the bus.

John took me to the teacher, told me to enjoy the trip and said that he'd see me at home time. He turned back and began walking even faster, as though I'd been slowing him down on the outbound journey. It was done too fast and he didn't hang around to watch my daily pre-school performance that he'd heard so much about at home from Mum.

I was on the bus and sitting down before I could even comprehend what was happening. I sat and cried as the bus moved away and didn't speak a word the whole way to Hunterston Power Station, about a forty-five-minute journey.

When we arrived, I was one of the first off the bus, and I immediately made a break for it. The teachers were obviously anticipating this and managed to grab me back and begin the usual routine of counselling me.

I was kicking out and screaming to be let go. I was creating a scene and workers and other visitors were looking over, baffled, whilst the teachers were embarrassed and trying to give off a 'move along, nothing to see here, folks' vibe.

I think there was even crowd of Greenpeace protesters gathered at the main doors of the nuclear power station who weren't demonstrating as much or looking anywhere near as pissed off as me. If they'd followed my lead, we could have had the place closed down there and then.

That night when my mum asked me how my trip was I told her it was 'fine', but in a way that made sure she knew it hadn't been fine. John had told her I had been fine as well.

She either knew we were both lying or thought it had been a breakthrough.

John's no-nonsense 'that's you at school, see you later' approach meant he'd missed the scene, and I knew I'd be in trouble if my mum knew about my display at the power station, so I left it at 'fine'. Besides, it was done now; this wasn't a time to be thinking about anything school-related. I'd block that out until the next morning.

The following morning my mum was taking me to school again, getting back to her hectic daily schedule. I admire her hard-working attitude a lot and although it was over twenty years ago and I was just a child, I still feel bad for putting her through so much unnecessary extra pressure. But she coped and she had everything done with amazing efficiency.

I think the home-help job suited her naturally caring personality. She'd talk to the elderly folk and make sure they were okay. If they needed anything, she'd go to the shops. She'd cook and clean for them. She did far more than was her remit. When the meals-on-wheels food wasn't up to much, she'd cook extra of whatever we were having and take it over to her elderly clients.

She became popular amongst the old people she looked after and at weekends I'd be dragged along to their houses with her whilst John and my dad would go to the Celtic games.

I'd sit and talk to them. Their houses always had the same smell, and their central heating was always cranked up to Mercury-like temperatures whilst they sat with a couple of cardigans on asking for the gas fire to be lit and complaining that there was a 'right nip in the air'.

My mum would always encourage me to speak and answer their questions. They'd ask how I was enjoying school. 'The happiest days of your life, son,' they'd say. I'd always manage to resist an urge to reply, 'You have got to be fucking kidding me!'

My mum would finish her work and make sure they were set for the afternoon. She'd flick through the TV channels and find them something to watch, usually a war film or a western. They'd often give me a 50 pence or £1 coin and tell me to get myself a bar of chocolate. I'd immediately feel guilty for not talking more and for feeling bored in their house. I've always felt a sense of protection when it comes to the elderly, probably stemming from going to work with my mum at this age.

I've been writing this book in cafés and become part of the 'during the day' crowd. The ones who seem to have too much disposable income to be students or unemployed, ordering coffees, sparkling waters, a green tea and then a peppermint tea when the caffeine starts messing with their heart rate.

I didn't really drink coffee until I started writing this. I started with ordering a double espresso as a way of paying the café some dig money for the use of the table as an office. If I tried to write from home I'd sit blankly staring at Sky Sports News all day, growing more and more depressed with every repeated cricket and Formula 1 story signifying another fifteen minutes gone by and still no shower and no sign of anything productive happening.

I love people-watching and cafés are great for that. Today, the café I've been writing in for the last week was far quieter than usual. It was empty except for me, two tourists having a sandwich and studying their map, and then just this one little old guy, about war-veteran age, sitting on his own with a bowl of soup, his napkin tucked in as though it was Christmas Day. He was looking perfectly content, but I couldn't help this massive feeling of sadness that came over me.

I had this feeling in my stomach. I started wondering whether he looks back on his life and whether he's done everything he wanted or still has more to do. I started wondering why this old guy was sat there on his own. Maybe his wife had died and his children were all too focused on their own children and their own careers to spend much time with their granddad.

It kind of rattled me and I could hardly concentrate when the waitress came to see if I wanted anything else, subtly letting me know the rent was due.

The old guy was probably having a great time, and I'd maybe watched too much Sky Sports News in the morning and slipped into one of my depressed moods. But whatever it was, it ruined my peppermint tea and put me off the idea of ordering the Parma ham and mozzarella panini from the specials board.

I don't know why I've told you that, but here's the lesson for all lonely men over seventy reading this: next time you're dining out please bring a hooker and spare us all the sympathy pangs by presenting yourself as a seedy old creep as opposed to a lonely, widowed old man.

After my mum had finished work we would get the bus to Clydebank for another customary trip to the shopping centre; we'd be headed primarily for Asda, but I'd try to drag her into a toyshop called Beattie's, which was opposite McDonald's.

A toyshop opposite a McDonald's! It was the epitome of everything a child could hope for from a Saturday afternoon, a primary school child's Vegas. Occasionally my pleas to be taken to Beattie's were successful; my mum would submit to my persistence and we'd make the grand entrance.

The place was mind-blowing – train sets, remote-control cars, water pistols, cap guns – and I'd ask for everything we saw. Trying to meet my demands at least a quarter of the way, my mum would usually buy me a Subbuteo team or some form of Subbuteo accessory, corner flags, dug-outs, a scoreboard or whatever else I felt was needed to take my living-room-carpet-based football club to the next level. I'd discovered John's old toys from when he was my age, and I gradually grew to neglect my Wrestling Ring and its figures and was beginning to develop an obsession with Subbuteo.

When we got home on a Saturday after my mum's home-help duties and our trip to the shopping centre, I'd lay the pitch out, put the goals up, sort the advertising boards and make all the other necessary match day preparations and then line Celtic up against whoever they were playing that Saturday.

If I didn't have a team with the correct colours, I'd tell my mum that it was their new away kit. I don't think she really gave a shite but it was a means of justifying the flaw to myself. I was usually meticulous in my attention to details, and maybe it was also a little bit of me hinting that I needed some new teams.

A way of letting her know that if my Subbuteo league were to be taken at all seriously, I'd need more financial backing from the chief investor.

We had to be home for 3 p.m. every Saturday afternoon or I'd begin to panic that I didn't have my Subbuteo game ready to run concurrently with the real game. If we were running late and my dad hadn't gone to the game, I'd beg my mum to phone home and ask him to put the teams out for me.

We would listen to the Celtic game on the radio and I'd react to whatever was happening. It kept me entertained throughout the match. I was pretty protective of all my Subbuteo gear. The first time my dad accidentally stood on one of my Celtic players, breaking the player off the little round plastic disc thing it was attached to, I was pretty pissed off. But he was quick to rectify the problem and used his cigarette lighter to slightly melt the plastic at the bottom of the player's feet, then stuck it back on to its base.

I mentioned that the player was now noticeably far shorter than the rest. 'He can be Brian McLaughlin,' he replied. Brian McLaughlin had just come on the scene at Celtic, a youth player who'd played the odd game here and there and who was no more than five foot six or seven in height. It made sense and we now had a unique team. I was soon snapping players from other teams and asking him for the lighter to correct this crucial detail that I'd overlooked.

I never actually played a game of Subbuteo, which would have required at least one other person. I'd try to get Mark and Gary into it when they came up to our house, but they didn't really get the attraction. They would carelessly break players, so the cigarette lighter would be out as soon as they left and another raft of Brian McLaughlin-types would be promoted from the youth academy.

Playing the game itself, I remember, was terrible and involved tapping the players gently towards the ball with the tip of your finger, the ball being about the same height as the players. I'd feel for Brian McLaughlin, who looked like a contender on *Gladiators* when the ball rolled towards him.

Nobody could comprehend my passion for Subbuteo, nor did anyone pay much attention to my constant live updates from the game in my head that I'd act out on the pitch. But it kept me absorbed on a Saturday afternoon, and my dad would be left in peace to listen to the football and check his pools coupon.

It was the early 1990s and in the middle of Rangers' 'nine league titles in a row' domination of Scottish football, a fairly grim time to be a Celtic supporter, as they'd regularly be finishing fourth and fifth in the table. I'd try to offer some escapism by going my own way and inventing better results on the Subbuteo pitch: 'It's six – nil to Celtic, Dad. Brian McLaughlin's got five, and Mark McInally scored from the halfway line.' Any player I'd hear him screaming and shouting at on the radio or TV would go on to have a great game in my head.

My fascination grew over the next couple of years and especially when my dad started to take me with him to my first few Celtic games. I was in awe of Celtic Park, the floodlights, the turnstiles, the scoreboard, the crowd, the advertising boards, the burger vans. I was there as the chairman of a proud, ambitious Subbuteo club. I didn't care about the game. I was there on a fact-finding mission, scouting for ideas on what we could be doing to improve, the methods we should use.

The only time my score updates were ever taken seriously was during the 1994 Scottish League Cup Final between Celtic and Raith Rovers. Celtic were fully expected to beat Raith Rovers, the underdogs who were in the league below. It would be Celtic's first trophy for a few years and the final was at Ibrox whilst Hampden was being renovated.

I was determined to put on a show on the Subbuteo field to run at the same time as the actual game. I had my TV men and camera-crew figures on the halfway line, beside the trophy. That was waiting to be presented to the winning team after they'd ascended the stairs to the middle of the stand, where I'd cordoned off a route for the winning team with masking tape.

The only trophy I had was the European Cup and it was the same height as five or six Subbuteo players standing on each other's heads. The makers of Subbuteo didn't make it easy for someone as obsessive and compulsive about the realism of the experience as I was. They probably thought these ridiculous flaws like the trophy and ball size would be overlooked by children just looking to play the game. Fuck that.

Still, other than the trophy and the ball, I found my own ways to enhance the experience and create some authenticity. I used to steal John's old Sony Walkman and put it under the Subbuteo stand. I'd again use masking tape to stick a headphone to each side of the stand. Then about thirty minutes before kick-off, I'd press the big Play button and turn it up full blast so that music could be heard coming through as the crowd began to build. The players would be warming up whilst the whole crowd were rocking to 'Female of the Species' and 'Mr Psycho' by Space. A breakthrough moment, and my early trips to Celtic Park were already proving beneficial, as our stadium was becoming a modern, state-of-the-art arena.

I'd use the little Subbuteo green fences for outside the stadium, to segregate the fans coming in. The last thing I wanted was a full-scale riot on the living-room carpet. I now had enough teams that I'd use players from that afternoon's non-playing sides as fans rather than the tiny official Subbuteo supporters who'd require patience to place them in their seats. When one was sat down, another would fall over.

With kick-off looming, my dad would watch me grow agitated as I tried to sit them all down without any of them lying on their side. 'He's had a bit to drink,' he'd joke. And I'd take it as a dig at the realism of my pride and joy. But that was it – another idea! The fans needed a pub, somewhere to meet before the game.

A shoebox was sourced. I coloured it in with Celtic colours, like the ones I'd seen in the Gallowgate and Parkhead areas of Glasgow during my reconnaissance trips to Celtic Park. The pub was decorated and ready for business in rapid time. It must have confused the fans, as it wasn't there before the game. But it was there, open, fully decorated and ready for business at full time.

I got rid of all the tiny little fans. I soon had four or five different Celtic teams. They'd kept getting snapped, and the cigarette lighter could save a life only once, maybe twice; after that I resorted to melting nothing more than a head on to a bit of round plastic.

I picked my twenty-two players as the official teams for the day's game, and kept them in their packets. The rest I'd place in the stand. They were the fans, along with any other teams I had whose kits could pass for Celtic and Raith Rovers colours. My Dundee United and Borussia Dortmund teams I'd used as stewards, due to the high-visibility colours of their strips. They'd be lined up between the fans against the masking-taped partition that was now in place.

I'd use VHS tapes, every single one in the house, to sit the stands on. I now had four stands, two for the bottom tier and two for the top tier. The VHS tapes would be laid out, some long ways on their sides with other ones lying across to make steady foundations. The stands would be carefully placed on them, and then the green lid of my toy box would be sat on the top so the fans were sheltered from the elements.

It was looking shit-hot. My mum, dad and John would laugh, but comment that I was very observant and had a great imagination. I was delighted that my hard work was finally being recognized.

John went off to Ibrox for the game and my mum disappeared to the shopping centre. She'd always try to stay from my dad, who turned into a bit of a screwball during big games.

The real game started, as did my Subbuteo game. 'One – nil to Celtic, Dad,' I told him after a few minutes, trying to calm his early nerves as he was already beginning to swear and change colour. 'Two – nil to Celtic' and then 'Three – nil to Celtic' quickly afterwards. The angrier he got at the real game on the TV, the better Celtic were playing in my head/ Subbuteo game.

Celtic had just gone four up in my game as Raith Rovers made it 1–0 in the real game. Shouts of 'Aww, for fuck's sake' and 'I don't fucking believe this' from my dad spurred me on to make it 5–0, 6–0, 7–0 to Celtic. Celtic then equalized in the real game, and my dad grabbed me and cuddled me. All was well again. The game went on and on, tied at 1–1, whilst mine was a goal fest. I think my teams went in at half time with Celtic 9–0 up.

The second half got underway and although there was still not much happening in the real game, Celtic were embarking on a world record attempt on the living-room carpet. The score line was the only area where I'd allow for fantasy, with everything else being kept as bona fide as I could make it. I think I really did feel for my dad and John, who'd constantly be investing so much, financially and emotionally, into a team that just seemed to upset them again and again.

With five minutes left and the real score and Subbuteo score at 1–1 and 18–0 respectively, Charlie Nicholas scored to put the real Celtic in the lead. My dad went mental, running around the living room. My game was almost abandoned as one of my players was seriously injured during my dad's celebrations. I was joining in cheering with him, but anxiously trying to find a substitute as I could sense this wasn't the time to ask for his lighter.

There wasn't long left in the real game and at 18–0 to Celtic, with central defender Mike Galloway scoring his seventh, I decided it was getting a little far-fetched. But it was 2–1 to Celtic in reality, so all was well. 'Raith Rovers have just scored, Dad,' I said, feeling that an 18–0 hammering was a little unfair and that they deserved a consolation goal.

'Don't say that,' he replied. He overlooked all eighteen goals in Celtic's Mike Galloway-inspired demolition, but this update grabbed his attention. He was a nervous wreck and it was probably more by coincidence than in celebration that he'd smoked a fag for each one of the Subbuteo Celtic's goals.

Almost straight away, after Charlie Nicholas's goal, which was supposed to be the winner, Raith Rovers went up the park and scored: 2–2. I felt sick. 'I was only joking, they didn't score, it was offside, I didn't see it properly, I think it hit the post.' I was quickly firing excuses at him. They were contradicting each other, but I wasn't thinking straight. Celtic could lose the Cup Final, and it'd all be my fault.

The real game went to extra time, and then penalties. I remember watching Paul McStay walking up to take his penalty and feeling something inside me pleading with him to score. The Raith Rovers keeper saved it. Shit.

It put a dampener on the Subbuteo Celtic's celebrations, and their planned ascent up the masking-tape-lined stairway to stand and gaze up at the gigantic trophy was postponed, as a mark of respect.

I began to fold up the pitch, put the players back in their pack and take the VHS tapes down – the standard sort of post-match de-rig which I'd usually have to be shouted at to do.

'I'm sorry, Dad,' I pleaded.

'It's not your fault, son,' he replied in a way that made it feel even more like it was my fault.

My mum came home to hear the news. My dad jokingly told her about how I had jinxed the game. She came into my bedroom. I was sat on the floor, devastated. I looked at her and said, 'Sorry.' She burst out laughing, hauled me downstairs and gave my dad a telling-off.

I don't think my dad knew how bad I felt, and he quickly started trying to cheer me up. He told me, 'That's what it feels like to support Celtic. They'll break your heart.'

My dad will mention this cup final every now and then, and I think he still holds me up there, along with a lack of financial investment and an average squad whose bottle crashed at the vital moment, as factors that share an equal proportion of responsibility for one of Celtic's biggest Cup upsets.

12

My family have always been football fanatics. Even my mum will sometimes watch a game and confidently contribute to a post-match discussion about a player's performance or a refereeing decision. That's probably down to the fact of growing up with Tommy and two brothers and then marrying my dad and having two sons.

I've always been a Celtic supporter; it's something I'm proud of and I grew up to fully understand what my dad meant. He never dragged me along to games or tried to force being a Celtic supporter on me. He took me to one or two games around about 1992 and 1993, just enough to get me curious. But after that I had to plead to get taken again and to have the new strip. I'd been allowed to wear John's old 1988 Celtic strip, which had been over-washed and had shrunk just enough to fit me, contradicting a famous Jock Stein quote.

My first few football trips with my dad were to watch Clydebank, our local team, who were in Scottish Division 1 at the time. If Celtic were away from home, he'd take me to Kilbowie Park to watch 'The Bankies'.

I wasn't really that interested and it wasn't much of a stadium. It was far too quiet and everyone seemed to be there simply to watch the game. My dad never got animated and was a totally different person from the guy who watched Celtic. He was relaxed and would explain things about the game to me.

Ken Eadie, Craig Flannigan and John Henry were the

three players I remember. They must have done something notable for me to check their shirt number with their name in the match programme. They were my local team so it was only right I knew a few of them for future Subbuteo purposes.

A match day programme, a 'kwenchie' cup, a hot dog, crisps, chocolate – I cost my dad a fortune on our couple of visits to Kilbowie Park, far more than at Celtic Park, where I had things other than food and excess consumerism to occupy my mind. That was much bigger, busier, louder, and everyone seemed to care a lot more about what was going on.

I didn't understand why they cared so much, but it was infectious, and also it was good to go into school and tell everyone I had been at a Celtic game.

At St Mary's, supporting Celtic soon became pretty competitive.

I didn't understand the connection between Celtic and Ireland. I didn't know what 'Ireland' was until everyone in my class with an 'Irish' name would start to stake a genuine claim to being the biggest Celtic supporter in the school.

I'd been to games and I had the 1988 centenary strip; what the fuck has Brendan Kelly done? He can't even name the full team. I was outraged at the new criteria being put in place. 'What's Ireland?' and 'Am I Irish?' I'd go home and ask my mum and dad.

They'd tell me I'm Scottish, but that my great-grandparents were Irish. Three out of my four grandparents were dead, so how dead were my great-grandparents? They were dead as fuck.

'Was Grandda Tommy Irish?' I was getting desperate, hoping for some sort of evidence. 'He thought he was,' they both laughed in a sentimental, what-was-he-like kind of way.

I'd heard enough, though. He was Irish now.

I started school in the 1990s, over a hundred years after the Irish potato famine brought thousands of immigrants to Scotland. A hundred years is a long time, but the depth of integration into Scottish society meant that even the most tenuous of Irish links were clung to.

Tommy was born in Scotland and was definitely Scottish, but he saw himself as Irish; his surname, Mullen, was Irish, he listened to Irish rebel music and he could sing the Irish national anthem, in English.

He'd actually even been to Ireland. Case fucking closed.

My now good mate Tony would go to extreme lengths to present himself as the number one Celtic supporter at St Mary's. He'd been to a few games, he had the home and away strip, alternating between them, and he always wore one under his school uniform.

He was a pioneer on all other fronts as well. His jotter was covered with a Celtic poster whilst everyone else had settled for wallpaper, the same soft, spongy, patterned council-house wallpaper that I'd clawed apart a few years earlier.

He had a Celtic pencil, a Celtic pencil case, a Celtic pencil sharpener; the man was blazing the trail. His surname, Clark, was Irish, but maybe not quite Irish enough for him. His crowning moment, though, was after an Old Firm game at Ibrox.

Going to an Old Firm game was unthinkable; that wasn't what anyone at St Mary's had done. John went to them all, but I wasn't allowed. I'd never even asked to be taken to one, and I was too young to know what the attraction was, so it didn't really bother me. I knew they were off limits for a good few years and it wasn't a place for a child.

The game at Ibrox was unique in that of the fifty thousand crowd, fifty thousand of them were Rangers supporters, the Celtic supporters serving a ban on account of damage they'd caused to the stadium on the last visit.

At kick-off, a plane flew over the stadium trailing a banner that said, 'Hail! Hail! The Celts Are Here', like one of those planes you see on holiday, flying over the beach promoting a local radio station.

The TV cameras caught it and it made all of the newspapers the following day. The game itself ended as a draw so the plane stunt was one of the main talking points, with the general consensus being that it was pretty impressive that someone had gone to the effort of chartering a plane, hiring a pilot, having the banner made, obtaining permission from air traffic control and having it flown across the stadium, just to show some support to their team.

On Monday at school, Tony told the class, 'That was me and my dad.' Everyone was blown away, a thoroughly impressed, collective 'Woooowww' from the class, with only the teacher and Tony knowing it was total bullshit.

I had my suspicions but I wanted to believe him; he'd done us all but I was proud of him. Get that one right up you, Brendan Kelly, you and your auntie from Donegal, I thought to myself.

Under the new flawed and innocently misunderstood rules of being a Celtic supporter, if your surname was O'Donnell or O'Neill you didn't even need to go to a game or own the latest strip.

You were already a front-runner in the Celtic supporting stakes, saving your parents a fortune in merchandise, tickets and chartered planes, and you wouldn't have to face regular interrogations from those suspicious at the lack of evidence backing your claims of being a season-ticket holder.

I'd taken inspiration from Tony's far-fetched tale being believed by the class and I followed his lead, determined to join him in pole position. I told the whole class one lunchtime that I had a season ticket and would now be going to every game.

Celtic Park had just been rebuilt and it was an exciting time, with everyone desperate to go up and see it. The calls of, 'Bring it into school, then,' I quickly answered with: 'My mum won't let me in case it gets stolen.'

I lacked Tony's total conviction and throwaway confidence and every Monday I'd be grilled: 'How was the game? Where did you sit? What was the first goal like?'

I could just about get through most of their cross-examinations, but they knew I was lying, they simply couldn't prove it. I'd quiz John about the game when he'd get home on Saturday nights, the same way they'd quiz me.

I was doing my revision so that I could go in prepared, totally bulletproof. But it was starting to get too much, and the only plan I could come up with to try to prove myself to the doubters was to steal John's season ticket for a day.

I grabbed it from the top drawer in his bedroom one morning and stuffed it in the inside pocket of my jacket. I knew it would be an ordeal to get it in and out of school and back into the drawer in the same condition and without my mum, dad or, crucially, John knowing.

I didn't even want to consider the consequences should it be stolen, lost or damaged.

It was a very delicate operation; I felt like a G4S/Securicor driver collecting cash from a city centre bank on a Friday afternoon. I'd planned to unveil it at playtime to a gathered crowd of sceptical classmates, and when I pulled it from my pocket there was genuine surprise. The crowd was taken aback.

They were impressed. I was cool. The rapid ascendency to 'number one Celtic fan' and hero status lasted only minutes, though. 'That could be anybody's season ticket,' a voice from the huddled masses challenged, leading to calls of, 'Check the name on it.'

My world had collapsed. I was a fraud.

Hands were trying to grab it from me. I managed to keep hold of it, but I'd no other choice than to open it up and show the inside information page: 'North Stand, Block 4, Row E, Seat 10 . . . John Bridges.'

It was humiliating. There were cheers of celebration, people pointing and laughing, looking at me, silently shaking their heads and walking away dejectedly, more disappointed than anything.

Writing this, and reading it all back so far, I can see I was quite a confused child and always felt a little bit lost. I was desperate to fit in and just be like everyone else.

If you're familiar with my stand-up, then you've maybe quoted my 'toughen up, ya wee prick' line at some point over the last few chapters about my early school years.

I'm surprised that I remember so much from then, given that I was so young, and I struggle to place events in order; they all merge into the same sort of period.

I probably spent too much time in my own company and my imagination was pretty wild, which is a good thing for a child, but I'd over-think everything, positive and negative.

Teachers for my first few years, Mrs McInnes, Mrs Reilly and Mrs Conway, would tell my mum and dad at parents' nights and in report cards that I was smart but needed to come out of my shell a lot more. They added that I'd constantly daydream and look as though there was something on my mind.

I'll never know what was up with me, and people who only knew me then would find it difficult to imagine that I'd be making a living performing live on stage to huge crowds. But even now I have the same sort of feelings as I did at that age, and I'd say I'm still quite introverted and an over-thinker.

People will laugh at what I was like and say, 'Look at you now', which is a compliment and to be expected. But I don't feel all that different, and, if anything, I'm quite proud of that confused, anxious, nervous wee guy. I didn't change and I figured things out my own way and in my own time.

13

In 1995 a lot seemed to change and a few things happened that resulted in me going on to feel a bit happier and content with myself.

My mum and dad managed to get the money together to take us on a family holiday at the same time and to the same resort as my Uncle George and my Auntie Maureen, Paul, Stephen, Mark and Gary.

The day we booked it I remember well because it was a Saturday and we were in Clydebank Shopping Centre, but this time my dad was with us. He asked the travel agent how much it would cost to go on the Orient Express. She answered, he laughed, my mum slapped the back of his head and a week in Majorca was booked.

We flew from and to Newcastle as it was a little cheaper than Glasgow, and we got the train down. It wasn't Orient Express standard, but my mum had made cracking rolls and chopped pork.

I remember our flight being delayed for hours, which meant I got to spend a lot of time with John. I'd try to pester my mum and dad with questions, so they'd give John more money to take me away to play in the airport arcade. It had a pool table, air hockey, shooting games where you held a toy gun and aimed at targets on the screen, a motorbike simulator . . . being on holiday was amazing. I'd have happily done two weeks self-catering in Newcastle airport.

The holiday actually got even better once we left the airport. When we arrived at about six o'clock in the morning at the apartment complex where we'd be staying, my mum, dad and John were exhausted and went off to sleep.

I was too hyperactive to sleep and assumed the role of their snooze button, checking if they were ready to get up and head to the pool every fifteen/twenty minutes until I eventually took the hint and went off to occupy myself in the apartment's living room.

I'd been allowed to pack my school bag full of my own stuff. I'd seen John packing his, and to prevent another equal-rights demonstration my mum let me pack mine. John had his Walkman and his bag space was taken up predominantly with his cassettes.

I didn't really have much shit that I'd wanted to take but, still, I wasn't missing out on an opportunity. My bag contained anything I could find when raiding my bedroom the night before we left. Toy cars, a packet of playing cards, a little glove-puppet monkey and a white fluffy soft toy that had been lying around the house since I was born. I'd never decided if it was a dog or a rabbit so I'd diplomatically named it 'Dabbit'.

I even took a few ornaments from our hallway window ledge – 'in case anyone gets homesick' I had explained earlier at Newcastle airport when my dad had opened my bag to stick a few cartons of cigarettes inside. They all found it funny, and I was chuffed with my sharp-witted response to their confused looks.

Again, I should mention here that this was back in the good old days – the days before budget airlines, before hand-luggage space was in demand and a necessity when trying to save being hit with a hefty charge.

I didn't have my Subbuteo. It was summer, it was pre-season and the lads needed a rest after a gruelling campaign. I noticed I had a toy plane and a few fire engines, like the ones I'd seen in the airport. I didn't have anything to make a runway with so I started to look through a suitcase that my mum had opened to sort out some pills and painkillers for my dad. The travelling had meant his joints had seized up and he'd been in a lot of pain.

I think my mum thought we were going on a United Nations aid mission to a devastated developing country, as she had assembled an impressive first-aid kit. I was raiding through piles of Elastoplasts, bandages, antiseptic wipes, TCP, cotton wool, sore-throat rinse, antihistamine, ibuprofen, factors forty and fifty-plus sun cream, after-sun creams, cold and flu lozenges . . .

I can't imagine anyone ever having sunstroke and a cold at the same time, but my mum can. The original Doomsday Prepper, she was prepared for any illness or ailment that could threaten our week in Majorca.

My mum put the 'para' in paracetamol.*

I wasn't stupid enough that I'd start messing about with my dad's boxes of prescribed medication or anything that looked like it would fuck me up. I didn't know what I was looking for, but I found a massive tub of talcum powder, ideal for lining out a runway.

I managed to get it open and started liberally pouring it over the marble floor, using a playing card from my school bag to divide it and thin it out in lines.

If the apartment's maid had popped in unannounced with an enthusiastic 'Housekeeping!', she'd probably have been quick to alert the local police and their narcotics squad, thinking she'd just busted a cocaine ring being operated in a holiday apartment in a three-star resort by a chubby, freckle-faced eight-year-old child in a pair of *Sonic the Hedgehog* pyjamas.

* Thank you, good night, you guys have been great!

With my Nana and my Uncle Kevin and Auntie Anne – my godparents.

My mum and dad's expressions further evidence that I was an accident –
my christening, 1987.

With my dad and John on the veranda of our old flat in Hardgate.

Clocking off after a hard day's gardening.

With my Granddad Tommy and my little cousin Mark, sitting at our front door on a summer's day.

With my mum, posing before complaining about having a 'wedgie'.

First day of school with Big Doc. I look slightly more at ease with holding hands than he does, again, with the shorts . . .

John going to high school and me going to primary school. The photographer content with just a headshot of me, keen to get the architecture in the background.

MUSIC	✓	
ENVIRONMENTAL STUDIES	✓	
RELIGIOUS STUDIES	✓	

COMMENTS
Kevin has developed in confidence and is adopting a more mature attitude. He is trying hard to overcome nervousness in certain situations.

| NUMBER OF ABSENCES | 16 | DAYS |

PARENTAL COMMENT

A report card from primary school with comments
that maybe still resonate today. Not the greatest attendance
record but at least I passed the three important subjects!

At the altar of St Mary's chapel on the day of my first holy communion in 1993.

Standing with my arm around Tony's shoulder, as
he drinks from a can. Our nights out haven't changed
a great deal, even after all the years.

Up to no good with my main man Tony at our first holy communion.

Fed up getting my photograph taken already, the four of us
on the morning of my first holy communion in 1993.

Christmas Eve, sometime in the early 90s, so excited that
I'm about to piss my pants.

My mum, dad and John woke up to see the whole floor covered in straight parallel lines of talcum powder. They perhaps feared the worst and checked about for any rolled-up peseta notes (it was my holiday as well, remember!) before noticing that my toy planes and fire engines were all parked and carefully arranged. 'Don't walk across the runway,' I warned.

My dad, who'd arrived at Palma airport complaining he was hungry, had bought a box of doughnuts. They were called 'Bimbo' doughnuts. I think he found that funny and would be heard throughout the holiday saying to my mum, when she was walking down to the supermarket, 'Get another pack of they Bimbos, Paddy.'

He has always referred to my mum as 'Paddy', in an endearing way. I soon started to copy him and everyone laughed, especially my mum, and it's what I still call her today.

He'd eaten the doughnut before going to bed and had dropped crumbs all over the floor, resulting in a swarm of ants showing up and helping themselves to an all-you-can-eat buffet.

Any of the ants that attempted to cross the runway at Talcum Powder airport perished, though. Every other family we met in the apartment block had been on the hunt for the travel agent's representative, to complain about their rooms being infested with ants. It was a problem throughout the complex but not in our room.

Paddy never went on a holiday again without insect repellent and mosquito sprays; it was an uncharacteristic oversight from her on this occasion, but I'd accidentally bailed her out and was left to take the credit for discovering a makeshift pesticide.

A great start to our first holiday.

We'd meet up with my Uncle George and my Auntie

Maureen every day. They'd come to our apartment or we'd go to theirs, or the beach. At night it'd be the usual package-holiday routine. We'd head to the tourist restaurants and then the Irish bars, the karaoke bars, the hotel bingo nights, hosted by a burned-out-looking Brian Bridges-type, and, of course, the happy-hour places with the Take That tribute act and the mechanical bull beside the gents toilet.

A mechanical bull and a 'hardest punch' machine: two universally recognized indicators that you're drinking in a fucking hellhole. Stephen, Mark, Gary and I would spend the nights drinking Fanta orange, eating crisps and feeding 100 peseta coins into the game machine and the pool table.

Paddy and my Auntie Maureen would get drunk, initially complaining about but later praising the sizeable measures of gin being poured by the Spanish bar staff.

My Uncle George didn't drink either so he and my dad would sit smoking their respective cigars and cigarettes, moaning at the lack of transfer activity from Celtic, both having read a printed-in-Spain copy of the *Daily Record* at the poolside that afternoon.

John and my cousin Paul were at the age where they'd head to pubs and do their own thing, which left Mark, Gary and me with the loose cannon, Stephen.

He was a little older than us and smart enough to dare us to do things that he didn't want to be caught doing.

Stephen was just a year or two below the legal drinking age and, although it was a holiday, my Uncle George and my Auntie Maureen wouldn't allow him to hit the bars and the clubs. Stephen had anticipated that he might be bored, so he had bought himself a plastic BB gun on the first night to keep himself entertained.

Strict on alcohol but relaxed about firearms, my Uncle George and my Auntie Maureen would have been great

Americans. He wasn't allowed to bring it out at night, but he always did. Only Mark and I knew he had it on him. Gary was the youngest and going through a phase of being a grass.

Stephen would give us a signal, and we'd all sneak off from the pub and hide behind trees and bins and start shooting at strangers. The little yellow plastic ball bearings weren't exactly fatal but still enough to provoke an 'Ah! What the fuck was that?' from unsuspecting tourists, which made us giggle hysterically before tiptoeing along to the next tree to find a new target. It was nerve-wracking and a proper adrenalin rush and probably the first time I'd 'broken bad'.

It was great fun until Stephen would get fed up shooting at strangers and turn the gun on us. We'd run back to the bar where the adults were, with Stephen giving chase and emptying a few clips on our arse cheeks.

Sa Coma, Majorca, in 1995 was a time I felt genuinely happy. I was laughing every day, and aside from having John and my cousins there, I started to make loads of friends, the way children do on holiday.

No one knew me, and it was like a fresh start. My confidence had been shattered from school, and I felt like I'd always be known for crying and trying to run out of class. I'd isolated myself at school and that made going even worse; I was in a 'Catch 22'. But here I was confident; I'd talk to anybody.

My mum and dad were pleased to see this side of me and encouraged it. They must have been delighted as well that I was finally giving them hope that I wasn't a total fucking oddball. Other parents in the apartments would tell them that their son or daughter had remarked that I was great at impersonating them and doing their accents.

I'd begin to speak in the accent of whoever I was playing with. There were loads of English and Irish, and I'd even unconsciously start speaking to my mum and dad in terrible Scouse, Geordie, Dublin and Belfast accents. 'What's the craic, Paddy?' I'd say to my mum, and everyone would laugh.

But I kept the cruder phrases I'd learned confined to my new social circle, who lapped it up. The Irish expression 'Show's your gee!' was a fond favourite. Myself and Mark would dare Gary to shout it when we were in a restaurant or bar. Neither of us actually knew what it meant, but we had a rough enough idea, which made it all the more risqué.

At the pool during the day we'd play it like the game 'Jobby', or whatever you called it – 'Shithead', maybe. I'd guess there are several variations of this game. The basic premise is that you agree on a crude word or term and take turns at shouting it, each one getting louder until somebody has to scream it out with every bit of air in their lungs committing to it, eyes watering and blood vessels bulging, so that it's audible to every single person in the near vicinity. Dogs barking, car alarms going off, the lot.

Immature, definitely, but at eight years old, fucking hilarious.

It was getting out of hand. It all came to an abrupt end when an Irish woman who'd been lying by the pool reading a novel walked over to my mum and dad and informed them what 'gee' meant.

'A gee is a vagina,' the woman told my mum.

'I didn't know that "gee" meant vagina,' I said innocently, but knowing this was something I shouldn't be saying.

'What's a vagina?' I asked, inquisitively and clearly, fully enunciating this great new word. I sensed I had an audience and could see people looking over their newspapers and their books, grinning and trying not to laugh at this surreal and comically tense conversation.

'Get back in the pool, son,' said my dad, more embarrassed than angry. I walked back to the pool, giving a knowing smile to those who'd overheard, acknowledging that I knew I'd entertained them and given them a funny story to tell. Still, nobody told me what a vagina was and I decided it best not to ask, but for the rest of the holiday we had a great new game.

Even as I'm writing this I've just started laughing to myself again, this time at the thought of standing up and, at an ear-piercing volume, screaming: 'VAGINA!'

I'm too much of a shitebag to do it now, but by all means you feel free, wherever you are. If there's any comeback just blame this book you're reading, and I'll take full responsibility.

Aside from the 'vagina' debacle, I did get a far more serious telling-off from my mum and dad on the last day of the holiday, one that could almost have ruined the entire break.

We were on separate flights from my Uncle George and my Auntie Maureen, who were flying back direct to Glasgow. We were leaving in the early afternoon, and they'd all come round for lunch and to see us off, before getting their own flight home later that same evening.

Stephen had been told that under no circumstances was he allowed to take his BB gun home with him, that it was just a holiday plaything and that it'd be taken far more seriously in an airport than around a holiday resort.

I wasn't aware that he'd been ordered to bin the thing when he pulled me aside, away from everyone, and said, 'Here, you can keep that.' I was gobsmacked. He had barely let Mark, Gary or me even touch it the entire week and now he was presenting it to me, as a gift.

'Don't tell your mum and dad.' He winked and gave me a playful rub on the head as I held it and stared at it in amazement. It was like a scene from a gangster film, a young capo being handed his first piece.

Could this week get any better? I naively thanked him with all my heart and stuffed it in my school bag, beside my planes, my ornaments, two stuffed toys, a shit load of my dad's cigarettes and, of course, my tub of talcum powder.

The big coach came to pick us up, the doors opening with the distinctive 'sshhhh' sound, the bus's way of saying: 'Holiday's over, everybody, so shut it and get back to work.'

My mum, dad and John loaded the bags in the bottom and we got on board. I had a lump in my throat and felt like crying as we pulled away. I was gutted it was all over.

We arrived at the airport and waited in the check-in queue. I said goodbye to a few of the wee pals I'd met as they went away with their families to the Liverpool, Dublin and Belfast check-in desks, exchanging addresses and promising to write letters to each other as soon as we were home – a final effort to cling on to the unique feeling of a great holiday with great people.

My dad lifted the bags up to be weighed, answered all the mandatory 'Are you going to blow this thing up?' questions, flashed the passports and collected the boarding cards.

Job done.

It was only at security that things strayed from the mundane.

I was first through and stood waiting for my bag coming out of the x-ray scanner thing and along the conveyor belt. My dad was being searched, and my mum and John were putting their belts, coins, watches in a tray and waiting for the nod to walk through to be searched.

'Whose bag is this?' asked the Spanish security officer.

'That's ours,' my dad replied enthusiastically, as if we'd just won a prize or something. The security officer stared at him for a few seconds, and my dad looked round at my mum, but not in a panicked way, probably imagining it had just been picked at random.

He was well within the permitted allowance of cigarettes to take home, and it was a bag packed by his eight year-old son. What contraband could there possibly be?

I didn't even think about the BB gun Stephen had given me, let alone imagine the reaction it would get from airport security staff; after all, it was just a toy.

'May I look inside?' my dad was asked and he nodded.

I'll never forget his face and my mum's face and the face of everyone behind us in the queue when the bag was unzipped and Stephen's BB gun immediately fell out.

It was grabbed by a police officer who gave my dad a 'What the fuck, mate?' kind of look and ordered the rest of the bag to be emptied out.

I didn't even consider that the airport security staff would so much as raise their eyebrows at someone looking to board a plane with a toy gun bought from a Spanish souvenir shop.

What trouble could it cause on the flight?

No one on the plane was going to be alarmed, surely.

No one would see it and then immediately put their hands up in the air and start begging, 'Please don't shoot! We don't know what you want but, please, drop the BB gun, those things fucking sting.'

'I didn't steal it. Stephen gave me it,' I said, thinking that my mum and dad's reaction was because they hadn't seen me with it before, and they'd told me no when I'd asked for one. I was pleading my innocence.

I didn't know the accusations were more serious than petty theft and that this was a terror alert.

I'll admit, it didn't look great, a plastic gun and white powder everywhere from the talcum tub that hadn't been closed right, and then, like a drug-trafficking traditionalist, the two stuffed toys.

I didn't realize how serious it was until the guy ripped Dabbit's head clean off and then ripped his back open as well. I had to stand back and watch as poor Dabbit was being decapitated, torn from 'earhole to arsehole', as is the term for such a brutally violent attack.

I got ready to intervene. I knew we were in serious bother, but I was fucking baffled as to why he'd do that. I was old enough not to be emotionally attached to a teddy bear or anything, but I still felt it was a little over the top.

It had registered on me that bringing a toy gun through an airport in your hand luggage wasn't encouraged, but I was far too young to understand the implications of carrying a bag full of stuffed toys covered in white powder.

My mum was hysterical, telling how she'd never seen the gun in her life. She was also too innocent to make a connection between talcum powder and class-A drugs. It was probably better that way because she'd maybe not be here today if she had.

A firearm and bag full of cocaine at an airport.

They took us into a room, and thankfully a bit of common sense prevailed from the security guys. They were laughing and joking now and even berating the guy who'd carried out the beheading for not seeing the talcum powder tub nor smelling the powder itself. It was a sitcom-like coincidence.

They binned the gun and one of them apologized to me for what had happened to Dabbit, suggesting my mum could maybe sew him back together for me. I remember thinking, 'Fuck Dabbit, wait until you see what happens to me when we get home!'

My mum has never been the best flyer, and her nerves

were truly shattered. Our flight was delayed again, which was pretty fortunate as it gave us all time to recover from the shock, and we eventually had a laugh at the surrealism of what had just gone on.

My dad took my mum to the airport bar and got her a big bastard of a gin to calm her down a little. It helped take the edge off, but she was still rattled, and it would have taken a shot to the neck with a tranquillizer dart to return her to a normal state of mind.

It could have sparked a terror threat; we could have been detained for hours, days, weeks, who knows. It was, undeniably, a classic bit of 'holiday banter' from Stephen, who I thoroughly and unashamedly grassed on when we got home.

He got me, though. Fair play. The prick.

14

I returned to school after the summer of 1995 feeling a lot calmer within myself, but I knew I'd struggle to be as popular in my class as I was around the pool in Sa Coma.

The first day back I had that sad feeling you get when the holiday memories are so vivid, but you know they're now consigned to the past.

I sat in my class wondering what everyone I'd met in Sa Coma would be up to, and then I remembered the English and Irish schools didn't go back until September, much later than ours. I was in it alone whilst they were probably still lying in bed until twelve, eating Coco Pops and watching *Saved by the Bell*.

The English and Irish schools not going back until September explained why there were still cartoons on the TV in the morning for the first few weeks of our return and why, in June, when the Scottish schools had finished, we'd have to sit and watch *Kilroy* and *Going for Gold* for the first weeks of our holidays, waiting for the English and Irish schools to finish before something decent was put on.

My class in St Mary's had changed, and I was now in a 'composite' class, which meant pupils from two different age groups sharing a class. There were about fifteen Primary 5s and fifteen Primary 4s.

I'd hoped Mark would have been one of the Primary 4s, but he wasn't, and it was the first year that I wasn't in the same class as Tony, a bit of a blow. But Gary 'Big Doc' Docherty was there, so that cushioned the blow.

We shared a group with a couple of others who hadn't been in my class, including Peter Gilroy, who one day showed up at school in tears, probably for reasons more serious than simply 'showing up at school', but I remember being delighted that it was someone else. He'd taken over from me as the cry baby; I was one of the cool ones, for this one day at least.

If only I'd built on it. That day I should have headed round behind the football pitches, lit up a fag and commented, 'What about that dick this morning, eh?'

I remember Peter being a genuinely funny guy; he was up for a laugh and would always carry on and do stupid voices, and the class really liked him. If only they'd seen me in Sa Coma, though.

There was Doc, Peter, Sean Quinn, who'd just moved to St Mary's from another primary school, and me. I became friends with Sean and used to try to make him laugh throughout the whole class. He'd always get caught laughing and say, 'It's him, miss,' to our teacher, Mrs Elliot.

She would never believe that I could be responsible for cracking jokes or carrying on. My reputation was as the shy one, the one who suffered from anxiety issues, the mummy's boy, so the new guy's card was marked as a troublemaker.

He wasn't a troublemaker, but he quickly achieved 'No Angel' status, which was enough to earn him his 'y' and he soon became 'Quinny'. I liked how Quinny hadn't been there for the first three years and just knew me as the one who'd make him laugh during class.

He became quite popular and was filled in about my past and my tear-filled mornings, but even when everyone was taking the piss out of me for it, he didn't join in or laugh along. He took me as he found me, and I was grateful for that.

I started to enjoy our group. We'd all sit and talk about football and I was beginning to excel in my work, with teachers not hesitating to push me up a level for writing and maths.

There was a thing called SRA. I can't remember what it stood for, which will probably undermine this next chapter, in which I tell you how I was shit-hot at it.

I've searched online, but it's quite a popular acronym, the top boys being the Sustainable Restaurant Association, who claim that they 'help their restaurant members become global leaders in sustainability' – a commendable act, so well done, lads.

A few pages into the search I've found a Yahoo answers page acknowledging SRA exists – they'll always bail you out. No matter how much shite you're speaking, you'll always find something on Yahoo answers to back you up. 'Yes, Chinese takeaway food is actually really healthy.'

SRA was a box of English language and grammar exercises, all multiple-choice; you had to pick which sentence was right and all that sort of stuff. All the cards had different colours and each colour represented a level of difficulty.

We were started off at Brown and Yellow. I remember that because of the unfortunate scatological connotations that saw them renamed. You didn't want to be stuck there for too long.

SRA cards were self-corrected. You'd mark 'a', 'b', 'c' or 'd' and when you finished the exercise you went to collect the answers card and marked it yourself.

A few in our class who'd been stuck on the Brown and Yellow cards, and who'd had enough of the sneering comments from their smug classmates, proved themselves to be far from thick by devising a scam.

If you marked every answer as a 'c', that letter could be most easily changed to an 'a', 'b' or 'd', with only the 'b' looking slightly doctored. But the key was not to get full marks anyway, as that would arouse suspicion. No one was trying to be a hero; just a step up from 'Shite' and 'Pish' was enough.

I never took part in the scam. I was doing all right on my own, and I'd managed to get up to the higher level colours – Rose, I think. I remember being delighted at the promotion. I was proud and couldn't wait to tell my mum and dad.

John had passed his Higher exams and had been accepted into Glasgow Caledonian University. Not Glasgow University. The Caledonian one. Every city has its good uni and its shite uni; the extra add-on, like 'Metropolitan', was the indicator that this uni was for those too thick for the good uni, but too arrogant for a call centre.

Regardless, he was the first in all of either my mum's side of the family or my dad's to have made it to university. We were all proud of him. I didn't quite understand what it meant, but remember talking about him at school and telling everyone of his achievement.

I'd start to put pressure on myself to follow him. 'What SRA group was John in, Paddy?' I'd ask, checking if I was on the right road. I'd begin to put my maths and spelling tests on a parallel with John's exams and I went through a phase of trying to make myself sick on the days they were taking place.

I would struggle to sleep the nights before the 'exams'. I'd always pass and do well. But it would just mean I'd put myself under even more pressure to improve on the next one, and there'd always be someone doing better in the school and that would be my new benchmark. Even though I'd stopped with the tears and the tantrums, I still took primary school far too seriously.

My mum and dad and a few of my teachers had noticed

that I'd developed a nasty-sounding cough and that I was getting out of breath a lot during PE. I was chubby and not the fittest; worrying was the only exercise I got.

I'd been to the doctor's, and he'd prescribed me a bottle of cough mixture. But the cough wouldn't shift, and I'd start to get wheezy just walking up a few stairs in the house or in school.

My mum had had enough and took me back down to the doctor again, demanding that he look into something more serious than a cough. The doctor made me blow into a white and red tube called a 'peak flow' that measured the strength of your lungs and your air flow. I struggled to get the little dial moving, and my result was well below what a healthy child my age should be reaching.

The doctor gave me an inhaler and a big clear-plastic, dome-type thing. I was to spray the inhaler into the dome and then inhale from that dome. It was quite a complicated-looking thing but my mum made sure she figured it out and that I took the recommended three or four daily doses.

I didn't feel all that much better, but I knew this could be an excuse to try to stay off school. On the very first night of this treatment, though, I woke up struggling to breathe and felt like I was suffocating. I didn't have enough air to shout and I began inhaling desperately. It was terrifying and I staggered out of bed and into my mum and dad's room.

My mum heard my difficult breathing noises, turned the light on and started shouting at my dad to get up and get me to the car. My dad is normally quick to tell my mum she's overreacting, but he woke up, looked at me and jumped straight out of bed. My face had turned grey, and I was really struggling to get any air into me at all.

We got in the car and I remember being sick all over the back seat and also over my mum, who was sat in the back

beside me. I tried to say sorry but couldn't. My mum was trying to act calm because she knew that if I sensed she was in
a state of panic it probably would have made me worse.

We arrived at Yorkhill Children's Hospital in Glasgow, and
I was put on a bed and rushed straight to intensive care. I
remember feeling dizzy and light-headed when the oxygen
mask was put on. It took about five attempts to find a vein to
put my drip in. The nurse kept apologizing, taking the blame
for every failed effort, but I knew it was me being overweight
that was making it difficult.

I began to come round enough to notice all the machines
I was wired up to and realize that something terrible had
happened. I started panicking, but the nurses and my mum
and dad managed to calm me down and give me some drink
that made me tired so I eventually fell asleep.

I woke up the next day with my mum, dad and John sat
beside the bed. I'd gone from not knowing I had asthma to
having a severe asthma attack. I was moved out of intensive
care after two days and then kept in hospital for the rest of
the week.

I couldn't eat or drink and remember pleading for a can of
Coke or water or anything. I had a feeling of thirst that I'd
never felt before, but anything I drank I immediately spewed
back up.

I'd got my wish of being off school, but I'd have taken
school all day over this; spelling tests, anything. Everyone in
my class sent me a card. People came up to visit me, and I
remember all the hospital staff being really friendly and making jokes with me.

I began to get into reading, mainly just comics, things like *The
Beano*, *The Dandy*, *Oor Wullie* and *The Broons* that people would
bring up from the hospital shop. I remember thinking they were
shite, but I'd have felt too unappreciative to tell anyone.

I made myself read them and kid on I liked them. I'd try bringing some authenticity to my act and show that I was getting into the characters, in an 'Oh man, those Bash Street Kids are quite a bunch, aren't they?' kind of way.

I always had a zero-tolerance approach to anything that didn't seem realistic or appeared out of touch. I'd read about Oor Wullie and how he was the local rogue. I'd read about him getting into trouble for things like stealing apples from his neighbour's tree.

Eddie Riley punched the fire alarm and called the janitor a dildo last Friday, I'd think to myself, and then imagine a comic called *Oor Eddie* and how it'd be more relatable to children my age.

I smiled at the thought and then reverted to confusion, remembering that I still hadn't found out what a dildo was. The janitor hadn't taken it too well, so I'd gathered it was offensive and a certainty to be shouted from the pool if we went on a holiday again.

I did enjoy reading and it would always spark ideas in my head, just daft ones, but they made me laugh, and I'd sometimes write silly stories down.

I never got to showcase my stories, as we didn't do anything like that at primary school. All the subjects seemed regimented stuff to me.

There were right and wrong answers, and that was that.

Even though I was coping comfortably with all the schoolwork, everything was like a competition and a test, and that's probably why it filled me with dread.

Leaving Yorkhill, I was given two inhalers and told to go and see the doctor once every few weeks for a check-up, which my mum translated as twice every week. She eventually got over the hysteria and later told me how she'd seen my chest swelling up through my T-shirt and how she'd feared the very worst.

The doctors recommended that I started going swimming regularly to help my lungs, so that meant every Saturday morning my dad and I would go to Drumchapel swimming baths.

I'd only been in a pool on our holiday, but loved it. So it was good that we'd be going every week. My dad would always take the opportunity to talk to me and try to get to the bottom of my emotional hang-ups. He'd tell me I should relax and enjoy school more and not put so much pressure on myself.

He's always had a laid-back attitude to life, with the exception of instances involving malfunctioning remote controls, assembling furniture and watching Celtic. His favourite quote, and a mantra that I'd say he lives by and has always tried to instil in me, is John Candy's line from *Planes, Trains and Automobiles*: 'I like me.'

15

But, in keeping with our family tradition of boots in the balls happening in quick succession, not long after my asthma attack, my last remaining grandparent, my Granny Jane, my dad's mum, had a stroke.

She was kept in hospital for weeks. She was allowed to return home, but was told she'd require twenty-four-hour care. It would have broken her heart to be put into a nursing home, and my dad was adamant that wouldn't be allowed to happen.

My mum put in a request to her bosses that she be my Granny Jane's designated home help. For some reason, friends or family weren't allowed to work as a care worker for the sick or disabled, some council official obviously concluding that the sick or disabled would much rather have a complete stranger bath them, dress them, feed them and spend hours in their home than someone they know and trust.

We'd go over and see her a lot before she passed away a couple of years later. The funeral was the only time I've ever seen my dad cry, but he and my mum had got to spend time with her. They'd spoken and laughed with her, and they'd all got a chance to say the things they wanted to say, so everything was peaceful.

My dad's arthritis had again deteriorated. Every doctor he saw was now recommending that he quit working altogether in an attempt to prevent further damage, which could potentially result in him being unable to walk and being housebound. The pain was getting unbearable for him; but he saw his work as a distraction, despite it clearly aggravating his condition.

It had been on the cards, but my dad was taken aback and got pretty depressed about it. He thought he'd be at a loss as to how to fill his days, and he'd beat himself up and feel emasculated because my mum was now the only earner in the house.

When I read today about benefit cuts and those on incapacity benefit being forced back into work, I fully understand how immoral it is and how it must heighten an already difficult situation for them.

Benefits, like most other things in life, are open to abuse, and to people finding and taking advantage of loopholes; it's the same with MPs' expenses and the tax payments of the wealthy. Of course there are people who'll be trying to get away with working and taking a few quid off the government. I say a few quid and not 'a living', as I sincerely doubt anyone can live a comfortable life on the rates being paid.

To create a society, where everyone who relies on this money to survive is degraded and made to feel like they're scum – that's wrong, and it's infuriating that more people can't see this.

Those who have gone through the shock and hurt of being told they are no longer fit and healthy enough to provide for themselves and their families are never mentioned with any sympathy or understanding. They're made to feel like they're begging, that they're a liability that society can do without.

The same with those who are paid off and simply can't find work. 'There are jobs out there. Just get out and find them,' people will claim. What kind of jobs, though? You can't blame a fully qualified electrician for not being enamoured of a potential new career in chewing-gum removal.

Maybe it's easier to have a rant and believe that everyone on benefits lives the high life and that you're the mug for working. It makes for readable articles and watchable television. The case studies being presented are more relatable to us than articles or TV documentaries about tax-avoiding corporations and individuals or corrupt bankers.

We're too powerless to have a go at multinational, billion-pound companies not contributing to the country. They have the government onside, and they're untouchable.

The forty-year-old guy in your street, living with his parents and pretending he's got a sore back so that he can lie in bed watching *Storage Wars* and eating Quavers all day, though, he's a far easier target.

Excess borrowing and greed is my basic understanding of the UK's financial troubles, with the people at the bottom taking the hit and paying to rectify the situation, the very same people who were taught from an early age not to borrow.

Most people who grew up in a predominantly working-class area will remember their ice-cream van having a laminated notice stuck to the window, just in front of the jars of penny sweets, that said: 'Please don't ask for credit as a refusal may offend.' Often accompanied by a more straightforward 'No tick, so don't ask' notice, written in black permanent marker on a piece of A4 lined paper. It made sense and people took heed.

That one sign could have prevented the banking collapse and the astronomical bail-outs.

They fucked it, and a part of you really has to admire the sheer balls of their recovery operation.

Let's devise some harsh government cutbacks to be implemented under the guise of 'ending the country's entitlement culture'. Get the backing of a few newspapers who'll use words like 'scroungers' and 'spongers'. Show some programmes like *Benefits Street* and let the Facebook outrage begin. The people who are only happy when they're raging about something – get them behind you, and don't forget to mention the asylum seekers.

Everyone's distracted and the coast is clear. Job done.

I was too young to understand the consequences of my dad having to retire on medical grounds. But looking back now, and with a social conscience, I realize it was a difficult time, and I'm forever indebted and inspired by how well it was handled by my mum, dad and John.

John started working in Asda. He had his wages and his student loan. He was supporting himself and that helped ease the burden on my mum.

I wouldn't feel comfortable writing about my family being poor; I'd feel disrespectful to my mum if I were to go down that road. I don't remember ever wanting for anything. There was always a fridge full of food, and I always had football strips and a decent pair of trainers.

At school I was eligible for a uniform grant and a school-dinner ticket. I didn't know this until high school, though; my mum would always make me my lunch or give me money to get myself something.

I don't know if she'd have felt embarrassed or if she'd thought I'd be laughed at for taking a free lunch every day whilst everyone else went to the ice-cream van or the chippy. Either way, people feeling ashamed about getting some help is something that shouldn't be happening.

For the first few weeks my dad would sit around the house, miserable and not knowing what to do with himself. He gradually got his head around it all and recognized that it wasn't just for financial reasons that his family depended on him.

We'd start to see a lot more of each other. It made school easier that he'd come over some lunchtimes. We'd go to the Villa bakery in Duntocher, get a few rolls and talk total nonsense and make each other laugh. If I was getting a hard time at school, I'd tell him. He'd always advise me to stand up for myself and to fight back if I was being bullied.

Contrary to the advice that is so often dispensed by parents, 'standing up' to bullies and 'fighting back' will only worsen the situation. I did try to follow his advice; if someone called me 'Fatty', I'd reply with a specky/ginger/skinny insult, where applicable. 'Who the fuck are you talking to, Fatty?' would be the reply, followed by a baying mob cranking up the war of words. Shouts of, 'Are you taking that?' provoking the aggressor to turn things physical.

Not even Don King, Frank Warren, Bob Arum or any other famous boxing promoter has ever been able to rapidly source two opponents and hype up a fight with as much enthusiasm and penchant for violence as a school child.

It maybe took away from the aggression and the bloodlust when the bout was scheduled for 'playtime', but that didn't matter. The rest of the class were ecstatic with anticipation, and the two contenders petrified, but not wanting to let it show.

There was no weigh-in beforehand, the pre-fight build-up focusing mainly on the talk of who was going to 'jump in' for whom, adding a raw, chaotic brawl aspect that is so often lacking in professional boxing.

I was beaten up a few times before I gave up on my dad's advice. I wasn't a fighter so felt it best just to keep my head down and get on with the work.

I had Doc, Quinny and the rest of the group in my class. So I had people to sit with, but they were in with the popular crowd. At playtime and lunchtime, I'd just wander around.

I'd try to play football, but I didn't have the confidence. I'd stand at the goals, drinking a 275 ml bottle of Irn-Bru from the tuck shop and hoping the midfield would provide me with the service I needed. I was a traditional number nine. I think I managed one goal in over a thousand appearances, so not the most prolific of penalty-box target-men, but it was still a great feeling.

At primary school, I found football ability dictated your social standing. If you could play at a respectable level, then you were fine; you could keep a low profile, fade into the background and be left to serve your time.

If you were one of the better players, you'd pick the teams at lunchtime, everyone wanted to be your mate, girls would write your name on their jotters. Being good at football came second only to being fucking mental when it came to the brutal battle for playground survival.

If you had managed to establish yourself as a good footballer and a nut job, then you'd hit the jackpot. We had a few of those at our school, the overwhelming majority of them later deciding to focus on the latter, less lucrative and higher risk of their two callings.

Being neither a nutter nor a footballer at school, I found there were very few alternative options in shaping the early years of your life. You could take early retirement from the game in pursuit of other lunchtime activities – hopscotch, skipping, British bulldog. This, I learned through the mistakes of others, led to something even worse than ridicule: total indifference.

Maybe they had the right idea, though. The people at your school who nobody bothered, the ones who weren't thick or smart, they just sort of blended into the background. No one really knew them; they hardly ever spoke and had no notable personality traits.

I probably should have gone down that road; it'd have made for a much easier life, but I had so many built-up frustrations and had a need to let them out.

Football and fighting were the only vehicles for expression and I was a long way off mastering either.

16

Having my dad around the house a lot more, I really started to admire his total carefree attitude and realize how sharp-witted and at the same time how daft he was.

It was like having a new pal to hang around with, and looking forward to meeting up with him at lunchtime would get me through the mornings. Maybe it was the same for him as well.

When I talk about John being the first in our family to ever make it to university, I reckon my dad couldn't have been far off it. He's always been intelligent, clued up on his history as well as current affairs, and he fancied himself as a writer. When he retired, he began submitting some funny poems and short stories to a creative-writing group and received great feedback. He was told they'd like to publish a few of them in a book they were putting together for charity.

We had a copy of the book in our house years ago. I have no idea where it is now and I've only just remembered it when writing this down. I didn't really get the humour. It was all stuff about being drunk and getting a kebab on the way home, and characters that were based on the guys he used to work with in Singer and guys who used to drink with him in the pubs. But I'd read his name at the end, over and over, and I remember feeling proud that it was my dad's name in a book.

I took the book into school one day. I didn't bother showing anyone in the class as I was thinking they wouldn't appreciate it and would probably just laugh at me and, worse, my dad.

But I wanted to show my teacher, Mrs Conway. She complimented the work and told me to tell my dad he should keep at it. I don't know why I showed her, really; it was as though I was acting as an agent and hoping that my teacher could get him his big break.

I think she told him this again in person, at a parents' night, which made me feel even better, because she hadn't just been humouring me.

When he was at the end of primary school, my dad missed out on sitting his exams, which would have seen him go to high school. In his day, you had to sit an IQ test-type thing that determined if you'd leave St Mary's and go on to St Columba's, the same high school that I'd automatically go to.

He'd been standing watching a Duntocher Hibs game at the 'Hibby' Park in Duntocher. This was a legendary local team who played at 'Junior' level. Juniors in Scotland roughly equating to Conference, Blue Square, LDV Vans, or whatever it's known as now, level in England.

They were well known for attracting large crowds and producing players who'd go on to be signed up to professional teams, with Paddy Crerand, who went on to play for Celtic and Manchester United, being one of them, and James Docherty, my Nana's brother and Big Doc's granddad, another. He also went on to play for Celtic.

There was a crowd of guys, a little older than my dad's crowd, who'd been drinking and messing about. For a laugh one of the crowd threw an old metal fence pole towards my dad and his mates. The pole hit the back of my dad's leg, pierced straight through his calf and came out on the other side like a spit.

He was in agony and was in hospital for weeks. He was operated on several times and was then reliant on a wheelchair for a while before making a full recovery. This was in the 1960s and they didn't have any way of sorting a date for some re-sits. He'd missed the exams and that was that.

The teachers probably could have pushed for him a little more, but he was a class clown and received 'the belt' on a daily basis. So they weren't too bothered and felt he'd be suited to staying on at St Mary's with everyone in his class who'd gotten an IQ score below the St Columba's entry requirement.

When he told me this during one of our lunchtimes, I couldn't believe that he hadn't gone on to do exams and that he'd left school very young and without qualifications. I was naive and still at the age when I thought my dad knew everything. I've since documented in my stand-up that I discovered not long after that he was, in actual fact, a bit of a bell-end.

He left school at fifteen and was dragged down to the Singer factory gates every morning by Grandda John and made to look for work. He eventually landed a start as a 'barra boy', which involved pushing a wheelbarrow full of materials and parts and responding to the shouts from the production line. He worked his way up through the ranks at Singer until it eventually closed.

He went on to do a course in joinery. But by then he'd married and had John, so he decided against completing the course as he couldn't make a living working for trainee wages, nor could he be attending college unpaid.

He landed a job working night shifts as a security guard, again at a factory. It was well paid, but the hours weren't ideal but he stuck it out for a while to bring home some decent money until something better came up.

His last job was as a social care worker, working with

people who were recovering from strokes and people who had arthritis and other disabilities. His job was to help rehabilitate the patients physically and, ironically, to try to reassure them that they would eventually be able to return to work and to a normal life.

I write this, and as much as it's sad and easy to think what my dad could have done with himself, he's never been bitter about any of it. He didn't want to be a hard-luck story and took positives from the situation, using his time to turn his focus fully on his family.

John was independent by now. He was out studying, working, having a good time and doing well for himself. But for me, spending so much time with my dad definitely helped me realize that life wasn't to be taken so seriously. I never remember having any problem or something worrying me that I felt I couldn't tell him.

Along with the regular Saturdays at the swimming, on Fridays we'd go to the local 'Boys Club' football training. I remember everyone from St Mary's being there, my year and the year above and below. We were all allowed to run wild in the wooden-floored gym hall, with a yellow indoor football flying around. If you got a touch of it, you'd had a good game.

My out-of-school hobbies were my imaginary Subbuteo empire and playing John's old computer games. Everyone else in the class had a Sega or a Nintendo, but I was besotted by the Amstrad, and in particular the game *Paperboy*.

Paperboy was as it sounds; you controlled a teenager on a BMX and your objective was to deliver newspapers. This was achieved by rapidly tapping the space bar and using the direction keys to steer the bike. You'd hit return or some other button on the keyboard to throw a paper and there would be points scored for every paper that landed successfully on a garden porch.

It doesn't sound all that exciting, especially if you've become accustomed to the standards of modern computer games. There were no Apache helicopters to fly, no fighter jets, no surface-to-air missiles to launch and no prostitutes to murder with a flame-thrower.

There were risks, however. Dogs could eat the newspapers, and I don't know how many times I cycled into the back of a bin lorry. It was thrilling enough for me, and I'd spend hours playing it.

John would set it up for me when I came home from school. It served as a distraction whilst he'd stay in his room playing the far more advanced gaming revelation, the *Commodore 64*.

When relatives would ask me what I wanted to be when I grew up, I'd always tell them, without any hesitation, that I wanted to be a paperboy.

If I'd eventually had enough of *Paperboy*, I'd play shooting and strategy games like *Dan Dare*. But I could only get so far before having to shout for John to come in and help me through certain levels.

It never felt right asking for assistance. So I'd grow more and more agitated before giving up and finding a new game. I had a brief affair with Gary Lineker's *Superstar Soccer* before discovering a game called *World Soccer League*.

Having a ten-year age gap between your older brother and yourself can have its advantages. You're allowed to be a pain in the arse with no physical ramifications – that is the first and the one which becomes apparent at a very young age and one that I exploited, to the very limit.

Sometimes crossing that limit . . . At nine years old, you don't quite comprehend how painful a kick straight to the balls can be for a nineteen-year-old.

As a ten-year-old in the mid-1990s, when everyone else in your class is bringing in Spice Girls and *Now That's What I Call Music* CDs, introducing the end-of-term class party to the Happy Mondays, Black Grape, Oasis and the Stone Roses is something I took great satisfaction in.

Stealing every CD in my brother's room and then handing them back with the discs scratched and the cases cracked is something I took great shame in, though; maybe not at the time, but now that I've grown to respect the great tunes and the pride that the pre-download generation took in their carefully assembled music collections.

I've often been referred to as 'an old head on young shoulders' and I think I've always thought ahead of my years. I owe a bit of this to growing up between two generations, thanks to John.

Ask anyone around my age to name their first favourite computer game and I'd imagine *Mario Brothers* or *Sonic the Hedgehog* would dominate the poll, whereas my choice would feature in the 'Other' section. It's tough to put any game ahead of *Paperboy*, but *World Soccer League* would edge it for me.

It was my introduction to what turned out to be a long career of highs and lows in the time-consuming, emotional, unpredictable world of football management.

Not real football management, obviously. Anyone can handle two games a week; few can handle the pressure of playing an entire season in a day.

World Soccer League was the most basic game imaginable. I'm not going to go nostalgic and tell you that it was great. If I were to load it up now, it'd probably last as long as a 'Ha! Remember that? Mad, eh?' before an anti-climactic return to the loft.

You could play as Celtic, Rangers, Man Utd, Liverpool, Everton, Arsenal or Tottenham. You'd play in a second division of world football.

The game still comes in handy for small-talk conversations. Recently I was talking to a Moroccan taxi driver, and I asked if he supported Far Rabat (a notoriously tough away fixture in the *World Soccer League* second division). Only crashing the car would have derailed the guy's enthusiasm. He genuinely seemed blown away that I knew his team.

I crumbled when he proceeded to quiz me about the current squad and their latest run of form. But, still, it was a nice minute or so, and it perked us both up. I left him with a generous tip and a 'Fuck Raja Casablanca, mate.'

I'd made a friend for life.

If you won a game in *World Soccer League*, your players' ratings would rise and your transfer budget would increase, and the opposite would happen if you lost.

I would always go Celtic and purposely sign a Dutch player and a Portuguese player, editing the names from their fictional generic computer game names to Van Hooijdonk and Cadete, after Celtic's two strikers at the time. I'd then begin the search for a German, an East German, since, according to my sticker book, that's where Andreas Thom, Celtic's exciting attacking midfielder, was born.

I didn't understand politics or the fact that the game was designed before the collapse of the Berlin Wall. I wasn't overlooking any form of detail, though.

Pierre van Hooijdonk, Jorge Cadete and Andreas Thom would join Simon Donnelly, who'd recently been renamed Kevin Bridges, in our attack as part of our attacking 4–2–4 formation. Attractive football was the Amstrad way.

Navigating promotion to Division 1 was always straightforward, and after two, maybe three seasons in the top flight, all the players would be on a fifteen rating and losing a game was impossible.

It wore thin and I hit a glass ceiling. I couldn't take the club any further. There are only so many times you can beat Newell's Old Boys and Fluminense 8–0.

This was a gateway game, and soon I was ready for the harder stuff of the *Commodore 64* and *Championship Manager*.

17

My last couple of years at St Mary's I do remember enjoying. My last two teachers, Mrs McFarlane and Mr Thumath, both commented in my school reports that I was working ahead of the levels expected at my stage and both mentioned me as one of the few in the year with potential to go on to further education, if I kept working at the same rate.

I was still pretty shy, even though outside of school I now had Big Doc to hang around with. His mum and dad would work late and he'd started going to his gran's every day after school. Her house was in the street just behind ours.

He'd go there, get changed out of his school uniform and come down to get me. Then we'd go out and play football and meet up with Paul O'Donnell. Paul, whom I didn't really know until he was in my class at school, also lived in Hardgate, in the next street up.

We also had Rory Montgommerie, who'd joined St Mary's halfway through Primary 6, after he, his mum and his older brother moved up from London. I'd feel a little sorry for the one or two people who'd come to St Mary's with different accents, people from the north of Scotland and a couple from England. They'd be laughed at and usually end up in a fight. Rory quickly became popular, though, and my mate.

Again, like Quinny, he only knew me as just one of the class and I had a fresh start. It was a bonus that he was another in the Duntocher-dominated class who lived in Hardgate.

When we got bored of playing football and all the spin-off

games like 'records', 'cuppy' and the more physical 'let's see who can do the worst tackle', we'd start to get up to no good.

Paul and Rory both had older brothers, so that would open up a new crowd to me. A crowd who were closer to my age, being a little older than me, but slightly younger than the Gravils.

We'd get up to *Oor Wullie* and *Bash Street Kids* type of mischief, playing all the usual games like chap-door-run-away. Every day someone would be dared to go to the top level of the flats in our area and chap every door from top to bottom.

I was also introduced to the 'Grand National', a game where everyone raced through the entire street's gardens, hurdling the hedges, and then back, the return leg usually resulting in a chase from some of the residents.

I was more of a flat racer, and I'd often abandon the return hurdle event in favour of running alongside the pack on the pavement. I'd run and run, closing my eyes and willing myself to speed up. Seeking motivation from the thoughts of what would happen to me if I were caught.

I was going so slowly and lagging behind the leading pack so much that I'd expect whoever we were running away from to overtake me. They'd see catching me as too easy and whizz pass, in hot pursuit of the rest of them.

'I know you. You're Patricia Mullen's boy.'

I'd be running and shitting myself even more upon hearing this – they even know my mum's real name! They must go way back. I'd be trying to shout ahead, pleading for calm and discouraging the rest of the mob from hurling abuse over their shoulders at someone who'd just professed to know my mum. I was too low down the rankings to have any influence, though.

I'd end up running out of breath and having to stand and

take the talking-to. Everyone would stop and turn back, laughing that I'd been caught and giving more pelters to the incensed adult.

'I've got a good mind to drag you back down and make you repair my hedge,' I remember one guy saying to me, obviously a proud gardener.

'Fuck's sake, mate, I'm not Edward Scissorhands,' I thought, wishing I was with the rest of the crowd so that I could say it and show that I wasn't scared of any adult and that I was one of the gang.

'The cheek they gave me . . . and their language!' would therefore be included in the version of events relayed to my mum at the Hardgate shops the next day.

All the same, I did enjoy getting up to no good, and it was a release from sitting alone, fretting about nothing. Paul O'Donnell was maybe the first bad influence on me, and I'm grateful to him for that. I was enjoying playing stuff like chap-door-run-away and the Grand National, even if Paul was moving on to the next level, things like throwing eggs at people's windows and at passing cars.

I'd always picture the consequences – envisage the driver's vision being obscured by egg yolk, their car swerving off the road and crashing. A horrible way to go and it'd be all because of me.

Beside our house was an old wooden hut that Tommy and my dad had built years earlier. It was used mainly for storing deckchairs, a lawnmower and other garden tools, but we'd decided to turn it into a gang hut.

We decorated the inside of our new-lease property with felt-tip pens and Tippex, writing our names and our nicknames. I didn't have a nickname, although I'd recently started being referred to as 'Big B' at school. We'd write O'D and

Big B and, of course, Celtic and CFC on any spare bit of wood we could find.

I'd never intended to become a twisted fire-starter – that wasn't me at all – but sometimes events just run away with me and take on a life of their own. That's what happened on the day we turned the hut into a science lab, a place where we could attempt to make a bomb out of a chemistry set that my Auntie Anne had bought me for my birthday. Again, I felt a little guilty; it was a nice present and one that was probably bought to encourage me to keep working hard at school.

I should have been looking through the guidebook, following the instructions and conducting the experiments as outlined. That sounded boring, though.

I'd make some fun out of it, but on my terms and not as suggested.

I'd been rifling through the house, gathering anything that could make a feasible claim to being a potential bomb-making component.

My dad's cigarette lighter was the top priority. He went for a smoke every hour, always out on the front doorstep rather than in the house, a concession he made following my asthma attack.

We waited patiently in the hut for him to come out to the front door for his smoke. When he finished, we heard the door shut and gave it a couple of minutes to let him settle back down in the living room. I then sneaked in through the front door, into the kitchen and over to the top drawer where he kept his fags and lighter.

I grabbed it and then had a quick look through the other drawers and cupboard where our boiler and a load of other tools and domestic, explodable-looking shit were kept.

There was a can of lighter fuel, but I didn't have the balls to steal that. Introducing it would definitely elevate our gang hut to terror-cell status. It was only a laugh and a wee bang we wanted.

We spent a while going through the chemistry set trying to find substances that would blow up. We'd use the powders with labels warning/promising us that they were 'extremely flammable'. We gathered them together and poured them all into a bottle.

We lit our fuse, which we'd made ourselves using kitchen roll and a roll of masking tape I'd borrowed from my Subbuteo box. The masking tape's initial role was simply to hold our bomb together but, as we excitedly discovered, it was highly flammable itself. No explosion, though. Nothing.

We emptied an entire can of Lynx deodorant that I'd stolen from John's bedroom, trying to encourage the bomb along, but we got nothing, just a small fire. The fumes from burning masking tape, mixed with deodorant and kitchen roll created a black smoke that drew our next-door neighbours out to their back door.

They'd seen the fire we'd lit and went to our front door to tell my mum. She was out doing her teatime shifts, so my dad answered the door.

The neighbours explained what was going on. He got a whiff of the fumes so walked round to see for himself. I thought we'd majorly fucked it and that he was about to lose his shit, but, surprisingly, he was quite calm about the whole situation.

He apologized to the neighbours on our behalf, told us to go and fill up a bucket of water, extinguish the flames and then sweep up the debris.

As we walked round to the front door to go in and get water and a brush, my dad shouted me back, asking where his cigarette lighter was. I thought he'd be pissed off if he knew I'd taken it from the top drawer, so I said that I didn't know.

Then, in a move that undermined all our efforts, he crouched down just above the remaining few flames and took a light. I couldn't believe how amateur we were being made to look as he casually lit his fag off our bomb. He stood at the door and watched us carry out the clear-up, finished his fag and then told us not to do anything like that again.

That was that. That was the fire-safety talk, and the hut was never used as a testing ground for explosives again.

18

As well as being my mate during the week and leading me into my first forays into arson, chapping people's doors, jumping people's hedges and browsing through abandoned porn stashes, O'D was, ironically, an altar boy at St Mary's Chapel.

Every Sunday I'd be sat at Mass with my mum and dad and sometimes John, if he wasn't hungover, watching *Gazzetta Football Italia* and promising to go to the evening service.

'He won't go, he's lying,' I'd plead with my mum and dad, trying to get him roped into going. It was his choice, though, and he wasn't a child any more.

But being an altar boy looked good. Rather than being sat, bored out of your mind, listening to stuff about Jesus and how he was the man, having to stand, sit, kneel, there were far better ways to be spending a Sunday.

Going up to receive communion was the only exciting bit – that's when I'd get to make stupid faces to try to distract O'D from his altar boy duties, or Tony, who'd also landed an altar boy job.

I didn't hang around with Tony much at the time, and we'd not been in each other's class since Primary 3. But it didn't take much to make him laugh, even flicking a sneaky middle finger would set him off.

Feeling self-conscious and knowing he shouldn't be laughing would turn his face red, ready to burst and ready to let out a huge cackle. It was great to watch and I hoped we'd sit beside each other in school again soon.

I told my mum and dad that I wanted to be an altar boy, so after Mass my dad said to the priest, Father Tartaglia, that I'd like to have a shot. We'd always hang around after Mass. I'd be keen to get home and trying not to look like I was losing the will to live whilst my mum and dad stood talking to their elderly relatives about who was dead or their tips on who'd be the next to die.

Father Tartaglia promised to let me know when they were looking for new altar boys. It took a few weeks, but I eventually got told to come along on a Sunday afternoon and he'd show me how to ring the bell, carry the cross, light candles and teach me all the etiquette, where to stand when Jesus said this, where to kneel when Jesus did that, and so on.

There were a few of us there, looking to be Duntocher's next top altar boy. The rumour in school was that it could be a lucrative number with money being made from serving at weddings and funerals.

Father Tartaglia's experience meant he knew the ones who were there purely for the fat packet and those whom he'd never seen at Mass before. I landed the job and got my start the following Sunday. I was assigned to 8.30 a.m. Mass and had to be there twenty minutes before.

Getting out of bed before 8 a.m. on a Sunday, unfucking-believable.

I can probably accredit a lot of the feelings of irrational guilt in my early life to my Catholic upbringing. It's maybe a little clichéd to go on about 'Catholic guilt', but since it's in the autobiography-writing manual, I suppose I'd better.

I was christened a Catholic, raised in a 'devout' Catholic

family. Devout being a word that you'll rarely see other than when describing how committed someone is to his or her religion. Devout is like an upgrade from the standard, economy-class Catholic.

I went to Mass on Christmas Eve last year, for the first time in years and mainly because I knew it would make my mum happy. I'm one of those Catholics now; I don't really believe in it all, but I'll go to the odd big game. Easter Sunday and Christmas Day. I don't go to the league matches, but I'll go to the Cup Finals.

Although I've never fully committed to the idea of being an atheist, I use religion nowadays more as a source of comedy than for any kind of spiritual guidance.

I don't mean 'a source of comedy' as in picking apart the Bible in the style of a condescending, long-term, open-mic comedian talking at the crowd like he's the first and only guy to ever consider that the Bible could be a pile of shite.

Go to any amateur comedy night and you're almost guaranteed a student with an exaggerated stoner tone in his voice, intentionally dressed scruffily, a beard and long hair. Militant atheists tend to look like Jesus. They don't believe he's the Son of God, but they dig his style.

I've been performing at a few comedy clubs recently, just messing around with new ideas and trying to stay sharp before touring again. I've been doing a new routine about the idea of God and his personality. Religious leaders and the Old Testament tend to make him sound like a bit of a cock, an all-powerful, all-vengeful being, ordering people to kill their own families to prove their commitment to him.

God doesn't come off well in a lot of these teachings, but maybe he'd be totally sound, a fucking top bloke; maybe he'll appear to clear his name one day.

I like the idea of God himself being an atheist, denying all that's been said about him and just being this cracking guy, showing up, having a few beers and holding court at the bar.

'No sex before marriage! Who said I said that? The fucking Pope said that I said that? . . . Just cause he canny get a bird.'

As everyone laughs in admiration, in total disbelief and hanging on his every word . . .

'Canny believe it's actually you, God! Any chance of a wee photo with me and the boays. Legend, mate!'

Religious leaders could do with presenting God as far more likeable, like your uncle that's never settled down, your mum's youngest brother who's got a bit of disposable income and still fancies himself as one of the young team.

I'd never intentionally mock someone's beliefs for the sake of it, and even though the world seems to be rammed with religious-fundamentalist, evil-bastard nutter types, there are people who follow their religion literally, to the book, and live fulfilling, peaceful and happy lives.

They don't do me any harm and religion is something that I don't really think about. Nobody will ever know what happens when you die. If there is a heaven, it'll probably just be full of your gran and her pals, and if there is a hell, there will be some interesting stories to hear and fucked-up people to confront.

'Here, Hitler. What the fuck was all that about, then? Bang out of order, mate.'

I'm pretty sure that absolutely fuck all happens when you die. But when it happens, you'll be dead, so who cares? Enjoy your life and try to be a decent person – that's as much thought as I give it.

I was an altar boy for just under a year, leaving before starting high school, my resignation being down to my anticipation of the hard time I'd get at high school if word got out

I was an altar boy. I'd made a bad enough start at St Mary's, and I was determined not to make the same mistakes at St Columba's.

It made Mass a lot less boring and the rumours were true that you could make a few quid, £5 for a wedding and £5 for a funeral being the going rates at the time. You could scan the obituary column of the local newspaper every week to see how many packets of football stickers you'd be buying – the good old days!

I learned most of my values and all that sort of stuff through my mum and dad rather than from any priests or teachers. Despite being practising Catholics, they've always been open-minded, free-thinking and pretty liberal.

I found the confession aspect of Catholicism a bit strange. Do what you want, but as long as you let an old guy know about it every now and then, he'll let you know the full extent of the damage in Hail Marys and Our Fathers. Say your penance and then you're sorted.

Maybe adults use it as a more therapeutic thing, a form of counselling, but I've only ever been to confession as a child and I found it fairly harsh.

I made my 'first confession' aged seven. For every lucrative landmark celebration like a first holy communion or a confirmation, there would be something like this.

The overwhelming majority of seven-year-olds have nothing to confess. Our school would even brief us and give us examples of 'sins' we may have committed. Using a bad word, being disobedient to your parents, lying and calling people names were the usual charges.

I think the last time I was in a confessional box was when I was just about near the end of primary school. It was on Good Friday, the Easter weekend being a peak time for a few confessions.

Every Easter weekend the carnival or 'the shows' would come to Duntocher. All the usual fairground attractions would be there, the waltzers, dodgems, candyfloss and hamburger stalls, and even some booze-fuelled knife crime, which would begin as the evening drew on and would eventually put a halt to the annual celebrations.

Everyone my age in the area would be hyperactive at the thought of getting to the shows, but with it being Good Friday it meant going to chapel and confessions first.

I was a little older now, so I'd moved on to more serious offences, like taking the Lord's name in vain and blasphemy, along with the standard swearing, talking back to my mum and so on. I got sentenced to three or four Hail Marys and an Our Father for my penance.

I left the confessional and in my excited state of mind, walked straight out of the chapel, forgetting to say my penance. Once I realized what I'd done, I mumbled, 'Aw, shit.' I got myself into a further panic; swearing was bad enough, but swearing on the chapel grounds? Unheard of!

I didn't know what to do. I headed back to the confessional and started all over again. 'Bless me, Father, for I have sinned. It's been two minutes since my last confession.'

The priest's baffled voice enquired, 'Do you have a sin in such a short space of time?' I explained the swearing incident, and rather than just laugh he hit me with another few Hail Marys.

I told my dad what had happened and, obviously a little annoyed at the priest for not seeing the innocence in the whole thing and laughing it off, he told me I should have told him to, 'Stick his Hail Marys up his arse.'

You'd probably be looking at a full rosary for that, though, so I'm glad I didn't. Still, what a humourless old guy. I was glad my dad had made me feel better about it.

Later that night at 'the shows', out of frustration at losing my entire budget of two-pence pieces in the quest for the elusive Tamagotchi that sat at the top of the pile of coins on that machine you always see at fairgrounds, I decided to use my knee to give myself an advantage. I knocked it gently enough so as not to set off the alarm but with enough force to recoup my losses.

So I'd indulged in degenerate gambling and theft in one go. If I ever go back to a confessional box, it'll be good to get that one off my chest.

19

By 1997 and my last year at St Mary's in Duntocher, I'd begun to tolerate going, maybe even verged on enjoying it, and my teacher for the last year, Mr Thumath, probably had a lot to do with that.

I remember Mr Thumath as being a teacher who liked to laugh at himself; he put a lot more of his own personality into his job as opposed to dishing out work, explaining it and then correcting it.

He had the respect of the whole class, the quiet hard workers and the disruptive ones; everyone would pay attention, and his relaxed nature meant he was approachable and easy to talk to. Nobody was ever made to feel superior or inferior. We were just his class, and his outlook seemed to be that he was in our lives for one year, and he was there to try his best to help us out for the future.

We'd jokingly call him Mr T and shout things like, 'I ain't getting on no plane.' He'd show his human side and laugh along, coming back with, 'I pity the fool who just shouted that.' The class would be in hysterics before he'd eventually revert to teacher mode and tell us to get on with the work.

Friday afternoons would be good fun, and he'd have us taking part in a general knowledge quiz, with prizes at the end. I used to enjoy them because I was good at them. I'd watch loads of TV quiz shows with my mum at night, and my dad would always be coming out with obscure facts that he'd read, and I'd manage to retain some.

I was still too young to install a filter in my brain for when my dad would talk incessantly, showcasing how much he knew about stuff you wouldn't think you'd ever need to know.

Some of it turned out useful, though, and I probably owe the Galaxy Caramel I won for correctly answering that Lee Harvey Oswald was the man who shot John F. Kennedy to my dad and his relentless regurgitating.

Mr T had a season ticket at Celtic Park so it was easy to distract him by bringing up the weekend's game or any transfer rumours.

In the 97/98 season Rangers were closing in on winning ten league titles in a row, breaking Celtic's record set across the 1960s and 1970s. I'd been going to more and more games with my dad now. But when I wasn't going and I saw the supporters' bus leaving with John and his pals on board whilst I was walking to another elderly person's house with my mum, I'd really begin to plead for a season ticket.

My mum told me that she'd given my dad permission to put both of us on the waiting list and when Celtic Park was fully redeveloped, if two tickets – parent and child – became available, we'd be in with a shout.

I didn't believe my mum, but one lunchtime, just after the Christmas holidays, I was having lunch with my dad. Right before I had to walk back to school, he said something like, 'Oh, here, there was a letter for you today.'

I'd never received a letter before, so that was exciting in itself. I opened it up and inside the envelope was a season ticket for Celtic, with my name on it. My dad pulled out another letter, addressed to himself, and opened it. 'They've sent me one as well,' he said, pretending to be surprised.

It was the happiest I'd ever felt walking up the hill towards St Mary's. I'd only six months left of primary school, and I'd now be going to every Celtic home game for the rest of the season. There were no Old Firm games left at home, but that didn't bother me and it probably meant my mum had saved some money on the tickets.

Celtic won the league on the last day of the season, Henrik Larsson and Harold Brattbakk scoring the goals on a roasting-hot Saturday afternoon against St Johnstone at Celtic Park.

It was my first year with a season ticket and Celtic's first league win since 1989. I suppose I should have felt a little for John. He'd been going to watch them through all the shite of the 1990s and here was I, rocking up just in time for the happy ending.

I had a massive lump in my throat when the whole stadium sang 'You'll Never Walk Alone', with the stadium DJ turning the song off after the first few lines and letting the supporters sing it themselves.

'Perfect Day' by Lou Reed was the next song he played, and I remember tears rolling down my cheeks. It didn't feel like I was crying, though. It was a kind of happiness that I'd never experienced before and it just felt special to be part of something that clearly meant so much to so many people.

Right there and then, it was the greatest day of my life.

I went home, raided John's CD collection, found the *Trainspotting* soundtrack and listened to 'Perfect Day' on repeat on his CD player throughout the whole evening, resuming the following morning.

A couple of days later, Celtic manager Wim Jansen left, and all the joy and enthusiasm of that day and the excitement of playing in the European Champions League had gone. Another summer of watching Rangers spend millions on players whilst we were left trying to find a new manager approached.

It was the two extremes of supporting Celtic in the same

week. The feelings of euphoria after winning the league on the final day of the season followed by the disappointment of having it all taken away again by the people running the club.

It didn't matter, though. I was hooked on it all. I'd just finished reading *Fever Pitch* by Nick Hornby, and I knew that being a football supporter was defined by these wild changes in emotions.

I have no idea if buying the season ticket for the second half of the season was initially meant as a one-off gesture by my mum. But after letting your son into something as incredible as that last day of the season, then not letting him return for more would have been verging on cruelty!

When the renewal letters came through, I remember making all sorts of promises. 'It can be my birthday, it can be my Christmas, my birthday and my Christmas, you don't have to get me anything,' knowing my mum would never hold me to these terms of agreement. But if she had, I genuinely don't think I would have minded.

Going to the games was the best form of escapism I'd discovered to date; I'd stepped down from my Subbuteo duties and moved on to the real thing.

My mum borrowed some money from the Credit Union, figured out a way she could pay in instalments and renewed my season ticket, along with my dad's.

I still got a birthday and a Christmas present as well.

I'm convinced she was cooking and selling crystal meth on the side of her home-help duties as I don't know how she did it all.

I only had a few weeks left at St Mary's and then I'd be off to high school.

For the last month of the term, the entire school had been

working on putting a show together to celebrate the school as it was due to be demolished and rebuilt that summer.

The show was to be a complete history of the village of Duntocher, going right back centuries, to the Romans and the building of the Antonine Wall, right up until the present day. It was to last for two or three hours, and performed on a Thursday and a Friday night, such was the demand. It was to feature every pupil and teacher in the school.

What was great for me was that Mrs Conway had asked my dad if he'd consider writing some stories and some dialogue for certain parts of the show. He was honoured to do so and really got into it. Bringing his book into school had paid off and I'd landed him a gig!

He'd been volunteering at a creative-writing class, which was set up for people in the same situation as him. The class took place for a few hours every Friday in a community centre in Maryhill in Glasgow.

I'd got to know all the guys in the class well, from school in-service days and public holidays when my mum would be at work and my dad would take me with him.

They were working towards staging a puppet show. My dad was writing the scripts and the characters and helping out with the building of a small stage for them to perform it. It was good fun, and I'd spend the whole morning playing pool. All of the guys would take a break and come in and give me a game. Jimmy, Angus, Davie and Wee Jimmy were their names.

They all had a good nature and their own characteristics. Jimmy would always swear and grow impatient with me for not following his pool-playing tips. He was a great pool player and with any shot I'd be preparing to take, he'd be shouting, 'Chalk yer cue, take yer time.'

The more passionate he got about pool, the more I'd find it difficult not to laugh. He'd start to ask, 'What's funny?' in a joking tone and go on to clear the table. I could never beat him but I did feel myself improving as a result of his coaching.

At lunchtime, Angus would go down to Greggs or a Greggs 'outlet store' as it was actually known. It was close to the centre so it was convenient, and everyone overlooked the fact that their pies, sausage rolls, sandwiches and cakes had been on sale the previous day, in a 'real' Greggs.

Angus would reheat the pies and sausage rolls in the small kitchen at the centre then we'd sit and have lunch together, and it was a novelty to be eating from a second-hand Greggs.

They'd make me the centre of attention and my dad would tee up stories for me to tell, about things that had happened at school, or he'd tell me to tell them a joke that I'd told him during the week.

I'd hate being handed an on-the-spot request to tell a story or a joke. I'd go bright red with embarrassment and start disclaiming the jokes as someone else's. I'd downplay my dad's build-up by claiming, 'It's not even that funny,' and look at my dad as if to say, 'That's the last time I tell you anything.'

Everyone would start willing me on, especially Jimmy, who'd gently coax me by saying, 'Just spit it out, for fuck's sake.' I'd panic and start telling whatever it was, but I'd be aware that my stories or jokes were only funny if you'd been there or if you were my age. So I'd try to add on extra bits and exaggerate things.

I always had funny thoughts. So rather than explain them, I'd put them into stories and credit the funny thoughts and lines to other people. Things I'd love to have said at the time in school, funny replies to names I'd been called, situations I'd thought of that could feasibly happen, but hadn't.

My dad and the rest of the group must have thought my class was full of characters and that every day was like a sitcom. I didn't want the credit, and I'd rather they just believed these things actually happened.

I would have felt like a dickhead saying, 'I thought this the other day' or 'I said this the other day'. I just liked watching people laugh and especially people who were much older than me, people my dad's age.

20

At school I'd started to get a reputation as being quite funny and a bit off-the-wall. But despite beginning to discover that I could make people laugh, and despite the confidence that began to build when folk like Quinny would tell everyone at playtime and lunchtime about the things I'd be saying during the class, I still couldn't get rid of my introverted nature.

My dad was over at the school a couple of times, sitting with Mrs Conway and a few other teachers and parents, contributing his ideas for the big school play, but he was the only one in our house who'd be involved.

Everyone was asked to write down their own ideas and choose which part of history they wanted to feature in. The World Wars were pretty popular as was the modern day, with a crowd from the other Primary 7 class putting together their version of BBC Scotland's football comedy show *Only an Excuse*.

They wrote their own script and had their cast together. I remember Tony playing former Celtic manager Tommy Burns.

I remember it sounding good fun, but they already had their characters and I wasn't in their class. I told Mr Thumath that I didn't want to be in the play at all.

He tried to persuade me and told me that I'd be the only child in the whole school not featuring. I knew this wasn't true because Kevin Marshall had told me in class that he didn't want to be involved, and we'd decided that sitting in the classroom watching videos was better than going to rehearsals, and that staying at home was better than having to come into school on a Thursday and a Friday night.

Mr Thumath knew I wasn't an outgoing type and that it didn't take much to make me anxious and worried. He knew I hated reading out in class, despite being a competent reader, and he knew how nervous I had been presenting my school project to the rest of my class a few months earlier.

I told him that I simply couldn't stand on a stage in front of an assembly room full of people. I apologized and said I'd even stay in school and do work during the rehearsals.

He agreed, but I could tell he was disappointed and determined to get me to feature. A couple of days later he asked me to stay behind for a couple of minutes at home time. He told me that there was a part going where I had to play an out-of-work school leaver during the Great Depression and that I'd need to say only three lines and that I'd be doing him a favour.

He told me Kevin Marshall had already agreed to take part and that I was now the only one in his class not participating. I later found out he was lying and had told Kevin Marshall the same thing about me.

I obviously wasn't doing him a favour – it meant nothing to him – and it was more that he was doing a favour to me as he knew I needed to be pushed a little in order to build some self-confidence. I was going to high school after the summer, and he probably feared I'd get destroyed if I didn't come out of my shell.

I agreed to take part and left the school with a horrible feeling in my stomach, the same feeling that I usually arrived at school with.

I sat around the house all night with my trademark worried look on my face, the look that I'd now made my own. I sat hoping my mum and dad would ask what was wrong.

They asked and I said 'nothing' while deliberately trying to give off a vibe that there was something wrong and that they should continue enquiring. I eventually told them. They both told me not to be so silly and that it was great news.

My mum told me she'd get me a cardigan and a 'bunnet' from one of the old guys she cared for and that it'd be great. She was starting to get excited and told me I'd need to make sure they got some tickets.

My dad start making jokes and telling me everything he knew about the Great Depression, and offering all his advice about acting. He'd never acted before – there are a lot of things he hasn't done, but he'll always have advice about how to do them.

'You need to become the character,' he said. I gave him a confused 'What the fuck are you on about?' look, and my mum gave him her customary 'Andy, shut up' look. She told me to look forward to it and that it would all be great fun.

I read the script and had about three, maybe four lines. We didn't do any rehearsals, because we didn't have time: I was only in as a last-minute substitute.

We were playing the roles of six guys standing around bored and fearing the worst about when they would ever find work and worrying if they would be eating that night. My character was the one who was trying to keep everyone's spirits up, a positive, upbeat optimist, a pretty demanding role for me.

I certainly didn't take a method approach to my acting debut. I had to be dragged out of the house on the night of the show and I felt sick with nerves. Even other people in the play, who were nervous as well and in the same position, would be telling me that it'd be fine and to relax.

I was scared I'd forget when to speak or speak too soon or

mix up my lines, scared I'd stutter, swear, faint, scared that I'd let the school down and let my mum and dad down.

My first line was in reply to Paul O'Donnell's character saying, 'I wonder what we'll be having for dinner tonight.' My line was: 'What do you mean, you wonder? It'll be steak and chips as usual!'

I had no idea if I'd said it right or what it meant. I just knew I had to say those words. I'd been so preoccupied with learning them and saying them to myself repeatedly that I didn't even take time to figure out the joke.

I didn't even know it was a joke until everyone in the assembly room burst into laughter. It took me by surprise, but it was a nice laugh and it didn't feel like they were laughing at me. I didn't feel like I'd fucked up. I'd got the first line done.

My next line was during a conversation about playing football and the mud and grass stains on our clothes. 'When my maw complains, I just tell her I was playing in goal.'

As soon as I said 'maw', I felt embarrassed, like I'd made a mistake. The word was 'mum', but I'd constantly speak in slang and be corrected by teachers and my mum when I was in certain company.

The crowd loved it, though, and saying 'maw' brought more authenticity to an unemployed young guy during a depression. I should have seen it as an improvisational masterstroke rather than a mistake.

After that line and when someone else was speaking, I felt a smile coming over my face and an urge to hit the giggles. It was probably a release from the nerves I'd built up and all the worrying leaving me. I was nearly done and actually quite enjoying it.

I can't remember the next lines as I don't think they were

jokes, the funny lines being assigned in equal measure to all the cast. We left the stage to massive applause, and afterwards everyone complimented us.

I'd made my stage debut.

This should be the point where I tell you of how I caught the bug of performing and how I felt I belonged on the stage, but it isn't.

Mr Thumath came over to say something like, 'It wasn't all that bad, was it?' I laughed and agreed, but I couldn't quite bring myself to admit that I'd enjoyed it. But although it hadn't been as bad as I'd pictured, I remember thinking I never wanted to go through feeling as nervous as that again.

St Mary's was finished. It finished happier than it started, and I was beginning to overcome the obstacles in my head that had made it so unnecessarily difficult for me and my mum and dad.

I'd heard scare stories about high school, about the fights, with everyone from other areas of Clydebank and Drumchapel fighting against each other. I felt relaxed about it, though. I wasn't a fighter. I'd keep my head down, and no one would bother me.

I was going there to work hard, get some qualifications and go on to university.

21

The summer of 1998 I remember being a good one. I was looking forward to high school and the fresh start. When John was out, I'd make his room my own. His bedroom was at the front of the house. His window faced out over Clydebank, and St Columba's could be seen in the distance. I'd play his computer games and all his CDs, especially, and then exclusively, Oasis.

I was starting to love their songs and pay attention to the lyrics. Everything was about confidence, the 'sunshine' and 'making it happen', being 'a rock 'n' roll star', being 'free to be whatever you want'.

'Live Forever' by Oasis became my favourite song that summer. It's still my favourite song of all time and I still get goose bumps sometimes when I hear it today.

I know musical purists will maybe scoff and deride Oasis, but you can only like what you like. They made me and millions of other young people feel fucking great and that renders any sneering music journalist's or any hipster's presented-as-fact opinion redundant to me.

I'd read a book called *Brothers* by the oldest of the Gallagher brothers, Paul. He described Noel as being insular and mentioned how he was a daydreamer who hated school and spent a lot of time in his room, writing songs and thinking of ways to break free from the mundane life being mapped out for him.

It was a good read, and they seemed to come from the same kind of area as Clydebank and got up to the same things as everyone I knew. I didn't yet know anyone who sniffed glue or who fired air rifles at people, but I figured that it wouldn't be long until I did.

I appreciated my relationship with my dad even more now, after reading about their old man apparently being a bit of a bastard to his three sons and their mum.

I'd met their dad at an Irish bar in Manchester the year before, when my dad and I were down to watch Manchester United and Celtic play in Brian McClair's testimonial. Someone had mentioned that the DJ was Noel and Liam Gallagher's dad.

My dad took me over to meet him when he'd finished his set and was having a drink at the bar. My dad introduced me as a big fan of Oasis and I shook his hand. I obviously had no idea what their relationship was like, nor did my dad. Anyway, I couldn't imagine my dad being abusive or being bad to me or John, or especially my mum.

I hung about the house a lot during the summer, annoying John and asking him to play the computer with me. His mate from university, Jim, had gone back home to Fife for the summer and had let John borrow his PlayStation.

John didn't talk all that much about university, but I sensed he enjoyed it and was having a good time. He'd come home drunk a lot and that gave me an excuse to play up to being the good son.

If John had been sick all over the bathroom, I'd hear my mum shouting at him in the morning. When she'd calmed down, I'd make sure I got in there with, 'Terrible! He woke me up, Mum. Sure, I'm your good boy.'

She'd agree with me whilst obviously thinking, 'What a manipulative little bastard.'

The only thing I remember hearing about John's university days was when he came home one day, sat down in the living room and burst out laughing, making the occasional struggle to hold it in and then dissolving again into a totally hysterical state. Tears were filling his eyes, and my mum, dad and I were all laughing at him laughing, which was making him laugh even more. 'What, what is it?' we'd all begin to press him.

'Nothing, just silly, it's nothing,' he'd just about manage to answer.

It was long past a 'nothing' reaction, and he was forced into telling the story.

It was about Jim's flatmate, Gus, and how he'd got a hold of some pretty powerful cannabis and put a substantial bit more than the recommended measure into yoghurt and ate the lot.

Jim had told John at a lecture that morning that Gus had been standing still in a trance ever since and that he'd need to walk back to their student flat to check on him at the first break. John, already laughing at the image, accompanied him.

Jim opened the door and there was Gus, still stood in the exact same spot, staring out of the window, his face not registering any emotion and not reacting to any noise. 'Gus, Gus, GUS!' Jim was shouting. John even tried to assist with a 'Gus, Gus, mate! You all right?'

Jim and John were scared to touch him in case he came to and panicked or anything. They decided it would be best to phone a doctor to come out and look at him. The doctor concluded that he was pretty fucked up, but that it'd be nothing too serious and he'd be okay. With Jim and John's assistance, he gently lay him down on the couch, and Gus just lay there before coming round a couple of hours later.

He'd slipped into a total trance, which they'd first feared might have been permanent. A 'permo', I later discovered, was the hilarious expression for such a reaction to psychedelic-drug consumption.

John described how Gus had been stood in the same spot for so long that his feet were imprinted into the carpet and how when he came to he didn't quite seem right. He looked alarmed and was answering every question in a distracted and monosyllabic way, like he'd seen something that had properly disturbed him.

My mum was laughing, but not as wholeheartedly as John and my dad, her maternal mind obviously seeing it from a 'poor boy, is he going to be okay?' angle whilst mentally preparing a drug-awareness talk for John.

I was laughing, but more at how John and my dad were pissing themselves. When the laughter was dying down, I said to John, 'Did anyone go up and say, "You all right? Goos, Goos,"' mimicking the little fat mouse, also named Gus, from *Cinderella*.

This made my mum begin to laugh just as much as everyone else now. It was great to have all four of us laughing so much. But it happened a lot and it was definitely the time when I was happiest.

Gus made a full recovery. It wasn't a permo, so that eased any guilt we felt when we quickly remembered what we were laughing at.

22

I'd spend my nights playing the PlayStation, but during the day I'd enjoy hanging about and watching John play it. I'd start to plead with him to play a two-player game with me or to let me have a shot. He'd give me a shot and then leave the room. But I'd get bored, turn it off and go back to hanging around with him.

I didn't really want a shot; it was more to be in John's company. I looked up to him and enjoyed asking him questions and listening to him.

He'd seen Oasis live, been to shit loads of Celtic games, home and away, he played golf, he had a big crowd of mates. It was all the stuff that I wanted. I suppose I always felt a little lost, and John gave me an insight into being normal and cool.

I liked John's company, but I realized that he enjoyed his own company, even if it took him snapping at me for me to respect that. I knew I'd pushed him far enough when he'd pause the game, turn round and tell me from point-blank range to 'fuck off'. Off I would fuck, to find a new way of entertaining myself and claim a new victim of my boredom.

I was starting to become a pest when I found myself at a loose end, and I'd always be looking for something to get up to, usually something that would land me in trouble.

I was now learning how to channel my inner nuisance, and I think I found a sense of satisfaction in annoying my mum, dad and John until they'd snap at me.

Getting my dad to snap was always the biggest challenge. I'd be impressed by how he could answer my rapid-fire questions, even though I'd no longer be interested in the answers and had moved on to asking questions for the sake of it or telling him stories about people from school.

But his tolerance levels would be at an all-time low when there was horse racing on. I quickly came to realize that you didn't talk to my dad when John McCririck was on the telly.

'Dad, Declan Munroe's dad has a house in Florida, and he's staying there all summer,' I'd say, and look for a reaction before going again.

'Dad, Declan Munroe's dad has a speedboat.' Still nothing, his face anxiously fixed on the television and his right arm held over his head with his hand rubbing his left eyebrow. This was my dad's unorthodox way of sitting when he watched TV.

He went through a phase of rubbing his eyebrow like this. It went on for months, to the point when there was a notable bald patch, and my mum would be on at him to stop it.

'Dad, Declan Munroe's dad has got two cars.'

'When Declan Munroe leaves school, he's getting a job working at his dad's company.'

Just as I was beginning to run out of facts about Declan Munroe's dad, he replied in a relaxed, throwaway manner, his face not breaking eye contact with the racing results: 'Declan Munroe's dad is a fucking arsehole, son.'

And another bookie slip was crunched up.

He then had my mum on his case for the bad language. 'Andy!' she shouted.

'Aye, well . . . Nae wonder.'

I quickly grew to see his point. The poor guy's just trying to watch his horses getting beaten, and he has to put up with this shit. I was no longer in awe of Declan Munroe and his family's wealth and opulent lifestyle, though.

His dad was an arsehole.

Just to avoid being taken to court here, I'll point out that Declan Munroe is a fictional character; any similarities are purely deliberate, though, and heavily based on all of the 'Declan Munroe'-type school children out there.

To get me out of the house, I'd sometimes be given a couple of quid to walk up to the Hardgate shops and get a few things for the house, usually just milk, bread or a newspaper. We always had milk, bread and a newspaper but the point of the trip was to give everyone some peace and quiet.

I knew this fine well, so I'd always haggle and try to get some extra money to get myself something, a delivery charge. I'd walk up to a newsagent called Emerson's. There was a newsagent closer to the house, but Emerson was the name of a Brazilian footballer who'd played for Middlesbrough a couple of years before, along with fellow Brazilians Juninho and Branco, when I'd developed a soft spot for them.

Emerson's, as well as selling all the essentials you'd expect from a local newsagent, sold loads of stupid shite as well. Things like cheap plastic water guns, cap guns, small plastic glider planes and loads of party stuff like party hats, party poppers and balloons. I'd always buy something from this aisle rather than buy a sweet or a packet of crisps, which my delivery fee was designated for.

It had been great weather for a few days during the summer, and when I left for Emerson's I'd seen that my mum had been lying out in the back garden, the only one in our family who'd ever take a suntan.

I'd pushed John to the edge by constantly bursting into his room as he tried to watch the TV or play computer games, and I'd felt sorry for my dad and his constant torment at the hands of William Hill.

I hadn't gotten my mum yet.

It was late in the afternoon, so the choice of newspapers

was limited. I bought a *Daily Star*. I noticed it had far more women with not much on than the *Daily Record* or *Evening Times*, so I even had a browse myself on the walk home.

A *Daily Star*, a Mother's Pride loaf and a one-litre bottle of Wiseman semi-skimmed milk – 'The green one,' I was told, 'not the blue one.' I didn't realize that the different-coloured labels indicated which was semi-skimmed and which was full-fat.

I knew it must have been something other than football. Surely the Celtic and Rangers rivalry hadn't descended all the way down to milk.

I had about seventy pence left. I was tempted to buy a Snickers or even confront my demons and buy a Lion Bar, but the idea of my mum sunbathing in the back garden and me filling up some balloons with water and heading round to give her a fright was too much. I sacrificed the chocolate in favour of carrying out a self-assigned dare and the adrenalin rush that it would bring.

Excited, I walked home, round past Paul O'Donnell's, past the Gravils' house and down to our street.

I dropped in the messages and was thanked and told 'good man' by my dad. 'That was quick,' he added, in a way that said, 'Fuck, he's back.'

I put him at ease by saying, 'I'm just going upstairs to get my ball then I'm off out to play.'

'Okay, son.' He looked relieved, and his mind drifted back to his horses. I grabbed my ball, to be used as a decoy and for evidence to support my case later.

The house was at peace: John on the PlayStation, my dad watching the horses and my mum out the back lying on a reclining deckchair-looking thing that was bought from the Asda garden department and stored in the hut, only to be used on days like this.

I walked into the bathroom, wrapped the top of a balloon around the tap and watched as it began to fill from the bottom and grow wider. I noticed they weren't water balloons; they were proper party balloons, much larger than the little hand-held water ones.

I sacrificed the first balloon to see how much water they could hold. It covered the entire sink. I tied it up, and when I tried to lift it into my arms it immediately burst all over me and all over the bathroom floor. I grabbed a towel and made a half-arsed attempt at drying the floor.

It was getting too exhilarating, and I didn't even consider that the wet floor and little burst balloon pieces would later count against me.

I grabbed the second balloon and filled it with just slightly less water than the first one. I tied it without any problem and carefully lifted it out of the sink, like a mother lifting a sleeping baby from a cot.

Taking my ball out with me was now impossible. I needed both hands and decided just to try to sneak out unnoticed. I didn't care if John caught me because I didn't think he'd care if he'd caught me.

My dad was sitting shouting at a jockey, so he was distracted. A quick check from the stairs, a peek round the wall and into the kitchen, making sure my mum hadn't popped in for a drink or anything, then down the stairs and out of the front door.

I was starting to laugh to myself as I walked along our street. The neighbours a few doors up were out in their garden having a BBQ, and a few others were cutting their grass. I gave a nod and looked back at my feet, giving off a strong 'don't ask, in a hurry' vibe.

I got to the grassy banking at the end of the street and began the parallel walk back down towards our house. I looked over the hedge and saw my mum lying there, dozing peacefully, her eyes closed. I couldn't stop laughing and my heart was racing. I was careful, though; letting out a snigger would definitely have woken her up.

I looked up at my bedroom window, which was wide open. I could hear shooting noises coming from the PlayStation; I wished I could have attracted John's attention so that he could watch the attack.

I couldn't risk disturbing my mum, and I'd have been distraught if John had been mature about it and called a halt to it all.

My first problem was that the water balloon was far too large to throw from any distance. If I missed, it would be a total waste and I'd still be in trouble for the intent – all the effort in vain. I'd have to get right down to the hedge and just sort of let it drop down and over. As soon as it hit my mum, I'd have to make my getaway.

I was starting to over-think it all now and was scared that she'd feel my presence. So I used my hips to put the slightest bit of momentum into the throw, and the balloon went over the hedge.

It was only in the air for a split second, the pull of gravity speeding up the proceedings and dragging the balloon down to land on my mum's face.

The balloon separated into several individual pieces of rubber and a massive, loud, shocked intake of breath confirmed the hit. My mum's face, her hair, her magazine, and the sun lounger, soaked.

I was laughing, but not as much as before I'd thrown it. I was now beginning to feel bad about it; I knew my mum didn't like being in water; she'd never come in the pool on holiday.

I ran up the grassy hill, heading vertically away from the

house as opposed to continuing along the grassy banking where I'd be hidden immediately behind the hedge of our next-door neighbour.

My mum's reaction had brought John to my bedroom window to see what was going on. He described my mum standing in the back garden, her hair, clothes and magazine all drenched. He said he was confused at first, until he looked up at the grassy banking to see my little fat arse as I was running and running with all my effort, my brain demanding more from my legs than they'd ever had to cope with before.

In my head I was running at blistering pace, but the grassy banking just never seemed to end and I was out of breath. I couldn't look back until I was sure I wouldn't see the house when I did. Now came the difficult part: how to return to the scene of the incident without being questioned as a suspect.

John had spotted me making my poorly planned getaway, my bursting, sweating, red face contrasting with the 'leisurely' speed I'd managed to accelerate to.

I walked around the street in the other direction.

I knew it would be best to go and face the situation soon. I was prepared to play innocent, but I knew I couldn't. I got to the house, where the front door was wide open, as was tradition on a sunny day.

I looked straight through to the kitchen to see my mum with a towel wrapped round her head and another one in her hands, drying off her face. She had a shocked look on her face and I immediately felt terrible.

'What happened to you?' I asked, with deplorable acting skills. I'd have failed every body language or lie detector test in any court on the planet.

'Your mum got a right shock there,' I heard my dad saying. I knew I'd overstepped it a bit and thought again about how much she hated the water.

'What a fright you gave me. I thought I was drowning,' my mum said. I was beginning to feel really, really guilty and regretted what I'd done.

'What a shot, though,' my dad added. 'Right in the coupon.'

I looked at my mum to see if it was okay to laugh. She smiled and called me a 'muppet'.

I'd never heard that as an insult before and found it really funny. My mum began to smile. John came down to the kitchen and told his version of events. He thought it was fucking great. I was delighted to have impressed him. My mum was now laughing as well and telling in detail about the shock she'd got.

'Look at my magazine,' she smiled and held up a soggy copy of *Take a Break*, with all the ink smudged and the headlines impossible to make out.

Again, it went down as a good story and it became part of the family-gathering set list: 'Remember the time Kevin hit me with the water balloon . . .'

I enjoyed hearing the story and being made to sound a bit of a bad ass.

A part of my brain was now assigned to thinking up ways to get up to no good and doing things for a laugh. It was like I was in training, getting ready for high school.

23

I left for St Columba's on an August morning in 1998. Before I left, my mum told me that I was going to the 'big' school now and that it would be different from primary school. She told me to look after myself, to try to enjoy it and, above all, to work hard.

She added, 'And don't be crying in there. They won't let you forget it.' I told her to 'shut up' in an outraged and embarrassed voice, as if I didn't have a clue what she was on about. St Mary's was put into a place in my head where it never happened, and it wasn't ever to be acknowledged.

My mum gave me my packed lunch and a £1 coin to get something from the ice-cream van, the ice-cream van in the playground!

This place sounded fucking great.

I'd asked John the night before if I could borrow his Walkman and his Oasis cassettes so I could have something to listen to on the way to school.

Off I went, out of the house, out of our street, turning left down the hill towards the main road and off to high school, and turning back to wave at my mum at the window. Once I was out of sight, I started the Walkman up and walked, almost swaggered, through the housing estate that led to the school, 'Morning Glory' and 'Supersonic' blaring in my ears.

I was eleven years old and, like John, I'd be leaving there after six years, at seventeen, and hopefully with good qualifications. I'd always been one of the youngest in my class at St Mary's and the youngest in the house, by far, but I felt like

I was growing up a little. I had some independence now and I was enjoying it. I would walk to school on my own, a much further walk than to St Mary's.

I left home at 8.30 a.m. and arrived at school about 8.50 a.m., in plenty of time for our first-years' assembly, where we'd find out our class and receive our timetables, and then go on to meet the teachers and the pupils from the catchment area's primary schools: St Mary's in Duntocher, St Joseph's in Faifley, St Eunan's in Clydebank, right next door to St Columba's and, finally, St Claire's in Drumchapel.

I didn't know anyone from any other school, only a boy called Darren Lee, whom I'd sat beside on the supporters' bus from Hardgate going to a pre-season friendly against Liverpool. It was one of the free-on-your-season-ticket games. My dad had decided to give it a miss, but my mum went with me. She hadn't seen the new Celtic Park so she was excited about that, and my dad had convinced her that she was entitled to take a day off.

My mum and Darren's mum had got talking on the bus up to the game and established that we'd both be in the same year at the same school after the summer. Darren and I began to talk as well, mainly laboured small talk that eleven-year-olds struggle to sustain before getting bored and annoying people.

On the way home, though, we were sitting beside each other when the bus drove past a bunch of drunken stragglers from an Orange Walk earlier that day. A crowd of them began to throw bricks and bottles and whatever else they'd sourced in anticipation of buses coming back from Celtic Park. Nearly every window on our side of the bus was smashed.

It was pretty full on. My mum was panicking and trying to block the glass from flying about. It seemed to be all over in seconds.

With it being a pre-season friendly match, the bus demographic was mainly young children and women, with only a few of the regular 'back seat of the bus' mob on board, most of them with their children as well. They were totally different guys from the ones they'd be if it had been a game versus Rangers.

I remember a girl, Claire, who'd go to every game and who never let her gender get in the way of a fight, kicking the fire door of the bus open and running off to give chase with a handful of guys following her. The guys were half-hearted about it and not as furious as Claire, but they probably felt pressured and a responsibility not to let a woman head off to hunt down the crowd of assailants on her own.

Claire wasn't your typical woman, though. She could out-drink any man, out-sing any man and now she'd challenged herself to out-fight any man.

It was fucking surreal to watch a female lead the charge of about four or five guys. The bus was parked up for a few minutes whilst everyone helped scrape the remaining glass out of the windows. When Claire returned, she was limping severely, with a guy under each arm helping her back to her seat. I was thinking, 'Surely they didn't beat up a woman,' but Claire was proudly showing off her swollen fist and telling how she'd punched someone on the back of the head. Then, when she tried to jump a wall to give chase as her victim had staggered away, she'd underestimated the height of the drop at the other side and she had fallen and torn her ankle ligaments.

The whole bus couldn't help but see the funny side. Claire was a bit of a local hero and now she'd managed to introduce a slapstick comedy element to sectarian violence.

It was a fucking scary few minutes, but it meant I'd met Darren and I now had someone new to talk to and something to talk about on the first day at St Columba's.

On that first day, I almost ended up in a fight with a boy from the year above me; fortunately, Darren Lee knew him and walked over to defuse the conflict, describing me as being 'all right'.

He'd called me a fat bastard or something like that and made fun of my jacket. I'd again tried to follow the common, easier-said-than-done, 'always stand up to bullies' advice that parents and teachers freely dispense and told him to 'fuck off'.

Aggressively, he began asking me to repeat what I'd said, daring me to do so. I'd anticipated that repeating myself would have resulted in physical assault, and I didn't have much faith in my ability to return with anything that could pass for a punch. So I was thankful to Darren for sorting it out and getting me out of the situation.

He was in with that kind of crowd, so I wouldn't see much of him. He probably didn't want to see much of me either, given that I'd just displayed some classic shitebag credentials and backed down from a square go. I'd got away with being beaten up on day one, and for now I'd settle for being known as a fat bastard with a shite jacket.

I immediately began to plead with my mum for a new jacket, though. Everyone else had sports jackets, the good makes like Nike and Adidas. Even Diadora, Kappa or Sergio Tacchini were cooler than my bottle-green and brown selection from the BHS Back to School range. I'd survived Primary 7 without any comments on it, but I figured it best to actively seek an upgrade.

I enjoyed playtime and lunchtime, but I'd feel like I was wandering around on my own or else trying to attach myself to a crowd, to be seen as being part of it, to blend in and not be a target.

I sometimes preferred to be on my own as I hated the feeling of 'tagging along'. Probably everyone felt the same, but I was far too self-aware and self-conscious to ignore the feeling and get on with it.

Again, I wasn't in any of Tony's classes. I'd still see him around at playtime and we'd speak about Celtic. He hadn't changed at all; he was still bursting with confidence and always laughing. I wasn't in any of Big Doc's classes, either.

In my class at St Columba's, from St Mary's there was Christopher Mochan. Mochan was a good guy, very intelligent and the kind of friend your mum and dad would encourage you to hang around with.

He worked hard, came from a good family and was clearly one of the smartest in our year. I'd managed to match his level for a while; but I would always fall slightly short of him in test results, and whatever mark he got for an essay or an exercise sheet, I'd score just under.

I didn't know him all that well from primary school, but now we'd sit together in nearly every class and we began to get on. I realized how hard he worked, and I'd try to distract him, usually by doing stupid stuff.

One of my things was to say 'Here, miss' at registration at a noticeably louder volume than the rest of the class, almost shouting it, as though I was in the military, and Mochan would laugh.

I'd also discovered over the summer that I could do a brilliant cockerel noise. I was always at my best when I was overwhelmed with boredom, and that's when I'd realize I had these new skills.

I showcased my cockerel noise once in a class when the teacher's back was turned. He turned round from writing on the blackboard and just sort of shook his head; he was more bemused than angry.

It was a great reaction and I remember really finding it funny that he didn't at least mention it. How the fuck could he just let a loud cockerel noise in the middle of a lesson go without comment? I sat staring out of the window for the rest of the class, thinking about it and it really made me laugh.

I would talk a lot during classes and I'd eventually begin to receive punishment exercises, 'punnies' they were called. Punnies became a currency in school. Getting one was quite cool, and if somebody had got more than one from the same class, they were respected in a 'he's mental' kind of way.

If you continued to get punnies, it would result in being given a 'referral', when a senior teacher would be made aware of your behaviour. It would usually result in a verbal warning and a stern talking-to.

But sometimes they'd act on it and you'd be sat in the 'exclusion room' and made to do your work away from your class; you'd be in a small classroom with pupils from other years who'd also been disruptive.

My cockerel noise never landed me in the exclusion room. I'm thankful for that, as it would have been a difficult one to explain to the school's genuine nutcases when being asked the standard, 'What are you in for?'

24

I'd enjoy conversations with Mochan. We'd talk about football and music. He could play the guitar and was into Oasis and the Stone Roses and most of the other indie 90s bands as well. We'd also talk about wrestling and, of course, computer games.

We'd start to hang around together at lunchtime, walking down to Adriano's chip shop. I'd use the £1 that my mum gave me to buy a roll and chips and drink the can of juice that was in my packed lunch. I'd bin the sandwiches that my mum had made and eat the crisps and the biscuit.

I'd feel awful for binning the sandwiches, so I eventually told my mum that she didn't have to bother making them and that I preferred doing my own thing for lunch. I requested a pay rise as £1 wasn't enough for the chippy and the ice-cream van.

She never mentioned that I was entitled to a free school dinner. But after a few weeks of school, everyone began to realize that the dinner-hall food wasn't all that bad and that the teachers would hand out dinner tickets to anyone, without checking the official list of who was supposed to receive one. I had the £2 and I'd get my dinner ticket too.

I was pretty flush and I'd usually spend the money on more sweets from the ice-cream van or on the way home from school. It only became difficult one morning when a deputy head teacher insisted on more stringent checks to see which pupils were legitimately to receive a dinner ticket.

Everyone who had been chancing it got busted. It was

then that I realized I was on the list and that my mum hadn't let on. I felt bad for still taking the £2 every morning, but not bad enough to tell her I was taking the dinner ticket she felt too ashamed to acknowledge.

As well as Mochan, I'd hang around at lunchtime with Stephen Henry, whose brother John had played up front for Clydebank when I'd been to see them with my dad. He'd gone on to play for Kilmarnock and Falkirk.

I remember thinking it was amazing to know someone whose brother was a professional footballer. Stephen himself was a great player, one of the best in the year. But I admired the fact that he didn't exercise his right to be a dick, a luxury afforded to anyone at school who was good at football.

Henry played loads of role-playing computer games, watched obscure movies and had a left-field approach to everything. He'd dress a bit differently and say things like, 'Did anyone watch *Ally McBeal* last night?' He was genuinely enquiring and happy to admit he was a fan of the show.

He wasn't annoying – he didn't put on a quirky persona or try to be random and wacky. He made me laugh a lot, and I could make him laugh. I liked how he was his own man and had figured himself out more quickly than most people do.

Henry lived beside Mochan. They were good pals and they played for the same football team, Mochan being a good player too. I'd feel a bit out of the loop when they'd talk about training and their games. I was hopeless at playing football, but obsessed with watching it.

Their team was successful. They'd win their leagues and their cups, and professional teams were scouting a few of their players. The team was made up of Henry and Mochan – the rest were the 'best fighters' in the year, the ultimate high-school honour.

I remember that standing with them felt like you were being auditioned. Everyone would change in their company and it felt as though you had to impress them and they would decide if you were cool enough.

Mochan and Henry had a ready 'in' and were respected because they played in the same football team, but I was just their pal. I'd stand at the back, not saying anything, trying to avoid being slagged. The background role never suited me, and I'd often just mumble an excuse to Mochan and wander off.

I'd sometimes hang around with a boy called James McKendrick who was in my 'section' class, the class you'd be in for subjects like Home Economics, Woodwork and PE, the classes that people would soon begin to avoid showing up to. The register was full of the names of people who had come in on the first day, never to be seen again.

No explanation, just gone.

In our section class as well were Joe Traynor and Martin Kelly, both of whom were pretty disruptive and could always be relied upon to do something that would have the whole school talking at lunchtime.

At St Mary's we didn't have all that many nutters, and the ones we had were nowhere near this level, so it was intriguing to watch. Joe and Martin were definitely known as the funny guys in the class. It was before anyone had discovered 'patter', and their off-the-wall style was blazing the trail and was what the people wanted.

I had my cockerel noise, and sometimes I'd also take a turn in the running joke of making up excuses for people who were absent and relaying them to the teacher when the register was being taken.

The excuses were usually an embarrassing illness or an injury. 'He tried to light a fart at the weekend, but it backfired inside him and he had to get an operation to repair his bum hole, sir', or 'A pack of dogs attacked him on the way to school and ate his uniform and he didn't want to come to school naked, miss.' It was stupid stuff that made you giggle when you were eleven years old.

Joe and Martin's humour was pretty slapstick. They'd generate laughs from throwing flour and eggs across the classroom or hitting each other with rolling pins, pots and frying pans.

Every Home Economics class became like an episode of *Bottom*. They were both regularly sentenced to some hard time in the exclusion room, but they were funny to watch.

It was always good to hear someone else talking back to a teacher and swearing loudly during a lesson, or to witness more serious things like a table being used where a paper plane would've sufficed, or a fire extinguisher being set off. I'd be enjoying the show, calm in the knowledge that it was nothing to do with me.

When the teachers couldn't find out who'd done something, they'd call in a deputy head teacher or the head teacher himself, depending on the severity. They'd always resort to the 'if whoever did this doesn't own up, the whole class will be suspended', innocents-will-go-down-for-this tactic.

Some people would usually crack and confess, but not the hardened Joe and Martin types. They were streetwise and knew the school couldn't possibly suspend the whole class. The teachers would back down and that'd be it.

Joe and Martin went to the same primary school as James, so I'd got to know them through him and we'd sit in the same group. None of them knew me from primary school, so I could be anyone I wanted.

I remember James being quiet and not saying much. He was popular, though, and everyone got on with him. I'd talk far more than him, attracting more attention and placing myself at risk of being put down and slagged by the rest of the class.

I took everything to heart, every insult. I'd got over being called fatty and all that. But when I heard a new one, I'd fixate on it and really over-analyse why the person had said it, contemplating whether it was a valid criticism.

For example, it was common to spend your change on penny sweets at the ice-cream van. You'd get a can of Irn-Bru, a packet of crisps and then spend the rest on whatever penny sweet you specified.

One playtime I asked for 'the rest in fizzy sticks'. Someone behind me in the mosh-pit-like crowd at the ice-cream van window mimicked how I'd said it – 'the resht in fishy shticks' – emphasizing the 'shh' like somebody impersonating a Dutch accent.

Whoever said it probably thought nothing of it and had something else in his head immediately after saying it. But I walked away with my can of Irn-Bru, my packet of crisps and my fizzy sticks, thinking I had a speech impediment, another thing to be insecure about.

When I was on my own later that evening, it kept popping into my head and I'd silently say: 'The rest in fizzy sticks, fizzy sticks, fiz-ee-st-icks.'

I got over it eventually, and I laughed at the thought of finding out who'd said it and letting them think they were dealing with a psychopath by walking up to them in the playground, looking them straight in the eye and whispering, 'There is fuck all, AND I MEAN FUCK ALL, wrong with the way I say "the rest in fizzy sticks", okay?'

At home, everyone was well aware of my hypersensitive nature and that I could be a hothead. John would always be able to get a reaction out of me on the rare occasions he was bored enough to play the PlayStation with me. We'd sit and play *FIFA Road to World Cup*, and I'd take it frighteningly seriously and hate losing to him.

We'd discovered a way of taking free kicks where you'd just pass to your player who'd be standing at the side of the defensive wall and the opponent would be unable to move anyone to mark him. He'd get the ball and immediately be one on one with the goalkeeper, nearly always resulting in a goal.

It was considered ungentlemanly to exploit this oversight in the game's design and an unwritten rule was that free kicks had to be a direct shot at goal.

We were drawing when in the last minute John got a free kick. Obviously being fed up and not wanting to play extra time, he committed the cowardly act, passed to the unmarked player, scored and did an annoying victory dance right in my face.

I booted his shins whilst shouting, 'Press start, press start,' frantically wanting the game to restart, so I could try to grab a dramatic equalizer. But the referee's whistle blew as soon as I kicked off, and that prompted further unsavoury scenes.

John was flicking his two middle fingers at me, right in my face, as I was punching and kicking at him, but he'd keep jumping back before going into his room and holding the door shut.

I was furious and sceaming at him. According to John, my words were, 'I hate you, I hate you, you're a cheating prick, I fucking hate you.'

All the while, he sang, 'Championees, championees!'

I was demanding that he play me again, and rattling off the stats for shots on target and possession, which were marginally in my favour. 'There's only one stat that matters, and I'm retiring as the champ,' he'd keep baiting me.

I couldn't get at him, so I booted his door. But I didn't mean to boot it so hard that my foot would go right through one of the wooden panels. I knew I'd gone too far, and my dad came up the stairs and lost the plot with me.

I went back to my room, still pissed off about the game, but knowing I'd overreacted and that I was in a fair bit of shit. To be fair to John, he explained how he'd been winding me up and made up that he'd noticed his door was beginning to crack anyway and that it was on its way out.

It still didn't get me completely out of trouble and I was given a proper talking-to and made to apologize to everyone, including John, the cheating prick.

I think this summed up how frustrated I could get.

I was the younger child so naturally I had a lot of built-up angst.

I was a bad loser. I'd lose so often at things that I should have got better at losing, but instead I became even more frustrated when I lost the precious few things I had left, like computer games.

25

Over the first two years at high school, I started to notice how much people were changing in reaction to the demands of the new peer pressure that is part of becoming a teenager.

People would sit in class and talk of how they were 'getting a drink' at the weekends and compare strategies on how to go about acquiring alcohol.

I'd sometimes see them at lunchtime on Fridays in the dodgy shops behind Adriano's, the shops that sold single cigarettes and would happily sell a three-litre bottle of cider to someone in a school uniform, provided they had at least a slight bit of stubble and were paying a few quid extra.

Asking a local alcoholic, or 'a Jake', to go into the shop was another sound bet. I'd always laugh at how fucking obvious it must have been to the shopkeepers that the alcohol wasn't for the old guy's personal consumption.

'A quarter bottle of Glen's vodka and two cans of Miller, a quarter bottle of Glen's vodka and four cans of Miller,' he'd be saying, rattling off everyone's order individually and not as a collective. The shop owner was probably confused and replied, 'So that's a half bottle of Glen's vodka and six cans of Miller, then?'

The old guy was obviously under strict instructions not to buy in bulk, as buying in bulk or taking advantage of special offers would create confusion in the camp as to how the alcohol could be distributed evenly.

This wasn't sociable drinking, this was drinking because it was a new thing and everyone wanted to see what being drunk was like.

On Mondays at school, there would be loads of embarrassing stories flying round, who'd pissed or even shat their pants, who had got off with whom, who'd been fighting, who'd been jailed, who'd wandered away from their group and sat alone, crying and wanting to go home.

Again, I was glad it wasn't me and being drunk didn't sound like something I'd enjoy. I was curious, but I could guarantee that I'd end up being the protagonist in one of the Monday stories. No one I hung around with had got into alcohol yet, so that was another reason not to bother.

On Fridays after school I'd usually get changed and walk round to Mochan's. We'd sit in his house and either play the PlayStation or games on his PC.

He had a game called *Ultimate Soccer Manager*. Again, it was a football management game, but one that focused on off-field issues as opposed to the objective of simply trying to build a winning team.

You could adjust the prices of your pies, Cokes and merchandise and also offer other teams bribes to lose games. I'd always find it funny to fuck around and set the prices of select items in the food stalls astronomically high but lower the prices of everything else.

We'd sit and laugh at the post-match accounts that would appear on the screen showing that eight pies had been sold at £100 per pie and ten thousand hot dogs had been sold at one penny each. We'd sit and laugh as though it was the funniest thing imaginable: eight people paid £100 for a pie rather than settling for a one-penny hot dog!

We'd start to make up stories, like maybe one of them was

a guy trying not to embarrass himself in front of his girl-friend. She'd asked him to go and get her a pie and he didn't want to seem like he was a tight-arse, so he took the hit.

'I thought you were getting a pie as well,' she'd say, looking at his hot dog.

'I changed my mind. I'm not really a hot-dog guy, but they looked nice,' he'd explain, trying to conceal his shock at the £100.01 bill.

I liked how Mochan would use his brain for this sort of daft stuff as well. We'd improvise to the point when it was taken too far, the guy's girlfriend saying, 'Yeah, that does look like a nice hot dog, and this pie is a bit too greasy,' dropping the pie on the ground and taking a bite of his hot dog, cuing him to snap and start screaming: 'A hundred pounds, that cost me, one hundred fucking pounds!' He'd grab the remainders of the pie off the ground, forcing himself to eat every last bit, rubbing the grease all over his face, crying and shouting, 'ONE HUNDRED POUNDS!'

At that point, stewards would come over to escort him out of the stadium and his girlfriend would walk away from him like he was taking a full-on breakdown. We'd be in raptures and holding our sides laughing, trying to think of the next bit of the story. Exposing a flaw in the realism of a computer game was always a satisfying feeling.

Mochan had a printer as well, which I'd find entertaining. If we were staying over at his house, we'd usually go up to the Global video shop and rent a few movies or games. We'd type things like 'OUT OF ORDER' and 'WET PAINT', and Mochan would alter the font size and colour, make them bold, and then print a few off.

We'd put the 'OUT OF ORDER' signs on cash machines and phone boxes and things that couldn't really be out of order, like postboxes, bins and bus stops. The 'WET PAINT' ones we'd use for traffic lights and handrails, things people would have to touch.

We'd make daft signs like 'MISSING DOG', with no photograph or even a description of a dog and no contact phone number. Just letting people know that there was a missing dog.

Compared to the other folk in the year who were getting into alcohol, sex and recreational drugs, Mochan and I were definitely still stuck in the *Oor Wullie* and *Bash Street Kids* phase of 'tomfoolery'.

Again, at twelve years old, it was what made us laugh, and having a laugh and good fun was now becoming a priority in my life. The energy I used to waste worrying, I was now using to think up ways of carrying on and making Mochan and, hopefully soon, the rest of my class laugh.

I'd occasionally still get caught off-guard by my anxieties, though. I'd think they had left me for good and I'd moved on, but my mood would suddenly dip when I wasn't expecting it.

Staying over at people's houses or 'having a sleepover' I'd enjoy playing the computer, eating crisps, talking shite, flicking through the five terrestrial channels, debating which channel was more likely to show a naked woman.

The search would soon be narrowed down to Channel 4 and Channel 5 and the remote would flick between them, looking for any sort of sign that nudity was imminent.

'They're looking at each other in the eyes, keep it on this,' but it would cut to a different scene, the guy going to a baseball game or something, cueing an impatient, 'Try Channel 4.' But there would be nothing much going on on Channel 4 either, maybe a bit of flirting or post-watershed innuendo.

For all Mochan's PC provided entertainment, home Internet was very much a luxury and hardly anyone I knew had it.

This would have saved a lot of hard work in the naked-woman hunt but, then, part of the fun was in the searching. It made it more rewarding, and a sudden, excited, far-too-loud, forgetting-everyone-else-in-the-house-is-asleep shout of 'TITS! LOOK!' made it all worthwhile.

It would be on *Ibiza Uncovered* or some show like that, and they'd be there for only a split second; it would be a montage of drunken British girls lifting their T-shirts up to the camera, but it was all we'd wanted.

A unanimous, satisfied verdict of 'Superb!'

Once we'd seen some tits, the night would start winding down. I'd always try to keep Mochan awake. I hated being the only one awake in a house that wasn't my own.

I'd start to think of how long it was until morning and how I'd be there for breakfast and it would be ages until I was home again. It was a strange feeling of homesickness, even though I'd only ever be a few streets away.

I'd lie awake for hours, feeling shit and just wishing I could fall asleep. That way I'd be home faster.

26

Outside of school, everyone else was beginning to have a social life and getting into chasing girls. I was far too shy for all of that and it meant I'd be called a 'VL', which stood for virgin lips.

Being a 'VL' was a tough obstacle to overcome; no one could quite see past it. Some people would invent stories about holiday romances, but unless you had concrete evidence, no one would let it slide. It was another thing to add to the checklist. I'd got a new jacket, I'd got rid of my sticker book – and now this!

Mobile phones were becoming more popular and comparing how many girls' numbers you had was the new thing. It was especially popular during classes that were a skive, the ones in which no one paid attention and the teachers had no control.

I didn't have a mobile phone, but I had a watch that I'd got for Christmas that could operate as a remote control for televisions. It was a massive, ugly big thing, but I'd shown it to a few people in the class when our RE teacher had wheeled in a television at the beginning of the lesson.

He told us we'd be watching a movie called *Stigmata*, about a woman who began to develop the same wounds on her hands as the ones Jesus had from being crucified.

The blinds were closed, the class was darkened, and everyone was whispering to me to start messing with the TV. I started to turn the volume down from my watch, and the teacher stood up, pressing the buttons on the front of the set and checking the cables at the back. I then began turning the volume up again. Everyone was giggling, so I went for it and turned the volume up as high as it would go.

The old TV was struggling to cope and started to vibrate. When the teacher began freaking out, I turned it right back down again to hear what he had to say. He was saying things like, 'I think this is some sort of sign,' and 'There could be a spiritual presence in the room.' The class were laughing uncontrollably now. What a fucking idiot!

'It's just Kevin Bridges' watch, sir!' I was grassed in, but I denied all knowledge.

'How could a watch control the TV, sir? I think it's Jesus!' someone said, and the class erupted.

I enjoyed being the orchestrator of this wind-up, especially now that it had got a reaction far beyond the realms of what anyone could have imagined.

The teacher began shouting that he was going to have everyone suspended, which was too ridiculous a threat to be taken seriously, and I remember thinking we were clearly dealing with a nutcase.

I started to lose interest in a lot of subjects, especially the ones where I didn't like the teacher or the ones where I didn't really know anyone in the class all that well. I wasn't good at PE, woodwork, graphic drawing or any of the classes that were supposed to be good fun.

But I enjoyed English, which was probably down to my teacher, Mr Ford. Mr Ford reminded me a lot of my dad. He was his own man and didn't pander to the class. He didn't shout and wasn't known for his hard line on discipline or anything like that. He had a sharp reply for any smart-arses in the class who'd try to give him some grief, and everyone quickly came to respect him.

He'd read us short stories that he'd written himself, stories based on his own childhood. He'd act out the voices and properly get into it. One of the characters, named 'Wee Hally', had a high-pitched voice and a speech impediment.

Mr Ford mimicking this would make the class laugh, but I'd notice how Wee Hally had all the funny lines and was the hero in every story. It was good that I wasn't just laughing at his voice. I liked Wee Hally and could picture him clearly in my head.

I could never really motivate myself or feign interest when it came to analysing and interpreting poems, so this was much more enjoyable. I admired Mr Ford and the classes seemed to go a lot faster than usual.

The personality of a teacher was definitely more of a factor in high school than at primary school. Some of them would lose their temper every day, which would gradually lose its effect and result in them being deliberately baited to provoke a reaction.

Then there would be the ones who'd try to be cool, the ones who'd let you know their first name and liked to talk about stuff that happened away from school. I could never make my mind up about those ones. They seemed to sense who was popular in the class and try to make more of an effort to be liked by them.

I had one teacher who'd always talk about and bad-mouth pupils who were absent, referring to one of them as 'Drum Scum' which, being a dig at the area of Drumchapel, went down a storm with the Clydebank-heavy class. Clydebank and Drumchapel were two 'rival' areas with crowds who would fight with each other outside of school.

That type of thing wasn't my scene. But I did find it funny that there would be violent clashes at the weekends, yet the opposing sides would be sitting together in school during the week. Chasing each other with golf clubs and baseball bats on Friday night, but on Monday morning they'd be in Home Economics making rock cakes together.

I was definitely being fast-tracked in terms of growing up and I'd find myself between crowds. I'd hang around with people who I could make laugh and who'd make me laugh. It was the only thing, apart from the schoolwork, that I'd found I was good at. I wasn't really known for being funny as I wasn't extroverted and I was a bit scared to try to hold court in a crowd. Mochan, Henry and James would find me funny but the ones who were popular would just see me as 'fat', a 'VL' and, because I was in all the top classes, a bit of a 'geek'.

The first two years of high school I find difficult to separate in my recollections. I didn't really have an identity. I was clever but I didn't push myself enough; I daydreamed too much and began disappearing into my own head.

I struggled, sometimes, to concentrate in class but I'd always pull something together during class tests and manage good enough marks for my work.

At the end of the second year I picked the subjects that I wanted to study for the next two years, for my standard grades, the Scottish education equivalent of GCSEs.

Careers advisors would come into school assemblies and speak about how we should be thinking about our futures and what qualifications we'd need, which subjects were relevant for what we wanted to do with our lives.

I'd feel panicked because I had never thought of the future and what I wanted to do. I was thirteen, I didn't have a clue, and it was just another thing to worry about. I'd done enough worrying, so I just picked the subjects that I'd enjoyed.

Third year was the first year that everyone was separated from their normal 'registration' class and split into classes according to what level they were deemed capable of working at, based on performance over the first two years.

Credit, General and Foundation were the three levels, and Credit levels were again divided into Credit 1, 2 and 3. I was placed into Credit 1 for everything and remember being happy to tell my mum and dad, who were proud and keen to encourage me.

The first period of the first day of the third year, I had English. I sat beside Mochan, my best mate out of everyone who was in the class. I was no longer all that driven to do well or thinking about getting qualifications and emulating John.

Mochan was the smartest; that was his thing. I'd given up on chasing that accolade so it was up to me to find another field in which to excel.

27

In the Credit 1 English class on the first day of the third year, I lasted a little under five minutes.

The teacher, Mr McPhail, had only just taken the register. I hadn't planned on shouting 'Here, sir' any louder than anyone else. This was the big league now and the joke wouldn't go down well amongst the class of budding young intellectuals.

Mr McPhail completed the register and my name hadn't been read out. I was alarmed and put my hand up to check that I was in the correct class.

Mr McPhail asked my name and checked through his register again, his face blank; he was keen to start the lesson. The classroom door was chapped. 'Come in,' Mr McPhail shouted, in the tone that only high-school teachers and doctors have made their own. 'Sir, Kevin Bridges is supposed be in Mrs Gribbon's class.'

It was Tony.

'Okay, well, good luck, son,' Mr McPhail said, as I grabbed my bag and jacket and left, escorted to my new class by Tony.

Tony's face had been bright red with everything in him fighting to hold back a fit of the giggles when speaking to Mr McPhail in front of a full classroom. Keeping a straight face at important times was something Tony never mastered.

I had only seen him in passing since we'd been best pals in primary school, but it was like nothing had changed in the five years since we'd sat together.

We walked into Mrs Gribbon's class. There were two spare seats beside each other, Bridges and Clark, B and C. The alphabet had brought us together again.

I'd already told my mum and dad I was in Credit 1 with Mr McPhail, a respected St Columba's veteran who'd taught John as well. How would I tell them I'd been relegated after one day?

I'd handed in a mediocre report on the book *Kes* by John Brines, at the end of the second year. I figured that could have been what cost me.

I enjoyed the book, but only as much as you can enjoy a book you have to write a report on and then stand up in front of the class and talk about.

This was a problem for later, though. I was reunited with Tony and that seemed more important.

The class started and, like we'd done in primary school, Tony and I began to talk incessantly. 'Let's see your time-table,' he asked. I handed it to him from my pocket, eyes focused on Mrs Gribbon like she was a prison guard and I was a con passing over an offensive weapon or class-A drugs.

Tony studied it quickly before handing it back. 'We're in the same class for English, Maths, Modern Studies, French and Computing.' We both laughed.

I sat beside Tony on that first day in English, and instantly I was fascinated by how he'd go into these intense laughing fits with only the slightest bit of encouragement.

There were promotional posters for books on the walls in Mrs Gribbon's class, with the author's name, a photo of the book cover, the title and some press quotes.

One of them was for David Baddiel's book, *A Time for Bed*. 'David Baddiel's brilliant debut novel,' said the blurb.

When the class was quiet and working, I turned to Tony and whispered, '*A Time for Bed* – David Baddiel's brilliant debut novel,' in a privileged-sounding middle-England accent, the accent that would later become my 'Leamington Spa' accent.

Tony had obviously noticed the poster as well, as he dissolved into one of his hysterical states; I didn't think it had been that funny, but I had never seen anyone turn this kind of colour before. I didn't know what to do. I was smiling and looking at him, thoroughly impressed by his reaction.

I was looking at him the way Jim Carrey looks at the big criminal guy who starts sweating and choking after they'd put the hot chillies on his burger in *Dumb and Dumber*.

He was silent and his whole body was shaking with suppressed laughter. It look liked he was going to explode just as he let out a massive cackle.

This drew the rest of the class's attention. I remember looking up at Mrs Gribbon to see her studying Tony with a look of concern, sliding her glasses down her nose and unsure whether to tell him off or to contact the school auxiliary nurse.

'Is something funny?' she said, giving Tony the medical green light.

This made me laugh. What kind of question was that? 'Is something funny? Look at the fucking state he's in,' I said, to myself.

Tony was still struggling to get himself together, but he managed a 'No, miss'.

'Something must have made you laugh, Anthony,' she probed further, more intrigued than annoyed.

'I was just laughing at that poster,' Tony said, which baffled Mrs Gribbon even more.

'Which poster?' she said, her eyes scanning the walls, going through the entire collection looking for one that could have generated so much hilarity.

I thought Tony would tell the truth, say the David Baddiel one and explain that I'd put on a voice and read it out to him. '*Howard's End*,' he said, which I didn't expect.

This, along with how farcical the situation had become, set me off into a fit of the giggles as well. I felt my eyes watering up, and I was helpless. I needed Tony to stop laughing, so that I could stop, and he was the same.

We managed to calm down, but only to the point at which we were both sat attempting to get on with the work, but sniggering in a *Beavis and Butthead* kind of way.

Mrs Gribbon and the rest of the class definitely thought we had lost the plot. We didn't even know why we found this all so funny, so what chance did anyone else have?

As an adult, I'd never describe anyone as my 'best' mate; it would feel like a snub to the rest. But hanging around with Tony again was like restarting high school for me, and for the three years that followed I don't remember much except laughing like this and finding my self-confidence gradually building.

We were both the same sort of size, but Tony was never called names or anything. His self-assurance would act as a defence. He was popular and very difficult not to like.

I suppose this rubbed off on me. His relaxed attitude was infectious, and after a couple of weeks we sat beside each other in every class we were in together.

I grew to worry less and tried to enjoy each day. I'd come home and go over what we'd got up to at school, what had made the class laugh and what other things we could be doing.

After competing with Mochan to be the smartest, this was my new challenge. I wouldn't say Tony and I were ever in competition, though; we worked far better as a double act. Teachers would begin to separate us, and we'd begun racking up an impressive tally of punnies.

We started walking to and from school together and hanging around with each other at playtime and lunchtime. Every morning Tony would walk down from his house at the back end of Hardgate with Big Doc, Kevin and George Marshall, Shaun Doherty and Chris McLaughlin, and they'd meet me at the fire station near the end of my street.

The rest would walk on ahead, talking about football and whatever else, whilst I'd be beside Tony, the two of us acting out sketches from *Chewin' the Fat*, a brilliant and massively popular Scottish comedy show.

Tony's impersonations of all the characters were spot on, and the walk to school would take us far longer than it should, both of us lagging behind at the back, correcting each other and making sure we got all the words to the sketches and the songs right.

The show would always be on TV on a Thursday night so we'd usually entertain whoever was in our classes on the Friday morning, fresh with the latest material from the show. We were both enjoying performing and some lunchtimes we'd even try a spot of busking.

We'd stand outside McGhee's bakery, near the school, singing old songs that for years I'd been hearing on Clyde 2 radio every morning before school.

'King of the Road' by Roger Miller became our big hit. I used to sing the song around the house, even if I didn't understand all of the words, and I had to mumble my way through some of the verses.

We managed to find the lyrics online in a computing class one day and we quickly learned them, adding some professionalism to our shows.

We'd always try to emphasize the pause after 'short' with a choreographed point of our right finger, right on cue.

If we both nailed it and the two of us got the timing exact, it would make us laugh so much that we'd forget the next line. We'd compose ourselves, though, and fast forward to the chorus, where we'd give it everything we had; at the top of our voices, we'd alert the entire 'top of the hill' district of Clydebank. I was playing to a home crowd, and I had them in the palm of my hand. I was in my element.

The McGhee's staff would now be out shouting at us to get away from their front door, and other school children passing by were tutting and muttering, 'Check the state of you two,' at us.

We didn't care. For every doubter, there was a fan who would be lapping it up. Old guys going to the Cleddans pub beside McGhee's, or to the bookie's opposite would stop and shout, 'Go on yourselves, boys,' expressing their rip-roaring approval.

We even got a few coins thrown down at our feet; I'm sure we'd have made more but neither of us had a hat.

The chorus would draw in the crowd and their enthusiasm would spur us on through the next verse.

A simple repeated click of the right fingers and a left-to-right move of the shoulders were the only actions needed.

McGhee's would always threaten to bar us. Unlicensed busking was just one of what would end up as a whole catalogue of similar misdemeanours.

But we'd usually finish to at least a ripple of applause and then join the queue at McGhee's with everyone else, looking forward to a post-performance pie and beans.

28

Martin O'Neill had taken over at Celtic and there was a huge excitement about going to the football again. Chris Sutton had recently signed for £6 million, and Henrik Larsson had returned from his injury, a broken leg, and looked better than he'd ever been.

The first Old Firm game of the season at the end of August 2000 was the first test to see if this team was the real deal or not. Rangers had won the league the season before by twenty-one points.

Celtic went 3–0 up after ten minutes. The game finished 6–2, with Celtic going on to win the two cups and the league, by twenty-one points.

Things were changing.

I still loved going to the games with my dad, but I'd imagine it being good to go with Tony as well. At school we'd both talk about going to away games and how great it sounded to be travelling all over the country on a bus and watching your team, especially this current Celtic team.

My mum and Tony's mum would only let us go if there was an adult accompanying us. My dad wasn't fit enough for the travelling, and Tony's dad had unpredictable working hours. John knew how much we both wanted to go and said he'd look after us. Everyone agreed. John sensed how annoying we could both be and said he'd look after us, if we stayed out of his way.

We agreed.

I knew it would be too much pressure on my mum

financially if I was to go to every away game. But I got to plenty of them, and John would help out with the money as well.

John's only ask in return was that Tony and I would occasionally make the trip to Celtic Park, outside of match times, to collect the tickets from the ticket office.

John worked from nine to five all week so he didn't have as much freedom as we had. Plus, it was never a problem; it was something we'd have gladly done anyway.

We'd take autograph books as well, hoping to see some of the players. We'd head up on the 62 bus, Tony, our pal Seán Doak, and I, on Sundays or Saturdays, whatever day the game wasn't on. Sometimes we'd go during school holidays or we'd even head there straight after school, missing last period if it was something that wasn't all that important.

We'd collect John's tickets, together with ours and whoever else had asked and then hang around for a bit, asking stewards if any of the players were around. Even if the players were still in the stadium and were due out soon, they'd tell us 'No'.

The stewards had obviously been briefed that under no circumstances should a group of school children get a scribble on a piece of paper from their hero.

'Henrik Larsson, Henrik, Henrik!' Tony ran away shouting.

I barely took time to think, 'So it is!' before I was running at Tony's back.

Henrik Larsson was hurriedly trying to get into his car, with a few stewards standing around him, encouraging everyone to stand back and leave him alone, making a bit of a drama over something that I'd imagine happened every day.

Larsson was pretty cool about it. But I'd left my autograph book in the ticket office when I'd gone into my pocket to grab the money John had given me, and I didn't think he'd be all that cool about being asked to wait for me as I ran back to get it.

I had nothing on me except my First Bus All-Day ticket. I handed it to him and he looked at me. I laughed and pleadingly said, 'It's all I've got.' He signed it, but the marker pen he had in his hand was far too thick for the thin little bus ticket and a tiny bit of the ink went on his light blue jeans.

I was embarrassed. I'd caused him to get permanent ink on his jeans. 'Sorry,' I sheepishly said, totally star-struck but also feeling like I'd let him down.

'It's okay, don't worry,' he replied.

In the moment, I'd forgotten the guy could probably afford a new pair of jeans. I was just thinking that if it had been my jeans, my mum would be shouting how she'd just bought them. Twenty pounds, they cost. They're good ones as well, from that Colors,' I pictured her saying.

I felt a lot better when he seemed cool about it. He got in his car and drove away.

I turned to Tony and Doak. The three of us were high-fiving each other and walking towards the bus stop, talking rapidly, but with nothing to say other than 'Henrik Larsson, Henrik Larsson', studying our signatures and then repeating his name again, over and over.

We were running on nervous energy and feeling ecstatic. It had all happened in seconds. Tony's vision and then a quick burst of pace from us all and – bang! – Henrik Larsson's autograph on a First Bus all-day ticket.

We stood opposite the Forge Shopping Centre at Parkhead, waiting for our bus back to Clydebank, still repeating 'Henrik Larsson' to each other. The bus arrived. Tony and Sean showed their all-day tickets and the guy just threw his head back in the slightest of acknowledgements.

My ticket, however, was defaced and drew his attention. I was probably the one out of every hundred that the drivers actually decided to check. 'I canny make out the date on that, pal.'

Tony turned back, outraged on my behalf. 'It's Henrik Larsson's autograph,' he pleaded.

In a city like Glasgow, things like this are a 50/50 call, a game of roulette. I was either getting on the bus with the ticket or being made to pay for a new single.

'Is it? He's shite. This is a Rangers bus,' the driver said, straight-faced, before smiling. 'On you go, wee man.' If it was a game of sectarian roulette, the ball had landed on the zero. Fair play to the driver for not narking on my buzz.

I couldn't wait to get home now and show everyone. The First Bus All-Day ticket was stuck on my wall, and I'd say is still somewhere in my mum and dad's house to this day.

I did get to a few of the away games with Tony over the next few years, going to all the different stadia. Seeing players like Henrik Larsson and Chris Sutton so close, as opposed to in a stadium as vast as Celtic Park, was a new experience, and one I preferred to the home games.

A lot of the Scottish Premier League stadia had capacities under ten thousand. So we'd be stood behind the goal, and it was amazing to hear the players shouting at each other and seeing how focused they looked.

I'd enjoy listening to people who didn't seem to enjoy going to see their team at all. They'd spend the whole game shouting abuse at their own players. It appeared to be more about the diversion and the therapy session it provided than it was about supporting their team.

It was an afternoon away from work and their families. How they reacted to a sloppy back pass or a missed chance was a gauge of how content they were with their lives.

On the bus, Tony and I would sit together, not quite at the front of the bus, but nowhere near the back. We respected the rules and we were aware that you had to work your way towards the back of the bus and you had to have something to offer. We might have been the heartbeat of the party at high school, but on the bus we were reminded that we were just apprentices.

On the way home from places like Dundee and Aberdeen, I'd stare out of the bus window, listening to everyone at the back cracking jokes and singing daft songs. We were only about fourteen and found everyone hilarious; I didn't yet know that there was a difference between being drunk and being funny.

It looked great and carefree, though, travelling around with a bunch of your mates, watching your team, no immediate concerns except trying to convince the driver to pull into a service station, one that sold alcohol.

I figured that it was something we had to look forward to and that we'd be the 'back seat of the bus' crowd some day.

29

As well as Mrs Gribbon for English, we had Mr Farmer for Maths and Computing. Mr Farmer was one of the good guys. He was very passionate about his job, and I felt he took a genuine pleasure in seeing his students progress.

He was the height of a professional wrestler, easily six foot five or six. He had a ponytail and a strong southern English accent; he was mad into outdoor sports like kayaking and rock climbing and was, to be honest, a pretty cool dude.

It couldn't have been easy for someone who stood out in so many ways to teach in a high school in Clydebank, and I don't think we made it any less of a challenge for him.

'Tony! Kevin! Get outside,' became like his catchphrase and a running joke amongst the other classes in the Maths department, who'd hear this nearly every day and then hear us both giggling in the corridor.

We were never cheeky to him. As much as I liked getting the class laughing, I'd appreciate how most of the teachers were good people. It was nothing personal; it was simply that they had the authority, and we'd be trying to push it as far as we could.

My work got me out of most of the trouble that my behaviour got me into. For all I was an emerging class clown and becoming preoccupied more with getting a laugh than a good mark, I would still hand in my homework on time and pick things up pretty fast.

I think this frustrated the teachers even more. Sometimes

they'd ask me to stay back after the class, and then talk to me. They'd tell me I was bright and full of potential, but that I was wasting it by acting like a moron.

I'd feel two-faced as I stood there, just one on one with the teacher. I became shy again. I didn't have my class, my audience; there was no one to impress.

I'd pretend to take their advice and encouragement on board, but the following day I'd be back playing to the crowd again. When the class had settled into their work and the noise of the radiator was all that could be heard, I'd put my hand up and ask stupid questions like, 'Mr Farmer, if you were a farmer, would you be Farmer Farmer?' It was delivered to the teacher, but aimed at the class, Tony especially.

I'd be at the back of the class and Tony at the front. The class would laugh, but Tony would take it beyond that and disappear into one of his fits again, unable to control himself, his face changing colour and his shoulders shaking before he released another bellowing cackle – Mr Farmer's cue to deliver his line:

'Tony! Kevin! Get outside!'

And off we went, out to the corridor again.

For French, we had Mr Rundle. We'd always be late into French as it was in the school's annexe building. We probably could have made it there a little faster, but we'd always go on a detour and find ways to be a nuisance. If we recognized someone in another class that we were passing, we'd chap the door and say that Mr Rundle wanted to see them.

It would usually be our mate Sean Doak. Doak was much quieter than us and he would get embarrassed pretty easily and sometimes tell us to calm down a bit. It would be good to get him roped in, though, and he was always up for a laugh.

'I haven't heard from Mr Rundle. What does he want to

see Sean for?' Doak's teacher would ask, but we'd never have a story prepared. That's probably what made it funny to us.

'Just to say hello, sir. He said it's been a while.'

The class would start laughing, and that'd be Tony away into his hysterical, happy place, leaving me to dig us out of a hole.

'So Mr Rundle wants to see Sean, just to say hello?'

I'd be on the spot, but determined not to crumble.

'Look, sir, I'm only passing on the message, and I think anything else is between Mr Rundle and Sean Doak,' I'd conclude, trying to sound assertive, fully aware that the class were enjoying my performance.

The full class would be laughing now, the teacher too confused to say anything other than, 'Get out of the classroom and get to your own.' We'd walk out laughing and continue on our way to Mr Rundle's French class.

When we'd get to the annexe building, up to the top level and into Mr Rundle's corridor, we'd dare each other to shout, 'LET'S GET READY TO RUNNNDLE', like a boxing announcer. We'd stand around giggling, encouraging each other.

'You'll be a legend,' as usual, was the deal breaker.

One of us would agree and then let it rip, at the top of our voice, even attempting a showbiz American accent to give it some pizzazz. We'd quickly compose ourselves and walk into the class as though nothing had happened. The whole class knew it was us, and it became the running joke.

The joke wore thin on Mr Rundle, and he anticipated it one day. We were both late again. It was no longer an exciting dare or as funny as it had been the first few times; it was more out of tradition than for the thrill.

I'd gone to routinely shout it and as soon as I'd got to the

'LLLLLLLLET'S GET RRRR –' Mr Rundle pounced out from the classroom and caught us there and then.

'Ah, Mr Bridges and Mr Clark, how did I know it was you two eejits?' he said sarcastically, satisfied that he'd busted us.

'*Pardonnez moi, monsieur,*' I said in an exaggerated French accent, hoping he'd laugh and let it slide.

He told us not to bother coming into the class. I don't think he'd taken offence or anything. It was more he was fed up with us, and being left to wander the corridors during periods wasn't a great place to be. Deputy head teachers and even the head teacher himself would regularly be on the prowl, predators looking for prey.

We were busted and then questioned by Mr Ingram. Mr Ingram was primarily a woodwork teacher, but his hard line on discipline had landed him a senior position amongst the school hierarchy.

I'm not sure what his official title was, but I always thought he was particularly good at frightening the shite out of people. He was like one of the angry cartoon sausages in the old Peperami adverts.

He'd been made aware of Tony and me by this time, and he knew we'd had some referrals for our disruptive behaviour. This was his first run-in with us himself, though.

He began to shout at us. It was nothing more than a fright he'd wanted to give us, a first warning, and to let us know we were on his radar. I'm sure he'd have marched us back to Mr Rundle's class after putting a bit of a rocket up our arses and that would have been that.

The problem was that only that same day, I'd noticed someone had scratched 'Ingram's a Ballbag' into the wood on the main door of the annexe, using a key or a coin or something like that.

Even Tony knew that Mr Ingram meant business and he went to a dark place in his head in order not to laugh. He managed to stand, blank-faced, and take the grilling.

I knew Mr Ingram was the real deal as well, but I just couldn't get this hand-carved graffiti out of my head. I think the fact that they'd written 'Ballbag' rather than the Scottish 'Bawbag' made me laugh even more. They'd formalized it, presumably out of respect.

I just couldn't help laughing. I felt my eyes watering.

I'd lost control.

I apologized numerous times in between my sniggers but even Tony was fearing for me now. I could feel him looking at me as if to say, 'It's Mr Ingram, man.'

Mr Ingram flipped his fucking lid.

It was like a scene in *Full Metal Jacket*. Mr Ingram was the sergeant and I was Gomer Pyle.

30

As a result of that, I was put in the exclusion room for two days, made to follow my timetable, with work being sent from my teachers for me to do in isolation.

The exclusion room was definitely a great idea for punishing pupils like me. There was no teacher, which took the fun element out of carrying on. Instead there was only someone checking in on us every now and then, handing us the new work at the beginning of the new periods.

It was in a room too small to be used as a proper classroom, but big enough to fit some desks, chairs and a couple of old jaded-looking computers in the corner, too ashamed to be seen in the company of the new, high-tech, multicoloured Apple Macs that the school had recently purchased a shit load of.

The window looked out over the school's red-ash football parks and towards the fields between the nicer, more affluent parts of Hardgate and Drumchapel.

It was mind-numbingly boring. No one knew each other, so there would be hardly anything getting said, and I felt out of place. The other four or five pupils in the exclusion room had either been fighting, vandalizing something or threatening a teacher, or they had proper behaviour problems and had been in several times.

They'd all done something more serious than my offence of hitting the giggles at an inopportune time. I was in there to be given a warning, though. I found it a bit harsh, and even Mr Ingram had said something like, 'You're clearly a smart boy, but if this is how you want it to be . . .'

The boredom meant I had no option but to do my school-work, and I got it all done and done well. I finished it quickly so that I'd have some time left over to sit and be bored again.

I was always at my best when I was bored, and I began to write a stupid story, like a prison journal, about my time in the exclusion room. I'd written it from the stance of an inno-cent being 'detained' without a 'fair hearing'.

We'd recently watched a documentary in Modern Studies about Amnesty International and their work, so that was probably my influence. I wrote about our 'inhumane treat-ment', like the radiator behind turned up to the maximum temperature and the old school windows being painted closed; the 'awful conditions' – chewing gum under my desk and the back of my chair had snapped so I couldn't sit back and relax.

I wrote about my 'cell mates' and how some of them had been struggling to cope and had started to crack. Some of them throwing their work on the floor, taking a stance and expressing themselves through writing on the walls and burning their names into the desks with 'smuggled in' cigar-ette lighters.

I wrote about the 'outside' and my plans for when I was 'released' and how some of my 'cell mates' may never get out. It was all stream-of-consciousness stuff with a *Shawshank Redemption* kind of theme, but it passed the time and I was pretty proud of it.

I handed it into Mrs Gribbon, along with my real English work. It didn't count for anything and she couldn't give me a mark, but she did mention that it had made her laugh and that it was very well written. She also remarked that I was 'too bright' a pupil to be in the exclusion room and that she hoped it was a one-off.

I'd begin to get loads of warnings like this, ultimatums even, being told I had two paths I could go down and that I should choose wisely between fulfilling my academic potential or continuing to treat the classrooms like a place to perform.

I enjoyed writing. Mrs Gribbon would often compliment my work, and English became my favourite subject. Mrs McGlinchey, my Modern Studies teacher, was another who'd encourage me and I enjoyed her classes as well.

In Mrs McGlinchey's Modern Studies, we'd often have class debates about topical news stories, and I'd try to contribute as much as I could.

Half of it would be to raise a laugh. I'd deliberately make silly points in an *Ali G* kind of way, but I'd be keen, as well, to make points and ask questions based on what I'd read and what I understood.

At home I watched the news most days with my parents, and my dad would always be reading the *Herald* newspaper, a Glasgow-based broadsheet. Our paperboy would have to be regularly reminded to deliver us one – my dad was probably the only guy on the street who read it.

I'd find it far too big; I knew it was more in-depth and intellectual than the other newspapers, the ones that would have plenty of pictures and football coverage and were easy to read. So I maybe used the *Herald's* size as an excuse not to read it when my dad would tell me I should.

I always quizzed my dad about what was going on in the world, and he'd soon be ranting and giving me his own theories and opinions. I'd drift in and out of paying attention.

I preferred it when John was there, as he and my dad would regularly have debates on whatever the main issues on the news and in the papers were. They were not so much debates as my dad going off on tangents, his heart dragging him into battles that his head couldn't win.

John wouldn't sit and humour him the way me and my mum would. Instead he'd take pleasure in calmly grinding my dad down with facts and counter arguments, and it would be funny for both my mum and me to sit and watch my dad get agitated.

He's always had strong socialist views and been a liberal-minded, each-to-their-own kind of guy. I always knew where he was coming from, as did John, who'd sometimes play devil's advocate just to get a reaction.

Both my dad and John knew their stuff, even if my dad couldn't quite get his point across without losing the plot. It was undeniably funny to hear him getting flustered and conceding arguments with grand statements like, 'You just need to look at him to know he's an arsehole.'

I know my mum and dad, especially my dad, were disappointed when I'd get punishment exercises and referrals and have letters sent home from school about me. I think it probably took my dad back to his own schooldays, to when he'd receive 'the belt' on a daily basis.

My dad was the one who'd sat and spoken to me during our lunch breaks towards the end of primary school, about relaxing and trying to enjoy school a bit more. I'd listened to him and took what he said to the other extreme. He'd now be talking to me about keeping the carry-on and the laughs for outside of school.

I'd go through phases of following his advice, but that's when school would become boring again, and I'd fade into the background.

I did enjoy being praised for my work, passing tests and getting good marks. There was definitely a sense of satisfaction there, but it didn't compare to the feeling of having everyone in an uproar and making people laugh.

It was becoming my thing now, what I was known for. I'd be disappointing everyone if I'd knuckled down and studied hard to pass my standard grades. I'd try to find a compromise and separate the classes that I should work hard in from the ones that I could mess about in. But all the most important classes I shared with Tony, so that was difficult.

At parents' evening, every teacher would now be telling my mum and dad about all the stupid stuff I'd done. They'd all emphasize that I wasn't a bad pupil and that they all liked me, but I was easily led and constantly disrupting the classes.

One teacher, Mrs Friel, my Business Management teacher, removed her glasses and began wiping her eyes. My mum and dad thought she was crying and, the way the parents' evening had been going, assumed I'd pushed her over the edge and she was having a breakdown at the very sight of those who'd created me.

She was laughing, though, heartily, and told my mum and dad about a story I'd told the class when she'd asked me to 'share what's so funny with the rest of us' after I'd been caught talking and laughing with my mate Kevin Marshall.

I don't remember what I said exactly, but it was some story I made up on the spot. They were usually about a fictional uncle that I'd created, an uncle who'd been everywhere, met everyone and lived a life littered with bizarre incidents.

It was the only good report of the night, but I was delighted with it. I'd made the teacher laugh the way I could make Tony laugh.

My mum and dad would come home and let me know how they were disappointed and concerned about where I was headed. My dad would shout at me, letting me know I was destined to be a waster unless I changed my attitude.

I'd try to defend myself, telling them how my work was still above average. I was maybe putting the bare minimum effort in, but they couldn't deny I was getting away with it.

I'd read books at home, only about things I was interested in. I saw this as part of my education. No one was telling me to read and that's why I enjoyed reading; it was my own decision. I'd write as well, silly stories, exaggerated and based on things that happened at school.

Nothing I'd ever show anybody, but I enjoyed it and I'd spend hours alone in my bedroom, listening to music and lying thinking about the future. I was no longer worrying about the future and what I'd do with myself, the way I used to, even though, according to my mum and dad and my teachers, I maybe had something to worry about.

When I'd talk back, defending myself, it infuriated my dad even more, to the point where he'd be shouting so much that John would come down to the living room. He'd tell my dad to calm down. It always helped the situation and John was always good to bridge the gap.

Being older he knew where my mum and dad were coming from, but he was also young enough to remember high school and see it from my point of view.

I'd tell my mum and dad that I could be much worse; I wasn't out drinking and hanging around the streets like a lot of folk in my year were now doing.

I knew I wasn't doing anything all that wrong. I was only making people laugh – what could be so bad about that? And besides, I was right, there were far worse people than me at St Columba's.

The fact that the school made the front page of the Scottish newspapers when two pupils were expelled for letting off a home-made nail bomb in the boys' toilets one afternoon only added weight to my argument.

My mum and dad couldn't believe the difference in the reports from a few years before, at St Mary's, when teachers described me as shy, nervous and introverted. I was still shy, nervous and introverted, really, but I'd developed a front now.

At first my confidence was all bravado and easily knocked. I was growing in popularity, but I'd still be picked on now and then and have my real self revealed. I'd blush and go quiet if I was being called names in front of a crowd. They'd pick on me for my weight, my clothes. 'How many birds have you got off with?' they'd ask and laugh before I could answer.

'I heard you used to cry for your mum at primary school' – that one would come up sometimes, obviously a tip-off from some of my old St Mary's classmates. I'd hate it, being humiliated in front of everyone; I'd be bright red and struggling to hide how much it was getting to me. It would rattle me for the rest of the day, and all the same feelings from St Mary's would return to me.

I wished I could fight, but I couldn't, so I'd try to stay away from the ones who'd give me a hard time. I'd tell John about it rather than my dad, who still couldn't see past the traditional, but outdated, 'stand up for yourself' advice.

John told me that at the end of the fourth year most of them would leave and that he'd enjoyed fifth and sixth years the most at high school; I had that to look forward to.

Getting singled out began to bother me less and less, and I'd soon begin to stand up for myself, at least verbally. I began not to really care about what was actually being said to me, or take it to heart; everyone got a roasting now and then.

I'd never hate the ones doing the talking; it was the ones who'd never speak I didn't like, the arse-lickers, the ones who tagged along with the popular crowd. They'd do anything for the 'best fighters' and do what they were told so long as they could remain a part of the crowd. I could see they were just as nervous as me, so I'd go for them.

In the dinner hall or in the playground or in a class, whenever one of the main men would make a comment – 'Where did you get your trainers, fatty?' or something along those lines – all the backing group would be laughing like it was the funniest thing that had ever been said. They'd repeat it to each other, '"Where did you get your trainers, fatty?" he said,' and laugh again, in awe of their hero.

'Well, I got these from Reggie's Sports,' I replied, in a pretend posh voice.

Reggie's was a budget sports shop in Clydebank Shopping Centre that specialized in the cheaper brands and was famous, locally, because of the owner's poor hygiene. He'd wear an old, ripped, ancient-looking grey suit jacket with both of the shoulders displaying an impressive collection of dandruff, and old Jack Duckworth-style glasses with an Elastoplast attaching one of the legs to the frame.

Shopping in Reggie's sports wasn't something anyone would openly admit to. My trainers weren't a 'good make'. I didn't know what was a good make any more, as it changed every day in accordance with these dicks.

I was getting to nearly every Celtic game, so I was fucked if I was putting my mum under any more pressure. I started to embrace my trainers, even learning how to properly pronounce the name of the brand.

My reply got everyone laughing, laughing at me. 'Ha, ha! He got his trainers in Reggie's, the fucking tramp,' one of the sycophants announced, looking round for approval and with a nastier tone in his voice than his leader had used when the issue of my trainers had first been raised.

He didn't get that I was being sarcastic, which was my attempt at self-defence. If I could be self-deprecating and laugh at myself as much as they could, then they'd leave me alone, I figured; it was the spoken-word equivalent of doing the 'truffle shuffle'.

They didn't get it, and I had to change tactics. 'Your mum was in front of me in the queue, buying a bra and pants,' I said, adding, 'I didn't know that Diadora made thongs.'

'Ha, ha! Your maw wears a Diadora thong,' the main, made man concluded, laughing at one of his own die-hard supporters right in his face, turning the whole crowd away from me and on to him.

He went red, his face raging. Everyone was laughing at him. 'Who the fuck are you talking to, fat tramp?' I could tell he was rattled, though, and desperately trying to save face.

'She was asking the owner if he'd help her pick a size, and he was all over her. I think he might be your real dad,' I continued, going in for the kill.

I was never good at 'slagging matches'; there was too much ammo against me. I could make something out of nothing, but I'd feel bad having a go at someone.

The next week, I heard the 'your maw wears a Diadora thong' line used by a bunch of first years. It had been added to the new range of playground patter. It was even used against me a few times in a less intense and more light-hearted way, a bit of 'gentle ribbing'.

It was ultimately a 'your maw' line and not my finest work. But it had got me out of an ugly situation.

3 I

Another thing I'd get a hard time about at school was not going out to hang about at the weekends. Towards the end of the fourth year, it seemed like I was the only one in our class who hadn't been drunk yet. I was fifteen.

Going to the football was the highlight of my weekend and afterwards getting a takeaway with my mum and dad and hopefully John, if he'd stayed in. I'd sit in my room playing on the PlayStation, Oasis blaring. I didn't feel like I was missing out on a lot not being out roaming the streets. I had a great time in the house.

I'd watch all of the late-night Friday television shows – *Eurotrash* and the Channel 5 erotic thriller, naturally, but I'd now stumbled on to a show called *Take the Mic* on ITV.

Take the Mic was a stand-up comedy show featuring amateur comedians who'd perform a few minutes of stand-up and then be given a critique by an established comedian.

The only stand-up comedy I'd ever watched was the Billy Connolly tapes that our whole family would sit together and watch at Christmas. I didn't get it when I was younger, but I'd repeat his swear words and laugh when he'd speak about 'farts' and 'jobbies'.

However, I'd begun to get why my mum, dad, John and my aunties and uncles laughed the way they did at him, appreciating how funny he was and how amazing it was that he seemed to simply walk on a stage and start talking.

That was Billy Connolly, though; he was famous. *Take the Mic* was just people, just these dudes that stood up and talked about their day. I knew there was more to it than that but that's why I was immediately impressed by how straightforward they made it look.

It was just people talking.

I'd tell John about the show and tell him to watch it. He watched it, but I don't think he found it all that funny. He knew more about comedy and had watched comedians I'd never heard of. He'd even been to a comedy club to watch Phil Kay.

I didn't know of him, either.

The guys on *Take the Mic* probably weren't that funny. I don't really remember laughing. I was more intrigued, willing them on, in full admiration of what they were doing.

I started to write down some stuff that I'd noticed, based on what it looked like they were doing. I wrote about three or four different 'routines' and walked into John's room the next afternoon, telling him that I had a stand-up comedy act and asked if he'd like to hear it.

It felt like it was a big thing for me as I'd never told anyone I wrote stuff. I was embarrassed and thought it was maybe a little lame that I kept what was effectively a journal.

I stood at John's door. He was lying on top of his bed. He refused to mute his telly to give me his full attention. A smirk kept coming over his face, and I could tell he wasn't taking me seriously.

I kept hesitating and saying, 'Naw, you'll just laugh,' pretending to walk out of his room, hoping he'd try to convince me to stay and encourage me to perform my 'material'.

He repeated, 'I'll just laugh?' and asked, 'Is that not the point?'

He eventually gave me his undivided attention, and I actually remember feeling nervous when he muted the TV, like it was time for the show.

It was my chance to impress my big brother.

He'd admire me, the way I admired the amateur comedians on *Take the Mic*. It was my big moment.

I started to talk, but in this strange, polite and proper-sounding voice, the voice that I used to answer the house phone when I knew it was someone from my mum's work.

I'd recently been relieved of my secretarial duties by my mum. The phone had rung, I'd answered, and it was my mum's boss, whose voice I knew. I shouted to my mum; she mimed 'I'm not in' and made a throat-cutting gesture with her hand.

'She said she's not in,' I told her boss, immediately realizing what I'd done. My mum had to grab the phone and make out that I was joking, attempting to squirm her way out of the situation.

Anyway, I can't remember my opening line. I think it was something about an advert that had been on TV a lot. John burst out laughing, though not at my observation – I hadn't even got to the joke bit yet; he was finding the situation itself hilarious.

His little brother standing there with a notepad, pretending to be a stand-up comedian, complete with a put-on voice and a style of delivery that had been copied from one of the guests on a late-night ITV amateur comedy show.

I felt humiliated, a rational voice in my head asking what the fuck I was doing. I dropped my notepad and I dropped my newly crafted *Take the Mic*-inspired façade of a stand-up comedian.

Then, in scenes only ever witnessed in the aftermath of controversially decided *FIFA: Road to World Cup* matches, it all kicked off.

I flew towards John, throwing punches at him and screaming expletives. He managed to block a punch with his knee.

But then disaster struck. I knew it was serious the split second it happened. We both heard a loud snapping noise: I'd broken a finger.

My first gig had been a fucking disaster.

If John was to offer any feedback on my performance, he'd probably mention that physically attacking the audience for laughing could set me back a bit on the comedy circuit.

Stand-up comedy wasn't for me. I'd leave that to the people on *Take the Mic*, I concluded.

I was only a class clown.

The weekends that John would be out and my mum would go to bed early, I'd sit up with my dad and we'd watch comedy shows like *Bottom* and *The Young Ones*. We both had a stupid sense of humour and loved how off-the-wall the shows were.

As much as I liked watching grown men smacking each other about with frying pans and blasting each other with cattle prods, my sense of humour was evolving, and I soon started to love *Only Fools and Horses* and comedy movies, especially Richard Pryor ones like *Stir Crazy*, *Hear No Evil, See No Evil* and *Brewster's Millions*.

We'd occasionally flick through the channels and come across movies that we'd never heard of, straight-to-video ones that were bad but worth it for the one funny line that we'd both sit laughing at. We'd always find something in them and sit making each other laugh, adding in our own wee comments.

A film called *Dead Man on Campus* was one title that I remember. It was a film about American college students who'd found out that they'd be given an automatic pass if one of their flatmates committed suicide during the term. So their mission was to find a flatmate likely to kill himself.

I don't think it was a classic, but there was a self-destructive, destined-to-die-young, loose-cannon, hothead character called Cliff O'Malley, who made us both laugh, and we'd quote his lines for the next few weeks around the house.

I forget the context of the line but it wasn't really important, it was just a funny thing to say. No one knew what we were talking about, like the way people would if we'd been quoting *Happy Gilmour* or *Dumb and Dumber*. Nobody was ever going to interrupt with, 'Oh, I take it you guys have seen *Dead Man on Campus* as well?'

I liked how it was our own private joke.

I did eventually start going out more outside of school with Tony, Doak and our other mate Graeme Wardrop. Wardy had been Tony's best mate for years. He went to Clydebank High School, so I didn't know him, but he lived in the same street as Tony and he soon became my mate as well.

We had a good crowd, together with Big Doc, Kevin and George Marshall, Christopher McLaughlin, Shaun Doherty and Luke Monaghan. Mony sat beside me in a few classes and was in most of the ones that I shared with Tony. He always had good patter, and we'd have loads of stupid running jokes.

When we'd all go out, I preferred it when we had somewhere to go and something to do rather than aimlessly wandering around the streets. I was landing myself in enough trouble at school, so I didn't need anything else that would get Mum and Dad further on my case. My dad did tell me to keep the laughs for outside of school, though, and it was another piece of his advice that I'd follow, to the extreme.

There was a point when, along with Tony, I was banned from near enough every attraction in Clydebank Shopping Centre. I maybe made Clydebank Shopping Centre sound like a holiday resort there; it wasn't Manhattan, but still we had ten-pin bowling, a cinema, the Play Drome swimming baths and a McDonald's.

We'd go to play ten-pin bowling some Friday nights, getting roped into three games for a fiver or some deal like that. After a few shots, we'd remember how boring ten-pin bowling was and start messing around, throwing the balls down someone else's lane and then apologizing as though it was a genuine mistake.

Changing our names on the scoreboards to obscenities and then loudly addressing each other by our new aliases: 'It's your shot, Colonel Arse Breath.' This amused us for a wee while, but we needed a bigger fix.

One night came when Tony dared me to throw the bowling ball as though I were taking a throw-in in a game of football, ball held with two arms at the back of my head and then thrown as far as I could.

I agreed. I'd do anything if I knew it would get a laugh.

I asked Tony to keep a look-out for staff – 'keep the edgy' was the term. I then did as he'd dared. The weight of the ball meant it landed just a few yards in front of me and made a massive thud noise.

Tony's 'edgy keeping' skills were lacklustre; the manager had stood there in disbelief and seen the lot. At first we hadn't realized quite how angry he was. But we soon saw that this guy was seething, shouting and hurtling towards us at pace. Tony and I have never been the most athletic, but we had the benefit of a head start and our lane's proximity to an emergency exit – and this was definitely an emergency.

He chased us straight out into the car park before giving up and screaming all sorts of abuse at us, saying he was phoning the police and all the usual stuff authority figures shout that makes 'getting a chase' so invigorating and so funny at that age.

The two of us stood there, breathless after the short sprint, laughing hysterically.

We then realized our trainers were behind the counter, and we were stuck with bowling shoes, those red, white and black abominations that they give you for a nominal 'shoe hire' price.

It all turned serious, neither of us daring to go back for the trainers. 'You threw it, you fucking go. It was your fault!' Tony said.

'I threw it, so he'll be after me. You'll be okay. Anyway it was your idea,' I countered. This is roughly how I remember the conversation going.

We had to walk to the bus stop and head home with our new footwear. I have no doubt we were banned indefinitely from the bowling alley, but we had no immediate plans to return. Ten-pin bowling is an unnecessary expense when you have new trainers to save up for.

I did feel a wee bit bad that maybe I'd caused damage to the wooden bowling lane, but hopefully the two pairs of used Adidas Stan Smith Velcro strap trainers covered the cost of any required repair work.

32

We'd also go to the cinema, sometimes to see a good movie, but most times we'd buy a ticket for anything that was on. It was just for an excuse to sit and be 'the wee arseholes at the back' ruining the experience for everyone.

I don't condone our actions back then, and I write this now as a big movie fan. A 'cinema lover' I'd describe myself as, if I was trying to sound interesting.

As you read these high-school chapters, as I navigate through 'that difficult age', I ask that you consult with your own teenage self before passing judgement.

We were pests, but we had a great time being pests.

We were aware of how annoying we must have been but we had a code of conduct. We wouldn't go to children's films or anything that sounded like it could be good.

The film would be granted about twenty minutes' grace before we'd arrive at a decision. If it was deemed to be shite enough, then we'd give the all-clear and start acting up, shouting things out, playing games of 'Jobby' and 'Show's Your Gee', a game that had easily survived the test of time.

Our cinema ban came courtesy of Tony, who'd saved up to buy an air horn to take to Celtic away games. We'd walked to Halfords in the shopping centre straight from school one Friday afternoon. Tony bought it, immediately removed the packaging and gave it a blast before we'd even got out of the Halfords.

It was pretty loud, so loud that gas-powered air horns like it were actually prohibited from Scottish football grounds, at least according to the terms and conditions on the back of most match tickets.

'If it's prohibited from a football stadium, then fuck only knows how a cinema would cope with it,' I said to Tony, my way of suggesting that he bring it with him on our pre-arranged trip to the cinema later that evening.

On the 81 bus down from Hardgate to the shopping centre, both Wardy and Doak knew Tony was up to something and that I was in on it. They'd always try to discourage us from embarrassing them and getting us chucked out of places, especially if there were girls our age there and we'd be blowing their chances.

Tony eventually showed them his air horn and they didn't seem as excited as we were about it. 'I'm not paying in, then — you'll just get us launched out,' one of them said. The other agreed.

'It'll be fine, just do it at the end,' I reasoned, getting in before Tony started doubting this great plan and backed out.

Men in Black 2 was the movie. Doak and Wardy suggested a couple of films that sounded like they'd be much better, but we knew our intentions and that it wouldn't be fair on the rest of the cinema goers.

Men in Black 2, though, was a movie that was only going to attract crowds of wee bastards like Tony and me, and self-conscious first dates, whose minds would not be on the movie and who'd welcome the disruption we'd bring as it would give them something to talk about.

We sang the chorus in exaggerated, deep voices, stamping our feet and clapping our hands like it was a football ground. The coming-soon trailers were the pre-match warm-up. The atmosphere was building.

We received our final warning before the movie had

started; Wardy and Doak were mortified and threatening to move away from us. 'First sight of Will Smith, let it rip,' I said to Tony, dismissing the terms of our verbal contract with Doak and Wardy.

Will Smith appeared as quickly as you'd expect Will Smith to appear in a *Men in Black* movie, and the two of us burst into life. 'GET IN THERE, WILLY BOY!' Tony shouted, like an old guy at the football, praising the team's midfield hard man after a trademark crunching tackle on an opposition player.

We followed it up with things like 'GET INTO THESE ALIEN BASTARDS!'

And 'LET THEM KNOW WHO THEIR DA' IS, SMUDGER!'

(Most people I knew with the surname Smith were called Smudger.)

'WILLY' and 'SMUDGER'.

Will Smith now sounded like an amateur Scottish boxer rather than a Hollywood A-lister.

After the pro-Will Smith/anti-alien chanting, I turned to Tony for the big moment, the air horn, and what was sure to be a cinematic first.

The first blast didn't work properly, and it sounded like the air horn's voice was breaking as it went in and out of two different tones.

'Again, again, quick,' I said to Tony, noticing the staff walking down from the back of the cinema hall. Just at that moment he nailed a massive, long, ship-coming-in type of alert, sending the noise bouncing off all the walls in the cinema. It was even louder than we'd expected.

The movie was stopped, the lights came on and easily six or seven cinema staff came in to drag us out, telling us that they were going to phone the police and that they had our faces on camera and we'd be banned indefinitely.

'We're just big fans of Will Smith, mate,' we'd jokingly plead with the guys. But they were treating it far more seriously than a routine weekend procedure of ejecting disruptive youths from the premises.

Doak and Wardy, who'd moved and sat away from us, left voluntarily. Quietly asking for a refund, they got their money back and were given a wholehearted apology on behalf of the manager, who deeply regretted their cinema experience had been marred in such a way.

We rejoined them in the car park, and we all concluded that it had been pretty funny.

It wasn't even eight o'clock, though, and our night looked to be over. We were at a loose end, and everyone was starting to snap at everyone else, looking for someone to make a plan for what we could do for the rest of the night.

It was Tony and I who'd landed us in this situation, nothing to do and nowhere to be, so it was our responsibility to come up with a back-up plan.

Tony's mind wasn't thinking very far ahead, and a plan for the evening didn't seem to be bothering him as he dared me to walk back into the cinema and steal one of the giant cardboard cut-outs promoting future releases. This sent Wardy and Doak off to get the bus in a 'not this shite again' kind of way.

Off they went up to Croft Park, to where everyone would hang around, drinking and whatever else. I'd never go up, to avoid getting into trouble, ironically. I duly accepted Tony's dare. I knew it was risky, returning to the scene of the incident and all that, but a dare was a dare and my only thought was about finding a funny cardboard cut-out. We didn't want to be carrying any old shite around all night. Tony held the door open. I ran in, quickly trying to scan my options. The staff had recognized me and were shouting, 'I thought we told you not to come back here!'

I looked up and saw a poster saying *Love Actually*, and, below it, a life-sized cut-out of Hugh Grant, the star of the movie.

It was a must, the only option.

I looked straight into his eyes, his blue eyes, his Mickey Blue eyes, twinkling at me.

Hugh Grant, Hugh fucking Grant.

He was there, gazing at me, with all his trademark, inimitable self-deprecating charm, looking debonair in his suit and tie.

It was easy to see how he was a darling of Hollywood and ideal casting for a romantic comedy; right now, however, it was time to cast him in his first thrilling, high-action role.

I grabbed it and rapidly bailed for the door.

I was back in the moment and a massive, wheezing laugh from Tony accompanied his excited shouts of 'hurry up, hurry up' as the cinema stuff realized we were back and came racing down to the foyer, radioing in for back-up.

We made it out of the cinema, both Hugh and me.

Tony grabbed him by the legs and I had a hand on both shoulders as we made our way across the empty car park towards the bus stop, hoping to catch Doak and Wardy and introduce them to our new main man, who'd be joining us for the next little while.

We got to the bus stop to see that it was empty; no Doak, no Wardy, no one. It had the deserted, post-apocalyptic feeling that bus stops have at that time in the evening, letting you know life had existed there just minutes before, that you've literally just missed your bus and you could be in for a lengthy wait.

My dad in Sa Coma, 1995, on a pedalo, about to go mental
the way only stressed-out dads on holiday go mental.

Inflatable water wings and a Donkey Kong T-shirt. Not many
could pull that look off with such aplomb. Sa Coma, 1995.

Carrying on, probably about to get into trouble,
with Mark and Gary.

Sitting on the couch with the shorts pulled up again, a look I firmly established as my own, with my goldfish, Jerry, who was grieving after the death of his pal Tom at the time.

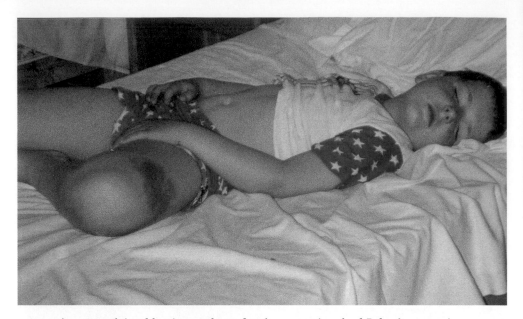

An unexplained bruise, and out for the count in a bed I don't recognize.
A situation I'd find myself in again and again as I got older.
What a night, though . . .

Pissed off in a restaurant on my tenth birthday in 1996.

John looking thrilled that I chose him to
be my 'sponsor' for my confirmation
in 1996.

My mum, dad, John and my Granny Jane at my confirmation in 1996,
another big pay day for a Catholic child.

Christmas Day, 1996. New bike.

Nearing the end of primary school and beginning
to come out of my shell. 'The cheek oozing out of me'
as my mum would say.

Showing off my toned physique. A shape that
I never managed to get back to!

We had the option of two buses that would take us to Hardgate, to Croft Park, where everyone would be. I'd never been up there on a Friday night before but I'd make an exception this time, if only to parade our new acquisition.

The bus timetable suggested that we wouldn't have to wait too long, but it was long enough for a police car to pull up first. The two police officers got out of the car, a man and a woman. They told us that they'd received a phone call from the cinema about us and asked our names.

The police were involved, but we knew we couldn't possibly be in any serious trouble and thought someone, in the very early stages of the course of justice, would see the funny side.

They asked our names. We all played a lot of *Championship Manager*, and in class a running joke would be to simply hit out with names of players who everyone would sign, players who were relatively unheard of in real football, but superstars in the game.

It wasn't really a joke, but it would always raise a smile of acknowledgement. It is hard to explain but, again, if you've played the game, you'll know what I mean.

I gave my name as Byron Bubb, a bright young hopeful who played for Millwall and who'd go on to great things in *Championship Manager*, providing he was given the right guidance.

'B-Y-R-O-N, Byron Bubb? B-U-double B, right?' the male officer double-checked with me, spelling out the second name with a humourless authority in his voice that indicated he'd go on to a long successful career in the force.

I couldn't fucking believe it. 'This guy thinks my name's Byron Bubb,' I thought to myself.

It was funny, exceptionally funny. I didn't even laugh, though, as I knew this could finish Tony. There was no doubt he'd find it funny, but maybe he'd find it too funny, far too funny for the investigating officer's liking anyway. A bit of fear came over me as I slowly turned away from facing the policeman's notebook to look at Tony, and just as he'd done so many times before, he went into a fit of laughter, a fit of laughter that only he could produce. The two police officers and I couldn't do anything except stand and watch until he was finished.

An apprehensive 'Tony, man' was all I could offer, a half-arsed but desperate attempt to get him to compose himself. The officer closed his notebook and told us both to get in the car.

'You can thank your pal for this,' he said to me, still thinking he was talking to Byron Bubb.

We were both sat in the back of the police car. The female officer got in the passenger seat. I tried to reason with her that the whole situation had gone a bit far now, a bit stupid, in the hope that she'd put forward our case, settle for an apology and we'd be let go.

She didn't say a thing. Her only response was to look over her right shoulder, past us and out of the back window of the car, to see her colleague wrestling with a cardboard cut-out of Hugh Grant. The cinema had obviously mentioned that we'd stolen it, and he was determined to be the hero and return it. They'd surely reward him with free tickets to see *Love Actually*.

It really did baffle me as to why she didn't find this at least a little bit funny: Byron Bubb in the back with his mate who couldn't stop chuckling, watching a police officer wrestle with a cardboard cut-out of Hugh Grant. He managed to fold it a little, with minimal damage, and placed it in the back seat between both of us.

Off we went, back to the cinema, me, Tony and Hugh Grant.

They then took us to the nearby police station and checked that they didn't know us and that we weren't on their records. They breathalysed us, and I had to reveal my real name, which got me a bit of a grilling and a lecture about lying to a police officer. It's fair to say the guy hadn't taken this whole episode too well.

Tony began to laugh again and that was it – the guy assigned us both a cell.

We'd laughed our way into jail.

It was serious now, and I remember instantly feeling terrified about how my mum and dad would react.

Fortunately, we weren't charged and we were allowed to leave after a couple of hours. It was a horrible feeling, though, lying on an old blue gym mat, staring at the ceiling, counting the individual glass panels in the roof, making up sums with them to stimulate your mind, wide awake and worried, reading the graffiti from the real criminals.

I was in the joint, man, doing time, unbelievable.

I'd laughed my way into the exclusion room and now this.

It didn't matter that the police officers had majorly overreacted and that it had been a fairly innocent series of events. It would sound like a far-fetched story and one that showcased all of the nonsense in my head that angered my mum and dad so much. All they'd conclude was that I'd been in police custody, and that the police must have had a valid enough reason.

Tony's dad came down to pick us up at about midnight. The car back was silent and I sat feeling ashamed. My mum and dad already knew I'd been in trouble with the police, as the officers had asked for the number of someone I'd want to let know where I was.

I obviously didn't want them to know, but Tony told them his house phone number so I said mine. I'd braced myself for a serious talking-to; there wasn't even a point in trying to explain the whole story.

Every Monday I'd hear about people being arrested, usually for fighting, drinking, possession of drugs. Now it was my turn, for letting off an air horn during *Men in Black 2*, stealing a cardboard cut-out of Hugh Grant, giving the name of the star of my *Championship Manager* team as my own to the police, and then the final charge: finding the whole thing funny.

After a couple of days of excruciating 'silent treatment', with my mum and dad barely talking to me, letting me know that I had a lot of thinking to do, they accepted my apology and my promise that I'd never see a police cell again.

My dad told me how much of his younger self he'd been seeing in me; he'd tell me how he'd go out and roam the streets and get into all sorts of bother. I hadn't done anything all that bad, he'd quickly concede, but it was more a concern of his that he didn't know what was coming next.

I was now immune to getting told off from teachers; I had my own ideas on how to do well at school.

I was sixteen; I had my standard grade exams coming up and then the summer holidays. After the summer holidays, standard grade results permitting, I'd be sitting my Highers.

Four or five Highers and I'd get to university. My plan was maybe slipping but I hadn't given up, not just yet.

33

The exam results themselves weren't great. I passed three subjects. I'd underachieved but, still, it wasn't a disaster.

My mum tried to take the positives from the results, focusing on the passes, despite there being only three of them.

My dad summarized the results with a dissatisfied 'shite' and said I should leave school there and then and get myself a trade.

I reasoned with them that I'd be sitting three Highers in fifth year and a level below that for two other subjects, which I could then go on to study in the sixth and final year at high school. I'd be leaving with five Highers and going on to university. I knew this was much easier said than done, and I knew they'd heard it all before from me. I was running out of lives.

As predicted by John, at the end of the fourth year at school, there was a mass exodus. Most of the leavers had college courses lined up and apprenticeships, the rest just wanted out of school.

I was now eligible for an EMA, an education maintenance allowance: the new government scheme to encourage children from lower-income families to stay on at school past the legally required age of sixteen. Dependent on attendance and performance, I was on £60 every two weeks.

Celtic played away from home every two weeks, so it took that burden off my mum. I had been aiming to stay on anyway, but it was an added bonus. It wasn't exactly a living wage, and if I had planned on leaving to go straight to work, then I doubt it would have made school all that tempting.

Our year was much smaller now; there was no one in particular whom I was glad to see leave but everyone that I was friends with had decided to stay on.

For classes, our year merged with the year above, and we were separated into Higher, Intermediate 2 and Intermediate 1 classes. The only difference between fifth and sixth year was that we had an extra year to fall back on.

I'd remind myself of this, a lot.

I was terrified at the thought of leaving school. I really had no idea what I'd do with myself, and despite the repeated reassurances I'd give to my mum and dad, I knew I wasn't going to settle down and get 'all that nonsense' out of my head.

I knew within myself how much of a target I'd potentially be if I didn't keep people laughing. I was popular in my year, but I still didn't feel like I could take my foot off the gas, especially now that I'd be sharing my classes with a whole new year, a new crowd.

I had to start all over again. From the year above us, I only really knew George Marshall. I'd known George for a few years; our families were friends, and we'd sit together on the bus to the football.

When George's younger cousin, Kevin, and myself would write out football coupons in class, George was our man to put them on for us. He was only seventeen but he'd been a regular in the bookie's for years. My dad had probably seen more of him than me.

He was one of the first to grow stubble, real stubble and not the pathetic, chillingly creepy-looking stuff, where all the individual hairs are spaced and you can count up the total number.

George wouldn't shave from Wednesday onwards so he could use his growth to add some years on to his appearance at the weekend, for the purposes of gambling and purchasing alcohol; he was an example to us all. George and Kevin and both their dads were into gambling. Even at primary school, they knew how to study the form, and we'd joke to them that their family coat of arms was three cherries.

I started to get into gambling as well, and with the growing number of Celtic's fixture dates and kick-off times changed for TV reasons, I spent a lot of Saturday afternoons with George, Kevin, Tony, Big Doc and Mony.

The day would start when Mony would walk up for me, just after *Football Focus* on BBC One, and we'd write out our football coupons and then walk up to the bookie's to meet with the rest.

George would put our bets on and we'd head across to his mum's café for something to eat. Sometimes it'd be Greggs, but we'd feel bad not giving our business to George's mum, especially after he'd put our coupons on and he'd be letting us sit in his house all afternoon, watching our teams getting beaten. However, sometimes a man needs a steak bake.

When the football was over, everyone's minds would turn to the night ahead, which would be my cue to make excuses and head home.

Everyone would try to talk me into coming out, even if I wasn't going to drink. It still didn't appeal to me, though, and I'd much rather have had a night in playing the PlayStation, listening to music and watching comedies with my dad.

The Goldenhill Park, just behind my house, was now the main meeting point on a Friday and a Saturday night. 'The Gowdie', it was known as. 'The Goldie' would seem like a more obvious abbreviation, but it's too late to change the name now.

I don't know where the 'w' came from, but that's been the name for years, and I'd imagine it would be too boring a story to ever ask anyone. The Gowdie, pronounced as in Gaudí, Antoni Gaudí, the legendary Catalan architect.

Its main features were a graffiti-decorated seesaw, a swing with the seat permanently wrapped around the top bars, and a death trap of a deteriorating climbing frame.

The rubber safe surface had piles of rubbish on display: an eclectic collection of different lager cans, crushed and fire-damaged, the victims of cannabis abuse.

It wouldn't be up there with Gaudí's finest works, and I'm sure he'd feel relief at the different spelling of his name, absolving him of the blame.

The Gowdie was very much the work of West Dunbartonshire Council and the youth of the surrounding estates. It was the place where Mony, George and everyone else would stand about drinking before getting on the 59 bus to Glasgow city centre to go to what became known as 'The Unders'.

City centre nightclubs would be open from 7 p.m. until about 10.30 p.m., specifically for under-eighteens. There was no alcohol sold, but everyone would get tanked up beforehand.

These nights would end in violence, obviously. Gangs from different areas – 'Young Teams' they'd be known as – would meet up, flocking to 'The Unders' from every park in Greater Glasgow.

At that age, someone being from a different area was a perfectly valid reason for beating the shite out of them.

Who knows who thought these under-eighteen clubs would be anything other than drink-fuelled mayhem?

Some naive club owner thinking everyone would be happy drinking Fanta and bingeing on Astro Belts, Cola Bottles and Wham bars, the DJ spinning 'I am the music man, I come from down your way'. Regardless of how grim it sounded, these clubs became the place to be on Saturday nights.

Tony would also go on to join the Saturday night 'Unders' crew. He was one of the last ones to do so and one of the last to discover alcohol and lose his virginity, leaving me on my own to take all the insults that accompanied being a teetotal, involuntary celibate in the latter years at school.

It was heart-breaking when your friends started losing their virginity. I tried to accuse Tony of lying about it, but it was half-hearted. He had credible witnesses, and the girl had even mentioned he was quite the lovemaker and had a bit of a weapon on him.

The little bastard had hit the jackpot.

I did start to feel that I was missing out on a lot and that there was something wrong with me, that I should have just gone with the crowd. I'd be plagued with guilt, though, if I lied to my mum and dad, told them I was staying over at someone's house and went out instead for a night, hanging about the parks, the streets or going up to the town. But there was also part of me convinced it wasn't anything that special.

Drinking, drugs, fighting didn't interest me; of course, I wished I was doing better with girls. I didn't change in female company, like a lot of our crowd did; they'd turn serious and paralyse themselves trying to act cool.

But I did feel a sense of injustice when I'd make a girl laugh all week in school and then find out my pal had banged her at the weekend. 'Him? He doesn't even talk,' I'd think to myself.

I'd try gelling my hair, wearing aftershave, wearing a polo shirt with a designer logo rather than the school badge, talking about dance music and making stuff up when they'd ask what my plans for the weekend were.

'I'm not sure yet, just whatever everyone else is doing,' I'd say, smooth enough to resist the temptation to talk about going to the Celtic game, complete with details of our supporters' bus dilemma: 'We're four tickets short for Saturday's game against Hearts at Tynecastle. They've cut our allocation. We're only getting the stand behind the goal this time. Sure, that's a disgrace!'

I'd also decide against discussing, in depth, Halifax Town's hopes of regaining the Premiership title in the 2019/20 season, or any other esoteric *Championship Manager*-related conversation.

Nothing I tried seem to work when it came to girls, so I'd just need to work on getting funnier. As a consequence of my self-imposed solitude outside of school, school itself became my only place to entertain. Sharing the class with the year above us meant I had to prove myself.

With George being the middleman, our crowd and George's mates from the sixth year merged and we began to hang around in one big massive group. I wouldn't say I fell in with a bad crowd. Bad crowds don't make it to the sixth year at school, but they were an older, more grown-up crowd.

They'd all been on holiday together, they went to pubs, they came to class stoned, and they'd drink and party the whole weekend: Friday to Monday men. School was just a place for them to kill some time before having to deal with the real world.

I was slowly realizing that I was there for the exact same reasons. I knew I was going to fail at school. Teachers no longer seemed as frustrated with me. They'd admitted defeat, even dropping the 'you're intelligent and full of potential' bits from their stern warning lectures. It was like I had already picked my path and going back wasn't an option.

I'm aware that there is nothing worse than the guy in the crowd who thinks he's the funny guy, the loudest one, and the one always battling for the limelight. I don't believe I was ever like that. I didn't try all that hard to make people laugh – at least until I'd started being told that I was funny. If I'd been told that I wasn't funny, I'd have shut up and probably got back to my schoolwork.

I'm trying to remember funny things I said or did, but I don't feel comfortable writing too many 'I remember the time I did this', like the funny guy at your work, the guy who's the hero in every one of his stories. Throughout the rise in my popularity at school, I was still the exact same person that I'd been in St Mary's and for the first twelve or thirteen years of my life, when I found it impossible to loosen up, relax, laugh and be carefree, be a child.

My favourite film of all time is *Stand by Me*, even though the general coming-of-age story of friendship wasn't something that I could fully relate to. Nor could I identify with the narrator's closing line about having friends like the friends you have when you're twelve.

I never had that many real friends at twelve years old; for me, it was the reverse.

34

I did find it difficult to fit in, in so many ways. It was difficult, but now I'd discovered a role for myself and I was making more friends than I'd ever imagined.

It did feel cool to be hanging around in such a massive group. There were far too many names now to mention, and I'd feel like a young Henry Hill in *Goodfellas* if I was to introduce everyone individually.

I'd almost given up on school, and I was now using my brain exclusively to think up ways of making myself laugh, which would, hopefully, make other people laugh as well.

I began writing short stories. I'd realized I had a creative side, and I began to neglect doing the assigned homework in favour of doing my own.

I'd been reading the local newspaper, the *Clydebank Post*, in our house one night. The front-page headline was: 'Post Office Robbed', and pages two and three had things like: 'Bus Driver Attacked', 'Drug Haul Seized', 'Drunken Knife-man Jailed'.

Then, on the following page, was the regular feature entitled: 'The Crime File'. What the fuck were the first three pages, then? The whole paper was a 'crime file', I thought.

I began writing down the story of a superhero who had come to rescue the Clydebank area. I was never into comic books or anything, so the story quickly changed direction. It evolved that the superhero surrendered the use of his superpowers in exchange for backhand payments from local gangsters.

He was corrupt and a total despot but content with

running only his own street and the surrounding streets that made up his 'bit', his 'scheme'.

One night, while I was on the PC, I'd sent a few stories to my mate, Danny O'Neill, through MSN messenger.

MSN messenger was the Facebook of its time, and it is at this point that it'll hit home, again, that you're reading the life story of a twenty-seven-year-old.

Danny was in the year below me but I'd started talking and getting to know him at school, through Tony, who lived in the same street as Danny.

Danny was regularly getting into bother outside of school. His gang, his 'Young Team', from the Hillshed area of Duntocher, was 'feuding' with their rivals from 'the top of the hill' which was, unfortunately for Danny, very close to St Columba's.

If he was ever wanted, they knew exactly where he'd be between 9 a.m. and 3.30 p.m., Monday to Friday. Danny wore a Berghaus jacket, a Marseille tracksuit, a baseball hat with the skip pointed upwards at an angle of at least 45 degrees.

I don't know who engineered the trends in fashion of the average Young Team member between 1998 and 2003, but there was no denying it was quite an eclectic mix of tastes, combining the merchandise of a respected outdoor clothing label, a French football club and a load of Major League Baseball teams.

He looked he was a middle-class drama student lazily parodying a 'Ned' or a 'Chav' for the amusement of his rosy-cheeked, fair-haired chums.

At face value, Danny was a bit of a bam. 'Bam' is a word I prefer to the over-used and clichéd 'Ned' and 'Chav', which tend to be used as a blanket term for anyone with a working-class accent or wearing a pair of trainers. A difficult word to explain, but a word I'd like to think captures something more light-hearted, a far more affectionate and less sneering term.

Danny was smarter and more articulate than he presented himself; we'd talk about films, books and authors, particularly Irvine Welsh. He would genuinely make me laugh, and we'd riff with each other, sending each other daft patter and stories and funny ideas every night on the PC.

After a few weeks of our online patter-sparring sessions we had an idea to make a website. We didn't have any money to register a domain or anything that would look professional, but Danny found one of those free, cheap-looking sites with the hosting company's name in the address.

It was all about the content, and it was a place to get all our stuff out there. The website was loosely based on my Clydebank superhero idea, but Danny had suggested giving him a name. We couldn't think of a made-up name that sounded authentic enough, so Danny said, 'What about Jimmy Hay?'

Jimmy Hay was Danny's mate, and they were in the same crowd that ran about wild, under the guise of the 'Hillshed Young Team'. He'd left school by now, and at first I don't think he was all that happy about his new, fictitious, mythical, legendary status that the James Hay worldwide website was perpetuating.

I should mention here, as an adult, that the website wasn't in any way ridiculing James. His name and his face just seemed ideal for the character we'd created. When it got out that it was Danny and me behind the site, he knew there was nothing mean-spirited about it.

Danny was just daft and funny. I didn't see Jimmy as much, but we'd always got on and, anyway, I wasn't a fighter, so he could have beaten the shite out of me at any point if he'd wished to show his disapproval.

Once he'd seen how fucking off-the-wall it was and how none of the articles we wrote could possibly be based on reality, Jimmy was cool about it.

The site became a local hit. We'd be writing new content every day and trying to keep it topical, reacting to news stories from the local paper with our own spin on how Jimmy planned to deal with the situation.

We'd print off posters in computing lessons and put them up in the school corridors, promoting the site. The whole school would be asking us when the next update was. Some would sneer and ask if we had nothing better to do with our time. We hadn't.

Some of the teachers had even got on to it. They'd laugh and praise the writing. One teacher, Mr Hughes, who hadn't ever taught me, so never knew how much of a pain in the arse I could be, stopped and asked me, in a complimentary way, how I came up with all the ideas. Another teacher suggested we entered writing competitions or sent the Comedy Unit a link to the website.

We sent some emails out to people, but we knew it was far too risqué and niche for anything a TV company would be expecting from 'new talent'. It was just good fun, nothing more.

It made us laugh and we enjoyed trying to outdo each other and ourselves. It felt good to be creating so much laughter by doing something that meant using my brain and my imagination, something that wasn't landing me in bother.

I'd added some professionalism to my clown duties, but I still wasn't averse to a simple, low-brow, cock and balls on the blackboard.

I had Mrs McGlinchey again for Modern Studies, this time in a Higher Class, Tony at my side once more. We'd been sitting, working away. It wasn't yet time for carry-on because we didn't know everyone in the class. We hadn't cased the joint yet.

Mrs McGlinchey had disappeared out of the class to go and use the photocopier or something like that; I was dared by Tony, as always, to do a 'menchie' on the blackboard.

A menchie was the name given to writing your name in your own personalized style; a 'tag', I think it's also known as. If your name or nickname ended with a 'y', then on either side of the 'y' you'd write the initials of whatever the gang from your area was called. Every gang had a three-letter acronym, the first letter always 'y', which stood for Young.

Young Clydebank Bundy, Young Faifley Team, Young Duntocher Fleeto, the spelling of Duntocher often changed to Duntoker, a nod to the 'Fleeto' members' penchant for cannabis.

I was eligible for member status of the Young Duntoker Fleeto, despite being from Hardgate and not being a fighter, a drinker, a toker or a shagger. They were our new crowd, and I was now an honorary member.

I didn't have a menchie either, another setback in any future I may have had as a member of the YDF. I didn't even have a nickname.

It was my first chance to make an impression on the class so I didn't want to embarrass myself. I had to think on my feet. I began writing in giant letters. I'd got as far as 'KEV' . . . and my mind went blank. I couldn't just write my name; that'd be a cop-out – the fans would want more. This was a new crowd, a tough crowd.

From behind me I could hear Tony laughing and I could feel the hushed confusion from the rest of the class. I decided to carry on with simply writing my name but in place of the letter 'i', I drew a cock and balls. A massive cock and balls complete with pubes and some detailed vein work.

I now had a menchie, and it had gone down a storm with the class. I quickly checked to make sure Mrs McGlinchey wasn't walking down the corridor on her return journey, and I got back to the job, adding my surname: 'BR-another cock and balls-DGES'.

Signed off with the ubiquitous 'YA BAS!'

I pushed the board up, so my artwork would be hidden until Mrs McGlinchey had run out of space and had to pull it back down.

For the rest of the lesson, each time she wrote on the board, there was a massive sense of immature, childish excitement from the rest of the class. She'd begun running out of space to write on and everyone was now desperate for her to grab the big plastic ridge that ran across the middle of the blackboard and unveil my personalized phallic masterpiece.

There were a few times she came close, a few false alarms, but at the end of the class came the grand showcase. She'd been telling us what the homework for the next time was. She'd been talking, facing us, as her right hand extended out from behind her, grabbing the plastic thing and unveiling my work to the class, the eruption of laughter prompting her to turn round and take a look herself.

'Kevin, wait behind after the bell, please,' she said, calmly.

I liked Mrs McGlinchey and I got the impression she really liked me. She hardly even spoke to me after the class, no disciplinary action, no warning. She just seemed disappointed, after having seen so much potential in me when she'd first taught me a couple of years earlier, that this sort of thing now meant more to me than anything she could teach.

She was laid-back and wouldn't try to force anything on me; if I didn't want to pass my Highers, then there was nothing she could do.

I'd try to show that I was paying attention, but only when it would raise a laugh.

Mrs McGlinchey was one of the first teachers who'd let us listen to music during lessons; she had a CD player at the back of her class and the majority verdict would be in favour of the dance and techno music that everyone was getting into at the time.

I wasn't into dance music and, to me, the only images it evoked were of a Vauxhall Corsa type of car, tinted windows, spoilers and alloyed wheels, parked at a red light, the bass-heavy, techno re-mix of a love song vibrating through the car, the driver and four passengers staring provocatively at pedestrians and other cars, a joint and a McDonald's cup passed from the back seat to the front.

I'd complain to Mrs McGlinchey that she should change the voting system used to decide what music was to be played, from first past the post to proportional representation, as the minorities, the little guys, weren't having their voices heard.

She agreed and worked out that some of the airplay should be devoted to the less popular choices. It meant we had to listen to a bit of death-metal shite from the school's remaining few goth/emo sorts, but it was worth it to hear Black Grape blasting from the classroom stereo during the last period on a Friday afternoon.

I'd got Tony into their song 'Submarine', and we'd both sing it word for word, complete with drugged-up-sounding Manchester accents.

We'd be standing up and dancing, pretending to be shaking maracas, vibing out to the melodies, bursting with excitement, knowing it wasn't long until the end of another week at school.

The rest of the class was thoroughly entertained and even Mrs McGlinchey would laugh and compliment our song and dance routine.

35

I became well known throughout the school. I enjoyed being the life and soul of everything, and a part of me was sad that I had only one year left and then it'd all be over.

Near the end of every year at St Columba's, there would be school-council elections. The school council would usually be exclusively for students studying advanced Highers, the ones who would come to school wearing a blazer and carrying a violin case.

The ones who would take great pride in their role and get passionate in school debates, saying things like 'we're not children, we're young adults', the ones you'd forgive the teachers for telling to shut the fuck up, maybe even throwing a little pretend punch, just to make them flinch.

At the election, I was nominated by my class to run for the head of the year. I agreed, despite the senior teachers being a little sceptical and raising their concerns about my behaviour record. But it was a democracy and the people had the power.

I won the class election and then the year election.

It had started out as a joke, but it had grown and spiralled out of my control. I rode the wave of popularity, and I was now an official member of the school council.

It was destined to be a shambles, and as much as I'd initially been up for the laugh, I didn't imagine it would get to the point where I was expected on stage with local councillors and school delegates, at a special school assembly, to discuss the 'issues affecting pupils of today'.

I sat behind the 'school council' desk, as the fifth-year representative, the one who'd go on to be the head of the school after the summer, when the sixth years had left.

I was sat there along with a few sixth-year pupils, who seemed to be entirely taken in with what they perceived as their bit of authority. They took the thing far too seriously and weren't impressed about the whole thing being made a mockery of.

I felt like a member of the Monster Raving Loony Party, or some local eccentric guy that had somehow managed to garner enough support, as though I'd been used as a protest vote against the current regime.

I had no idea what to do, but I knew the hype was building around the school assembly and the crowd would expect their newly elected representative to speak on their behalf and have their voice heard.

The entire school was there, the head teacher, all the deputy heads. One of the deputy heads pulled me aside and warned me not to be showing off and embarrassing the school in front of the attending Education Chief from West Dunbartonshire Council. He let me know he'd be watching me and that any slip-up would be dealt with severely.

I was well out of my depth, and I even felt nervous.

I couldn't just sit there and be another fucking plant-pot 'young adult'. I'd been elected for a laugh, and that's what I owed my constituents.

I knew it had to be funny, but really funny.

Like always, I'd get the laughs now and deal with the punishment later. I knew that, at the very least, I could be doing some serious time in the exclusion room, if this one went well.

I gave the deputy head a nod and a slight shrug of my shoulders; we both knew it would be a shambles.

That's why I'd been elected.

The head teacher was welcomed to the stage by one of his deputies. He spoke about how great a year it had been for St Columba's and about all the school had achieved; the football, the netball, and the hockey teams had all won trophies.

It was a positive speech, and he thanked the Education Chief from the council for attending and mentioned he'd be sitting on the board and overseeing the events. I was now wondering what the fuck I was doing. I turned round to the crowd and saw everyone looking at me, smiling, excited, waiting for me to do something.

I couldn't believe the air of importance surrounding this assembly. The sixth years beside me were scribbling notes, the head teacher was still talking, surely aware that everyone in the assembly room had long since switched off.

The Education Chief was sat there, analysing, nodding his head. I felt myself about to laugh but I managed to contain it. I had *The Simpsons* in my head, and I kept thinking of Superintendent Chalmers and Principal Skinner when I looked at the Education Chief and Mr McLaughlin, our head teacher.

I opened a bottle of water and poured some into my glass. This wasn't meant to be funny or anything, but I heard a few people laugh and begin to whisper. It wasn't my time yet, though. I'd wait until I was spoken to. I didn't want to be an ignoramus.

We were introduced, one by one, my crowd being far more vocal, shouting encouragement. I gave them a clenched fist like I'd seen Tommy Sheridan do on a school trip with Mrs McGlinchey's class to Edinburgh, to see the Scottish Parliament.

Eventually, it was the turn of the school councillors. A couple of the pupils started to read from their notes, mentioning things like the facilities and how there should be more plays and theatrical productions put on by the school. I couldn't get over the fact that they were leaving for good in a month – why did they care?

Regardless, their questions prompted long droning answers, the kind of answers that you'd expect from an 'Education Chief', a guy with the politician-like knack of making everyone forget the initial question, go to their own happy place and then silently nod in agreement at the end of the answer, attempting to show they were listening, relieved that it's over.

'Any other questions?' we were asked, as a group. I was the only one who hadn't spoken yet, and it was clear they were keen to move along and not bring me into things unless they absolutely had to.

I put my hand up.

'Yes, Kevin Bridges, our fifth-year representative who'll be in sixth year after the summer.'

I realized I had nothing prepared. I had no notes, nothing to say. I hadn't really been listening to anything either.

'Well,' I said, trying to put on a serious demeanour, even giving a little cough as though I was about to say something fairly important.

This made the assembly room laugh. The Education Chief, unaware that I was the school's designated dick, looked around at the room, probably a little wary at the sudden change in atmosphere.

I started speaking, the way he'd spoken, pausing after every word. I was trying to think of every politician I'd heard speak, and to use that same dull, deep tone they had in their voice.

It was going down a storm.

'First of all, let me begin by saying how much of an honour, and a privilege, it is to be sat here today, representing my year, who I'd like to thank, from the bottom of my heart, for their faith in me.'

This cued a massive round of applause. I almost hit the giggles, and I knew I couldn't look out to the crowd, as I'd see Tony or someone else.

I'd always been able to keep a straight face, during prank calls and in situations like this, and I was always doing silly voices and accents. Anyone could come up and say a few words and then walk off laughing, but I wanted this to go as far as I could take it.

'I can't promise results, but I can promise that I will be fighting with everything in my power to ensure there are changes made, for the better,' I continued, with a rhythm in my voice that would manipulate another cheer at the end.

I didn't realize how closely I'd studied politicians and their contrived rabble-rousing. I was even using my hands to emphasize my points, getting right into character. The crowd applauded again.

I was running out of things to say, just as the Education Chief interrupted and asked what kind of changes I'd like to see. 'Fuck knows, mate,' was all that was in my head, but again that would be a waste of an opportunity and wouldn't be in keeping with how polished my performance had been until now.

'The toilet facilities at this school, with all due respect to Mr McLaughlin, are nothing short of abysmal,' was the first example of one of the changes I'd 'fight with everything in my power to ensure is made'.

It was the first thing that had popped into my head. The crowd were now laughing, but I felt I'd been too obvious, going down the toilet road.

So I quickly backed it up, making things a bit more daft.

'We need toilet attendants; we need them distributing complimentary mints, aftershaves, deodorants, wishing us a good day. Going to the toilet in this school used to be a pleasant experience . . .'

I was cut off, the assembly hall was now rocking, and the job was done. One of the deputy heads apologized to the Education Chief and described me as one of the school's 'characters'.

I remember how rattled everyone looked, unsure of how to react to my manifesto. It was like I'd made a mockery of a World Peace Summit.

It was only a school assembly, I reassured myself. I'd probably be in a bit of bother now. Perhaps not for this specific incident; I technically hadn't done anything all that wrong, and for all they knew I was deadly serious. I was an elected voice, after all.

I figured they'd be out to get me, however. I'd embarrassed the school's Illuminati and I was running out of lives. It had undeniably been a fucking belter, and that was all that mattered.

There are loads of stories like this, stories that are now badly told and exaggerated by people whom I didn't know and who weren't there.

I'll even hear entirely made-up ones about things I was supposed to have done. It's a compliment, though, and if they're funny, I'll take the credit.

I'm sure you get the point, and you can relate me to someone from your own schooldays. I wasn't unique; I know that. I wasn't all that different from anyone else.

School was full of funny people. The only thing that maybe separated me from them was that I knew making people laugh was all that I had. As self-deprecating as that sounds, I knew that I could easily be a loner if I didn't keep outdoing myself and finding new ways to be funny.

Towards the end of school, I was told regularly that I should be a performer, an actor, a comedian, but it wasn't something I would listen to or take seriously.

If they'd tell me I should be a comedian, they'd tell the nicest-looking girl she should be a model, tell the guy who could play the guitar that he should be in a rock band. I saw it as false praise and I felt I had limitations.

36

At family nights in our house or in Uncle George's or Uncle Kevin's, my younger cousins Mark and Gary would tell stories about things I'd done at school.

Mark was in the year below me, Gary in the year below him. My cousin Nicole was in the year above. We knew the same people, but weren't in any of each other's classes. 'Your cousin's mental,' they'd be told, before hearing another story about me. I was proud, again, to hear my work praised.

My mum would tell me off after every story. I knew she'd found them funny, but had to save face by being seen to condemn my actions.

I'd sit trying to look embarrassed, but I'd like watching my dad laugh. 'Don't you encourage him, Andy,' said my mum, keeping up the pretence.

I didn't mind everyone hearing about what I'd done. It was only when the story was told badly or if details were missed out that I'd interrupt and give the real version of events.

Neither my mum nor my dad could deny that I was happy and popular. It was good that they'd get to hear the same sort of things they'd hear about at school parents' evenings, in letters home and meetings with the school, but from a different point of view, from Mark, Gary and Nicole, who'd find everything I'd do hilarious. I was still promising that I'd grow up and that sixth year would be my year, my last year.

Martin O'Neill's Celtic had gone on a European run that no one had anticipated, beating Liverpool 2–0 at Anfield in the

UEFA Cup quarter-final second leg. That was the moment when everyone began to think that the current team had it in them to go the whole way and win the thing.

John had been to a few of the European away games, and I'd been saving and constantly on at my mum and dad to let me go to another one. I'd been with my dad to see Celtic get beaten 3–0 by Porto two seasons before and been desperate to go to every one since.

They'd agreed to let me go to see Celtic play VFB Stuttgart in Germany with John and his pals. But an incident involving Tony, a firework and me meant that didn't happen.

We'd bought a packet of rockets for £2. Like everyone else our age, we weren't buying them for the colourful display or the noise; we were buying them because we were warned not to mess about with them.

We'd snap the sticks off and throw them around, not even considering the dangers. I'd thrown one, and in a freak accident it landed in the inside of Tony's unzipped tracksuit top.

They were only cheap rockets, but, still, I couldn't believe it and we were both shocked. Tony was unharmed but his tracksuit was scorched. It had been his birthday only a few days before, and this was one of his presents.

I felt awful.

I went home and had to tell my dad. I don't know why I had to tell him. I wasn't thinking straight, and I probably could have got away with it. He phoned Tony's dad and apologized, letting him know that I'd be dealt with and that I'd be paying for a new tracksuit.

I wasn't allowed to go to Stuttgart, but I wasn't even bothered about it any more. I was just glad nothing more serious had happened, and getting my mum and dad to speak to me after a couple of days was all I could hope for.

It was just another thing in what was a never-ending series of incidents. It would only be at times like this that I'd panic and look around at how much bother I was causing. Every day I'd be in trouble for something. This was the worst kind of trouble, though; there was nothing funny about it. I had no defence.

My heart was still set on getting away to another European game, and the longer Celtic's run continued, the longer I had to save up money.

I had my EMA money. But I also had a financial boost because I'd managed to get a part-time job, working in the clothes shop TK Maxx. Now, helping people try on clothes was not the most taxing job on the planet, but it was going to help me get to Europe with Celtic. My roles included sorting the footwear section into some sort of order. This meant matching every single shoe with its partner.

TK Maxx customers would treat the merchandise with the upmost disrespect, so this was much more challenging than you'd think. We wouldn't get to leave until it was done to a level that the managers deemed satisfactory.

I'd be wandering around with a size 5 Caterpillar boot trying to find another size 5 Caterpillar boot, often settling for anything within two sizes. It was my first job and, fuck me, it was mind-numbing.

I was earning, though, and my mum and dad were delighted at that. It would help me grow up and knock 'all that carry-on' and 'nonsense' out of me.

My dad had helped me type up a CV. He'd asked me what I felt was my USP, my unique selling point. I laughed and told him he was watching too many late-night movies on Sky.

It was a job at TK Maxx I was going for. It wasn't Wall Street or Silicon Valley; it was Clydebank Shopping Centre.

The term stuck with me, though: what was my unique selling point? 'All that carry-on' and 'all that nonsense' – that was my USP, that was the only thing that made me stand out.

After a few shifts, I'd got on well with my colleagues, especially another guy called Kev, a giant of a guy who was a few years older than me, closer to John's age.

Kev smoked a shit load of grass and this came across in his outlook. He was a bit more mature than me but we had a good laugh together. He was one of the most laid-back, chilled-out big guys I'd ever met and working with him made the hours go a bit faster.

Being older, he probably needed the money a bit more for real-life stuff like rent and bills, so Kev wasn't as reckless and as wide open for the sack as me.

Like always, I'd be caught doing everything.

Even small things, like when I'd hold up a stupid-looking jumper and shout at him across the aisles. We'd both laugh and I'd say, 'Who the fuck is going to wear one of these?' Then I'd turn around to assist a customer, who'd been standing right behind me all along, looking to try one on. I'd find their size, walk them to the changing room and then have to grovel, saying things like, 'It actually looks great when you see it on someone.'

When Kev wasn't working, I'd have to make my own entertainment.

There would be pop music on nearly every day, the same songs every day, the tunes that became synonymous with work.

I'd be in charge of the changing rooms on some shifts; one of the store's intercom phones was in the changing room, with a button to hold and a speaker for when a manager wanted to do a 'colleague/customer announcement' message.

It was easy to work and on days when it was quiet and I was ready to crack under the intense monotony of it all, I'd speak into it. I was unsure at first, so it was just a 'Hello'.

I'd see a few people's heads turn; they'd look around, wondering if they'd imagined hearing a voice say 'Hello', before getting back to whatever had caught their eye on the shelves.

I figured that if I held the buzzer in, spoke fast and released the button quick enough then it would sound like I was talking over the song, like a radio DJ.

A song that was always on was 'Set You Free' by N-Trance, an essential Vauxhall Corsa anthem. It had the sound of rain pouring at the very beginning, with a piano playing slowly before a female vocal of 'Oh, oh, yeah' confirming that it was 'that fucking song again'.

When the dance bits cut in, I'd hold the speaker and in an English nightclub-DJ voice, I'd start saying things like, 'It's Sunday, it's TK Maxx,' releasing the button again to let a few more seconds of the song play.

'Come on! You can do better than that. Let me hear ya, Clydebank!' and release again. I'd start to add 'drink promotions at the bar' and 'let me hear you scream' — just things I'd heard the pub DJs on holiday say.

I was forced to step down from my changing-room duties and placed in the stock room, away from the customers. I had no audience now; again, like the teachers at school, they'd easily figured out how to disarm me.

My final shift at TK Maxx was a Saturday morning. I was excited and looking forward to my 1 p.m. finish and going to meet with Tony, George and Big Doc.

I was in the stock room by myself, lifting the stuff off the lorry, the lorry driver standing with paperwork and asking me questions that were well over my head.

I went and got a manager for him, the forms were signed

and I was told to 'get a move on' with the stock, to hurry up with tagging the products and taking them out to be stacked on the shelves.

This day we'd received a massive delivery for the children's section. I looked around at all the toys; I was in a particularly daft mood, which wasn't helped by the sight of a box full of skateboards.

I quickly cut the boxes open, tagged the skateboards and piled a few in my hands. Three or four, I'd be able to carry. Then, in order to get the job done a bit faster, I decided I'd skate out on to the shop floor on top of one. I opened the door and shouted to one of my co-workers to watch.

He was at the side and at a perfect angle to capture my entry.

I went back into the stock room and then came flying out of the door, on top of a skateboard and carrying three.

I panicked because I couldn't slow down, then the top skateboard fell from the pile I was carrying and landed in front of me, causing me to collide with it and fall off, narrowly missing a whole shelf full of lampshades and household accessories.

I'd fucked it now. My colleagues laughed, but quickly got back to work; they backed off, knowing that I was in serious shit and that I'd be going down alone.

I was called into the top manager's office and given a grilling about how I wasn't mature enough for the workplace and how I had a lot of growing up to do.

I'd heard all this so many times that I'd impersonate their voices in my head as they spoke, playing a game of guessing what line was coming next, to make it entertaining: 'You might be impressing your little friends out there but . . .', etc.

I'd find it hard not to smile when I'd successfully predicted what they'd say.

I don't know why but when the manager asked what I had to say for myself, I denied the crime. I'd taken the flak for it and then denied it; very strange, she must have thought.

I was always good for owning up to things, but I figured I'd try to be like everyone else who'd get into bother and deny all knowledge. It was up to them to prove it, I thought, like a seasoned criminal.

'Okay, let's take a look at the camera footage, then,' she said, telling me to get back to my shift and that she'd speak to me at the end.

I should have just left, but I'd be guaranteed the sack if I did that. I re-emerged on the shop floor. The rest of the staff were laughing, but surprised to see me back to work so quickly after what was a major health-and-safety breach.

'Colleague announcement . . .' I was called back up to the manager's office. I walked in to see my boss sat there. She told me to sit down and pressed Play on the monitor with the camera footage.

There I was, sitting watching a CCTV video of myself riding a skateboard, whilst carrying skateboards, down a TK Maxx aisle, losing control and crashing.

I was issued with a full written warning. I wasn't sacked but told that I'd be on the minimum number of hours, four hours per week, and should start looking for alternative work.

37

My mum, who knew all of the staff in the Co-op store at the Hardgate shops, had managed to get me a part-time job stacking shelves.

It was closer to my house, so the money I'd save on bus fares subsidised the 30 pence drop in wages to £3.50 per hour. I was sixteen, so still not eligible for the minimum wage.

I left TK Maxx and what could have been, for a fresh start in the working world. I behaved myself a lot more, on account of the links with my mum. I didn't want to let her down, but also there was no one else anywhere near my age there, except on the occasional shift I'd share with my mate Del.

Celtic had made it all the way through to the UEFA Cup Final, to play Jose Mourinho's Porto team in Seville, in the south of Spain. It was like everyone was going (it's estimated that between eighty thousand and a hundred thousand Celtic fans travelled).

I'd saved money but nowhere near enough. I'd underestimated the opportunism of all the airlines and all the travel companies who were rapidly chartering planes and putting day-trip packages together. There was also the issue of trying to get tickets for the game.

If I didn't get to this game, then what was the point in going to any? This was as good as it would probably get for years, decades. Celtic hadn't been in a European final since 1970.

Money, flights, ticket were all obstacles, and then, in a sickening blow, the date of the game turned out to be the day of my maths exam and the day before my computing one.

That was that, then.

I'd been to nearly every one of the home and away games for the past few seasons. But people who hadn't been to any would be talking about their travel plans and how they'd managed to get tickets through contacts.

It was the usual feeling-sorry-for-yourself story that anyone who's ever passionately followed a football team will know. I didn't have a valid passport either. I was fucked.

I'd come home from school one night and was sitting in the living room with my dad. He told me that he'd met George McClymont in the bookie's that day.

George McClymont ran the supporters' bus and was the man in charge of tickets. He told my dad that he was confident he had four tickets: one each for my dad, John, my Uncle George and me, the four who'd applied.

My dad obviously hadn't told him we couldn't go and his name had been kept on the list. My dad had missed out on the European Cup final in 1967, when Celtic won. He made the 1970 one, when they lost. He'd always regretted missing out on 1967, in Lisbon, and was well aware of how rarely these special things happen.

I jumped up off the couch, smiling, and asked, looking for confirmation, 'Are we going?'

I knew he wouldn't be telling me this if we weren't. My dad told me to wait until my mum had come home from her teatime shift and he'd speak to her.

My mum told him he'd lost the plot, quickly rattling off the list of stumbling blocks, minus the one about not having tickets. My dad had struggled with going abroad. His joints would seize up after being sat on a plane for too long and he'd struggle with walking and climbing the stairs, my mum warned, her replacement problem for the resolved ticket issue.

He'd be fine and we'd get taxis to and from the stadium and the airport, my dad reasoned with her. I could sit my maths exam again in sixth year, he continued, paving the way for me as well.

I still had time to get a passport, I added, and I was round at my work to use the photo machine that same night. The application form was sent off the following morning.

I had around £200 saved up. The day trips were more than that and we'd need spending money. My mum had a Credit Union bond that she offered to cash in – she'd agreed to it.

I gave her a massive cuddle and promised her that I'd make it up to her. I'd study hard in sixth year, once and for all, and I genuinely felt that I meant it this time.

Celtic lost the game 3–2 in extra time. The feeling after the game, sitting in the airport, knowing that I had my computing exam first thing in the morning, wasn't a nice one.

It was a massive comedown.

The excitement, the experience and everything about it was special, and I let my mum and dad know how grateful I was to them for making it happen.

I failed the computing exam.

I also failed my Modern Studies exam. I passed English but only just and I passed Business Management. I returned to school after the summer, but I was the only one. All my fifth-year mates had gone. Tony, Mony and Doc had all left a year early, to start apprenticeships.

I was in sixth year now and I didn't know anyone in fifth year.

I was on my own.

I should have used it as an opportunity to finally 'knuckle

down' and let some advice sink in, but I couldn't get motivated. It was no longer going to be fun and all the life would
be sucked out of me.

I got into trouble a couple of times, not for anything
major, but it was enough to give the school what they'd been
looking for. I was called into a meeting with the head teacher.

He felt it was time I left.

The game was up.

I asked for one last chance. He said it wasn't up to me any
more. He told me that if all five of my teachers signed a
form stating that they believed I would behave and conduct
myself like a senior pupil for the coming year, then he'd consider one last chance.

I had until the end of the week to report back to him.

Two of the teachers signed it.

One of them said he'd need to think about, clearly enjoying the hold he had over me and wanting to string it out a bit.
He told me that I'd acted the fool and given all my wee pals
a good laugh, but I'd get found out in the real world.

I don't write that sentence in an 'I showed him, the prick'
sense. At the time, his words hit home and really rattled me.

I had a final meeting with the school at 3.30 p.m. on a Friday afternoon, mid-August 2003.

Everything I'd done was brought up; I was reminded of
everything I'd been in bother for over the past few years, as
though they were reading out my charges.

I was told I wasn't being formally expelled and that it
wouldn't be on my record, so long as I left there and then. I
was introduced to the school's career advisor, who began to
grill me about what I wanted to do.

I just walked out.

It was after 3.30 p.m. on a Friday, normally the happiest
time to be walking out of the school gates.

I was gutted.

I was trying to think of how to tell my mum and dad.

I'd been expelled; it was worded as 'advised to leave', but it wouldn't matter.

I was out of school and that was it.

A part of me was annoyed that they hadn't thrown me out before the summer. They'd let me come back for sixth year, obviously knowing that I was on ice deemed too thin to last another full year.

It was my own fault. I'd found out that I could be popular by being willing to do anything for a laugh. The last three years had been great, the glory years. I'd done everything to make other people happy, but I was left to try to clear up the mess. It was a proper fall-from-grace story and if it was a movie, my walk home through the eerily quiet housing estate beside the school, alone, would be the closing credits. I was as miserable leaving school on my last day as I was arriving for my first day, nearly twelve years earlier.

Still, it wasn't a time to be down about it. I was only sixteen, and I had my Highers in Business Management and English.

I wasn't exactly ready to take on the world, but that was maybe because I hadn't figured out what I wanted to take it on at yet.

38

On the walk home from school, like every other day, I stopped off at the newsagent halfway between my house and St Columba's. It was one of those shops that does the majority of its trade off the back of their close proximity to a school.

To work there, patience was required, and it must have been hard for the staff to keep their composure, being terrorized by loud and obnoxious school children in three short intervals every weekday, once in the morning, once at lunchtime and once more later in the afternoon.

The calm had settled now, but about twenty or twenty-five minutes earlier, the shop would have had a 'maximum of three in at a time' policy and one of the till workers would be working as a door steward, enforcing the entry policy and keeping a watchful eye on any goods leaving the store having not gone via the cash register.

'Good afternoon,' the shop owner said to me, barely even looking up from the back page of an early edition *Evening Times* newspaper. I'd never be in this shop as a school child again, the thought hit me, in a brief moment of sentimentality. It hit me, and also reminded me of why I had a feeling of dread.

I bought a Topic; I don't know why I bought a Topic.

I'd never tried a Topic before. I was out of school; I was my own boss, so fuck it. I had a 50 pence coin and needed change to use the phone box. I think a Topic was slightly cheaper than a Mars bar or a Snickers, but a more substantial snack than a Taz bar or a Freddo.

It was the ideal selection for a man on a 50 pence budget who was looking for an ample enough fix of chocolate that would still leave change to make a phone call.

The phone call I made was to my mate Jamie. I'd been good friends with Jamie ever since the merger of the fifth and sixth years. I'd sat beside him in English, and we first bonded after he'd unashamedly grassed on me over a profanity-ridden, gratuitous poem I'd written for his entertainment.

He'd been asked by the teacher why he was laughing and told the teacher, 'Kevin wants you to see what he's written, sir.'

I was mortified. I couldn't believe he'd just stuck me in like that.

Still, we became close friends.

I phoned Jamie because he'd told me a few weeks before that he'd been accepted into a college course that started at the end of August, an HND course in Business Administration, which I think required two Highers and respectable enough standard grades.

An HND in Business Administration meant you could enter university at third year. So, really, I was going into first year at university.

I wasn't deluded enough to even begin to try to convince myself that I was still on the right track. I didn't want to study Business Administration, but I didn't have many choices and this would help me buy some time.

I told Jamie on the phone that I'd been chucked out of school. He laughed and asked me what had happened. He knew it would have been nothing serious, but I sensed he wanted to hear a story about something stupid that I'd orchestrated. He was probably already feeling nostalgic for school himself.

I told him I'd tell him later and that I was phoning from a phone box because I had no credit in my mobile phone. I'd used it all up, mainly through doing prank calls to local pubs and businesses.

Jamie laughed again, called me a 'fanny' and gave me the number of his college, the full name of the course and the name of who to ask for. The course started on the coming Monday morning. I figured this would cushion the blow a little for when I told my mum and dad that it was game over for me at school.

I can't say my mum and dad were shocked at the news; they were angry with me and they also seemed angry with the school. My dad wanted to phone the head teacher and go over for a meeting with him in person.

I asked them not to bother. My head was elsewhere, and it would have taken a staggering effort on my part to last a full year without landing in trouble again.

I admired how much my mum and dad would always stick up for me, but I knew I was in the wrong and I knew I'd let them down. They both warned me that I wouldn't be allowed to lie in bed all day and hang around the house.

I told them the news about the potential college course, starting on Monday. I used the house phone to call the number Jamie had given me. There were still spaces left, and I was told to arrive on Monday morning with my exam results and photographic ID.

The college course was only three days a week with Tuesdays and Wednesdays my days off. I walked round to the Co-op and asked to be considered for any Tuesday and Wednesday day shifts from now on.

This was it: The Real World.

On the Monday morning, at the end of August 2003, I met with Jamie and our other mate, Sean, who had enrolled in the college along with Jamie, just before the summer.

Sean's dad was a teacher at St Columba's. I'd been on the wrong side of him a few times, and I don't think he was too enamoured of the fact that I was now a potential distraction to Sean and his college work.

Sean wasn't exactly a shy academic type, though. He was full of energy, and at eighteen years old he still took enjoyment from slapping people in the balls and administering 'nipple twisters'. He was always looking for an angle to take the piss out of people.

I was the youngest out of the three of us, the youngest in the whole class, so I'd come under scrutiny from Sean every day. He'd be looking for some fault – the wrong trainers, the wrong T-shirt, not wearing hair gel, wearing the wrong hair gel.

I never really managed to figure out my hair. When I tried to put some gel or wax in it I didn't get the same style as the barber had managed at the end of the original haircut; I'd spend too long chasing the losses.

It was five minutes every morning that I could be using for sleep; cashing them in for vanity purposes seemed like insanity. I didn't really care what I looked like. Obviously I wanted to lose weight and feel a bit healthier, but other than that, clothes were clothes and hair was hair.

Sean could be a pest, a serious fucking pest, but he had good heart and the bus trips to college became something to look forward to in the mornings.

Although I got on well with Jamie and Sean, I'd known them for less than a year. I'd been their friend, but only within a massive crowd. They had their own jokes, their own stories; they'd been on holiday together and knew loads of people whom I didn't. It didn't bother me, and I was the one who'd attached myself to them by signing up for the same college course.

I'd look around our class and wonder who I'd be mates with if I'd come on my own, instead of with ready-made pals who I'd naturally be inclined to stick with.

I felt like I'd defeated the purpose of the whole thing when here was an entire class: Scottish, English, Chinese, Indian, and an American!

We even had a Yank. 'How funny would that be, hanging around with an American dude?' I'd sit and smile, imagining inviting him down to Clydebank at the weekend.

I'd say these things to Jamie and Sean during the lectures. Jamie would always be stoned, having smoked a joint for breakfast before boarding the bus in Duntocher, so it'd be mainly him I'd target.

I liked being in the company of stoned people. I'd never really enjoyed the couple of occasions I'd drunk alcohol but being stoned looked far more appealing. It was a drug that interested me.

Everything seemed to become funnier and silly things became hilarious. I'd read online about the effects, and the only thing deterring me was the smoking part itself, and also the unique case of Gus.

My dad had smoked since he was thirteen. My Granddad John, when he first caught him, had tried the traditional parenting solution of the time, the perhaps once-revolutionary method of buying your son or daughter a full pack of cigarettes and watching on, smugly, until every single one had been smoked. The idea being that it'd make your child sick, thus instantly putting them off smoking for life.

My dad proudly tells of how it didn't work and how he gratefully appreciated the ten free fags and how that was him until the present day: a heavy smoker.

I knew how my mum, John and even me were on my dad's case about quitting and spamming him with the health risks, so I'd have felt hypocritical smoking myself, let alone smoking a joint.

Still, though, cannabis looked great, like a performance-enhancer for patter.

I remember a Friday morning on one of the first weeks, when the class was quiet and the lecturer was talking, rapidly rattling through the course work, his voice and his irritating marker pen the only sounds, along with an occasional interruption from our new American classmate, Mo, asking a question about the subject matter, establishing himself as the top pupil – he was here to get results.

I knew this silence meant a stoned Jamie would be at his most vulnerable. In the most exaggerated Californian accent I could manage, I started to whisper esoteric Glasgow slang expressions, to create an image of Mo having fully immersed himself into his new city's culture.

'You guys getting mad wae it on Friday, or whit?'

Jamie laughed; he had a great, silent laugh, when just his face would crease up. He started playfully punching me in the side and trying to get back to writing his notes.

I knew he had a cackle in him, so I kept going.

'Man, I was oot my nut, I ended up getting a chase aff the polis.'

I watched him trying to bury his head so the lecturer wouldn't notice he was laughing. I saw his shoulders shaking and I knew he was laughing, so I kept going.

I knew a cannabis reference would go down well and finish him off; I leaned in again and whispered: 'I had a hawf ounze on me tae, pure jail bait.'

Jamie then let out a massive, exotic-bird-sounding noise.

He quickly clapped a hand to his mouth and looked down,

his face going red, then whispered: 'You're a dick, you're a fucking dick,' still laughing and looking shocked.

I turned straight to my notes, looking up, scrutinizing the white board as I pretended to write, getting right into the character of a focused, hard-working student, in anticipation of Jamie turning informant again and testifying against me to the lecturer.

The lecturer looked up only briefly, and then turned his attention back to the board, carrying on, perhaps thinking he'd imagined it, or, most likely, not being bothered enough to ask any questions.

It was like school all over again except that the lecturer wasn't interested in telling us off. It was his job, and if we didn't want to listen, he didn't care.

It wasn't compulsory for us to attend. There was an unwritten 'shut up or fuck off' agreement in place. I picked this up almost immediately and, as much as there were similarities with school, this was a class full of adults for whom getting an education meant much more than I could ever imagine.

The lecturers would never seem bothered about anyone having a laugh and they'd even join in with the jokes. One of the lecturers, Gavin, who wanted to be known only as 'Gav', billed himself as 'one of the lads', and every Monday he'd talk about being out partying at the weekend in a 'you know how it is, eh boys?' kind of way, double-checking that he sounded cool.

He was totally laid-back and he'd have little joking digs at me. I was by far the most outgoing and confident student, aided by the fact that I had Jamie and Sean with me, and I'd got to know the rest of the class, so I was the one he'd go for.

I'd always be answering questions, finding the balance between correct answers and total whoppers, deliberately trying to confuse him and steer him on to non-related issues.

He'd call Jamie, Sean and me 'the Clydebank boys', adding a hint of wariness in his voice, as though Clydebank was the 'hood or the ghetto.

I'd play up to this and in a reference to the film *Dangerous Minds*, I'd tell him he was our Michelle Pfeiffer, the only teacher who ever managed to get through to us.

I'd learned to time things better. I knew when to shut up now, not for my own benefit, but for the rest of the students to whom this course was important, especially the overseas students.

I'd talk to our Chinese classmates: Paton, his girlfriend, Sarah, and their friend, Scott. Paton would laugh at me, and call me 'silly' in an affectionate way and we got on well. He'd tell me to come into his work and he'd sort me some free food, his work being a Chinese takeaway on Sauchiehall Street in Glasgow.

I'd wear him down with my questions about China and life over there, but he was patient and I think he took it as a compliment that I was so interested in his homeland.

It was obvious that he wasn't here to waste time; he had a lot more at stake, along with Sarah and Scott. They had complex visa issues and, effectively, they had one shot at this college course or they'd have to return home to China, which none of them seemed too keen to do.

I couldn't believe I had a friend from China and one from America as well; this was much more of an education than school.

I'd talk to Mo. Mo was in his thirties and was one of the oldest in the class. He seemed impressed that I was sixteen and doing the same college course as people who were double my age, but maybe it was more to reassure himself that he was doing okay.

I told Mo about how great his accent sounded to us, and

we'd try to teach him local slang. He didn't need to be encouraged and was soon shouting things like, 'Whit ye uptae, ya wee prick!' when he'd see one of us in the corridors or in the cafeteria.

It made me laugh every time and I'd give him a new word, acknowledging his progress.

'Bam pot? Bam, bam pot, like a pot of bam? What's bam?' he'd ask in his movie-star, cool-as-fuck voice, eager to learn.

Our lessons would get more in-depth, and he seemed genuinely intrigued by what the people of Glasgow had done to the English language. He was fascinated by Glasgow's totally liberal use of the word 'cunt' and how charming the most offensive word in the American-English vocabulary could be made to sound.

'So I can say, "He's a good cunt", and that's cool, but if I say he's a cunt, that's bad?' He'd be double-checking, still a little unsure.

'A cunt can also mean a person, Mo,' I'd tell him; he was clearly baffled by the number of definitions, especially the affectionate ones.

'So I can say, "That cunt, he's a good cunt"? But I can also say, "That cunt, he's nothing but a cunt,"' Mo would summarize.

'Correct,' we'd tell him, and he'd add it to his repertoire, saying it at any opportunity, over and over again, but still managing to retain the excitement of someone from a country where 'dropping the C-bomb' remains largely uncouth and frowned upon.

39

To be honest, we had a great class, and I was starting to embrace the freedom of it all.

I found the work straightforward. It didn't interest me all that much, but I'd make sure I handed in good essays, for Gav and for the other lecturer I got on with, Pete.

I knew the HND and then university path wasn't the one I wanted to go down, not studying Business Administration anyway. But I'd decided to stick it out. I enjoyed the whole scene and tried to take as much from the whole experience as I could.

Even getting the bus into Glasgow city centre in the mornings excited me, as opposed to the short walk through a housing estate to school every day.

Spending lunch breaks on Buchanan Street in Glasgow, people-watching, walking round the shops, seeing how fast everything moved – it brought me out of my own head, and I started to love Glasgow. I was the young kid from the backwater making his way in the big city.

No one knew me, no one knew my family, and it wasn't like a walk through Clydebank Shopping Centre, where I'd spend my days off and where parents of my old schoolmates would stop and talk to me.

I didn't have much luck with my Co-op shifts. They'd never be on my college days off, so I'd have to go in straight from college on a Monday and the same on a Thursday, with a weekend shift somewhere as well. Tuesdays and Wednesdays became like my weekends.

Two days off, but two days off with a stigma attached.

'I heard you left school, that you got expelled, is that right?' a faux-concerned mother of a St Columba's sixth year would ask, as I stood trying to figure out whose mum it was.

I'd actually been 'asked to leave' but I didn't have it in me to correct her terminology.

Whatever I said, I knew she was looking at me like I was a waster. She'd caught me wandering through the shopping centre, wearing a hooded jumper or a tracksuit, on my way for a look around the shops, killing time before planting myself in the bookie's for a couple of hours of escapism.

'What did your mum and dad say about that?' she'd want to know, the second question already lined up before the first was answered, the second question reminding me that I'd let my mum and dad down.

I'd be embarrassed; it wasn't worth trying to explain about my college course and how it was going well, or to give her my 'it's just the same as being in first year at university' rhetoric.

She'd be quickly on to telling me of how her son or daughter had been accepted into a university, passed all of their exams and were going on to be a systems analyst or a risk surveyor or some other career I hadn't fucking heard of.

I was aware of the pitfalls of having too much free time to myself and I definitely spent too much time in the bookie's. I wasn't interested in horses as the races lasted too long and it just reminded me of being bored as a child, watching my dad study the form and shout at jockeys.

I'd put on football coupons, but only really to provide an interest in the games during the week or on Saturday after-noons at George's; it was a sociable thing more than anything else.

I liked betting on greyhounds because it was fast and

267

didn't really require that you knew anything about grey-hounds. A lucky number, a funny name, the dog doing a shite before the race, these were the only factors I'd consider before deciding who my money was going on. Despite being two years below the legal betting age, my gambling wasn't all that bad, at least to begin with. But it wasn't long before I discovered the new touch-screen virtual roulette machines.

You could put in a £1 coin and turn it into £20 in minutes. The money was won or lost as fast as you could hit the screen with your finger, pressing the numbers you wanted to bet on, every tap of the screen equated to 25 pence, with the option to change that to anything up to £10 per tap.

I'd see loads of guys in a pretty bad way, donating their entire month's wages into this little metal box, trusting their right index finger to decide what number every 25 pence they'd worked for was going on.

They'd hit Bet and stand back, oblivious to anything else, ignoring their phones ringing, probably their wife or their boss wondering where they were, occasionally booting or punching the machine out of frustration and storming off. They'd receive a verbal warning, never a ban, though, and off they'd go, out of the door, but only to return, apologetic and armed with more cash.

It was grim to watch and a part of me was relieved that I didn't have the kind of money these guys had.

I didn't have the initial start-up capital required for a gambling problem, but I'd stick in a couple of quid from my lunch money and I totally understood the attraction. These things were addictive and my fascination with them began growing gradually over the next few years.

I'd spend my days off a lot with Jamie. Sean had landed himself a labouring job with his dad's mate for Tuesdays and Wednesday so we didn't see much of him.

He'd passed his driving test and bought a car, so on the occasional time he did have a day off, we'd go for a drive in his car, along with whoever else was at a loose end. We'd be headed for nowhere in particular, except maybe a McDonald's with a drive-through, but not our local McDonald's, one further away, to extend the road trip. A drive for the sake of going for a drive, because we could go for a drive, was part of the novelty of the first one of your mates getting his own car.

I'd usually shout things out of the window at strangers, to justify my place in the car; I was still the new guy so I had to earn my place on the team. I didn't shout abuse or anything; it'd just be things like, 'Stevie! Have you lost weight?' Or, 'Davie! Are you going to this thing on Friday?' We'd laugh and watch the guy in the mirror, or out of the back window, standing staring at the car as we drove on into the distance. He'd be confused, wondering who I was and wondering who I thought he was.

On days off when Sean wasn't with us, and we were back on foot, Jamie would walk round for me and we'd both head off to where our other mate, Halpin, lived.

Ryan Halpin was also in Jamie's year at school. He had a reputation for being a great fighter. He was tall and naturally well-built, but constructed more like an athlete than a big, freak-looking, protein-shake-guzzling meathead.

I'd heard of him before I'd spent any time with him, but he didn't seem to be aware of his reputation, or else he was embarrassed by it, like he had grown up faster than the ones who championed the legend.

He was one of the happiest and friendliest big guys I'd met, the opposite of anyone else with a 'best fighter' title I'd come across. He'd always smile and his smile would be so wide that it looked like it was sore, like he was asking too much of his face. It was easy to instantly relax in his company.

He was constantly laughing and laughing at himself. He was disarmingly daft, mispronouncing words and coming out with ridiculous statements and theories.

He watched the Discovery Channel and the National Geographic Channel religiously, so he'd retained a vast assortment of facts and statistics about animals, wars, weapons, history and conspiracies.

He knew what he was trying to say, but he'd struggle trying to get it across in his own words without everyone laughing. He'd offer concise summaries of historic battles and major world events as though he was reporting on a fight between local young teams: 'Aye, but then Napoleon decided to bounce down and the whole lot of them done the off.'

Or hilariously blasé understatements like, 'Here, Hitler was bang out of order, man, a total cock.'

We'd sit in Halpin's bedroom, a loft conversion in his mum and dad's house. We'd play computer games, watch films and talk a lot of shite. If I was the new guy, Halpin was the main man, but I'd never be made to feel that it was like that. He wasn't a bully, unless he was bullying a bully.

The only fights I'd heard of him being in were with people who'd taken liberties and, for no reason, beaten up someone he knew. It was like hanging around with a superhero.

Jamie was the middleman. He knew Halpin better than I did, and he knew me better than Halpin did. He'd tell Halpin about stuff I'd done at college or on the bus or in Sean's car and Halpin would laugh and look at me, nodding in approval, as though to say, 'I like this kid.'

Big Doc would come up sometimes as well. He was a first-year apprentice electrician, and on the days he was at Clydebank College he'd come and join us at Halpin's at lunchtime.

If there was a lull in the conversation or if we were bored of the PlayStation, Jamie would tell me to do a prank call.

I'd be embarrassed, because I didn't know Halpin all that well, but he'd join in with persuading me, laughing, excited, and looking around his bedroom for takeaway menus or a local newspaper, to find numbers for me to phone. I'd get nervous, hoping the prank call would be a good one. I didn't plan out anything to say, I'd just phone and start talking.

We'd scan the *Clydebank Post*, and if any local pubs had entertainment booked, I'd phone the pub pretending to be the act's manager and make outlandish demands and rider requests.

We'd sit and laugh at the image of a Rod Stewart tribute act showing up for his sound check at some shit-hole pub in Clydebank to be met with an apologetic manager who was unable to track down scented candles and a yoga mat in time but cheerily announcing that he'd managed to procure a multi-pack of Salt 'n' Shake crisps, all opened, salted and ready for consumption, as requested.

I'd pretend to be a furious father and phone the lost-property department of a local nightclub on behalf of my teenage daughter.

'Okay, can you calm down, please, sir? What is it she's lost?'

I'd look at Jamie, Halpin and Doc, all covering their mouths and trying not to laugh as I had the guy by the balls. 'Her virginity, she lost her virginity!' We'd have the manager on loudspeaker asking, 'What the fuck do you want me to do about that, mate?'

Which suggested he wasn't skilled in the field of customer service.

The customer is always right, unless the company is a money-laundering front for gangland activity.

'I'll be coming down there to get it back, or I'll be taking yours,' I'd conclude, proudly holding up the phone to hear him return fire, an incoherent volley of abuse. This was the cue for Jamie, Halpin and Doc to stop suppressing their laughter; they'd erupt, letting the guy know it was a wind-up.

As soon as I'd hung up, the shouts would come to do another one, everyone scrambling through their mobile phone contacts, looking for a number.

Opposite Halpin's house there was a takeaway called Frank's. What gave it its appeal for a prank call was that the owner had a hilariously short temper. I'd wound him up before and we'd formed a Moe Szyslak/Bart Simpson relationship with each other.

From Halpin's living-room window we could see right into the shop, so we could watch the guy, live, losing his shit. It was a prank-call first.

His nickname became Frank the Wank and then Frank the Fruitcake, on account of how easily he'd snap and start shouting threats. 'You think you're a hard man? Hiding behind the phone, eh?'

The sheer venom in his voice would make it difficult not to laugh. I was becoming fascinated with people who could take themselves this seriously.

We went down Halpin's stairs and into his living room. His mum and dad were both at work. I dialled the number and we watched Frank the Fruitcake shaking the chips about in the fryer, wiping his hands and walking towards the shop phone.

'Get it on loudspeaker!' Jamie, Halpin and Doc were whispering, covering their mouths again. Any laughter would ruin what had the potential to be a ground-breaking prank call.

I was aware that he might know my voice from previous

wind-ups, from when Tony and I would phone to noise him up. This was big-time now, though; the art form of the prank call had evolved since then.

I changed my voice to a deeper, more serious-sounding, mature voice, like the ones I'd heard on the bus to college in the mornings from people living in Bearsden and Milngavie, the more middle-class areas between Clydebank and the city centre.

'Listen, I just popped in for lunch there, in my taxi. I opened up my sausage supper and, well, I'm afraid to say the chips didn't appear to be cooked thoroughly.'

That was all it took for Frank the Fruitcake to have one of his meltdowns; his demons came rushing out, the red mist had descended.

'Well, why did you not say anything at the fucking time, then?'

Unbelievable. One fairly trivial complaint from a polite enough voice, and it'd got him swearing at the customer.

'Are you swearing at me?' I asked, trying to sound thoroughly outraged.

'Look, mate, fuck off. If there's a problem with the food, then you come down the shop.'

He'd finished, and was about to put the phone down. I had to be quick or this was an opportunity wasted.

'I'm on my way down. Fuck you, mate, we'll sort this like men,' I said, changing my voice to match his menacing tone.

'I'll be right here waiting. Come ahead, come a-fucking-head!' He was screaming at me now.

'Black taxi, mate. I'll be outside in five minutes.' I hung up.

It hadn't been the most creative prank call, although the sheer abuse and aggression from Frank the Fruitcake had ensured the hilarity. But I had a twist.

I phoned a local taxi number. I didn't bother with the

273

loudspeaker since Jamie, Halpin and Doc would hear all that was important.

'Hi, taxi, please . . . Frank's . . . As soon as possible.'

I then phoned Frank back. 'That's me on the way. We'll see who's the big man now.'

The three of them began pissing themselves, but in shocked realization of what had just been set up. Everyone was now clambering for a space at Halpin's living-room window, to get the best view.

I immediately began feeling terrible, thinking of the worst possible outcome, images of violence flashing in my head – anything could be about to happen.

An innocent taxi driver showing up, whistling, parking outside Frank's, tooting his horn, patiently browsing the back page of his paper, and then suddenly being dragged out of his cab and beaten to a pulp by a crazed, lunatic, chip-shop owner.

A few taxis passed, but none were ours. All three of us must have looked away from the shop at the same time because we heard a horn first, which made us instantly return our focus to the shop. I felt even worse now that the poor guy had given a playful toot of his horn. He'd done a little tune; it wasn't the sound of a man down to settle a score.

I went to grab my phone, to phone Frank and let him know I was a sixteen-year-old boy, showing off in front of my friends, but it was too late. Frank was out on the pavement, accompanied by two of his staff. Frank himself was quite small, a definite case of little-man syndrome, but his workers looked as fierce as he sounded.

They stood at the passenger side window, talking to the driver for a few minutes. I was glad they were appearing to ask questions first; hopefully it would become apparent to all parties that this was a misunderstanding.

They spoke for about two minutes in total before the taxi drove off, the driver obviously explaining that he didn't know what was going on. He'd just received a call to pick up a hire at Frank's, and Frank hadn't recognized him from being in the shop buying a sausage supper earlier. There'd been a few flaws in my idea, thankfully.

Frank and his two henchmen returned to the shop. I was relieved.

I was pumping with adrenalin after thinking I was about to be the cause of a brutal attack. Frank obviously wasn't as psychotic as his telephone demeanour suggested, so that was good.

I phoned him back, to round it all off. He answered, clearly a little pissed off, but, above all, confused. I simply whispered, 'Shitebag.'

'You again? Fuck you! I don't know what the fu —'

I held up the phone again, letting him hear how much entertainment he'd provided in Halpin's living room.

40

I'd go home at the end of these days and have dinner with my mum and dad. I'd feel sometimes like I was wasting time, but all my college work was done, and I'd work any shifts I could get at the Co-op. I was enjoying being out of school and the independence that came with it.

As much as I didn't know where I was going, I felt like I was progressing and learning. There were so many things I wanted to do and to see that maybe school or university or a career would hold me back. Of course, I'd want to get out and earn a wage, like Tony, Doc, George and everyone else serving apprenticeships, but I wasn't yet old enough, or mature enough, to think about practical issues, like money and earning a living.

I was still a daydreamer.

I had no one to guide me now, no teachers and no one to report to, except my mum and dad, but they could only offer advice; the rest was up to me.

I was the youngest in our house, I was the youngest in college and I was the youngest in the crowd I hung around with. If anyone had time on their side, it was me.

I'd try to read as much as I could. I'd talk about books with Jamie and he'd read ones that I'd recommend. It was no longer cool to be thick, like it had been at school sometimes.

I liked reading real-life stuff or at least books with a message, a moral. As well as Irvine Welsh, I liked Chuck Palahniuk after enjoying the film adaptation of *Fight Club* and discovering it was based on his book.

I wasn't a nihilist or anything, but I did like the overriding message of not conforming. I was going through an impressionable phase of relating to the protagonist in every single book I read. So after reading *Fight Club*, I went on to the ubiquitous read for a sixteen-year-old feeling a little detached, *Catcher in the Rye* by J. D. Salinger.

I tried to move on to slightly lighter, upbeat reads. I loved Roddy Doyle. I'd read *The Van* and *The Commitments*, again, after watching the film versions; I loved the Irish attitude, their humour and their swearing.

I'd never been to Ireland, but I knew from the people I'd met on holiday that it was a place I'd love. Roddy Doyle's books made me think of my grandparents and their lives and upbringings. I knew that I'd like one day to see the places where they came from.

I enjoyed all of his books, especially *Paddy Clarke Ha Ha Ha* and how it was written from the point of view of a ten-year-old child growing up in Dublin. I liked reading about his childhood. It was something I could relate to, and, although it was a sad read, it made me appreciate, again, my mum and dad and coming from a stable family.

I almost mentioned that 'we didn't have a lot of money, but there was a lot of love in our family' and how 'we had each other' there, but we've come this far without all that many autobiographical clichés.

For a seventeenth-birthday present my Auntie Anne had given me a £20 voucher for Waterstone's bookshop. It was enough potentially for four books, if I was astute enough and didn't recklessly dive in to the new-releases section.

I can remember only two books, but I'm sure I bought at

least three. The one I'm struggling to remember obviously didn't make that much of an impact and it's probably still in my bedroom at my mum and dad's house, the promotional offer sticker still on the front cover, obscuring part of the author's name.

The other two books were autobiographies, Paolo Di Canio's and Frank Skinner's.

I loved Paolo Di Canio when he was at Celtic. I liked watching passionate players, the guys who were a bit mentally unstable. It wasn't just a job to them, and you could feel they cared as much as the supporters.

I'd pick up his book and read a few chapters at a time, looking for similarities with my own life. He was the youngest in his family, he was overweight growing up, and he'd suffer panic attacks and anxieties.

I enjoyed reading about his early life and his time at Celtic, but then gradually lost interest in it. I don't think I even got as far as his now infamous Mussolini comments and political views, or I raced through them.

I'd tell everyone I'd read the book and they'd ask me what he'd actually said, and I wouldn't know. It was a bastard when things like that happened, like being back at school; I'd forgotten to study the bits I'd be asked about.

Frank Skinner's book was left lying there, in immaculate condition, on top of my chest of drawers or on the floor beside my bed, along with the other, unknown title.

I liked Frank Skinner. I liked how quick he was and how he always seemed to enjoy getting a good line in. I'd never seen any of his stand-up; I'd only heard that he was a stand-up.

I knew him from *Fantasy Football* on Friday nights, from when I'd go with my dad to pick John up from his work in Asda and the three of us would watch it together when we got home.

His ITV chat show was on at the time and I'd always sing the opening song about playing the fool at school.

If my mum and dad heard me singing it, they'd laugh and remind me how much of an understatement the lyrics were, in my case.

I was proud that Frank Skinner played the fool when he was just a boy at school. I admired him for that; he'd done well out of it and represented guys like us. I had no idea how important his book would turn out to be, as it sat there, for weeks, while I went to college, went to the Co-op, went to eighteenth-birthday parties, went to house parties, empties, doing everything that someone my age should be doing. I'd loosened my stance on not hanging around the streets, and I'd started drinking at the weekends.

I'd only just turned seventeen, but I'd receive sarcastic applause when I'd hand my £5 note to whoever was going to the shop, the seasoned veterans acknowledging the novel sight of me drinking.

Jamie, Sean and Halpin had all turned eighteen now, so they'd be served legally, not that there was ever a problem with the off-licence at the entrance to the Gowdie, where Halpin had been served for years, probably because of his size and build.

I'd been behind Halpin in the queue on the weekend of his eighteenth birthday, pretending not to be with him whilst he bought mine and everyone else's drinks for the night, cans of Miller, bottles of Mad Dog 20/20, and bottles of Buckfast for the experienced drinkers in the group.

With a nod to the substantial amount of alcohol he'd placed on the counter, the shop owner cheerily asked Halpin, 'What's the occasion?'

Halpin told him it was his eighteenth birthday and he replied, 'Happy Birthday!' before snapping out of shopkeeper, small-talk mode as it hit him that he'd been selling Halpin alcohol every weekend for two or three years.

Halpin was subsequently banned from the shop. He'd been served alcohol since he was fifteen, but now, on his eighteenth birthday, he was told to find somewhere else to purchase his drink.

I'd never feel comfortable as we stood drinking up at the Gowdie.

Every couple of hours, wherever we'd be standing would suddenly be lit up by headlights. No one would hang around to confirm if it was a police car or not. Everyone would be off, fleeing the scene of the crime, or at least fleeing the scene of the minor offences.

This was the bit I'd dread every night. I wasn't the fastest and I wasn't great at climbing fences. I'd be taking the hit on behalf of everyone and it would be just my luck to get in bother with the law on my rare outing as an underage drinker.

I don't think the police would have come down that heavy on us. We'd probably be booked again, they'd pour out our alcohol, I'd give my name, my real name, and it would be fine. I wasn't hanging around to see if I was right, though; I would run, because everyone else was running.

If it wasn't the police hassling us it would be a crowd from a different area who'd come up, intentionally looking for bother. I'd see people fighting, being chased by folk carrying golf clubs, baseball bats and the usual assortment of sport-ing equipment.

I'd seen a badminton racquet used as a weapon before. It broke and bent on impact and seemed quite a humane way to beat the shite out of someone, but this was more serious now. Most of it was pre-meditated and at almost all of the eighteenth-birthday parties that seemed to be happening over a series of consecutive weekends at the time, there were incidents.

I usually managed to get out when the atmosphere turned nasty, when the bass-heavy dance music would stop, making way for the sound of bodies hitting the ground, shouting and swearing, guys who weren't involved being held back, glasses smashing, the victim's name being confirmed by a crowd of hysterical, screaming females.

It was at times like that I'd think to myself: 'What the fuck am I doing here?' I'd see it from my parents' point of view, especially my dad's, and understand their concerns.

I had friends who'd been stabbed and friends who'd been caught with large amounts of drugs that they were looking after for people higher up the chain of command. There were times when it would hit me just how off the rails and indirectly involved in all this shite I could end up.

I enjoyed holding court and it was addictive. I now knew everyone. I knew mental people, dodgy people, people who had reputations. At these parties, everyone knew my name. They'd laugh and say, 'Give us some of your patter', or challenge me: 'I hear you're funny, let's hear it, then.' I'd go silent. I couldn't just be funny on demand. I was only funny to my mates and people I knew well, and in certain circumstances.

This would annoy me; how the fuck could they expect me to just start being funny?

41

If I was out with my mum, she'd be amazed at how many people stopped to talk to me. At John's work, people would ask him if he was 'Bridges' big brother'. Everyone was known by their surname. John was known as 'Bridges' first, so I was 'Bridges' little brother', but he'd say yes and they'd smile, impressed, like I was a local celebrity.

For all my mum, dad and John had been told about me, the negatives and the positives, the underlying message seemed to be that I was popular and a good laugh.

They had no parents' nights or any letters home now for them to hear anything more specific than that. They knew I had quite a witty sense of humour and they knew I'd read and write a lot. They knew the real me. It was maybe an act I'd put on outside, terrified of being picked on and terrified of going back to the shy and reclusive child I'd been.

My life had changed, rapidly, but I was aware of not being easily led. I never tried Ecstasy, thinking I'd probably be the guy who'd hit the front pages, another fatality. I never tried cocaine; I didn't like how seriously it turned people. If cannabis was a patter-enhancer, then cocaine was patter-repellent.

I eventually tried cannabis and, like I'd read online, it did make everything seem funnier. I couldn't smoke a lot and I could smoke it only in the right company, but it helped me to calm down a little. All of the negative effects that I'd read about, I was affected by already. I was a scatterbrain, I was clumsy, and I'd think too much.

I also had an increased appetite, big time.

I knew I wouldn't smoke it all my life, but it was enjoyable and far better than being drunk. I had never seen anyone smoke so much grass that they'd attacked somebody with a golf club, unless it was in a computer game.

I played a lot of games; I'd pass whole days sitting in good company, funny company, playing *Grand Theft Auto*, *Pro Evolution Soccer*, *Fight Night*, *Tiger Woods* and any games that would get competitive and usually end in someone going into a mood.

I was listening to music more than ever, still Oasis, but now, in particular, their B-sides, along with any bootleg CDs of their live concerts I could get from my mate Stevie, an HMV worker whom I'd met at his work and with whom I'd stand and speak about music, books and movies every time I was in.

I was normal and no longer trying as hard to fit in. I was one of the lads, but at times it felt underwhelming and I'd get a horrible sense that this was it; you did this for a while, got a job, settled down, got married, had children, and then you watched them repeat this cycle.

My cynical outlook was well beyond my years. I'd maybe matured slowly in some aspects of life but rapidly in others, or maybe I was reading too many books and I was starting to think like Holden Caulfield or Tyler Durden.

On one of the days between Christmas Day and New Year's Eve in 2003, I was lying in my bedroom, at a loose end. I didn't know whether or not to go out and see everyone. I felt like I should be doing something, something sociable. I was under the pressure that comes with the festive season, when you start to look forward to it all being over but the child in you is disgusted at such thoughts.

I had a couple of text messages and some missed calls but I felt like I couldn't move. I was fucking miserable but I couldn't figure out why. The TV had all the usual, nostalgic, family-Christmas stuff: *National Lampoon's Christmas Vacation*, *Willow*, an Indiana Jones film.

'There's that *Toy Story* on at teatime, Paddy,' I'd hear my dad say, obviously scanning the channels in the living room, shouting to my mum in the kitchen.

It usually made me laugh how my dad loved animated movies so much. I'd walk in and he'd be sitting watching them on his own. 'Your mum won't watch this with me; she says it's just a cartoon!' he'd say, outraged that anyone could be so indifferent towards such iconic cinema as *Toy Story*.

I enjoyed animated films as well, especially the Pixar ones, but my dad was fanatical about them, and he'd sit, gripped and fully tuned in. If he wasn't in his mid-fifties and didn't have rheumatoid arthritis, then I'm sure he'd be sat on the floor in front of the TV, legs crossed and his face just inches from the screen. After *Toy Story*, he'd probably suggest *It's a Wonderful Life*, his all-time favourite film.

I was lying on my bed, staring at the ceiling, feeling like I was about to burst into tears and I didn't really know why. I couldn't be bothered watching *Toy Story* or *It's a Wonderful Life* with my mum and dad, but I thought back to the times when I could be bothered, when I'd moan at John for not joining us, choosing to go out to the pubs with his pals instead.

Downstairs, one of the old men whom my mum would care for, Sammy, was getting ready to head home, and my dad was going to drive him round to his house just behind ours.

Sammy didn't have any family, so my mum would invite him down for dinner over Christmas, usually on Christmas Day. But for some reason he'd cancelled on us this year and rescheduled for a few days later.

The thought of being his age and having no family to

spend Christmas with was heart-breaking, so my mum would make this a yearly thing.

I could always tell Sammy was having a great time, and he'd be knocking back some old cheap-looking lager that he'd requested and a few whiskies.

I'd hear them getting his coat for him and his slightly slurred, tipsy voice thanking my mum for the dinner, my mum running out of 'you're welcome' and 'don't be silly' responses, as he'd repeat himself, the cheap-looking lager and the whisky making sure he expressed his gratitude thoroughly. The thought of him – heading home to an empty house, to his lonely bed, and waking up to no one, sitting around for a few hours, waiting on my mum to arrive and make him his porridge for breakfast – would all add to my new feeling of sadness.

I'd think of how good a person my mum was, and how maybe I didn't let her know that enough. I didn't know how to go about it. If I tried to express some gratitude there and then, I'd feel like it was only a short-term attempt to rid myself of this unique sense of guilt.

I'd probably walk down the stairs, say, 'I love you, Mum, and thanks for dinner,' and break down crying, just as *Toy Story* was starting.

This would give them more to worry about. 'He's lost the fucking plot,' they'd be saying to each other after they'd consoled me and I'd gone back to my room.

I was lying there, thinking of all the bother I'd caused. I knew my mum and dad got over everything. They'd shout at the time of the incidents and warn me to get my act together, but they'd always let things go and wouldn't use them to beat me up.

We'd argue a lot, but I understood that they were right and only had my own interests at heart. They knew I loved them, but I wanted them to know I admired them, and thought they were great people.

I couldn't think of how to say all of this, but then there was no point in saying all of this, I realized. I thought it, I acknowledged it, so I should act on it.

Ideas would play in my head about how they deserved more. My mum hardly knew anything other than working and running a house and looking after my dad, whose arthritis had begun to flare up every couple of weeks to the point when he couldn't move. During the nights I'd hear him lying in bed, in agony; I'd go in to see if he was okay, and he'd be embarrassed that he'd woken me up.

I knew it hurt my mum when she'd be stopped in the street and at the shops to be told of how I'd been seen running around in a crowd, being chased by the police or drinking in the street.

The stories were exaggerated and some of them wouldn't add up, like when I'd been at home on the night I was supposed to have been out wrecking and pillaging the streets of Hardgate.

My mum knew fine well that these were the kind of people who'd only speak when they had bad news, but, still, I didn't want her to be embarrassed and upset.

She knew I wasn't a bad person and I knew that as well. I couldn't see past the fact that I was making people laugh, and that was all I wanted.

My phone was ringing, someone probably looking to see where I was, to come out, get a drink, have a laugh. I ignored it. I turned my phone off. As much as I'd like to say for the good of the story that this was the moment I picked up Frank Skinner's autobiography, which had been lying beside me all through my episode with these intense, manic thoughts of dread and self-loathing . . . it wasn't. The book that contained the solutions was left there, unopened.

It wouldn't be for long.

But right then, I went down to the living room, just in time for *Toy Story*. 'Oh, are you joining us?' my mum said, pretending to sound posh and clearly in a good mood.

I told her I was, but only if she gave *Toy Story* a chance. She was relieved that I wasn't going out and agreed. We watched it, and if my mum didn't enjoy the 'cartoon', she enjoyed the company. It was a nice night, and I woke up the next day feeling like a weight had been lifted and the awful feeling in my stomach had gone away.

I stuck on some music and *Championship Manager* and had another day to myself. I didn't need to be running about wild. I needed to chill out, to take a back seat and slow things down.

Another film that we'd always watch as a family, usually over Christmas, was *Ferris Bueller's Day Off*. It was a feel-good film, one that Granddad Tommy apparently loved. The image of him preferring a film starring Matthew Broderick to any old black and white western or war film made me laugh. I loved the film and its message of taking a step back now and then.

42

I returned to college after Christmas. I didn't have any repeat episodes of my mini-emotional breakdown, but packing shelves on New Year's Eve in the Co-op, with the song 'Mad World' by Gary Jules playing repeatedly, was a tester.

I'm trying to rearrange a shelf of Princes ham, with the earlier sell-by dates at the front, the later dates at the back, in keeping with the store's 'facing up' policy, and all the while this is playing, the in-store radio doing its best to make sure there was nothing left in me at the end of my shift, at the end of the year.

For sure, 2003 had its high points and low points, but if it had gone down to the last round for an overall decision on the year, Gary Jules secured the victory for the 'low points' side.

Then 2004 started in a wild house party, an empty. I got drunk. I saw someone lean against shoddily fitted patio doors and fall right through them, on to the decking outside, cigarette in his mouth, lighter in his hand, lying staring at the sky.

Unintentional, costly damage, caused by someone too drunk to shout at about it, or even to remember it, was a stipulation of any great empty.

I fell asleep on a couch, watching a 1996 VHS tape of Oasis live at Maine Road that my new friend that night, Jordy, had gone home to his house to get, following a drunken conversation we'd had about Oasis and live music.

I was watching Liam Gallagher walk on stage in a cotton Umbro tracksuit, in front of thousands of people going mental, a guy who had made it, a superstar. They were one of the biggest bands in the world and here was the lead singer in a cotton Umbro tracksuit. I remember loads of people wearing the exact same cotton Umbro tracksuit in Clydebank in the mid-1990s.

Oasis were superstars, but they weren't from a different planet. They weren't born superstars; they'd grown up in Burnage, a suburb of Manchester, a place I imagined wasn't all that different from Clydebank.

I'm aware of sounding contrived here and trying to re-create an epiphany, but I was seventeen years old and I had no idea how life was going to turn out.

The concert made an impact on me, along with a case of Red Stripe, which I ended up sharing with Jordy. It was the least he deserved for introducing me to the beauty of being drunk in a stranger's house and having a heart-to-heart with someone I'd just met. As the sun starts to come up, watching a concert of your favourite band, live in their home town, gives you an amazing feeling that there's so much to look forward to, that you could be a rock 'n' roll star as well.

I should mention again that I never tried cocaine, but I'd imagine this was what it felt like, except it didn't wear off.

It was over the next few weeks that I read Frank Skinner's book.

Jamie and Sean were attending college less and less. Sean's labouring shifts were providing money he could be doing with, making labouring more appealing than wasting his time on a course he wasn't interested in, and Jamie was struggling with Monday morning hangovers and the temptation of Friday afternoons in the pub.

Usually, I'd get the bus on my own at least one day a week.

I'd deliberately take the 59, a double-decker which took about forty-five minutes; the 17 was known to do Hardgate to Glasgow city centre in half an hour, not bad for a bus, but I wasn't in a hurry.

I'd sit on the front seat of the top deck of the 59, for the near-panoramic view of the different streets, different areas and different people.

I'd be listening to music and reading about Frank Skinner's life, about stand-up comedy, reading about this guy called Chris Collins, who'd gotten into trouble a lot at school, who'd always liked to play the fool, a guy who discovered he could be funny and went on to take it as far as he could.

Like Noel and Liam Gallagher, he'd come from a working-class area where people weren't expected to do something different. He wasn't selected to be a comedian, no one came to him. He'd gone from being chucked out of school to signing on. He was going nowhere, but now he was Frank Skinner, the guy from the TV, the guy whose chat show I watched every week.

I admired him. If I'd seen similarities to my own personality in the characters of any books I'd read before, this was the most accurate. He was a guy who could describe the feelings of wanting to make everyone laugh, the feelings of neediness, as pathetic as it sounds.

He didn't seem ashamed. It was his talent, being funny, and he'd embraced it and it had taken him much further than he'd ever expected. He'd stuck with it, learned a craft, a craft you can only learn, live, in front of rooms full of strangers.

I'd been told I was funny, by my friends, my teachers, my parents and John, and people at work and college who didn't know me as well would laugh and pass comment that I'd made them laugh.

This was something I barely thought about any more. I'd hear it all the time and I'd rather be known for something more than being an idiot. I didn't want people to take me seriously, fuck that, but maybe I felt that I should stop treating life as a big joke.

I now took it for granted. It frustrated me, though, like it'd be better if I just didn't talk to anyone – then I wouldn't have the urge to start making them laugh and I could get something productive done. Being funny had held me back so much that I was beginning to see it as a negative.

I finished Frank's autobiography and then began to read it again. I'd flick through all the other stuff; there was a lot about sex, particularly anal sex, that I couldn't relate to, as much as it made me laugh. It was the sections about stand-up that I was fascinated with.

I didn't consider myself skilled enough, confident enough, clever enough; I knew I could be quite funny but nowhere near funny enough to be a comedian, an actual comedian. I was even amazed at the thought of having that as a job, of being 'a comedian'.

I also had far too much respect for him and anyone who made a living as 'a comedian' to think: 'I could do that.' Instead, I'd picture myself doing stand-up comedy and think: 'Imagine if nobody laughed.'

I always had his book with me, in my college bag during the day and at the side of my bed at night. Any chance I could get, I'd scan through it all again, looking for any bits about comedy I'd maybe missed, about the writing process, the travelling, the bits about how he'd drive to London and sleep in his car, just so he could do stand-up at night, the bits about the tough gigs, nobody laughing . . . How the fuck do you come back from that? It would destroy me; again, my respect for stand-up comedy grew.

The frequent cutaways to his current life didn't captivate me as much, where he'd talk as Frank Skinner, the guy I knew from TV. He'd mention being in his London agent's offices and waiting for his driver to take him to a TV studio for a recording.

It sounded nice; but when he spoke about what it was like walking on stage in a pub packed with strangers, and making every one of them laugh, live and in the moment, not singing, not reading poetry, not telling jokes, but speaking, just speaking about your day, your life – it made me think of how incredible a feeling that must have been.

'Imagine if nobody laughed' was replaced, for a few brief minutes, with a feeling of 'Imagine if everybody laughed.' It was quite rare that I'd find a positive from a negative like this; that was usually my dad's department.

Strangely, though, the thought of everybody laughing at me, at whatever I was saying, strangers in a pub or a comedy club, filled me with adrenalin, a nervous energy.

I was more nervous picturing myself ripping the roof of a gig than I was about the thought of being stared at, in complete silence, heckled even and getting a 'You're shite, mate' from someone much funnier in the crowd, who'd climb up on the stage, grab the microphone off me and tear me to shreds.

I was nervous because I imagined the high was something that I could only dream of. It was unlikely to happen – but there was that slight chance that everything would click.

Dying on my arse, however, was almost a certainty.

I'd be sent back to my pals, humbled and silenced, my dreams shattered. I'd be thinking of every teacher whose class I'd disrupted, every parent whose child I'd distracted, the staff from the ten-pin bowling alley, the staff from the cinema, the police officer who'd heroically rescued Hugh Grant from kidnappers.

I'd be thinking about the parents of my old classmates

who'd stopped me in Clydebank Shopping Centre. I'd be thinking of how well their sons and daughters would be doing now, compared to me. My mum would be out, walking from house to house in Hardgate and Duntocher, being stopped in the street: 'Oh, I hear Kevin was up on stage at the comedy club. I heard nobody laughed? That's such a shame. Wasn't he quite funny at school?'

She'd have to try to defend me – 'he wasn't that bad' – but they'd have their story by now. It didn't need changing; someone had failed at something.

I'd soon be the former class clown in my new role as the pub funny man, with a descent into the grim world of being a local 'character' inevitably beckoning.

Selling golf balls, wearing a purple and green anorak, trying to tell jokes to passing teenagers, not real jokes. I'd try to disguise that I was telling a joke until the end, the funny bit when I'd hope they'd laugh.

'I'm just back from the doctor's there . . .' I'd start, or: 'I'm standing here sweating like a . . .' Things like that, and I'd look for their reaction, desperately hoping for their approval.

Maybe they'd buy a few freshly washed Pinnacle or Dunlop balls, even if it'd be just to humour me, so I'd go away. The sons of my old schoolmates – 'My dad went to school with him and said he used to be quite funny' – would walk by me, passing comment.

'I've got Nike ones, boys, and Titleist. Only the best, lads,' I'd be shouting after them, desperately pleading, looking for a sale but, above all, for their approval and a few minutes of their time, when I could tell my jokes.

The lonely old guy, who fucked it up and let every opportunity in life pass by. He'd had a good laugh but his audience had moved on, on to the real world, with their wives, their children and their careers.

They'd speed by in their cars, tooting the horn and waving at me; they wouldn't want to stop and have a catch-up, the toot of the horn and the wave being enough, an acknowledgement, a 'thank you for the laughs when we were children' and a 'sorry it never worked out for you'.

43

I didn't want to be in attendance at eighteenth-birthday parties, listening to dance music, watching people being booted in the face as they lay on the ground out cold, seeing people, my own best friends, stabbed.

Who the fuck would take a knife to a party?

I didn't want to get into fighting, taking drugs, or even drinking.

I always felt I was a good person and that there were far worse people than me out there. In fact, I knew there were; I knew them, and I was now seen as one of them.

I was the same as the guy who took a knife to an eighteenth-birthday party, in as much as I dressed the same and spoke the same, but that was enough to be convicted in most people's eyes, enough to be labelled as a Ned, or whatever.

I didn't want to go back to the loneliness of childhood and being worried about something different every day,

I could maybe speak to a therapist to really figure out what went on in my brain back then, but there would be no point. It had landed me here. I'd worked through it, but this was a new battle, one about where was I going next.

I'd discovered a way of making friends and being popular; it was all I had, but now what?

Signing up for a spot at an amateur comedy night would have to be the most terrifying thing I'd ever done in my life. Six years earlier I was begging not to be included in a school play; and here I was considering volunteering myself to perform on stage?

This time, it wouldn't be in front of my primary school teachers and classmates' parents. This would be a room of strangers, people who wouldn't be as supportive, people who didn't know me.

Plus, I was an adult. I was young, but not a child, and I didn't imagine there would be as much goodwill towards me because of that as there was in the St Mary's assembly hall. Also, there was no scriptwriter; all of that was down to me.

I thought, in depth, about what would happen if the gig didn't go well. I acknowledged how it would feel so I was prepared for that; it was highly likely I'd need to be.

Even thinking about it, my nerves would kick in. If it went well, then I'd prove a point, to myself, first of all. I wouldn't be the loud, confident, centre-of-attention, class clown at St Columba's who'd thought he was funny enough to make strangers laugh, discovered he wasn't and then hit a downward spiral, too proud and deluded to admit to his failings, to grow up, change direction and accept that life isn't just one big joke.

I was interested in how much work was behind a stand-up routine. I didn't have any stand-up routines, but how did I know that? I had never been in a position where I'd required a stand-up routine, the position being on stage, in a comedy club.

Every doubt that came into my head, I had an answer for, like it was someone else willing me to just go for it. I had two consciences, one of them representing me and what I was like, a little unsure, a little scared but, above all, realistic.

The other conscience was far more daring, far more up for taking a chance, a gamble, and the arguments for finding a comedy club that would let me try stand-up just kept on coming forward. There was no boss, no one to tell me how to do it; my only requirement was to be funny. That hadn't been a problem to me in any other environment, so why would it be a problem in a comedy club?

I wasn't going to get in trouble in a comedy club, unless I *wasn't* funny. I'd laugh at how great a 'comedy club' sounded. I was smiling and beginning to listen to this new conscience. It was my conscience, it was me, and so what if I failed? I'd failed at everything else. I couldn't think of anything I was good at, and, as pathetic as it sounded, that didn't bother me. I was funny, but this would be risking it all. If I tried stand-up and it didn't go well, it would change me forever. I'd finish the first year of my college course and then get out, get a job, a job doing anything, just working, working because people worked, that's what they do.

There'd be no more thoughts of escapism, well, thoughts, maybe, but none that were ever to be acted on. I'd work, make money, pay my mum her dig money, work harder, make her and my dad proud. I'd save up for a flat of my own, maybe even meet a girl and have children.

If it was good enough for everyone else, it was good enough for me.

Frank Skinner's first gigs didn't go well, but that was Frank Skinner. As much as I felt like I knew him, he was still a star, he was on television. He'd made a great career out of stand-up comedy and maybe he was only saying that his first gigs didn't go well to make any budding young comedians reading his book feel better.

A normal life, that was the deal. I'd try stand-up and that was the worst thing that could happen. Afterwards, I'd have a normal life. It wasn't all that bad; there was far more to gain than there was to lose.

I'd convinced myself.

I didn't imagine what would happen if it went well, like really well, the whole place laughing and clapping, at me, at the things I was saying, at the things I thought, the things I noticed, the stories I told. I didn't waste time even thinking about anything that would happen; the most important thing was trying to make it happen.

Frank Skinner was thirty when he first tried stand-up. He wrote that he'd hate to reflect on life in his later years and ponder, regretfully, what would have happened if he'd only given it a go.

Right, then, before I'd talked myself out of it, I plugged in the PC in our house, went online and began searching: 'Stand-up comedy Glasgow', 'Amateur comedy night Glasgow'.

I'd been using the computer for research ever since my new fascination with stand-up comedy, and broad, generic searches such as 'How to write stand-up comedy' and 'How to be a comedian' were still on the PC's browsing history. That was an oversight from me; this was top secret and deeply personal, I didn't want anyone to know.

I'm sure my mum and dad would have reacted positively, but it didn't matter. Their encouragement would be just as likely to put me off booking the first gig as their dissuasion would make me more determined.

I didn't want anyone to know.

I knew how easily it could be a disaster. I could drop the microphone. I could faint. I could forget what I wanted to say, someone would maybe shout and I'd have no idea what to say back. Everyone else could be hilarious, and I'd be the only one who struggled. I didn't want anyone I knew to witness anything like this, especially not my mum and dad.

I was ashamed. It was as though I'd admitted I was funny and funny enough to go and try to perform stand-up. So I made a deal with myself to do one gig, to satisfy my own curiosity, before following the clear, well-mapped-out, low-risk path to my future.

I found the Stand comedy clubs in Glasgow and Edinburgh. The one in Glasgow was on Woodlands Road. I didn't know where that was but I'd figured not finding the venue was the least of my concerns for now.

I sent an email. I think it was an email to the box office as I couldn't find any 'Are you considering performing?' kind of option anywhere.

Still, I sent my email, explaining that I was seventeen and at college and a big fan of comedy. I wasn't a big fan of comedy, but I thought it would increase my chances of landing a spot if they thought I was.

I'd seen only a few stand-up comedy shows before, on video. I had read Frank Skinner's book, and I hadn't even seen his stand-up. I asked to be considered for a gig anytime soon and that it would be appreciated if they'd let me know if anything came up.

I left my mobile phone number; usually I'd leave the house phone number that I knew off by heart, but I didn't want a comedy club to phone the house. That would be a pretty silly way to be caught out.

And that was it, the email was sent.

I deleted the computer's browsing history as though I'd been watching animal porn and went to bed, hoping I'd awake to the phone ringing and I'd be booked in for my first ever attempt at stand-up comedy.

44

I woke up feeling like I'd made a huge mistake. I was seventeen years old; there were no comedians at seventeen years old and, if there were, they were probably annoying, extroverted drama students with a love for anything that involves being on a stage.

Frank Skinner was thirteen years older than me when he tried stand-up; he'd been to university, he'd been an alcoholic, he'd been in relationships and he'd worked proper jobs. What had I done? What could I talk about?

It was a huge mistake to contact a comedy club; it had been late at night and I wasn't thinking straight. It was the morning now, and I was a realist, thinking rationally and feeling mortified about my late-night 'gazing at the stars' and 'believing' about 'following my dreams' – all that shite that you hear about in pop songs.

I was awake now and I had half an hour to get in the shower, brush my teeth, find my black trousers, black shoes and my white shirt and then walk round to the Co-op for a few hours of packing shelves. That was my life. I'd hopefully go on to a better job, but this was it for the time being, at least.

I was embarrassed and checked the PC to see whether the email had definitely been sent. It had.

I read it back: 'I'm seventeen, at college, and a big fan of comedy.' I felt myself ready to break into a sweat. I was panicking. Now, if I wanted to try stand-up when I was thirty, they'd remember me as the guy who messed them around. I wasn't thinking logically enough to consider how many emails they must receive, from people like me, dreamers and escapists, deluded or not, but looking for their chance to be a star, for their ticket out, and how unlikely it'd be that they'd remember my name and my email, thirteen years later.

I decided to leave it and forget about the email, in the hope that I'd have no further correspondence. The contract I'd made with myself was no longer binding, and I wished I'd just gone to bed, or *Championship Manager* had distracted me when I put on the PC and I'd never got round to sending the email.

My bottle had crashed, and I hadn't even been booked for my first gig.

About a fortnight later, I'd stopped thinking about comedy. I was trying to block it out. I was too scared and it embarrassed me that I was the funny guy when I wasn't supposed to be, but when it had come down to it, I'd ducked out.

To be fair, it was the comedy club who hadn't got back to me. My enquiry was still with them, but I wasn't going to chase it up. I was relieved to have dodged a bullet and hoped it had gone straight to their junk mail.

I'd finished college early, and it was one of the rare days that Jamie had decided to show up. We got off the bus at the Hardgate shops, strolled across to Greggs and then walked round to mine, up to my bedroom to play the PlayStation.

During one of our games of *Pro Evolution Soccer*, my phone began ringing. Our games were usually intense encounters, so there was a blanket ban on using phones or pausing the game unnecessarily.

We'd both mastered how to break rapidly on the counter-attack with a Mexican chicken oval bite in our hands, squashed against the control pad.

It would have taken a major incident for play to be halted,

even for a few seconds. I looked down to my carpet, at my phone, a scratched and battered grey Nokia 3310, with a missing number 9 key.

If I'd to call a number containing a 9 I'd have to use a pen to press it in.

I'd always dread the day that I'd ever have to phone the emergency services. There'd be panicked screams of 'Someone, quick, phone an ambulance!' and I'd be replying, 'I will, stay calm – do you have a pen that I could borrow?'

It made texting any words with a letter 'w', 'x', 'y' or 'z' frustrating, but also educational. I'd expanded my vocabulary looking for alternatives. They weren't the most popular letters, not the ones you'd be looking for when watching *Countdown* and playing along; it could have been worse.

I didn't recognize the number, so I paused the game.

'What the fuck? I was about to play him in there, cheating prick,' Jamie shouted, before picking up his own phone. 'That'd better be a bird,' he commented.

The number began with 0131, an area code I didn't recognize; 01389 or 0141 was as far as my phone had ever been in contact with.

I panicked and answered quickly. It was the Stand, Eva from the Stand, phoning from their head office in Edinburgh. I immediately began talking properly, and my already red face grew brighter when I heard Jamie giggling at my pathetic, 'Yes, Kevin speaking' and several repetitions of 'yeah'.

It felt horrendous. It was not how I wanted the call to go, and all the apprehension about doing the gig came raging back. I couldn't get out of it now.

I had Jamie here, who I didn't want to know anything about this. But I had to try to crack a joke on the phone. It was a comedy club – what kind of comedian was I going to be with my 'yeah' and my 'uh-huh' and my excruciating 'let me just grab a pen'.

I had nothing. I was speechless and just wanting to be off the phone and for Jamie to go home so I could be alone, to lie on my bed and figure out some form of a solution.

Eva mentioned they'd got my email and I'd been put on the list to perform; she asked if I'd like to confirm a spot for Tuesday, 10 February.

'Yeah,' I said. 'That works for me.'

I don't know why I was speaking like this, so proper, like the way my mum would talk to her boss when she phoned the house. I felt like a character in a shite Scottish TV drama show.

I just didn't want Eva to think I was a fucking bam. What kind of comedian would I be, sitting holding a control pad of a paused PlayStation, eating a Greggs, trying to speak proper whilst my stoned mate sat giggling at me, desperate to hear who I was talking to?

I looked at my phone when I hung up; it was Monday, 2 February. I told Jamie it was just someone about a job that I'd applied for and how I had an interview on Tuesday, 10 February. This was kind of true. He hadn't spotted the 0131, which was handy, as I didn't have to add an Edinburgh element to my story.

I remember letting a 1–0 lead slip and being beaten convincingly when play resumed in our game. My mind wasn't on it. I was shell-shocked.

I thought I'd got away with it, but now I had just eight days to get ready to perform stand-up comedy, in a proper comedy club, with proper comedians, in front of a proper audience.

I couldn't have said anything funny there and then.

I felt like the least funny, least cool, and most terrified, tragic figure on the planet. Why had I agreed?

I'd been caught off-guard; the call was unexpected. I'd been having a nice, easy day, eating my Greggs and playing the PlayStation.

The easy life, but I'd gone and fucked it now.

If Jamie hadn't been there, maybe I could have relaxed and explained that I didn't consider myself to be ready, yet, but maybe in a few years I could have a go.

I could have asked Eva for some advice. I could have maybe even gone up to see the place first, to watch a live comedy gig. I hadn't been inside a comedy club before; now my first time inside was to be as one of the performers.

It was a long eight days. I'd struggle to sleep, and when I slept I'd dream about it, I'd dream about the audience being full of people whom I'd annoyed, people who'd love to see me fail.

In truth, I don't think there were all that many people who'd like to see me fail. I did feel a lot of goodwill towards me and if I'd put the word out that I was doing stand-up comedy, in front of an audience in a comedy club, I'd have packed the place out.

But what would the point in that be? My mates found me funny. I was their mate, I found them funny. That's what mates are, people you share laughs with. I remembered the deal I'd made with myself and I got over the fact that it was done, booked in. I couldn't cancel. I could cancel, but it would be pathetic, like someone in a water park or a theme park who'd waited in the queue, climbed all the way to the top and then decided they were too scared to slide back down. The worrying was in the waiting, but it would be worth it for the short burst of pleasure. If it wasn't pleasurable, then there would be no need to ever go through it again.

I started trying to view it more positively; it was only five minutes I'd be on for, or 'up there' for, if I wanted it to sound more daunting. I was facing a fear; I was about to do something far more challenging, exciting and potentially rewarding than anyone I knew had ever attempted.

I grabbed some paper from my college notepad and began searching online again, about how to write an opening joke and how to write a routine. Everything seemed so complicated and it was freaking me out.

What Frank Skinner made sound so appealing about stand-up was the freedom of it all, the freedom that you can say anything, literally anything, so long as you respect that the audience are under no obligation to laugh and they have every right not to.

I didn't know who these comedy experts were, on online blogs and forums. They knew far more about stand-up than I did, but they'd write too much, and it was putting doubts in my head.

I wrote 'Hello' on my paper, and then 'Good evening'. I started to laugh. I'd never greeted anyone with 'Good evening' before, but this was show business. I said it a few times out loud, 'Good evening', and I felt a warm grin slowly come over my face.

I started to look forward to the gig now, to standing in front of a packed crowd, people who I'd never met, people who I'd hopefully entertain, even if only for five minutes.

Other than my smooth-sounding 'Good evening', I was fairly light on material. I didn't know about writing routines or how many routines would equate to five minutes, but I just played it out on my head. After 'Good evening', what would I say?

I had nothing. I walked away from the piece of paper; I still had time so I'd wait and see what came to me.

For the next few days, I'd walk around saying, 'Good evening', and hoping something funny would come racing out behind it. I'd be packing shelves, or on the bus to college; I'd deliberately be late so even if Jamie or Sean were both going in, I'd be on the bus after them, on my own.

I had some thinking to do.

45

On the Monday, the day before the gig, Eva called me again. This time I was on my own, walking from the bookie's to the bus stop at the bottom of Clydebank Shopping Centre, but she didn't need to know that and I could talk more freely now.

She asked me to confirm my age, mentioning that my email had said I was seventeen years old. I told her yes, I was seventeen, and gave my date of birth.

I began to feel anxious: what was wrong, why was she asking that? I didn't want it to be cancelled now. I'd prepared and it'd been all I was thinking about. If I'd been told to wait until I was eighteen, I wouldn't have bothered. I'd been running on nervous energy for the past week, just thinking about it. Now I'd have to postpone that and then go through it all again.

She mentioned that because the club had an alcohol licence I'd need to be accompanied by an adult. She laughed and made sure I didn't feel patronized.

I laughed as well; I was still getting to perform so that was a relief. I told her that finding an adult wasn't a problem. It was a problem, a major fucking problem, but as long as the gig was still confirmed and everything was going ahead, then I'd figure it out.

She apologized and wished me luck, asking if it was my first time doing stand-up. I told her yes, and she said, 'Well, I hope you have fun.' I'd never heard anyone with as friendly a voice before, and I hoped it wouldn't be the last time I heard from her.

I had to find five minutes of jokes and an adult I could trust, someone who I could fail in front of and who'd understand. I'd have to explain everything; how, just because I'd read a comedian's book and everyone told me I was funny, I thought I should try stand-up comedy. I would sound like a dick. I had no choice, though. John had been to comedy clubs before. He knew more than me, but the last time I'd tried stand-up in front of him, he'd been assaulted.

I'm sure he'd have put that ugly episode behind him by now, but I was terrified he'd see me as his daft wee brother up there, trying to be funny, his pain-in-the-arse wee brother.

I knew he'd be supportive, but I'd worry that if it went badly, he'd lie and try to big me up. I didn't know what to think or what anyone would think. It was a shite situation, and I wished I'd just lied to Eva and told her I was eighteen.

I couldn't exactly phone back and say, 'Eva, listen, did I say seventeen? Ha, I wish! What am I like? I forgot I was eighteen ... desperately clinging on to my youth!' I'd be laughing falsely, like a car salesman or an estate agent, the kind who, the friendlier they force themselves to be, the less you trust them. I got home after the phone call, and it was only my mum who was in the house. I told her I had something to tell her, that I needed advice.

She looked alarmed. 'What is it, son, what's wrong? Is something up? Tell me.' Her mind was jumping to the worst possible scenario – I was in trouble, someone was after me, I'd been in bother with the police, I'd got a girl pregnant, I was pregnant – anything, her mind quickly churning out women's magazine-type headlines: 'My seventeen-year-old son, pregnant, to my husband'.

Her panicked reaction had made her stop everything she was doing and turn to look me right in the eye, so I hurried up and got to the point. I told her I was booked to perform stand-up comedy at a comedy club in Glasgow.

She looked at me, too confused to be relieved. I could tell she wanted me to answer the questions she hadn't even asked yet. 'It's something I've been wanting to try. I've read a lot about it and it's only five minutes. The reason I'm telling you is that I need an adult to come up with me, because I'm not eighteen and the club has an alcohol licence.'

Showing up for my first gig with my mum would be removing the entire rock 'n' roll element. But showing up with your dad had a bit more kudos, a father and son thing. I went to the football with my dad. I'd never played football, so we'd never had anything where he could come along and support me, but maybe this could be it.

I told my mum how it wasn't ideal and I'd rather go myself, but that it was my first time, so I didn't want to piss off anyone at the comedy club. My mum thought I'd gone a bit mad; she looked unsure, but tried to sound supportive. 'I'll tell your dad. I think he'd like to come.'

I thanked her. I disappeared out of the house again, to go for a walk and to think about what I was going to say the following night, hoping that when I returned to the house my dad would be home and already briefed about my latest venture.

I wouldn't have to squirm and explain everything. Hearing myself talk about doing stand-up made me realize how ridiculous it sounded. I knew I was being daft, but there was that little bit inside me, willing me to go through with it.

My dad was delighted. He was intrigued and wanted to know everything. I was relieved that he hadn't called me an idiot. I don't even know why I thought he would. He'd always been into Billy Connolly, and he started to tell me about how he'd got up one night on stage in a pub in Blackpool and tried to tell a few Chic Murray jokes.

There had been a comedian on, who'd been struggling. My dad and the rest of a stag do that he was with had been heckling the guy. So the guy challenged one of them to go up on to the stage and see if they could do any better.

Everyone in the stag do turned to my dad. Obviously he was the funny guy in his crowd, or at least the daft guy, like me, who'd be the most likely to get on the stage.

My dad told me how he'd been drunk and full of confidence, but immediately froze on stage. He'd been drinking since midday, but instantly felt sober. He tried a few Chic Murray jokes that didn't go over. He was heckled himself before handing the microphone back to the comedian and apologizing. He told me how he felt embarrassed and had nothing but respect for the poor guy.

I'd never heard this story before. My dad had heckled a comic, got up on stage himself and proceeded to die on his arse, using someone else's material.

'They say it's the hardest job in the world, comedy.' My dad would sit there, making this grand statement, 'they' being a source for most of the knowledge he'd acquired over the years.

I didn't know who 'they' were. But from what I'd read about stand-up, heckling the comic is frowned upon, as is challenging a heckler to come up on stage, and the biggest faux pas of the lot is using someone else's material.

My dad's Blackpool trip sounded like a dark night for the art form. I think I'd won his respect already, by volunteering myself to go up on a stage, stone-cold sober, and at the age of seventeen.

I could tell he was excited and couldn't wait until the next night.

My mum quickly told him to leave me alone when he moved on to talking about ideas for stand-up routines. She could sense it was making me uncomfortable. A sharp, authoritative 'Andy!' was all that she needed to say. 'Sorry, son.' My dad put his hands up. 'You do what you feel comfortable with.'

I was looking forward to the gig even more now; nervous, of course, but there was an excited feeling as well. If I'd enough riding on it already, knowing that my dad was going to be watching was further motivation to push myself, to give it everything I had.

46

I woke up on the Tuesday morning and went into the Co-op. I was working from 9 a.m. until 1 p.m. When I got home, I was the only one in, so I used to the house phone to call the Stand.

I pretended to be a curious audience member. It wasn't Eva who answered so I didn't have to change my voice too much in order not to sound familiar. 'I was just phoning, just wondering, who are the performers at the club this evening?'

I wanted it to sink in that I was on stage, that I was booked, confirmed, that I was going to try stand-up comedy.

'Jojo Sutherland, Robert Parker, Vaqas Qareshi, Quentin Reynolds, Derek Lightfoot, Kevin Bridges . . .'

She continued and there were about ten people on the bill in total.

I felt goose bumps when she said my name. It was genuine; I was booked in and on the list. I hadn't heard of the other comedians, but I started to imagine what they'd be like. I'd be sitting backstage with them, all us funny guys, together.

Jojo Sutherland, the first name the girl on the phone had mentioned, was 'compering'. I didn't know then what a compere was and presumed she'd said 'comparing', implying there was a judge involved. I figured if I got there early enough, I could ask all these questions.

I now had my original piece of paper with 'Hello' and 'Good evening' written down and other scrap bits with notes, stuff I'd noticed in the town and on the bus.

I'd written down a short 'routine' about always getting an erection for no reason on a bus, and the rush to get it to go down before your stop. I also had a bit about chocolate liqueurs and how bad they tasted – why do two good things, chocolate and alcohol, combined, make a bad thing?

I'd top it off by saying: 'Two wrongs don't make a right, but two rights make a wrong. My favourite pastimes are masturbation and gambling, but you won't see me standing in William Hill, tearing the head off it.'

I had a couple of things about being seventeen, being old enough to have sex but too young to watch a porno. And a routine about the Glasgow tour bus, complete with a mock, hypothetical commentary: 'On your left, you'll see a vandalized phone box . . .'

The show started at 8.30 p.m. I didn't know what time I was due onstage but I wanted to be there for at least 8 p.m. I didn't know what to wear on stage. Wearing tracksuit bottoms would have got me off to a terrible start and I had to try to look older. So I decided on jeans, my only pair, from D2, the shop in Clydebank that sold jeans big enough to fit my waist.

I didn't want to wear trainers. The trainers I had were old, faded and horrible-looking but I had a pair of Timberland boots I'd got for Christmas a couple of years before, so I gave them a rare outing.

I had a white Puma T-shirt that said, in red letters, 'Bedford Track'. I don't know why I picked that – maybe because it was loose and baggy enough that I could relax wearing it, not worrying about it being too tight and highlighting my size. I put on my watch and a silver chain that I used to wear, and there I was, looking and feeling sharp, a stand-up comedian.

We drove up and the car was pretty quiet. My dad was

talking and still offering his advice, but he quickly sensed that I needed some time to get my thoughts together. He'd snap a few times – 'See these arseholes that don't indicate at red lights when they're turning right?' – but quickly apologize: 'Sorry, son, just ignore me.'

I was deadly serious about getting this right. It wasn't like going up for a shot on the karaoke. It was much deeper than that to me. I'd wasted my academic potential at school; I was headed for a dead-end job once college finished. I doubted I would graduate, and I didn't know how I'd function in an office environment. I'd almost been sacked from a part-time job at TK Maxx, for being an idiot, for playing to the crowd.

Tonight, I could turn all that into something constructive. I'd thought about nothing else for the past eight days, since Eva's phone call, and even before that, throughout the course of Frank Skinner's book. But it was only a fantasy, a product of late-night, left-field thought, reading a book with a little voice somewhere in your head encouraging you to go for it, that it could be you.

Now, it was me, and regardless of how this first gig went, I'd have tried it.

I didn't want to be the pub funny guy, the guy who should have been a stand-up comedian but who 'got too nervous standing up in front of a crowd'.

I knew all of those guys, the guys who 'could have been' professional footballers but they 'didn't have the right attitude', they 'liked a drink too much', deciding, instead, to pursue their calling as the local bore.

I was trying not to think about it being a disaster. I was only thinking positively. It was going to be over soon; it would last five minutes, and I'd be free, one way or another.

I felt sick in the car, my legs were shaking, and I just

Photographic evidence of one of my 'holiday romances',
to quash any VL rumours.

On holiday sometime in 1998. My dad ready to shout
camera-operating instructions at my mum.

My stage debut in 1998. Playing an out-of-work
school leaver, a role I'd soon get used to.

With John, my cousins Paul, Stephen, Mark and Gary, and
Paul's future wife, Ashley, at my mum and dad's twenty-fifth
wedding anniversary in 1999.

Me and my dad on holiday, with a few photographs
left to take on our disposable camera.

Me, my dad and John, looking Scottish as fuck,
at Paul and Ashley's wedding in 2002.

My first ever photo shoot, for the *Sunday Herald*'s
'People to emerge in 2005' special feature.

My autumn/winter collection catalogue pose. A 2005 promotional
photo for the Stand comedy club's website.

'You guys have been great, good night!'
On stage at the Stand comedy club.

My twenty-first birthday. My Auntie Maureen and
my friends George and Jamie.

Tony's birthday night out,
October 2013.

My mum and dad finally making it to the Orient Express,
even if the train left without my dad, at Innsbruck station in Austria.
An arsehole but a good arsehole, May 2013.

couldn't concentrate on anything. I was picturing myself, speaking, saying my jokes and an audience laughing.

The feeling of nervousness was getting pretty awful and all that kept me going was the fact that I just had to do it now. It was like I was punishing myself for everything at school, everything I'd done for a laugh before.

I realize now, at twenty-seven years old, ten years later, that I was being extremely harsh on myself, but that's always been what has driven me on.

I write this in a café in Sydney. Tonight I play two shows at the Enmore Theatre, so over three thousand people will watch me perform, in a country I never imagined I'd get to see.

I didn't know, on the drive up to the Stand, on Woodlands Road in Glasgow, in my dad's Peugeot 106 mobility car, that life was about to become so exciting. I couldn't have begun to imagine all the places I was going to travel to, all the people I was going to meet, and the education, in stand-up comedy, and in life, that I was signing up for.

I was about to learn a trade, an unpredictable, frightening and rewarding trade, one with no set answers and no set way of doing anything, one that is wide open to any sort of interpretation.

47

We found the Stand, no problem: we drove along Great Western Road, the same route that the 59 bus would take, and then we turned right, down past a few cafés and the Shish Mahal Indian restaurant. 'They got a good write-up in the paper,' my dad said, nodding towards the glass windows, again apologizing for distracting me.

He didn't need to apologize, and I was grateful that he was trying to keep my mind off the gig.

The restaurant was packed, full of couples and groups of friends, catching up, laughing and relaxing.

If I'd just shut the fuck up, kept my head down and worked, that could have been me, living a life of contentment, doing normal stuff, but instead I'm driving past, feeling ill, petrified, like I'm on death row.

The thought of eating Indian food almost made me retch. I loved Indian food but not right now.

I hadn't eaten since an omelette my dad had made me in the afternoon, after my Co-op shift, and no matter how good the write-up in the paper had been, I couldn't even imagine being able to eat a poppadom without spewing everywhere.

We couldn't find anywhere to park. My dad managed to keep calm and we parked down the hill, behind the Shish Mahal, opposite the entrance to Kelvin Bridge subway. 'There, your name up in lights already!' My dad pointed at the neon sign above the station entrance, a wee joke, his attempt at relaxing me. It didn't work, but it was appreciated.

He asked me if I was okay. 'No one is forcing you to do

this, you know? There's no shame in turning back now. I'll go in and explain to them, if you want,' he reassured me, as we got out of the car.

It was tempting, really tempting, and I was so close to breaking down in tears, agreeing, and saying sorry, like I'd let him down.

But if I bailed now, I'd only be letting myself down.

I remembered my dad complimenting me a couple of weeks earlier. He'd told me I looked smart, in my white shirt and black trousers, my Co-op uniform. He said that he was proud to see me out working.

I had nothing to prove to him; he was behind me whatever I did.

I could go on to be the best fucking shelf stacker the Co-op had ever seen and he'd be standing there, watching, shouting, 'That's my boy!' as I was bursting open crates of baked beans and tinned soup, ripping the plastic off with my bare hands and firing them up on the shelves, screaming at the guys unloading the delivery lorry to keep them coming.

I'd maybe even make it to the tills, scanning every bar code on the machine at the first time, every time, with no hesitation.

I had built things up in my head so much that my emotions were all over the place. I had to get in there, get backstage and begin to prepare, to focus on my jokes rather than on my nerves.

The Stand is in the basement of an old trade union building, with only a small wooden sign, attached to a lamp, to confirm we'd arrived at our destination.

We walked down the stairs. There was no queue, really, just a few students handing over their £2 and walking in, taking each other's drinks orders, going to the bathrooms, looking at the posters of upcoming shows.

I said my name to the girl at the ticket desk, who ticked it off on the running order behind her, and I looked up at my stage time. I was due on at 9.25 p.m., shortly after the first break.

My dad paid his £2 and we walked on through; there was a bar on the left and the curtain for the dressing room on the right.

I didn't want to just barge in but I was worried that people would see how lost and terrified I looked and then see me on stage. How could they laugh at this distressed-looking figure?

'Look, it's him, the nervous-looking guy who didn't know where he was going,' I'd imagine them shouting.

I felt my heart bursting; I didn't exercise a lot so my heart must have been wondering what was going on.

At that moment, I'd never respected comedians so much in my life, any comedians, from Frank Skinner to the guys I was about to go in and introduce myself to. How do they go through this? Or why, why did they go through this? Because they had to, like me: what else could I do?

Maybe I was a bit mad; I certainly had my emotional hang-ups, as I made clear all through nursery and primary school.

At high school I'd figured out how to deal with them, to hide them, but they'd never gone away, so I was still the exact same person, and now here I was, in this dimly lit, hidden-away basement off Great Western Road. The 59 bus from Hardgate didn't turn down past here; it kept going, the same route, every single day, as though this place didn't exist.

I'd never heard of the Stand. In fact, I never knew Glasgow had comedy clubs; nobody ever mentioned that they'd been at one. People had been to comedy shows, of course, but only to see people from the TV, in theatres, not at 'comedy clubs'.

I'd never heard anyone talk about the Stand; it could be my own 'fight club'. I wouldn't talk about it, and it was my first night, therefore I'd have to fight.

My dad went to the bar and ordered a diet Irn Bru for himself and an Irn Bru for me, before saying, 'Hold on,' to the girl at the bar and asking if I'd like a pint instead, in a 'don't tell your mum' kind of way. A pint would help calm me down, was his logic, I presumed.

I didn't want a pint – I had to think clearly – and I could have a pint afterwards, if the offer still stood.

I was hoping to find him a seat so he wouldn't have to stand for a couple of hours. I knew his joints had been aching and even the uphill walk from where we'd parked was maybe a lot. I felt selfish, I hadn't considered slowing down a little, and he'd forced himself to keep up, feeling selfish if he'd held me back.

I asked the girl at the bar if it was okay for me to walk through the curtain and sit backstage. She asked if I was performing, so I told her I was and she laughed as if, well, obviously.

I felt like a dick, asking a stupid question, but I didn't care. I just wanted to be away, in my own company, or at least in the company of other people who were nervous.

I walked backstage, just as the manager of the club, Paul, or Docsy, as I'd soon know him, was making his way from the dressing room out to the bar.

He looked at me as if I'd arrived to rob the place, or like I was only popping in briefly to sell a few pills and a bit of weed, collect some cash and then head back out, into a Vauxhall Corsa, dance music kicking in as soon as the engine started, wheels spinning back down towards Clydebank.

I'd thought I looked like a comedian when I was getting ready in the house, but once I saw what comedians looked like, I had to concede that I still looked like a bam.

I understood Docsy's wary expression when he'd seen me. 'Are you Kevin?' he asked.

I shook his hand and introduced myself properly.

'You're seventeen, is that right?'

I told him I was and that I'd spoken to Eva at the Edinburgh office and she'd said it was okay as long as I brought an adult with me.

I was panicking, hoping everything was still going ahead. 'My dad's out there,' I said, ready to go and find him.

'No, it's no problem, and the bar staff have been briefed not to serve you any alcohol. The red light above you will flash when you've done four minutes and that's your cue to finish.'

I nodded and said, 'That's fine, no problem,' as politely as I could, stopping short of calling him sir.

I felt incredibly out of place and I just didn't want them to think I was a dick.

I was now feeling under even more pressure. I had a warm glow in my head and my face felt like I'd been blushing, but it was as pale as it had ever been.

I entered the green room, and it amazed me how tiny it was: two small sofas, some paintings on the wall, loads of graffiti and a small fridge with cans of soft drinks.

Everyone was civil and welcoming; a woman introduced herself as Jojo Sutherland, a name I recognized from when the line-up was read to me on the phone.

I didn't tell her but I'd imagined Jojo being a guy's name, a nutcase guy, a nutcase who'd been in and out of prison, the top nutcase that nutcases went to when they needed an issue resolved.

She was friendly and smiley and she didn't look like she would throw someone into the River Clyde for a nominal fee, as I'd pictured a 'Jojo' to look.

She couldn't believe my age and she seemed excited that it was my first ever gig.

I felt a bit more relaxed now and asked Jojo if she was 'comparing'.

She laughed and said, 'Yeah, comparing you to him', and pointed at one of the other comics, who laughed. Jojo laughed. I looked at the guy and back at her. I didn't get it. Was I up against this guy? I didn't understand the format.

She could tell I didn't get the joke but didn't want to embarrass me. 'I'm the compere. I'll be on in between all of you guys, introducing you,' she explained, before quickly changing the subject: 'Do you want me to mention that it's your first gig? Sometimes that helps.'

I was on the bill, and it didn't matter about experience. I'd signed up and the only thing I wanted guaranteed from the night was an honest reaction.

I asked her not to mention that it was my first gig and that I didn't want sympathy laughs or anyone in the audience feeling nervous on my behalf.

Jojo laughed, and told me that was wise and that she respected my attitude.

I felt like a dick again, like I'd come across as too self-assured, or something.

I backtracked and said that I didn't know what was best.

She laughed again, told me to relax and said that she'd let the audience know at the end that it was my first gig; that way if it didn't go well I'd have an excuse and if it went well it would be even more impressive.

That was fine by me.

Anyway, it wasn't about what she said, it was about what I said.

Everyone began cracking jokes and talking about other

gigs they'd done, and other comedians. They'd bring me into the conversation by talking about their own first gigs.

A couple of them sat and told stories backstage that they then repeated, word for word, onstage. That was strange, but no one was thinking straight; it wasn't a natural situation.

It was impressive how they'd managed to force their material into a conversation. I wouldn't know how to do that as smoothly; there would be nothing subtle about the nervous, seventeen-year-old new guy sitting in the dressing room and casually remarking that he 'got a hard-on on the bus again today' before explaining and demonstrating his struggle to conceal the offending object as his stop approached.

I found it hard to sit still, then the show started and I didn't know if it was frowned upon to go out to the bar and watch.

I heard laughter and applause every five minutes as the acts were walking on and walking off.

I thought of my dad and hoped he'd get a laugh from these dudes, even if not from me.

The atmosphere in the place was great.

There was an excitement, an expectant silence at the beginning of every comedian's set.

The crowd seemed to have a nervous energy as well as the comics.

It wasn't like watching a singer or a band, when you can get up and dance, sit and speak, sing along or do nothing, just sit in silence, knowing that it won't affect the performer.

Watching stand-up comedy was totally different: you had to listen, you had to buy into the person on the stage. They had to connect with you and you had to relax and trust them.

The comics who showed signs of nerves would make the

audience uncomfortable, I noticed. As soon as the person on stage showed any sort of vulnerability, unless it was part of the act, it was done.

The audience definitely shared my admiration for anyone who'd give it a try, but once the night got going it was a laugh they wanted, amateur night or not.

Watching someone die on their arse was intriguing in its own way. It's what everyone, myself included, automatically fears when they picture themselves doing stand-up, imagining how awful that feeling must be.

Even if I didn't get up on the stage, if I was the work-experience guy who wasn't quite trusted to do the job unsupervised and was left there to watch and observe, I'd feel like I'd learned a lot more about stand-up comedy in this one evening than any books or any online blogs could teach me.

After the show started, listening to everything going on took my mind off my own set, but the fear would hit me every couple of minutes, reminding me that I should be shitting myself.

I had to keep my mind off it for now, knowing that, if my heart had kept racing the way it had been when I'd walked into the place, then I'd have nothing left in me by the time 9.25 p.m. came.

I'd be burned out, shattered, and it'd be a shambles. I'd faint and wake up backstage, my dad standing over me, waiting for me to come round so he could take me home, saying, 'You tried your best, pal.'

I looked over my notes every now and again and tried to ask questions. I was aware of not distracting anyone from their own preparations and I knew how compulsive I could be once I took an interest in something; stand-up comedy was my new interest but it was becoming an obsession.

I asked one of the other comics how many people he reckoned were in the audience.

He peeked out through the curtain, beyond which was the walkway to the stage, and took a good look around, then, whilst still facing through the curtain, as though he'd noticed something else that required further analysis, he told me, 'There's about a hundred out there, quite good for a Tuesday.'

I asked about the busy nights and how many would be in; he told me he'd never done a weekend but that Jojo had just been booked to do her first weekend sets.

The weekends were for professionals only: twenty-minute sets with one, shorter, ten-minute spot allocated to someone working their way up.

He'd been performing for three years and reckoned he wasn't far off landing a ten-minute weekend spot; tonight going well would strengthen his case, he told me.

I wished him luck and genuinely hoped he got it. He was friendly and three years seemed such a long time.

The first interval arrived.

I wanted to go out and speak to my dad, to see if he was okay and to see how it had been going, from an audience's perspective, but I still felt too nervous to be seen by the rest of the crowd.

Backstage was louder and there was alcohol now. The comics who'd already been on would be sitting with their pints and talking more naturally, talking about the crowd and dissecting their own performance and each other's.

My support network had shrunk in numbers with only three people and me left, nervous, and still waiting to go on.

After us there was the headliner, who hadn't arrived yet; he could do what he wanted, I figured. Beside everyone else's name it said five minutes, but the headliner was down for twenty minutes. It amazed me: twenty minutes of material, how did he remember it all?

I moved from the green room down into the little cheap-looking, wooden-board tunnel that divided the performers' area from the audience.

I imagined how many people had stood there, the point of no return, and I imagined how they felt.

It was where I'd wanted to stand the whole night but I felt I'd get in the way; it seemed a great place to take it all in, though, because you could hear the comics and the audience and still be hidden away.

It was where Jojo stood when the comics were onstage.

She'd stand close to the curtain that led to the stage, accompanied, in total silence, by the comic who was on next, the comic pacing up and down, looking at notes, drinking water, doing breathing exercises, with Jojo leaving them to it, waiting to hear the opening few seconds of Jackie Wilson's 'Reet Petite' being played by the sound tech, her cue to go back on, ask the audience to applaud for the act they'd just seen and introduce the next one.

I'd done well so far to block out the reality that I was going up on the stage. The act before me had just started; he was getting laughs and it sounded like there was an even better atmosphere now than during the first section. I can't remember anything he said. I don't think I took any of it in.

Everyone had stand-up routines that sounded slick and polished and I was just going on to say a few funny things.

I'd thought of saying, 'I'm only seventeen and I just got sold a pint at that bar, so get it up ye!' as my opening line. It just popped into my head and it was funnier than 'Good evening' and it would lead me into my jokes about being seventeen years old. I had that. It didn't help me relax but it made me desperate to get on there to say it and get going. Five minutes and it would be over.

The act before me finished. Jojo opened the curtain and walked back on to the stage. She repeated his name and they applauded again. The guy took a sip of his glass of water, looking exhausted; it had been only five minutes but he was sweating and looked really rattled.

He told me, 'Have a good set.' I liked how he said 'set', implying I had a set, implying I was one of them.

I took another look at all the graffiti on the wooden board that marked the border between audience and performer, just as Jojo was beginning to introduce me: 'Now, ladies and gentlemen, we're going to keep it moving and bring on our next act . . .'

48

My heart felt like it was going to burst through my T-shirt and my legs were shaking, as they'd done when I'd been sitting at an awkward angle on the edge of my chair in school. I held out my hand; it was still.

I wouldn't call anything in those thirty seconds a relief but while I knew I could hide the shaking legs, if my hands were to make a scene, I'd look pathetic.

I'd look like a seventeen-year-old who'd never done this before but who thought, because he'd been funny at school and with his pals, that he could do it.

I noticed a drawing of Homer Simpson that someone had doodled. It was impressive how accurate it was, and it made me think of Homer, which made me smile.

Five minutes and this is over.

I needed to make this worth it. 'Think of Homer,' I kept repeating to myself, smiling, trying to keep at least calm enough to get to the microphone.

'. . . and please welcome Kevin Bridges.'

I was out of the traps and off before it had even hit me how surreal it was to hear my name announced over a PA system, followed by the sound of a crowd applauding.

I couldn't see anything. I could only make out enough to get up on to the stage.

I took the microphone out; everyone else removed the microphone and then lifted the stand out of their way. I'd made a note to do this but I'd forgotten, being too preoccupied with getting my opening line out.

'*It's good to be here,*' I said, from nowhere, no good evening or hello. '*I'm only seventeen and I just got sold a pint at that bar, so get it up ye.*'

The audience burst into a huge laugh, like a real fucking belly laugh. It surprised me how loud it was, like I'd really said something funny.

I quickly followed it up with the 'get it up ye' gesture, left hand across the bicep of the right arm. It was a thing myself and a boy from my college class, Ryan, used to do to each other every morning; we'd laugh at how universally offensive it was but how it made no sense, and wonder where it originated.

The crowd kept on laughing. It didn't feel like a separate laugh, they'd continued, their laughter rolling on from my first line.

I was almost panicking but every note I'd taken down, every little thought I'd had kept coming to me, racing down from my head but managing to form an orderly queue to get out of my mouth.

I could have easily melted and mumbled everything out, an incoherent re-mix of every note I'd taken, rather than a routine.

I suddenly thought about what to do with my other hand, my left hand, when I was speaking.

I panicked that I was even thinking about that and quickly placed it across my chest and into my right armpit. It must have looked awkward and a little unorthodox but I felt I could self-destruct at any second, the slightest thing could throw me and I had to keep pushing through, to keep this momentum going

'*Seventeen, it's a shite age.*' The audience's laugh grew louder again and I was learning to pause, to let them laugh, to think whilst they laughed.

'*I'm old enough to legally have sex but I'm too young to legally watch porn.*' Another laugh. I remember feeling relieved that I'd decided to add in 'legally'. I don't know why, but it sounded better and the joke worked: my first idea for a 'routine'.

'*You can maybe tell by looking at me that I don't get my fair share of the action,*' I added, before pausing again and looking down at myself. The crowd seemed to really laugh and I made eye contact with the very front table, where a guy was laughing uncontrollably.

I couldn't fucking believe this was happening. I started laughing myself, then the crowd laughed again, even louder. '*Not only can I not get any, I'm not even allowed a wee swatch at the topless darts.*'

The crowd broke into applause.

The applause really threw me. Suddenly it was like I was determined to sabotage myself, but I knew I couldn't let this go. I didn't want to even think about my dad, sitting there watching. My mind then went totally blank as the reality of what was going on finally caught up on me. I looked around, back at the guy who'd been laughing; he was smiling and leaning in for the next line, looking like he'd have laughed at anything I said next, but I couldn't think of anything to say.

It seemed like ages.

'*If you could just keep laughing at that one until I think of something else.*' This made the crowd erupt again, at the audacity of it all. They knew it was amateur night but that was a trick shot, something a professional would maybe say, knowing full well they had control over the crowd and knowing full well what they'd say next.

I didn't feel in control but I didn't have a clue where it came from, it was instinct almost; the adrenalin and the warmth from the crowd had bailed me out.

I started my Glasgow tour-bus joke. The first laugh had

stopped and I'd reset. I didn't know how long I'd been speaking for but I hadn't noticed any light flashing, in fact I didn't know what light I was to look out for, so I figured I'd do my tour-bus idea and then finish, hoping it had been five minutes.

'*I can understand Edinburgh having a tour bus, they have the castle and the Scott Monument.*' I didn't know what the Scott Monument was. I'd asked my dad a few days before for some examples of Edinburgh landmark attractions, other than the castle, and he'd rattled off a few, not asking why I was asking, but now he'd know.

'*What have we got, though? On your left, you'll see a vandalized phone box, and if you look to your right, you'll see a famous Glasgow tradition, the midday rammy! Imagine trying to explain to a bus full of tourists why there appears to be a youth chasing a man with a golf club, shouting, "Mon then!"* '

The crowd applauded again, the light flashed. I had been on for four minutes.

I finished by saying I was getting a lift home, because I kept getting an unwanted erection on the bus, which led me into my routine about walking down from the back of the bus, like a duck, with a hard-on tucked between my legs: '*I always have to tuck it and duck it.*'

I mimicked the walk, crouched over with my arse sticking out.

This made the crowd applaud, louder than the first few times.

'*Ladies and gentlemen –*' I started to wrap up. I'd never said 'Ladies and gentlemen' before, but it was showbiz, in the same mould as 'Good evening', and I was part of it now.

'*Thanks for listening, good night.*'

A roar went up from the crowd. I didn't feel like I was inside my own body; I was looking down on myself. The five minutes had gone so quickly, and it was only now that I could take it all in.

The applause made every hair on my neck stand up. I'd goose bumps, my legs and hands were shaking now, more than before.

I'd done it, I'd fucking done it. Now it was sinking in.

Jojo re-appeared from the curtain, looking taken aback. 'Wow!' she said as she passed me, to get back on the stage.

I went to walk through the curtain and she shouted at me: 'Don't go anywhere, stay there.'

'Ladies and gentlemen, let's hear it again for Kevin Bridges.'

The crowd hadn't stopped applauding since I'd finished but there was a surge in the applause, with another, louder, roar.

I didn't know what to do, all my confidence had left me and I felt embarrassed at the attention. I was a superstar for that five minutes but now I was back to the seventeen-year-old Co-op worker, back to being the guy who didn't know what a compere was, the only performer who'd asked the staff if it was okay to go backstage.

I just stood there, my hands pulling at my T-shirt, feeling and probably looking uncomfortable and awkward. I gave a little wave and walked towards the curtain, looking back at Jojo to make sure it was okay to go.

'That was Kevin's first ever gig, his FIRST EVER gig. I don't think it will be his last, so remember the name,' she continued as I arrived backstage.

The entire dressing room applauded me when I walked back in.

I didn't know where it had all come from. I was shaking still but I could relax, for the first time in eight days, for the first time since sitting in my bedroom playing the PlayStation and eating a Greggs with Jamie.

I immediately thought of my dad. I wanted to go out and see him but there was another act about to go on stage and I didn't want to be disrespectful and just disappear.

It was his turn now and I knew what he was going through.

I told him, 'Have a good set.'

He finished the section and Jojo announced the final interval before the headliner.

I didn't know what happened next; should I speak to someone before I left? I asked the other acts.

Some of them began to volunteer phone numbers for people to contact, about other gigs.

I began to write them all down. 'Phone Billy Bonkers, he runs Saturday nights at the State Bar, and tell him that I said to call,' I remember one of the guys, known as Vaq, telling me.

I thanked them all. Then I took a can of Irn Bru; I hadn't felt it was my place to help myself before the show but I'd earned it now, I thought.

I was beginning to come back to feeling normal, relieved but thoroughly fulfilled. I'd proved a point to myself.

I got out and my dad had been standing at the back of the club, near the door, talking to a younger couple. He introduced me and they told me well done, saying how they couldn't believe it was my first gig.

They'd been sitting beside my dad the whole night and before I was on he'd told them his son was performing, which was a gamble and could have been pretty awkward if it hadn't gone well.

My dad looked delighted. I suggested we make a move. I would have liked to stay, to watch the headliner, but I wanted to hear what my dad had to say.

We were in the corridor, about to leave the building, when I saw a poster for the Glasgow International Comedy

Festival, with pictures of Jimmy Carr, Jerry Sadowitz and other comedians I'd heard of. The festival was the following month.

I asked one of the staff at the door how I went about performing at the festival. He smiled and told me that it was all booked up, but remarked: 'Maybe one day, if you keep that up.'

As soon as we stepped outside my dad turned and put out his hand. 'Let me just shake your hand.' I laughed, embarrassed, and we shook. 'That was fantastic, fan-fucking-tastic! Let me see your mobile to phone your mum.'

I handed over my phone, he dialled the house and we walked slowly out of the gates, underneath the wooden lit-up sign: 'The Stand Comedy Club'.

I had a look around, taking in the surroundings that I'd raced by on the way in, and I looked at the listings board. 'Tonight: Red Raw, 10 amateur comedians.' It had Jojo's name and the name of the headliner. I smiled and thought that I'd be on the listings board one day.

'Paddy . . .' I heard my dad say. 'Aw, unbelievable, incredible, awesome, hilarious . . .' He went on and on.

I felt like my mum could have listened to him all night. It was great to see my dad this happy and I knew my mum would be ecstastic as well and she'd wait up until we got home, to hear more.

'Aye, I'll maybe even take him for a McDonald's,' my dad said, laughing and turning round to look at me, a reference to all the times he'd taken me somewhere as a child, football training, the cubs, karate, loads of passing hobbies that I hadn't ever lasted at for more than one attempt before giving up.

Tonight had been different, though.

'The best of the whole night, by a mile.'

My dad handed me back my mobile phone and I put it in my pocket, complete with all my new contacts, my comedy contacts.

We got to the car. I knew my dad had to say how good it was but he started to quote some of the lines: 'The midday rammy! I nearly ended myself at that, and the topless darts – how did you come up with that?'

I asked him if he'd actually laughed. I just presumed he was so happy to see other people, strangers, laugh at his son and that he had a feeling of pride, but then he went on, analysing the performance itself: 'And the way you stood, the pausing, you looked so relaxed, ice-cool.'

He told me about how nervous he'd felt the whole night and how much of a relief it was. He said a couple of the acts had struggled and he'd been thinking of how he was going to pick me up if I'd done the same.

I would have never put myself through anything like that again, unless it had gone as well as it had. I had an in, to the world of stand-up comedy. The first gig was done but now I had to do it again. It was a long road, I was well aware of that now, not just from Frank Skinner's book but from everyone I'd spoken to backstage.

Finding my second gig, as soon as I could, was my new priority.

We drove up the hill, away from Kelvin Bridge station and on to Great Western Road, heading back down towards Clydebank.

My dad's voice started to crack a little as he went on remembering something else from the five minutes I'd been onstage. He seemed emotional and I'd never seen that before. I felt emotional as well but I couldn't have us both sitting in the car fucking crying.

'Right, I get it, it went well.' We both laughed, a release of pressure. I changed the subject and mentioned that I hadn't eaten since lunchtime.

We pulled into the McDonald's halfway down the road, my dad announcing it was his treat, and we sat and spoke about comedy. He'd noticed things I wasn't even aware of, the way I'd used words like 'rammy' and 'swatch' – proper slang vocabulary, specific to Glasgow, that had endeared me to the crowd.

I was aware that I'd stood out, that I was raw. I hadn't watched a lot of comedy or been to a comedy course like some of the other new guys.

I hadn't worn a black suit jacket, jeans, Converse trainers and designer glasses. I hadn't read the manual. I wasn't trying to be a stand-up comedian. I was only trying to be funny.

When I go back to open-mic amateur nights now, if I'm warming up for a tour or a TV show, I see how my first gig worked and I can see myself in a lot of new guys.

I didn't know if I had material or if I'd just said things that made me laugh, or maybe that was now classed as my material?

I didn't want to be anyone; I tried to dress a little smarter but that was it. I used words like 'rammy', which means a mass brawl, by the way, and 'swatch', which means a look at.

I didn't do this intentionally, it was just how I spoke with my mates, and the crowd that night took to that, they bought into it and I'll be forever grateful that they did.

It's like playing a game of golf: no one has any empathy for the guy who'll show up wearing all the latest gear, using the top-of-the-range clubs and the best ball to shank his tee shot into the trees, whereas the *Happy Gilmour*-type will win everyone over.

Someone who doesn't look polished but has some funny lines is more endearing to an audience than the person who only wants to emulate their comedy idols, the person who'll hide behind a character. These people will manufacture a personality and, maybe as a defence mechanism, they'll try deliberately to be offensive or surreal: 'Okay, you're not going for the rape jokes, then, so I'll try something safer,' they'll announce, patronizing the audience, conscious of the other comics at the bar, thinking they'll be impressed at someone talking down to the crowd like that.

The open-mic comedy scene can be a pretty grim place, with a lot of fucked-up, deluded people and people who've failed at everything else and who need an escape. It was my new world now.

The following day, I'd been sitting writing some more notes and listening to my dad, who was still going on about the gig. He'd been whistling in the house all day and saying things like 'How's the comedian?' every time he passed me. 'Eh? Chucked out of school for being funny – you'll need to remember that for when you're writing your autobiography!'

My phone rang, at about midday. It was the 0131 number again.

'Hello, Kevin. It's Eva.'

I was a lot more relaxed this time and managed to talk naturally.

'I heard last night went well; we've had some great feedback,' she said. I didn't know what to say. I didn't want to confirm this and sound too desperate, or arrogant even, but I definitely didn't want to deny it.

Eva asked if I was available to come back for another spot the following Tuesday. Of course I was available. My second gig was booked.

Eva recommended I try to find a gig somewhere else in between so I told her about the State Bar and how I had a number for Billy Bonkers. I tried to mumble his surname, in case it was a wind-up, but she said, 'Yeah, that would be good. Give Billy a call.'

I hung up and then saved the Stand's number in my phone.

I phoned Billy. He sounded slightly less professional than Eva. 'Aye, get yourself up here on Saturday. Eight-thirty, we start. Have you got ten minutes?'

I didn't have ten minutes, but then I didn't have five minutes until I needed to. 'Aye, ten minutes is fine. See you on Saturday at eight-thirty, thanks.'

Three gigs in one week – in my first week.

I needed another five minutes now. I had to think of some more funny stuff.

I had a day off college and a day off from the Co-op. It was Wednesday but it felt like a Friday, it felt like every Friday there had ever been.

I left the house, my headphones in, music blaring, and walked down to get the bus to Clydebank Shopping Centre, to go for a walk, to fuck around. I wasn't wasting time, though; I needed ideas, I needed to get out and think. I needed ten minutes.

I didn't care who I met or who'd think I was a waster.

I felt like I'd seen the light, a way out.

I couldn't wait until Saturday.

49

Billy Bonkers Madcap Comedy Club was a long-running and well-known night on the Scottish comedy scene, established downstairs in the State Bar, just off Sauchiehall Street and near the King's Theatre.

Billy compered the shows himself, like a lot of independent promoters, probably to save some money on paying a comic to compere and, more often than not, so that they could get some stage time.

A lot of them didn't get booked anywhere out with their own gigs so this was their big show and they were in charge.

My dad didn't know where the place was and didn't feel comfortable driving in the city centre. He hadn't been feeling all that great during the day, but John volunteered to take me.

I'd happily have gone on my own but I'd admired my dad's in-depth feedback and the things he'd noticed; he'd wanted to go and I think he felt bad that he wasn't feeling totally up to it but I told him it wasn't a problem, as did John.

John had been keen to see me try stand-up after hearing my dad's rave reviews, and he knew the State Bar.

John borrowed my dad's car and we drove up, parked just at the bottom of Sauchiehall Street and began the walk up towards the venue of my second ever gig.

Sauchiehall Street was mobbed, full of people my age going out in the town, excited at the novelty of getting into bars and nightclubs for the first time.

Again, like the folk in the Indian restaurant next to the

Stand, they looked carefree, like they were having the best night of their lives.

I'd had to make excuses all day. I'd had text messages and phone calls from Tony, Jamie, Doc and everyone else, looking to see what the plans were for the night. I was going to my uncle's birthday party.

I knew that if I continued doing three gigs every week, or more, I'd have to be prolific with my excuses.

An uncle's birthday party seemed feasible enough, but I'd have to be more imaginative if the gigs kept coming in. I'd eventually run out of uncles.

I only had two of them.

I'd have to invent some more, but I had experience of creating fictitious characters from out of town, usually girls, from when I'd get a hard time at school and was being called a VL.

I would need alibis for going AWOL at weekends, but this was a problem for later; for now it was one gig at a time, and one excuse at a time.

It was still top secret and only my mum, dad, John and the hundred people in the audience at the Stand during the week knew I was trying stand-up comedy.

It was still my Fight Club, my escape route, and right now I needed to find an extra five minutes of material.

Watching young people pleading with bouncers on Sauchiehall Street helped with that. I'd imagine a seventeen-year-old saying, 'ID? Oh, I think I left that in the car, it must have been when I was dropping off the kids.'

I wanted to run this past John but I was scared he wouldn't laugh and think, 'Is this what I'm in for all night?' I wanted him to hear my material for the first time, live, on the stage, in front of a crowd.

I made a note to add this new bit on to my 'I just got sold a pint at that bar' opener, which I figured I could use for another nine months, until I was eighteen.

We got to the State Bar. The bar itself was an island in the middle of the pub, and it was mobbed and difficult to make out who was in the queue to buy drinks and who had found their spot for the night.

It was noisy and full of smoke.

John went to the bar to get himself a lager tops and a can of Irn Bru for me. I looked around, looking for a stage, looking for a green room, another performer, maybe someone who'd been on at the Stand on the Tuesday. I didn't know then just how many budding stand-ups there were on the Scottish open-mic circuit and how it would be a while before I'd start sharing bills with the same comics again.

John handed me my can of Irn Bru and as we began to walk back out of the door I asked him where he was going, and he pointed at a 'Comedy Club Downstairs' sign.

I was relieved. Upstairs didn't look like it would be ideal for a comedy gig, but, still, I'd go on to perform in worse environments, and whilst it wasn't the Stand I'd have got up and tried to make the most of it, taking any opportunity to perform, riding on the euphoria of Tuesday night.

Downstairs was empty. We opened the door and a voice from behind a speaker said, 'The doors aren't open yet.'

'I'm one of the performers. I'm looking for Billy,' I said.

'I'm Billy, are you Kevin?' He stood up and walked over, we shook hands and he asked if I'd help him lift another speaker from across the room.

John volunteered to help out as well but Billy told him it was fine and to take a seat. John wasn't performing so why should he have to help set up, seemed to be Billy's thinking. We were nowhere near the level where we could expect someone else to do all this; you had to work for the right to get your ten minutes of stage time.

I figured the experienced acts hadn't arrived yet, realizing that the 8.30 p.m. start time was ambitious. The doors were to open at 8.00, and it was 8.15 before we'd finished setting up. I stood talking to Billy, whilst John was at the bar, talking to the Irish barman.

It was just the four of us in the basement of the pub.

We'd set up the speakers and tested them out, with Billy performing some material for the sound-check. I'd laughed and he kept going, like he was perfectly comfortable performing to just me, John and the barman.

I hadn't known what to do so I gave a thumbs-up, but of course I could hear him. I was only five yards away. The room was tiny and I didn't think a microphone and speakers were even required.

Maybe they weren't there for amplification purposes and more to create the illusion of a performance.

Without a microphone we'd just be guys talking in the corner of a pub.

When the basement door opened, Billy started going up and down, announcing that the comedy club would be starting in fifteen minutes, and we'd hear music, laughter and conversation from the drinkers upstairs, where the bar was bustling, as it was outside.

The first few people through the door were comedians, Scott Agnew and Neil MacFarlane. They joined John at the bar in the corner, and the barman greeted them both by their first names; they were regulars at the State Bar and didn't seem fazed that John was the only audience member and he was with me.

The show eventually got started just before 9 p.m. About twenty people had been persuaded to come by Billy, who'd been in the bar upstairs, and even out on the street, talking them into a night of stand-up comedy.

I was nervous, really nervous, but it wasn't the same nervous excitement I'd had at the Stand and I didn't think that a reaction anywhere near Tuesday's was possible, but I'd try.

The gig looked like it could go either way, but this seemed more how it should be and I felt I'd got it easy playing a purpose-built comedy club for my first gig.

I quickly realized, for myself and through talking to Scott and Neil, that the Stand was the main venue and everything there was designed by people who knew stand-up. The co-owner, Jane Mackay, who I'd soon meet, was a comedian herself and compered the prestigious weekend shows.

I got the sense Billy loved stand-up. He was an honest guy and definitely seemed a bit eccentric, exactly like you'd imagine a guy who called himself Billy Bonkers to be.

He opened up the show, doing his material whilst smoking what he pretended was a joint. He had curly hair and glasses and looked like the dad from *Honey, I Shrunk the Kids*.

Billy got the crowd settled and managed to form the basis of a comedy show out of what had been a bunch of self-conscious strangers, all unsure of what was going on and wondering how they'd found themselves in a pub basement on a Saturday night.

Neil was on first. He was polished and professional-looking, and was the first comic I'd actually watched live, having stood backstage at the Stand, only listening to the acts.

He didn't look as nervous beforehand and was obviously much more experienced than the guys from Tuesday night. He went through his twenty-minute set, a pint of Guinness in his hand and looking like he'd done it all before. He got the crowd laughing, finished his set and told the audience they had 'a great night ahead of them'.

I was on next. I felt my legs shaking and my heart racing, like on Tuesday, but I felt I had to try to hide it a lot more.

There was no green room to sit in and no graffiti-ed wooden partition to protect me from the audience. I didn't want them to see a terrified-looking teenager, in Timberland boots, jeans and, this time, a navy blue Reebok T-shirt, until I was at the microphone – I needed to get out a funny line before they had any opinion on me, by which time it'd be too late, because I'd be off and flying through my material.

I was conscious of how nervous I was feeling, and the audience, seeing where Billy had been standing and where Neil had walked to the microphone from and returned to, had figured out that we were the performers.

I quickly crouched down behind the bar, looked over my notes and put them back in my pocket, along with a bookie's pen.

I went through my set in my head again, making sure I knew it all.

I didn't obsess on trying to have it word for word, but as long as I knew how to get to the first laugh and what came next, I would build towards the next one.

The laughs were my checkpoints.

I'd get to them all successfully and I'd finish when it felt like I'd done ten minutes. I figured I wouldn't be caught up in the moment at this gig and I wouldn't be able to ride the adrenalin; it was a much smaller, quieter crowd and it wasn't billed as an amateur comedy night so there was a little more expectation.

Billy introduced me as making my State Bar debut and how I was 'quite new' to the comedy circuit. He didn't know it was only my second gig or that I was seventeen.

I opened up with my line about being served at the bar and the crowd laughed, but not for as long as the crowd had laughed on Tuesday. I didn't feel confident enough to do the 'get it up you' gesture so I quickly added in the bits I'd thought of on the way to the gig, about the underage drinkers arguing with the bouncers.

This kicked my set into life. The audience laughed and I carried it all the way through my 'Seventeen, it's a shite age' routine.

The laughs weren't as loud as they had been on Tuesday but I could see everyone's faces – there weren't any stage lights like there had been at the Stand – and they were all looking at me, laughing and appreciative, waiting for the next line.

I didn't have any mental blocks and the lack of atmosphere meant I didn't get too carried away. My heart was still racing but I was taking my time and thinking about what I was saying.

Again, I'd look for people who were laughing the most and laugh at them laughing.

I moved on to my Glasgow tour-bus routine and the audience continued to laugh; they didn't break into applause but I felt like the set was building and I was climbing through the gears and racing towards the checkpoints.

I had an idea during the week to use my line about 'tucking it and ducking it' in a situation where I'd been woken up by my mum shouting at me to come to the phone, as it was one of my pals to see what my plans were for the day.

This happened nearly every weekend and I began to really describe the situation.

' *"Kevin! Kevin! It's the phone for you," my mum's shouting. I'm up, but I'm not the only one that's up.'*

I nodded downwards and the audience laughed. I was in, they knew where I was going, and it was up to me to paint the picture.

'*I look down from the top of the stairs, my mum's standing there, she's shouting, "Would you hurry up, I'm going to burn the breakfast?" You see, my mum thinks she needs to hold the phone until I get there, rather than place the phone on the wee table that's purposely designed to hold the phone. I'm getting myself into a frenzy. I can't walk down with this . . . What am I going to do? "Kevin!" My mum's getting louder and now the smoke alarm is going off. I have no option other than to tuck it and duck it.*'

The audience were really laughing now. They'd bought into the imagery and the laughs were rolling into each other rather than being separate and resetting at the end of every punchline.

This encouraged me on and I really got into the walk. I went off to the right of the room, beside one speaker, then walked back across to the left speaker.

'*By this point the next-door neighbour's at the door, to see if the house is on fire. My mum is there; my dad is there as well now and he's not doing anything to calm the situation: "Patricia, that cooker's broken," and my mum's snapping: "It's not broken, it's just needing fixed."*'

I'd then look serious, like I was trying to make sense of that sentence from my mum. '*"It's not broken, it's just needing fixed"?*'

The crowd was now laughing like the crowd on Tuesday.

I could see a few people throwing themselves back into their seats and turning to each other, nodding in recognition, as though their mums said things like that as well.

It felt good that it was something they could relate to and, again, I was laughing watching them laughing.

'*I arrive at the phone, bent over, my hard-on tucked and my arse ducked, and it's just one of my pals, after all of this. The smoke alarm has stopped, the smoke is clearing and the telephone conversation goes:*
'*"What you doing today?"*

' "Don't know, what you doing today?"
' "Don't know."
' "Cool."
' "Cool, see you later." '

The audience broke into applause and it felt like a nice point to end it. I wasn't sure if it was ten minutes but it seemed much longer than Tuesday night's set. I looked over to the corner and saw Billy smiling and clapping his hands along with the crowd.

He looked ready to come back on. I thanked the audience and walked off. The applause was warm and I could tell the crowd had appreciated my short set. It wasn't as rapturous a reception as the first gig but I'd dug in, I'd worked hard and listened to what I was saying. I was raw and confident but, more importantly, I'd developed my material and I knew the jokes were getting laughs on their own merit. When I'd settled down after Tuesday night and my focus had turned fully to emulating it, I'd had self-doubts and a feeling that maybe I'd fluked that first gig, that everything had simply come together, that I'd got the perfect spot and I'd caught the crowd at a good time.

I'd done it again now, so that was a relief.

Plus, John was there and he seemed taken aback. John isn't the sort of guy who'd be forthcoming enough to say as much but I could see I'd surprised him and he respected the fact that I'd got up there for a start, and, of course, that I'd made the twenty strangers in the room laugh.

50

I didn't feel out of place. Neil and Scott and Billy himself all complimented me and seemed impressed that it was my second gig and that I was only seventeen.

Billy told me he wouldn't have asked me to do ten minutes if he'd known it was only my second gig, but when I came back he'd happily give me another ten-minute spot.

I asked John if he'd mind if we stayed behind to watch the rest of the show, and he was all for it, even though he was driving and had already finished his lager tops. I think he was as intrigued as me, watching a full comedy show from an insider's perspective.

The open spot on after me was a character act, introduced only as 'Prudence'.

Prudence, like myself, hadn't read the manual about how a comedian should look; he had parts of his hair shaved and the rest of it in clumps, like his last haircut had been against his will but he'd eventually managed to struggle free from the barber.

He came on stage wearing a dressing gown, an oxygen mask and wheeling an intravenous drip.

He hadn't stood with us before the show, in the corner, at the end of the bar.

No one knew him, except Billy, who maybe only knew him as well as he'd known me, before booking him in for a short spot.

It was pretty disturbing and I didn't quite get the point of what he was trying to do. It kind of freaked me out a little, and the audience too.

I looked at Neil and Scott, who were both laughing at my reaction; my face was shocked and I couldn't figure out what was going on, but they were obviously both used to watching these cry-for-help appearances by mentally unstable people on the open-mic comedy circuit and knew that this was my first experience.

I really didn't get it and if I'd looked composed, mature, confident and well above my years on the stage, then, right there, I must have looked like a child, a petrified child watching something I shouldn't.

We were only just off Sauchiehall Street, on a Saturday night, one of the busiest and most vibrant places to be in Glasgow, but I felt like I was in a horror movie.

He spoke about how he'd just escaped from a mental home and it was as if he was too convincing, that maybe this wasn't an act.

Prudence finished and walked back to the cupboard.

He'd exorcized all of the goodwill from the room.

Billy introduced the interval and half of the audience left, escaped, even.

Scott Agnew closed the show. He'd been performing for only a couple of years himself but he went down great and made the most of the ten people left in the room.

Scott was easily nineteen or twenty stone. He had a deep voice and had been standing talking about football with John and me during the break.

It was a surprise to me, and to the audience, when he announced that he was gay and went on to talk pretty graphically about his sex life.

He played up to how no one ever believes him when he tells them he's gay. 'If I start acting camp and mincing about, furniture gets broken' being one of the lines I remember laughing at.

The audience loved it and I loved how honest he was and how he didn't seem to care.

I'd got on with Scott before the show. He was full of encouragement after my set so it was good to see him do so well.

Scott finished his set and then came over, took a massive drink of his pint and got back to talking about comedy with both John and me. He was down to earth and it was actually really funny how straight he was, for a man who'd just been standing yards away talking about homosexual orgies and underground sauna parties he'd been to.

We had much more in common than our stand-up material would suggest, but I figured Scott was from an area similar to Clydebank and he'd maybe got a hard time growing up, on account of his sexuality.

I knew how brutal school had been for the few boys in my class who were a little camp and spoke a little differently from everyone else.

I'd got a hard time for a lot of things but it was stuff I could control, like my weight, and I admired Scott, for representing those guys and going for his dream.

Stand-up was his escape as well. The State Bar was his Fight Club.

He'd go back to his work on Monday and what would get him through was the thought of his next gig.

We were both in this for the same thing: we loved making people laugh and we could both laugh at ourselves.

Scott became my first mate in comedy. We swapped numbers and he told me he'd send me some contact details for other promoters. He repeated again how I had something and how I should keep on at it, keep writing material and perform anywhere and as often as I could.

As we left the State Bar John said he agreed with everything Scott had said, that it'd been great. He wasn't as emotional and effusive in his praise as my dad, but they were two different people, and I knew John was delighted and proud. I thanked him for taking me.

It had been another great night and it was only three days until the next gig.

When we got home my mum and dad were up and wanted to know how it all went.

I left it to John as I felt a like a knob talking about my own gig going well, and he explained that everyone had loved it, the audience, the other comedians and the promoter.

I went to college on Monday and I felt great. I knew I couldn't tell anyone but this made it even more special.

I had the Stand the following night, something to work towards, a break from the mundane and something that I had total control over. No one was telling me how to do it, it was all on me, good or bad.

I'd daydream about it on the bus, I'd be quiet, I'd listen to everyone talk, I'd take notes of small things.

I'd notice signs saying: 'Please give up this seat if required by someone less able than you.' Then I'd imagine a young guy offering his seat to an old guy and pointing at the sign, the old guy taking offence and inviting the young guy to step off the bus for a square go. 'We'll fucking see who's less able, son.' Silly thoughts like that, silly thoughts that could now become material.

I didn't feel destined to be a loser any more or like I was lost. I knew where I was going now. I had a goal.

I wouldn't say the first two gigs were like therapy but it was a release, a release of all this neurosis, and the comedy clubs were somewhere where I could shine.

I didn't even consider a gig going bad now. I had a two out of two hit rate and I was getting the hang of it.

I was thinking only of how to improve on the last show.

The show at the Stand on the Tuesday went great, the best show yet.

I'd managed to combine the skills I'd used to get through a more reserved but polite and supportive audience at the State Bar with the confidence I'd taken from the reception the previous Tuesday.

The audience were no different, although perhaps they were even more receptive, but maybe that's because I went in there not looking just to survive, like I had done the first time, but looking to better the reaction.

I knew what I was capable of and I'd got all the doubts about the first gig being a fluke out of my head after the Saturday at the State Bar.

I went on and got my first laugh and I took the time to enjoy it all. I used my new routine about answering the phone with an erection on a Saturday morning. I'd added in lines and built on all of the other material I'd used the week before.

The audience laughed and clapped like they had done the first week. It felt great and I was getting a bit addicted to the feeling of it all.

I just wanted to get back out and do it again and again.

My dad was there, feeling the same, bursting with encouragement, patting me on the back and deconstructing the whole set again, picking out all the bits that had improved.

The other acts, the compere and even the headliner told me that if that was only my third gig then I was a natural. They'd tell me I was the youngest comic they'd seen and that I had a bright future.

I couldn't believe what had happened, in just one week.

As I was leaving the club, the manager, Docsy, mentioned that there was a journalist in from the *Herald* newspaper, who was writing an article on the modern-day amateur comedy scene in Scotland and wanted to know if he could ask me a few questions.

My dad answered before I even had time to think about it: 'Aye, of course, go on, tell him, son. Where is he? This could be your big break!'

I'd never spoken to a journalist before, I'd never been in the paper, and even the Hugh Grant incident hadn't made the *Clydebank Post*'s 'Crime File'.

This was the *Herald*, the newspaper my dad read, the newspaper I found too difficult to read. It was well respected.

The guy asked me why I was trying stand-up. I didn't know what to say and I stuttered and mumbled my way through an answer.

I was panicking talking to him. I'd been bulletproof on stage but now I was back to feeling as though I was in St Mary's again. It hit me that people would read this article, all my friends, and I'd be busted.

It wasn't my big break. It would finish me.

The journalist sensed how uncomfortable I felt. I asked if he'd change my name and my dad interrupted and said, 'Don't be stupid. We'll deal with all of that. Stop thinking so negatively.'

I could tell the journalist was surprised, used to dealing with people who'd kill to get their name in the paper.

I told him I was from Clydebank and studying at the food technology college in Glasgow and that this had been my third gig.

The following day, my dad woke me up, with the newspaper open at the relevant page.

. . . And seventeen-year-old Kevin Bridges takes to the stage for just the third time in his life, a food technology student from Clydebank, his confidence astonishing and his patter truthful, natural and hilarious.

I read it and burst out laughing. I couldn't believe it was about me. I kept reading my name, again and again. Seeing it in print felt strange but it was nice.

My dad kept reading it out loud and my mum came in behind him. 'Have you seen it?' she was asking, delighted. 'When can I come and see you perform?'

I knew my mum and dad wanted to go and show everyone the article but I asked if they'd keep it quiet. They agreed but let me know how proud they were.

I was due in at the Co-op at 9 a.m., and the first thing I did was hide every copy of the *Herald* underneath the other newspapers and magazines, doing my bit to try to keep this top secret, as though the article had exposed me as a sex offender.

I knew none of my friends would read the *Herald* but someone somewhere along the chain would and it would spread, rapidly.

I finished my shift at the Co-op and when I came home my mum, who knew I'd been worried about everyone in the area finding out I was doing comedy, handed me about twenty copies of the *Herald*; she'd been out working and bought every copy from every shop she'd been in.

51

I told my mum I'd give her the money from my Co-op wages at the end of the month, but she said not to be silly and to pay her back when my first comedy wage came in.

I knew she'd done it partly as a joke but it meant a lot more than that to me and I was grateful. I felt like I had a good team behind me.

My phone hadn't rung all day. I'd been hoping Eva would have phoned, as I didn't have anything else booked in at the Stand. I had this rave review in the paper and my first three gigs had gone great but now I was back to where I'd started. I asked my dad if he thought I should call them but he told me: 'No, they'll call you. Be patient.'

Eva didn't call me. I was panicking.

I phoned Scott and asked for some numbers for gigs, and he told me that a pub called the Vault in Pollokshaws, on the south side of Glasgow, ran a Monday night open-mic comedy club but that it struggled to get an audience.

I didn't care.

I needed some gigs to keep this momentum going.

I phoned the guy, whose name I can't remember, but he was pretty dismissive and sounded fed up speaking to desperate amateur comedians who phoned him every day when he was at his work.

He told me to get to the Vault on Monday for 8 p.m. He didn't ask my name or number, nothing.

I had a gig, though, so that was a relief, even if it wasn't for five days.

I phoned Billy. He told me he'd have me back in a few weeks and that a week was too soon to return to his club. He added that it had gone well and he wanted to see more of me.

I then got on to the Internet, searching for clubs and phoning them up.

Most of the numbers would ring out or wouldn't connect, and the ones that answered didn't know what I was talking about. 'I think there was a comedy night in here a few years ago' was the best I could get.

I spent hours trying to find places. I'd walked past Jongleurs Comedy Club between the bus stop and college, but I couldn't find a number for them other than the box office, who didn't deal with the booking of the performers and didn't know the number for who did.

I typed a letter and printed it off, to post through their door when I was next going to college on my own.

I was disappointed that Eva still hadn't phoned but I decided to listen to my dad's advice and play it cool. I doubted myself, though; maybe last night hadn't gone great, maybe I'd pissed someone off.

I was feeling paranoid.

At college on the Thursday I noticed one of the bar staff from the Stand standing outside, smoking a cigarette.

I didn't know he went to the same college as me.

It was definitely the same guy, with his long, blond dreadlocks and general stoner appearance. He was unmistakable.

I was with Sean and I felt myself break into a sweat.

If he spotted me, he'd talk to me.

Sean would ask how I knew him and I'd have to come clean.

Hiding all of this was becoming stressful.

Eva still hadn't phoned.

I had only one gig booked in.

I was beginning to feel down about it and the excitement was turning to fear: what if this was it?

What if the *Herald* article was the highlight, the pinnacle of it all, and no one had seen it? I'd be reduced to walking the streets of Clydebank, handing out the twenty-odd copies my mum had stashed safely in the house.

'Read all about it! My patter is truthful, natural and hilarious, look, see? That's the *Herald* saying that, a respected paper, none of your shite. Take a copy, read it and pass it on.'

John, again, volunteered to take me to the Vault, although neither of us knew where it was. John hadn't heard of it but we got the address and left the house just before 7 p.m.

The Vault didn't have a backstage area and it didn't even have a separate room for the comedy.

It was a pub and every Monday night someone put a microphone in the corner and anyone could get up and try some stand-up comedy. On other nights of the week the same rules applied for music; they also had a poetry night, a spoken-word night, rap battles and whatever else.

The pub was quiet. I didn't know who to speak to.

Anyone could have been a comedian.

There was no instantly recognizable crowd of misfits huddled together and no one setting up speakers; all of that had already been done.

I figured we'd got there pretty early but 8 p.m. came and still it wasn't any busier. I asked someone at the bar if the comedy show was definitely happening.

She told me that it usually started around 8.30 p.m., and pointed at a guy at the end who, she said, knew more about it than she did.

I felt like leaving there and then, but John had given up his Monday night and we'd driven from Clydebank, we were here now.

A couple of people heard me asking about the comedy show and introduced themselves. They were performing as well.

Eight-thirty came and there were now about six of us there to perform and two couples sat in the bar having a drink.

It was put to a vote. Two of the comics said they didn't fancy it, the rest seemed to be undecided and looking to see what the consensus of opinion was.

I asked John what he thought and he told me to go for it but I just didn't see how it could possibly work.

There were only the comedians and then six other people in the pub, the two couples, who didn't seem to be there for comedy, John and the girl behind the bar.

If I'd had another gig coming up then I definitely would have sacked it and gone home but I had nothing. I hadn't performed for six days.

We were talking to an actress at the bar who'd been performing stand-up for a year. She'd recently won a competition and was signed to an agent, she proudly told the rest of us.

She didn't need to be here, seemed to be her message, and she finished her drink and went home.

The headliner for the night, Raymond Mearns, who'd been performing stand-up for ten years, had now arrived and convinced everyone that the show should go on.

He'd played to even smaller crowds, he told us, and I thought that if I wanted to be a real comedian, a professional, like him, then I couldn't pick and choose my gigs.

If I left, what would I have gained? I'd have gone home and lain in my room, thinking about comedy, worrying about Eva not phoning and about when my next gig would be and about whether this had been it, my week of stand-up comedy.

357

If I stayed, the gig would be difficult but at least I'd have done it.

I'd have done another gig.

'There's going to be a lot of love in the room. We'll all sit up at the front and we'll do this,' Raymond announced, like a coach rallying the team together.

The show started, the compere went up, and before trying to make a joke or starting a routine he began asking the couples to come forward and sit closer to the stage.

I was nervous but it was a defeated sort of nervous, a fear. I'd resigned myself to defeat, like I knew I was going up to take a bullet. I was going to be standing up where the compere was, going through my routines, and it would be my last ever gig.

I wouldn't have the hunger for it now. I'd waited six days, for this, then I had nothing else. It was my sad, farewell appearance.

I was introduced after the first few guys had done their five minutes before placing the mic back into the mic stand and walking off.

The show went exactly how I'd imagined.

'*I'm only seventeen and I just got served a pint at that bar,*' I announced.

I immediately felt like a liar. I knew the girl behind the bar wouldn't have cared and knew it was only for a joke, but I didn't just get served so why was I saying I did?

I began to listen to my head as I carried on with my '*seventeen being a shite age*' routine, '*too old to have sex and too young to watch porn*'. I'd look at everyone, all of the other comedians, and they were staring at me as if thinking: 'Is this the guy who is supposed to be truthful, natural and hilarious? How can a seventeen-year-old be funny, what does a seventeen-year-old know about life? Look at what he's wearing.' I'd find a voice in my head agreeing with them all and turning on me as well.

This is real stand-up comedy. I felt a sweat go down my back and my mouth go dry. I was drifting in and out of concentration. I was managing to say the words that I now knew so well but only occasionally did I arrive back in the room.

'. . . *I'm not even allowed a swatch at the topless darts.*'

I was getting to the laughs, the checkpoints, but there was nothing coming back and it forced me to say things like 'So' and 'Anyway' and 'What else'. I could feel my face freezing into a concerned look. I wasn't making myself laugh either. I started talking to a couple, asking them if they'd seen the Glasgow tour bus, trying to tee myself up to talk about it. They looked at me and said yes. They'd seen how much it meant to me, they'd have loved to laugh, but I was just being brutally unfunny. I was rigid and stressed-looking.

I was talking too fast and I had a voice in my head telling me to get off.

There were no hecklers and no one to tell me to fuck off, which made it worse. This was the worst heckle of all: utter silence.

I could see Raymond looking at me, unsure, and the comics who had been on looked relieved to be watching someone else struggle.

I was their consolation.

The ones who were still to go on also watched, analysing me, concerned at how hard I was making this look, because they were up next.

I finished on a routine about a bunch of guys I'd seen smashing up a bus stop to kill time waiting on their bus and then going mental when the bus refused to stop for them.

' "*There's no bus due for fifteen minutes. What are going to do for fifteen minutes? Someone find me a brick.*" '

It was the first time I'd ever tried it. It got me a couple of chuckles and made one of the couples smile, but it was more that they were acknowledging my endurance than finding what I said funny.

I finished my act. I almost said sorry, but I felt that would have been too harsh. I could have fucked off home, like some of the other comics had done. I felt devastated, humiliated and burned out. I could sense a headache coming on and a horrible sweat, but not a rewarding sweat, not like I'd done something worthwhile. It was cold and fucking awful.

My confidence was shattered. I felt like tomorrow's *Herald* would print a front-page apology for lying to their readers, like word would get back to Eva about this and I'd never be allowed near the Stand again, like even Prudence could have handled the situation better.

I couldn't think of anywhere I wanted to be.

I wanted to see no one and just to block it out.

I sat beside John and he patted my knee and said, 'Hawl,' when he saw how distraught and pale I looked. 'You did your five minutes, but there was nobody here to laugh. Come on.' I appreciated his words but I just couldn't see a positive.

The other guys went up to take their bullet as well.

I don't think anyone had a good time.

Raymond finished the show and I remember laughing. He had loads of routines I could relate to, one about taking glass bottles to the ice-cream van and a story about someone calling him a 'fat junkie' and how much of an oxymoron such an insult was.

The comics laughed, and laughed a lot; he was well known amongst them.

He riffed off the two couples and improvised around them, on the spot. It was excellent to watch.

He totally broke down the performer/audience barrier

and it looked effortless. It was ten years of experience, right there.

I told him well done as I was leaving and he shouted me back. He handed me some notes and talked me through my set.

I wasn't interested, though.

I'd already made up my mind. I'd chucked it.

I didn't want to go through that again.

He was a professional comedian and I was everyone's funny pal.

The first three nights and the *Herald* review were forgotten, dragged to the recycle bin, erased from my memory.

'This is a hard, hard, craft. What I did there tonight, that's ten years of this, playing shit holes, dying, failing and failing and failing again. Learn your trade. It's an apprenticeship.'

I shook his hand and thanked him but I couldn't look him in the eye. We got back in the car and the drive home seemed to take hours, John tried to pick me up but he could tell I needed silence, to gather my thoughts.

I wished I'd never picked up Frank Skinner's book.

What chance did I have in a crowd like that, at my stage, my fourth gig? If I'd nailed that gig, then I'd be a freak, the man who mastered stand-up comedy, at seventeen, after just four gigs.

I wasn't thinking rationally enough to acknowledge this at the time.

I had the day off on Tuesday and I felt low all day. I kept replaying the gig in my head and thinking what a monumental failure it had been.

I went over and over how my voice had changed, my face had contorted, the horrible dry mouth, that ice-cold sweat. The more I thought about it the worse it got.

My dad was convinced that it couldn't have been that bad and John had reassured him it hadn't been.

I just felt like an idiot.

I decided never to think about it again.

I put my notes away, I stopped reading online about stand-up, I stopped phoning clubs and pubs. What was the fucking point if it was just going to be shite gigs like that?

52

On the Wednesday afternoon, my phone rang. It was Eva.

I let it ring out.

She'd left a voicemail but I didn't bother to listen to it. I left my phone at home and went out for a walk, up to the Hardgate shops and into the bookie's.

I put a few quid into the roulette machine and sat around, betting on greyhounds and feeling sorry for myself.

Spending all day in the bookie's was an easy life; if I ran out of money I could just walk around, watching other people playing the roulette machines. I could offer them advice, like the old guys would offer me: 'After two a zero normally comes out, mate.'

I started to snap out of it when I realized how much of a parody of a 'sad clown' I was being.

That was it? One bad gig and I was finished?

I was just as bad as the ones who'd left before the show started, the ones who'd escaped death row.

Were they feeling like shite today? Were they even thinking about the gig?

No.

They'd be somewhere, in their work, at an acting audition, at a Pilates class, in a café, talking about all of the gigs they'd stormed, talking about their agent and their big plans, superstars in their own barbershops.

I got a grip of myself and decided to go home.

I left the bookie's and started walking, and as I began to panic about how I hadn't got back to Eva yet I walked faster, then I broke into a jog. I thought about it, that missed call, that voicemail lying there, ignored. The gigs now offered to someone else and me forgotten. 'Does he think he's too good to get back to us?'

I started to sprint.

I ran across the Goldenhill Park, where I could have been standing smoking dope on Monday night instead, a much easier life. That would have been failure.

At least at the Vault I had a slight chance.

I ran down the grassy banking behind our house, climbed the hedge at our back garden and walked round to the front, in through the door and upstairs to my room. I grabbed my phone and immediately called Eva back. I apologized for the delay and explained that I was at work. I didn't think it would be wise to tell her I'd died on my arse two nights ago and had been sitting in the bookie's dwelling on it.

Eva offered me three gigs.

One, a five-minute spot at the Stand's 'Best of Red Raw' showcase as part of the Glasgow International Comedy festival, one other five-minute spot at another Red Raw, and one, a five-minute spot on a Sunday show, which seemed like a promotion.

She asked if I'd done any other shows and I told her yes, the State Bar and the Vault. 'One victory and one defeat,' I added. She laughed and said that was good going and to get on the phone and find more stage time.

I agreed to the three gigs and it gave me a massive lift. I could think forward again.

I went down to the living room and told my dad. He gave me a big exaggerated cuddle, like I was a five-year-old that'd fallen and skinned his knees.

It made me laugh and I felt like I'd been a bit immature about it all.

'Of course you'll die on your arse, but learn from it and move on,' he said. 'Footballers have bad games, boxers get knocked out, but it's getting back up and going again that makes them.'

I laughed at him and his motivational speech; he laughed at himself and seemed happy just to see me smile again.

I told him about what Raymond Mearns had said. He agreed, and told me to listen to the professionals. I told him about the 'fat junkie' and we both laughed. Comedy could be easy; it was simple things that were so funny and as long as I got my head right and realized that not every gig was going to be smooth, I'd be fine.

'Your patter is truthful, natural and hilarious, your confidence is astonishing, ASTONISHING!' he was shouting as I walked away back to my room, laughing.

Fuck it! I'd failed on Monday night, but so what.

Raymond was right.

This was going to be difficult but what else was I going to do with my life other than get stuck in and at least go down with a fight, because of course I'd fail again.

I'd have even worse deaths than that Monday night at the Vault but I'd have even better gigs than the first three.

I needed mental strength and that would only come through performing.

The shows at the Stand went great. I was yet to have a bad gig in there and it was becoming 'my happy place'.

The 'Best of Red Raw' showcase had sold out and the owner of the club, Tommy, was there and watched me for the first time.

He told me to 'keep at it' and that I had 'incredible potential' but I needed to keep on gigging.

He told me they'd book me for more Red Raw spots and some Sundays, but that 'it's what you do in between that will improve you'.

I wanted to improve every time I returned to the Stand. I no longer considered dying on my arse in there; I was going in to be the best of the night, to have new material, to try things that the professionals would try. The Stand was my home gig, my home game, it was my crowd and I was fearless.

The Sunday show I was booked for was on a bank holiday weekend and the place was totally sold out.

It was the first time my mum had ever come to one of my shows and it was comfortably the best gig so far.

The reception was as loud as the first night, maybe even louder, and the crowd began shouting for more.

The compere, Michael Redmond, Father Stone from *Father Ted*, came back out and asked, 'Who the fuck was that?'

It was also the night that I met Greg McHugh, who'd later go on to star as *Gary: Tank Commander* in his own BBC show.

Greg told me he was going to phone Eva the following day and let her know that they should 'keep an eye on me'.

I thanked Greg sincerely. He didn't know me, and he didn't owe me anything. He was just genuinely impressed.

He was true to his word and Eva mentioned that Greg, Michael, Jojo, Tommy the owner, and also a few of the staff at the club in Glasgow had all been talking about me

I began to spend entire days on the phone, chasing up gigs.

I phoned big Scott again and between him, Greg, Michael and a few other comics at the 'Best of Red Raw' showcase, I obtained even more contacts.

I'd phone them, leave messages and text them. I didn't tell my dad, as he was too proud and would tell me to let them come to me. I knew it didn't work like that, though, at least for a good few years.

I took on everything I could get.

I had five- and ten-minute open-mic spots booked all over

the place, pubs in Glasgow city centre, pubs in areas of Glasgow like Easterhouse, Pollok and Castlemilk.

Patrick Rolink ran a lot of gigs in North Lanarkshire, pub gigs in Airdrie and Coatbridge and anywhere else near there, where he was from.

Mac Star ran gigs all over Scotland, as far north as the Highlands and as far south as the borders; he'd run shows on islands, and in any pubs in the centre belt he could find that would let him set up a PA kit for a few hours.

Every day I'd tell my dad about a new gig I'd found. He'd mention the logistics of getting to these places, but he was excited. 'I was there on a summer holiday when I was ten, and there's a good chippy there,' he'd say, reminiscing and looking forward to making his return.

I knew it would be difficult finding transport because John had work commitments and my dad wasn't fit for longer drives.

My mum told me that she'd let my Uncle George and my Auntie Maureen know how well my comedy was going and had let them read the *Herald* article that she'd held on to – I think she even gave them one of her copics.

She was apologetic and told me she'd sworn them to secrecy. 'I'd sworn you to secrecy,' I said. She laughed and I laughed as well.

I knew she was only telling them because she was proud but she mentioned that they'd love to come and see me and that my Uncle George was used to driving all over Scotland, through his work, and had offered his services if I ever needed to be driven to gigs.

My Uncle George was delighted with the *Herald* article and told me himself one night that it was 'absolutely no problem' to take me anywhere and that he'd 'even give me some jokes'.

I laughed. It was how everyone was going to react to the news: a little unsure, but supportive.

There were nights at these gigs when I'd brought the majority of the audience with me. There would be my Uncle George, my Auntie Maureen, my mum and my dad, a few other comedians and then a couple of stragglers from the pub, again, unaware that there was comedy happening.

Showing up with your mum and dad and your auntie and uncle looked pretty uncool but it got me to the gig so that was all that mattered. However, when I was asked to do a longer set, sometimes fifteen minutes, I had no option other than to finish on my 'waking up with a hard-on' routine.

Doing the 'tuck it and duck it' walk in front of eight people, four of them related to you, one of them your mum and one your auntie, was pretty embarrassing and was thankfully never mentioned on the car journeys home.

I couldn't drop it; I needed it for the time and I knew it was a good routine, even though it was physical and much better in front of a larger audience.

The smaller gigs meant I had to work on sharp lines and subtle observations. There weren't many performance skills that could win over a small crowd. You were judged on material, jokes and stories, alone. It forced me to write better.

Doing a funny walk up and down the stage or anything too over the top would just look strange in front of eight people.

I'd start to write things like this in my notepad.

It wasn't specifically a notepad for jokes and ideas. It was now my guidebook.

I'd analyse the gig and rather than beat myself up when it didn't go well, I'd write why I felt it didn't go well.

If the gig went great, I'd write why I felt it had gone great rather than basking in it.

I'd enjoy it, of course, but if I wanted this to be my job, my profession and my craft, then the gig going great had to become the norm.

I was careful not to suck the fun out of it so I'd raise my standards after every show.

What I could class as a great show was changing, my expectations were rising, and that would become the fun part: outdoing the last gig.

53

Another family day out was a gig I landed in a pub in Edinburgh, where I was to go on stage during the interval of a quiz night.

I was to do my routine whilst the quizmaster marked everyone's answers and counted the final scores.

It was tough. No one listened to begin with, but towards the end some of them would shout at me and I'd have responses; this would get laughs and I'd be able to seamlessly move into material and finish on a high.

I was learning how to think on my feet, how to be live and in the moment, how to react.

It could be hard and my heart would sink when I'd walk in and see the set-up in some of these places, but what kept me going were the gigs at the Stand.

I knew that if I could survive all of these situations then by the time I returned to the Stand, an actual comedy club, I'd be sharp, I'd be on fire.

I'd be learning faster than anyone else I was on the bill with, the guys who hadn't performed since their last time at the Stand, the ones for whom it was a hobby.

Their friends would play badminton on a Tuesday night, they'd do stand-up comedy.

There is nothing wrong with that. They had their real jobs and this was just a bit of fun to them. I had nothing else, though. I needed this.

I was climbing the ladder at the Stand, rapidly.

I was booked to play my first full weekend of gigs in the

summer of 2004. I was being paid to perform, paid to make people laugh, in a place I hadn't even heard of four months previously.

The Thursday night had gone great. Raymond Mearns, who compered, had remembered me from the Vault and mentioned that it was 'a shite night', but, again, reiterated the importance of getting through the shite nights.

He complimented my set, my material and my 'stage presence'.

Another of the comedians had struggled a little, opening the show, but he didn't seem to care; he told me that opening the show is always tough.

He gave me feedback.

I felt my set had gone down much better than his, but it was my first weekend and he'd been doing it for years.

He told me to drop my left arm and not to put it across my chest and into my right armpit, like I'd done at every single show since the first night.

I was confident in my own ability by now, but not so arrogant that I'd dismiss advice from anyone. 'It's negative body language and makes you look like you're protecting yourself,' he told me.

Fuck. He was right. It was my natural defence. It reflected how scared I was on that first show. The audience maybe didn't see it like that but then how often did they watch stand-up and how closely did they analyse the comics? They didn't, they just wanted a laugh.

I immediately thanked him and told him I'd bear that in mind.

The following night I had the best set yet, easily the biggest reaction I'd had from an audience, and it was in front of Jane Mackay, the weekend compere and co-owner of the Glasgow and Edinburgh clubs.

I hadn't been feeling well all that day and I felt worse when I woke up on Saturday.

I'd noticed my glands were beginning to swell up and I kept feeling like I was going to faint.

I didn't tell my mum before the Friday show because I knew she'd tell me I was taking too much out of myself, arriving home at all hours and then going to college – well, getting a bus to the city centre first thing in the morning. Feeling nervous all day, thinking about the gig, my mood going rapidly up and down, depending on the shows, and running on adrenalin every night, wasn't the healthiest lifestyle.

When my mum saw me on the Saturday she immediately phoned to get an on-the-day appointment at Drumchapel hospital.

I had the mumps.

The doctor told me to rest, to stay in bed and not to do anything that would exert me too much.

I couldn't cancel the gig.

It was my first weekend and if the Friday had gone well, then the Saturday would be even better.

I knew what kind of reaction was in the audience, and by all accounts the Saturday night at the Stand in Glasgow was one of the best gigs, if not the best, on the UK comedy circuit.

I had picked a few things I didn't do as well the night before and thought of some new bits.

I couldn't cancel because of the fucking mumps.

What would that say about me?

They'd think I'd bottled it.

The seventeen-year-old? 'It all came too soon for him,' they'd think and I wouldn't get to play any more weekend gigs at the Stand for a while.

I stayed in bed all day, I took antibiotics, I ate fruit, drank loads of water and orange juice.

I felt awful but I knew I could last ten minutes; the excitement of the gig would carry me through and I could outdo the Friday night.

I'd be booked back again and again and maybe even promoted to open the show.

I could stay in bed all day Sunday.

I didn't have a gig until Tuesday night, at a pub in Ayr.

I didn't want to cancel that one, never mind a Saturday night at the Stand, even though I'd played at the same pub a couple of weeks before and no one listened; they sat with their backs to me, watching a Champions League game on the television.

They'd listened at half-time but the guy on the stage was a regular drinker in the pub who I'd recognised from the first time I'd done the gig, as he'd heckled all through the night. He didn't have any jokes but passed his time by asking every couple their favourite love song and then singing it, but with the word 'love' changed to 'cunt'.

The crowd gave up on him after a couple of polite smiles at lyrics like, 'I don't care too much for money, because money can't buy me cunt.' Too worn down to even heckle him about prostitution, exposing the flaw in his lyrics.

They'd listen in spells but quickly turned back to the TV, an entire pub facing the television, pretending to be engrossed in a Heineken or a Ford advert, to avoid eye contact with a distressed-looking, bald, middle-aged man putting everything he had into power ballads like, 'Can you feel the cunt tonight'.

The vibration of the speakers was making everyone rub a finger in their ear and look at each other, suggesting: 'Shall we go somewhere else for the second half?'

A difficult act to follow, one that drove the punters in their numbers out the door and made the bar manager seriously reconsider booking the comedy night. It didn't stop me going back again and again.

Cancelling a gig wasn't an option.

I showed up at the Stand at the same time as the night before. The Saturday show started at 9 p.m., though, thirty minutes later.

My dad had come to the shows on Thursday and Friday so this was his third show in a row. I think he was secretly pleased I hadn't cancelled the gig as he knew how big a night it was for me and how unfortunate it was that of all the shit-hole pubs in fuck-knows-where that I'd been performing in, it was a night like this that I wasn't feeling great.

My mum came as well on the Saturday. She'd been out and got her hair done during the day and was looking forward to it.

I was entitled to one free ticket but Eva had told me it was okay for two. The weekend shows always sold out in advance so this saved any extra hassle of trying to find a ticket from somewhere.

My mum was concerned and on the journey up she kept asking if I was okay.

I was feeling better but only because I was thinking of the gig now and not my swollen glands, my temperature or my nauseous, light-headed state.

There was a long wait backstage and the only time I could stop myself shaking with nerves about the gig was when I'd try to move and feel dizzy, like I was going to be sick. The mumps and my pre-gig anxieties had been introduced and were getting on great with each other, uniting to fuck me over.

I had to keep reminding myself that the gig would sort me

out, whilst going over my set, which served as a distraction from the symptoms.

Everyone else in the green room was sympathetic when they saw the extent of the swelling. The other acts tried to reassure me that it didn't look that obvious unless you were close up, and they didn't think the audience would notice. I was quite chubby anyway, so that helped.

Jane told me that I didn't have to do the gig and that it wouldn't have any effect on me being booked again.

But I was here now and I had to make it worth it.

I had a reference all ready about looking like the character Sloth from the movie *The Goonies*, and I'd practised his 'Hey, you guys!' catchphrase in case anyone heckled me about my appearance.

I wasn't going to raise the issue if no one else did, however.

I had ten minutes and it had to be tight.

Every joke had to work, every line.

Jane got the crowd whipped up, like no one else I'd seen. She'd skilfully take the piss out of everyone in the front row, and even if she sounded harsh, they'd laugh, knowing that this was her way of letting everyone know she was in charge.

She wasn't like a school teacher, like a lot of comperes, who'd rattle off the rules – no mobile phones, no talking, there will be an interval for all of that, and so on – issuing these humourless, boring warnings as though they were a member of the cabin crew on a budget airline.

Jane didn't really need to do all of that. She gave off an aura that if you spoke, or your phone went off, you'd be destroyed.

She'd speak to the front row, ask them about themselves, and then bounce the information off her own jokes and bring other people in, forming a united audience out of a collection of strangers.

This created an excitement, a feeling of anarchy. This was live comedy and no one else was part of it, only the comedians on the stage and the two hundred audience members in this dark, basement room, drinking and smoking, their big night out after a long week at work, excited but listening, desperate for a laugh.

A reaction was guaranteed, either way.

I can't bring myself to write in detail about another gig going well, but the Saturday went well. It was like the Friday but even more polished. I'd gone in thinking of the rewards if I could get through this, with my mum and dad there. My mum was still on at me to get a back-up plan; college had finished and comedy was just my hobby, my dream, for now. It wasn't my job. But I knew it was going to be if I could keep working and progressing at this pace.

The crowd began shouting for more and Jane MacKay told them, 'Calm down, calm down, he's okay, for a spam sandwich. Any more of that we'll need to pay the little fucker.'

It was a line befitting her character, scathing but with a smile in her eyes.

She told one of the bar staff to go and get me a pint, despite my routine about being seventeen. It was my first pint in the Stand, my first post-gig pint. I was underage but it was bought by the owner and drunk backstage.

I didn't know what a 'spam sandwich' was but I guessed it was a reference to being working class.

Jane gave everyone equal abuse; that same night she'd referred to a sketch group as 'posh little cunts wasting Daddy's money'.

Maybe I was a 'Spam sandwich'.

I didn't know I was working class until I met middle-class people, through comedy, but by that time all we were judged on was whether or not we were funny, not our backgrounds.

Jane handed me my brown envelope of cash, £50 in total: £10, £15 and £25 for ten-minute sets on the Thursday, Friday and Saturday.

I signed the little bit of paper and put the envelope in my pocket.

She asked if I was signing on.

I told her I wasn't old enough, not getting that she was joking.

It was pretty amazing how rapidly I'd turn back to being shy and quiet after a gig, after making two hundred strangers, all much older than me, laugh, applaud and cheer. I'd then feel embarrassed and humble when they'd grab me after the show, telling me well done, asking my name, promising that they'd look out for me.

Girls would talk to me but I wouldn't know what to say; I'd feel my face turn red when they'd ask if I was single.

I'd say, 'Aye,' and not know what to say next. I couldn't offer to buy them a drink because I wouldn't get served.

They'd sense I felt awkward, then smile at me, tell me well done and walk away, to find someone who could hold a conversation without staring at the floor.

'You were in there, mate,' guys who'd been watching would shout.

I'd laugh and walk away.

I didn't care. Not a lot else in my life mattered. I wasn't missing being out with my friends, going to pubs and clubs, or even girls.

54

After the shows I'd go home and my dad would always make toast and we'd sit and talk through my material and aspects of the night's performance.

Everything was always positive with my dad, but he'd notice times I'd doubted myself, when I'd hesitated during certain bits.

'Relax, look around. The crowd love you. Just be yourself and laugh,' he'd always say.

Every day, at some point, me, my mum, dad and John would sit talking about my gigs and comedy.

John had started coming to most of my Glasgow shows and bringing his mates along.

At first I thought he came just because I was his little brother, but he told me that I genuinely made him laugh; he'd tell me which bits he'd laughed at most and I'd be delighted.

I was still his pain-in-the-arse wee brother, but I was doing something with myself that John admired.

I'd run all my new ideas past him and he'd give me feedback.

If he didn't like a certain bit, I'd usually tell him to go and fuck himself and then make it my priority to get the bit into my act and make sure it worked. He was usually right, though.

My whole family was involved now, and I think it gave everyone a boost, something to look forward to.

It was an exciting time and this drove me on even more.

I didn't know exactly when all of this was going to end, but if anything was chasing me, trying to drag me back, back to where I was before 10 February 2004, then I wasn't hanging around to be caught.

I was in a hurry and now I'd hit another landmark, my first paid gigs.

I'd only been paid £10 before for a show in a pub somewhere near Falkirk. I didn't count it as my first paid gig, though, because the promoter told me that, as it was £5 a ticket and he'd let my dad and my uncle in for free, I should ask them to pay me my money.

I didn't tell my dad because I knew he'd have made a scene and told the promoter that I'd bailed out his night, that the other acts were terrible and that I deserved to at least be given my fee from him, no matter how small, and not made to go and beg for it.

Paid gigs were still to be the exception, for now, but it was a sign of progress, a stamp of approval.

I made it to the gig in Ayr on the Tuesday night and struggled through my set to another single-figure 'crowd'.

It was frustrating that not every gig could be like the Saturday night at the Stand, but that was the nature of it all.

I was gathering momentum and the first gig seemed like years ago.

I'd now enrolled in a new college course, studying Social Sciences at Glasgow's Stow College. But I had zero interest except for reading the odd thing about psychology, criminology or politics, areas that could maybe spark ideas for material.

I didn't hand in essays on time. I'd sit at the back of the class and not say much, just look out the window and think about my next gig. I could sit in the class, not listening, but writing notes and reworking routines. The lecturers didn't care and they'd rarely interact with the class.

It was good to have the structure in my day.

My mum bought me a diary and every day I was filling it up.

I asked for more shifts in the Co-op and I started taking a packed lunch with me to Glasgow, putting the money I saved towards my travel fund. My packed lunch, my Sony Discman, my sleeve of CDs, stolen from John, and my notepad.

I'd found a use for my brain, my daft side and my love of making people laugh.

It felt like something incredible could happen in my life but I knew I had to work for it.

I started to attend college less and less.

I'd still get up in the mornings, I'd still get ready and still get on the bus to the city centre, but I wouldn't go near college.

I'd walk around Glasgow, for hours. I'd walk up Sauchiehall Street to the Buchanan Galleries, down Buchanan Street and on to Argyll Street.

I'd walk along to the Argyll market and up towards Trongate, the border, just where the city begins to get mental, where Glasgow becomes 'Glesga'.

I'd look at people, groups of young guys, groups of young girls, couples, guys on their own, women on their own, the elderly, Asians, Africans, students, bams, goths.

It was exciting and I'd feel happy walking through Glasgow thinking that someday every one of these people could know my name and I'd be known as a comedian, the funny guy.

I'd be at my happiest listening to music and playing out my material in my head, stopping to take notes, to add lines to my existing routines and to write ideas for new ones.

I'd picture myself on stage, and what I'd say, what I'd do if something happened, if a glass smashed, if someone shouted 'you're shite' or 'fuck off, fatty'. I wanted to have everything covered.

Every detail.

I'd always react to disruptions individually and try to have a unique reply for every occasion.

This was something I'd remembered Frank Skinner mentioning.

A stock heckle put-down always sounded pretty lame: 'Really? That's what your mum was saying last night.' Or, 'Don't disrupt me at my work – I don't come to your work and knock guy's cocks out of your mouth.'

Lines that were probably funny and the person who first said them deserved a laugh, but why the fuck would you say it, if you knew everyone else said it? It was like primary school again: 'Your maw's got baws and your da loves it.'

It was better to have nothing, than to use one of these.

Say what you feel and be honest about it. I'd find I could always get out of situations with my own lines and that would help my confidence build even further. I don't remember ever using a line I'd thought of during these long walks, but it wasn't about having a witty retort prepared, it was about feeling comfortable, about feeling bulletproof on stage, in front of four people or in front of two hundred people.

One night, at a gig in a pub in Glasgow, I mentioned at the beginning of my set that I was from Clydebank and then later referred to myself as a Glaswegian.

A bald guy in the front row interrupted and shouted, 'Clydebank's not in Glasgow.' The gig was going well and the audience groaned and shouted at him to shut up. They were on my side and I had to repay their faith in me by doing the guy myself.

I don't know where it came from but I replied with something about a bald guy 'splitting hairs'.

I don't remember the exact line but the crowd loved it.

It was a skill I had to learn fairly quickly, given that I was playing so many gigs to people who weren't interested in comedy.

Comedy was now my apprenticeship. My friends were apprentices and so was I. They were apprentice electricians, joiners, plumbers and I was an apprentice comedian.

Their apprenticeships were paid and mine wasn't, aside from the odd weekend spot here and there, but as long as I felt I was learning something from every gig it didn't bother me and I'd find money from somewhere.

I knew it would be increasingly difficult to keep everything a secret, locally.

I'd received some more positive reviews in newspapers and magazines and my name was now appearing in their listings sections.

In Clydebank Shopping Centre I'd been asked a few times, by people who'd seen my name in newspaper listings for local comedy nights, people who knew what I'd been like at school and could acknowledge it wasn't all that unlikely that it could be me.

I'd laugh and deny all knowledge, even though I'd be squirming and wishing they'd change the subject.

I'd much preferred it when they thought I was a waster, when they didn't take an interest, when they'd talk about themselves or their children and how well they were doing before leaving me to get on with my day.

Friends would ask as well, and the first to hear was George Marshall, who, like most of my mates, I hadn't seen much of since the gigs started racking up.

George told me his driving instructor had been telling him

that he'd been to a comedy club and a young guy called 'Kevin Bridges' was on, 'seventeen and from Clydebank'.

I laughed but I couldn't bring myself to lie; it was fairly easy lying to people who I only knew by name but not to someone who'd been there all through the good laughs, at school and at house parties, and who'd always said, 'You should be a comedian.'

I told George about the gigs and how they'd been going well and I was moving up the ranks.

He laughed as well, surprised but then not that surprised as he began reminiscing about funny and stupid things I'd done.

I told George everything and it felt good, a relief, seeing how interested and supportive my friends might be. George promised he wouldn't tell anyone and asked if he could come to my next gig.

The next gig was a Wednesday night, a notoriously quiet night at the Stand. I started to explain how the weekends were the prestigious gigs and how being booked for the weekend meant . . .

I realized I was bombarding him with information that wasn't relevant to him. He didn't want to make his way on the comedy circuit, he just wanted to know when and where he could watch me.

There was no point trying to talk someone out of coming on a Wednesday night and going on a Saturday instead. People would come and see me whenever they wanted, not when I wanted. I just had to accept that.

I took George finding out as a sign of progress; word of mouth was going round and the 'insecurities' in me wanted to know if George's driving instructor had enjoyed my set, and if so what bits, and what bit about those bits?

I stopped myself and told him I'd text him the address and the times for the Wednesday night.

George never told anyone, and it made things a little easier, knowing that at least one of my pals knew.

I knew everyone in the area would soon know and that I'd need to get better, fast.

55

Near the end of 2004, Eva phoned me up with a whole load of bookings, some of them well into the new year.

I was booked for more weekends, in the Glasgow and now the Edinburgh clubs, fifteen-minute spots and even my first twenty-minute spot, headlining Red Raw, the amateur night where I'd started.

There was a bit of hype around me now and the *Sunday Herald* had contacted the Stand, asking if I would come to their Glasgow club on one of the days between Christmas and New Year for a photo shoot and an interview as part of a special feature on Scottish talent and 'people to emerge in 2005'.

I knew that agreeing to this would finally 'out' me to all of my friends and to everyone else within a one-mile radius of my front door.

A few mentions in a review section were okay and had managed to go under the radar but this was to be a special piece, a festive pull-out, with photographs and a profile on me.

Someone would see it and that'd be all it would take.

Comedy would no longer be my escape.

The first rule of Fight Club would be broken, and in a national newspaper.

Despite how well everything had gone, in my head I was still in St Columba's, sitting at my desk, or outside in the corridor.

I wore trainers and T-shirts on stage. I had a short back and sides.

I wrote my routines on the bus, with a bookie's pen.

I lived with my mum and dad and I was at college, doing my second course in a year.

A 'people to emerge in 2005' profile piece was something for the rest of them.

The ones who'd embraced the showbiz lifestyle, the ones who knew a short-cut and could by-pass the spirit-crushing pub gigs.

'You're not still doing that gig, are you, for him? Is he paying you?' They were wary of all the shady promoters; they knew that they should be getting paid and what they should be getting paid.

They'd sit and talk backstage about signing to agents, auditioning for acting roles, writing scripts, having meetings with television executives.

They'd been to London, they'd been to the Edinburgh Fringe, they had degrees, they met famous people for coffee, and they seemed connected to this industry.

I felt like an imposter when it came to anything off the stage.

I could do the job and do it well and that's all I had to justify my place in their company; thinking about anything else made me realize how surreal it was that I was about to be interviewed and photographed for a newspaper.

It would be ridiculous of me to turn down this request, as much as I wanted to do.

Even the staff at the Stand seemed a little surprised when I asked if I could have a think about doing the interview first, and then phone them back.

I spoke to my dad about what to do and he more or less told me to get a grip and lose my narrow mindset, to think about the wider world and to take the fact that a newspaper wanted to write about me and photograph me as a reward, reminding me of all the nights performing to tiny crowds with no one listening.

This was progress and I wouldn't have to do gigs like this for much longer, he said, with total assurance.

I went for the photo shoot and interview and, despite my dad's words, I hated every pose I had to 'strike' and every answer I mumbled my way through.

It was eerie being in the Stand out of hours, with no audience, no microphone and no way of justifying my place there.

A guy just a little older than me was in there, loading cases of alcohol into a small downstairs room behind the bar and hanging around for a signature from one of the managers. He gave me a nod. I wanted to talk to him, to explain that I was embarrassed at being interviewed and that this was all strange to me as well.

I felt like I should be working with him, at least as his apprentice. I'd be sitting in the van right now, messing around with the radio, waiting for him to come back and drive us to our next licensed premises.

I wanted him to hurry up before the interview questions began.

'When did you realize you could be a comedian?'

I hadn't realized yet. I didn't feel like one right then. I looked over at the brewery delivery guy, as if I was apologizing.

I knew I was no better than him and I didn't want him to think that I thought I was.

'Were you funny at school?'

To some people, but so was this guy. He was probably hilarious at school and now he was doing what funny people from school do, they drive vans and make deliveries.

'What do your friends think?'

They don't know yet, but telling them via an interview in a newspaper felt like an excruciating way to tell them.

I remember apologizing after nearly every stuttering, uncomfortable answer, and sounding more like a lower-league footballer giving a man-of-the-match interview than an 'up and coming funny man'.

I didn't have an ego in that I could see this interview as a 'fuck you' – a fuck you to all of the teachers who'd decided I wouldn't amount to anything.

I was over all of that.

I hadn't even listened to teachers when they'd said things like that, which was part of the problem.

I couldn't sustain something for as long and with as much dedication if it was only built on a petty notion of revenge.

'This one is good. I like the moody expression, very thoughtful and contemplative,' the photographer was saying, inviting me over to her laptop to see myself standing looking lost, ashamed, guilty, like it was a photograph for the *Clyde-bank Post*'s 'Crime File'.

It was a face I'd only ever seen on my passport, from when I'd been frustrated and ready to lose the plot with ASDA's photo machine.

With every question they asked I felt like I was under pressure, as though it was a quiz, that there were right and wrong answers and it wasn't my own story.

The interviewer and the photographer finished and they offered me a drink, as a thank you for my time.

I told them I was okay and that if I left now I could catch my bus.

'The bus? Are you not doing your driving lessons?' the interviewer asked, playfully and off the record, just hoping for a witty response from 'Scotland's new comedy prodigy'.

I forced myself to laugh like it was the funniest thing I'd ever heard anyone say.

'No. Not yet, mate. Maybe that can be my New Year's resolution,' I replied, extending this horrible laugh right through the sentence and then mimicking my pathetic response back to myself in my head.

I'd have instantly formed an eternal respect for the interviewer if he'd calmly walked over to me and, with everything he had in him, cracked me with an uppercut, sending me right over the bar, smashing into the gantry.

'Don't you ever, ever, answer my questions like that again. Now go, go and catch your fucking bus.'

I left the Stand feeling like I'd just done a gig and I'd died on my arse.

I didn't know what time the bus was due – who the fuck knows what time a bus is due?

I'd just wanted out of there.

The feature went out and I was officially, according to the *Sunday Herald*, 'one to watch' in 2005.

I couldn't look at the article until my dad had assured me it read well and that the journalist had either made up quotes on my behalf or that I'd come across much better than I'd feared.

I was relieved. The journalist had obviously recognized how new all of this was to me and not mentioned that I seemed socially inept. He hadn't told me at the interview that he'd seen me perform, which would maybe have relaxed me and made me feel like I had less to prove.

In the article, though, he wrote that he had seen me on a couple of occasions, that I'd improved each time and that he was a fan.

I was glad I hadn't turned down the interview request; it

could only help my progress. Also, it hadn't gone on to be as much of an exposé as I'd feared.

There were a couple of enquiries but it was only when the schools returned after Christmas and one of my old teachers brought a copy of the newspaper into her class, to show everyone in a 'former pupil done good' kind of way, but with a strong 'what the fuck?' element about it, that they realized they'd now have to pay to see me do what they used to throw me out of their classes for.

Again, the irony of this made me laugh, but school was another life. I had been a nuisance and it was right that I'd left.

There were no hard feelings and I was doing all right.

I'd met all sorts of people, fucked-up, neurotic, funny, crazy, insecure, but, all in all, like-minded people. I'd been to places I'd never heard of before. I was doing something I enjoyed and that I took pride in.

I can't imagine my last year at school would have given me as much of an education as my first year in stand-up.

I didn't know if I would 'emerge' in 2005, nor did I know what they meant by that or who'd decide if I did or didn't, but it gave me something to look back on, and if nothing else came of my stand-up dream, 2004 had been the most exhilarating year of my life.

56

My first gig of the new year was in a pub in Largs, a popular seaside holiday resort in North Ayrshire. This time the venue was the pub's function room and in front of a packed audience who had paid to see stand-up comedy.

It was Raymond Mearns who'd booked me, having seen me a few times since we were first on a bill together at the Vault.

The gig was my highest paid yet: £50 to open the show and do twenty minutes.

I'd written more new material over Christmas as I was keen to drop all of my old stuff; the jokes about being seventeen had all expired now and I'd been getting fed up saying them anyway.

I opened by acknowledging that Christmas was done and how everyone's minds would turn to their holiday plans, which led me into talking about family holidays.

The routine wasn't getting any laughs and it felt like I didn't have anywhere designated for the crowd to laugh, even if they'd wanted to.

I was just talking, and there were no punchlines, no checkpoints.

'Speak up,' I heard a woman shout. I was starting to get nervous and rather than speaking up, I sped up, racing through my new routines, clambering to get to a tried and tested joke, to get to safety.

'We can't hear you!'

A few other people were shouting as well but I was going on and on, sweating and wondering what the fuck was wrong.

391

A gig not going great heightens all the senses. A friendly pointer from an audience member, like, 'We can't hear you,' can easily be interpreted as, 'We fucking hate you.' Then the paranoia kicks in. It's not just that they don't like your jokes, they hate your jokes and they hate you.

I didn't know what to do. I tried to block it out and pretend I hadn't heard anything.

I'd become complacent and I'd been caught out. I no longer thought about struggling at gigs. After all, I was supposed to be the one to emerge in 2005 and I was booked to headline the Stand; I didn't die on my arse any more.

I hadn't expected any turbulence. I hadn't familiarized myself with the safety instructions prior to take-off. I'd thought I could fly but I couldn't even get off the ground here. I'd stalled on the tarmac.

I was thinking of the £50: 'I'm being paid £50 here, for twenty minutes, that's £150 an hour I'm on, and I'm not getting the job done.'

I tried to avoid looking at Raymond. I was letting him down.

Out of all the pub gigs I'd done, for no money, in front of nobody, I'd chosen tonight, in front of a nice crowd who'd paid for a laugh, to have a meltdown.

I saw Raymond signalling at me. 'Is he telling me to get off?' I began panicking.

I'm being fired, fired on the job.

Raymond could see I looked rattled and he shouted, 'Turn the microphone on. The button, at the bottom.' He was laughing, in a supportive way, like he'd been trying to get the message to me all through my unnecessary struggle.

I held the microphone upside down and, as I moved a little switch, a light turned from red to green, literally, and, with regards to the gig itself, metaphorically.

I asked, 'Is that better?'

Hearing myself ask the question was my answer.

The crowd cheered.

'Thank fuck for that,' I said, and they laughed, my first big laugh. They knew I wasn't joking and that it was genuinely a relief.

I managed to salvage the gig, but it had been a slap in the face, a wake-up. This was live comedy and anything could happen.

Raymond gave me some advice about not opening up with new material or going into long routines without first connecting with the crowd.

He was right and was, again, full of constructive criticism and constructive praise. He handed me my £50 and told me to wait around until after the show, then he'd buy me a pint and we'd speak about comedy.

Getting to know Raymond definitely had an influence on the direction I would take for the next couple of years.

He was a professional comedian, as in he didn't do anything else for work. He supported his family and himself solely through his income from making people laugh.

I loved watching him. He had so many routines that I knew all of my friends would love, and when I eventually came clean and revealed my secret life to them, I'd make sure they came to a show that I was on with Raymond.

He was from the east end of Glasgow and told me that he'd seen his younger self in me. He seemed to enjoy my story, of how I'd been told to leave school, found myself at a loose end, read Frank Skinner's book and gave stand-up a try.

'You're living your fucking dream, wee man.'

I'd ask him about certain promoters and if he felt there was any point in returning to the same gigs for the fifth and sixth times, where I'd be shouting over drunks and struggling to just hold their attention, let alone make them laugh.

Raymond asked if I was getting paid at these gigs. I told him not really, but that stage time was important to me, showing that I'd taken the advice he'd given me almost a year earlier at the Vault.

There was stage time and then there was taking the piss, seemed to be Raymond's point, along with my dad's. Dad'd get frustrated at me when I'd come off stage dejected and beating myself up about the gig, when there was no gig there – a microphone in the corner of a pub, maybe, but not a gig.

Raymond always concluded these post-gig conversations with: 'Get to London, whilst you're young.'

Raymond's thinking was that there weren't enough quality gigs in Scotland for anyone to make it as a great comedian, a great comedian like the guys who I'd watched headline the weekend shows at the Stand, when I'd been in the ten-minute spot.

John Fothergill, Simon Evans, Jason Byrne, Owen O'Neill. These were the ones I remember from my first four weekends.

They were comedians who performed every night of the week; they played the London Comedy Store; they'd play three or four shows on Friday and Saturday nights in London; they were solid acts; they had to stay sharp and work constantly. They were from a circuit where you had to perform amongst the best and never stand out as the weak link, because there would be someone else doing something different or doing what you do but better, coming right behind you, to take your place.

I'd never been to London.

I knew it was massive, though, and busy.

The thought of it frightened me and I'd always smile and say, 'Maybe one day,' and Raymond would grow more adamant about it every time we spoke.

A couple of days after the Largs gig, I was at home and logged on to the computer to see that I had messages, from nearly everyone I knew, asking if it was true that I was working as a comedian.

I wasn't working *as* a comedian. That was the dream.

I was working to *be* a comedian.

I didn't correct anyone; this was a distinction only I made.

It would be impossible to relay everything that had gone on in the past year, every gig and everything I'd learned about comedy, via the medium of MSN messenger.

I heard you were at the comedy club one night and the comedian was trying to take the piss out of you but you took the microphone off him and tore him apart. That's brilliant, mate.

I had to laugh at, and then deny, all sorts of stories like this, and during the following weeks I'd be stopped, like a local celebrity, by people who hadn't met me and who hadn't seen me perform, but who'd been told: 'That Kevin Bridges, Andy and Patricia's son, he's a comedian now.'

This information was their starting point, their base. They'd add their own details, customized to their liking, and then pass it on, down the production line, the conveyor belt of local gossip.

'He gets that from his dad, his dad was funny.'

'His grandda Tommy, he was funny. I remember we were at a wedding with Tommy . . .'

'I met him in the bookie's on Saturday; he wasn't that funny.'

'A comedian? He must be loaded. When is he on the telly? He can't be very good if he's not been on the telly.'

'I saw him in the post office the other morning, standing there thinking he was something. It's all gone to his head.'

'He's not as funny as my nephew – *he* should be a comedian. Honestly, the stuff he comes out with! He told me one the other night, what do you call a . . .'

As well as a lot of this, there was loads of support, especially from my friends.

It turned out that the *Glasgow Evening Times* newspaper had also printed something about me and this was the one that most of them had read. One of the first phone calls was from my mate Halpin, who had an immense, baffled pride in his voice as he told me: 'I'm just taking a shite in work, reading the paper, and it's saying you're the next Billy Connolly?'

He was laughing excitedly, adding, before I could say anything, 'A mad comedian, mad Bridges. Right, I'd better go, I'll phone you later.'

This made me laugh, giggle, even, at how much I'd worried about what everyone would think, and at the image Halpin had created.

It wasn't something bad I was doing and Halpin's reaction had summed it up: 'A mad comedian, mad Bridges'.

I had to enjoy everything that was happening and to keep going, to see how much further I could take it all. Keeping my new life on the stand-up circuit a relative secret for almost a full year was pretty impressive, a good run. I'd started and I'd got to a level where I was confident they'd enjoy my performances.

That night I went down to Halpin's house and everyone was sat there, eager to quiz me and hear some of my stories.

I told them this was why I hadn't been out at weekends,

why I hadn't been to the pub or to anyone's house to watch the football, why I wasn't out for a few pints on my eighteenth birthday – I'd been performing in the bar of an arts centre in Peebles – and why I'd been the only one out of us all who hadn't gone on holiday to Majorca in the summer.

57

On their first night in Majorca, I was in the Isle of Skye, trying to sleep, in the back of a van.

Our gig hadn't sold any tickets. We arrived late and the owner of the hotel, where the gig was to be, subsequently cancelled the accommodation, refusing to put us up as there was no show.

The promoter refused to pay for our rooms out of his own pocket, and the rest of us had a total of about £20 between us. The headliner for the night had agreed to the gig under the condition that we drove up in his work's van, so that first thing in the morning he could deliver office materials to a few businesses and clients his company had on the island.

So that was it decided: we were staying overnight in the back of the van, myself and another comedian, Paul Pirie, whilst the promoter and the headliner landed the luxuries of the front, with somewhere to sit and, importantly, a heater.

We'd driven up with the shutter at the back of the van only open enough to let a little light in, but, crucially, closed enough so as not to be seen by any police who might be alerted to a potential human-trafficking offence.

I hadn't met Paul before so at least there was a lot there to fast-track us through the small-talk stage of forming a friendship.

We couldn't do much but laugh at the situation. We were both new comics, this was the furthest we'd travelled for a gig and it would take more than being crouched in darkness in the back of a van for seven hours to break our spirit.

Picturing ourselves performing our ten-minute stand-up routines and hearing a few people, hopefully even double figures, laugh at our jokes, helped keep us strong.

The promoter knew we were pressed for time after we'd been caught in bad traffic, so if we needed a piss we were told to find a spot in the back of the van; stopping wasn't an option, he told us, on the phone, from the driver's seat.

We were both almost rolling around now, desperate to piss, trying to distract ourselves until we felt we could make another phone call to the front of the van, for a progress report.

The vehicle seemed to be stationary for far too long, so there must have been an accident or roadworks. We couldn't see but we knew we were nowhere near a place to stop, even if the promoter permitted a stop.

We were faced with no choice but to piss in the corner at the back of the van, without even a consideration that the back of the van might be our digs for the night, our twin room, complete with our self-designated en-suite.

It felt wrong and it felt disgusting but we didn't know what else to do. It was too dark to make out exactly where we were aiming so it was decided that we should stand for the remainder of the journey, as any sharp turn could result in a tsunami of piss coming towards us from the corner of the van. Which was now off-limits. If we stood, it was only our feet that would take the tide.

The situation was pretty bleak, and even prisoners are allowed a designated toilet break. We were open-mic comedians, though, and stage time was more important than human rights, which made the cancellation of the gig the most sickening part of the entire episode.

The comedy circuit wasn't said to be glamorous and if you wanted to get good and make progress then it was to be a difficult journey, rife with occupational health hazards, physical and mental. But lying awake, in the back of a van, shivering and inhaling the remaining fumes of your own urine and the urine of someone you've just met, with no gig in between to at least provide a purpose to the trip and an outlet for a for-once-genuine 'A funny thing happened on the way here' story, was as low as it got, surely.

I told everyone in Halpin's house this story, and loads of stories like it. Everyone was intrigued, even impressed, and seemed to form a respect, as I had done, for comedians and the commitment required to make a career.

My road stories were in contrast to their initial lines of questioning.

I didn't get girls after the shows. I didn't make a fortune. I hadn't met anyone famous.

Talking about the tragic nights always seemed to be easier than recounting the great nights, and, with time, and in retrospect, they always became the funniest nights.

I gradually began to follow Raymond's, and my dad's, advice, by pulling back on the gigs that were a waste of time.

I'd feel uncomfortable turning down gigs and I still felt like I should be grateful to anyone who was willing to book me, even if it was a five-hour drive away and for £10.

At the stage I was at, no matter how horrendous the set-up was or how few people were in the audience, doing a gig would obviously, if only marginally, provide more progression than sitting at home playing the PlayStation or sitting in someone's house or a pub, drinking and talking shite.

One promoter, who'd been promising that the next gig I did for him would be paid, had phoned me on a Saturday afternoon, saying he had a last-minute cancellation and that he needed me to support a more established act as part of a comedy festival he'd put together.

There was no fee, as 'the established act's management company was refusing to pay for a support', I was told by the promoter, who also informed me that he didn't have the budget either but he'd make it up to me and that it would be a 'huge favour'.

He also knew how eager I was to make it in comedy and added, 'What else are you going to be doing, sniffing glue with the rest of the Clydebank Neds?'

I asked my dad's advice and he snapped at me, 'If you don't tell him to fuck off, then I will.'

I hadn't mentioned the patronizing line about the glue-sniffing and the 'Clydebank Neds', as I knew that would send my dad off his head entirely.

'I'll be disappointed if you do the gig. If he wants you that badly he can pay you. Fuck him,' my dad concluded more calmly, explaining that it was frustrating for him, as a father, who was much older and more streetwise and who'd met manipulative guys like these cowboy comedy promoters all through his life, to see his impressionable son being used.

I grew to see my dad's point and I admired how much he'd look out for me and, effectively, act as my manager.

I didn't follow his advice in this instance, though.

I didn't tell the promoter to fuck off.

I phoned back and told him I'd do the gig, but that I felt it was about time I moved to paid work. I felt horrible saying things like that, but I was realizing that if I didn't speak out, nothing would change, no matter how well the gigs went.

The promoter told me that if the gig sold out, he'd give me £10. It was better than nothing and I felt a satisfaction that I'd stood up for myself.

I told my dad I'd turned down the gig and he said, 'Well done, son,' and apologized for snapping, explaining again how I'd only understand when I was a father myself.

I could tell my dad felt a little bad thinking that I'd turned down the gig and maybe that he'd sucked the fun out of it. I knew he had a point. I knew that to go forward again I'd need some quality control on what gigs I did. Constantly doing the same gigs was no good, and I was thinking more seriously about trying to get to London.

I told him I was heading round to someone's house, but then I realized that with my jeans and my boots on I was dressed a little formally to be sitting in a house, so I quickly got in there with 'and we might go to the pub', my mind still sharp from a year of lying about where I was going. I suppose I was missing the thrill of my double life – this was a final fix.

I left the house and got the 62 bus up to the city centre, to the venue. The gig went well, really well. On the Monday morning my dad asked me how my Saturday night had been. I was taken aback about why he seemed interested.

'Fine, just the usual, a few pints.'

He held out another newspaper, with a four-star review, of me.

They explained that they wouldn't normally review a support act in his or her own right but that they'd been impressed and keen to see more of me.

If at eighteen, you have learned to play down your punchlines and flesh out your gags then you're already good, not just promising.

Kevin Bridges is a born stand-up.

These were some of the quotes I remember my dad reading out.

'You little lying bastard,' he added, laughing, delighted at the review.

The show hadn't sold out, and I hadn't been paid £10, but a review like that was worth more than £10.

I told my dad I had totally seen his point and that I just didn't want to be stuck, bored, in a pub or in my room, when I could have been gigging. He understood and mentioned that he didn't mean to sound harsh and that I had the right attitude.

We both knew we were a team, though, and this was to be a rare disagreement. We were in it together.

58

I started trying to find out more about gigs in London, by reading online and by asking other comics.

Most of them acknowledged that it was the unknown and that London had probably the most congested and competitive comedy circuit in the world.

It wasn't as easy as phoning a promoter and asking for a gig.

Even the open-mic clubs were booked months in advance and you'd be lucky if anyone ever answered the phone to you.

A lot of comics I spoke to were quick to point out that, as prestigious as it sounded to do a gig in London, a lot of the gigs were awful, with the audiences made up mainly of performers and their friends and uninterested tourists only in for a drink or something to eat.

The size of the place, I was told, meant that even if I had a run of London gigs booked in, getting from one end of the city to the other could take hours, costing more money in travel. Then there was getting back to the accommodation, at night, after the shows. London had some dodgy areas and they weren't the kind of places you wanted to be a lost, eighteen-year-old, amateur comedian from a small town like Clydebank.

If the idea of staying in Scotland and well the fuck away from London hadn't been sold to me already, I'd also hear of how difficult it was for a Scottish comedian to play in front of a 'London' audience.

By everyone's accounts, except Raymond's, I was wasting my time.

Raymond was a professional and despite his profile amongst comedians and his contacts, he rarely played in London.

He'd often say the reason for this was that no clubs paid for accommodation for their comedians in London and that he could make better money in Scotland and in the other cities of the UK.

For me, this wasn't an issue. I wasn't making money anywhere. Largs had made me £50 and a few gigs for some of the more genuine independent promoters would pay similar, but I'd be lucky if I got a payday like this once a month.

The Stand paid me for every gig as well now. It wasn't a lot, at my stage, but with them it was more about the prestige of playing the top club. It was the place to be seen and the most enjoyable gig, by far.

But going to London made sense to me, somehow.

It was a new challenge and I'd give it a go for myself, fully prepared for failure.

I had nothing to lose, and it could only make me a better comedian, however it went.

I made the phone calls, again, for entire mornings and afternoons.

I sent the emails, attaching my reviews from the *Herald* and the other newspapers and magazines.

I phoned Eva, to ask if I could use her name as a reference.

She told me by all means use her name, but that she didn't know what good it would do as most of the comedy promoters in London took no interest in what went on outside of London, especially not as far as Scotland.

I'd phone places every day, repeatedly, to the point when I was harassing them.

I'd read the websites and some of them even had instructions for open-spot comedians chasing gigs, to help them cope with the demand for stage time.

Phone between 10 a.m. and 11 a.m. on a Tuesday, and ask for Nige.

Send a video of you performing to the email address below. If you don't hear from us, don't contact us.

Email Trev. You must have references from at least two professional comedians.

We do not book anyone we haven't seen, sorry. No open spots.

This is NOT an open-mic night – don't waste our time or your time.

I phoned Nige at a minute past ten every Tuesday morning, writing a note to remind myself to do so every Monday night before going to bed.

I didn't have a video of me performing but I still sent my email, and when they didn't contact me, I'd contact them.

I didn't have two references from professional comedians, so I'd work on getting them, but for now I'd email Trev, and the email he ignored I'd follow up with another email.

I'd phone the 'no open spot' places looking for an open spot.

I had my answer-machine message as polished as a stand-up routine and every time I heard the beep at the end of the promoter's 'If you're an open spot, looking to perform then please note that we only book . . .' spiel, I'd relay it again.

Making faces and getting animated on the phone kept my tone upbeat as I burned through top-up cards like I was entertaining a packed living room with prank calls.

'Hello, my name is Kevin Bridges. I've been performing stand-up comedy in Scotland for a year now and I'm looking for some gigs in London. I found this number on your website and I was wondering if you had any open spots available in the coming months.'

The people who'd actually answer the phone would usually be immediately dismissive: 'Where have you done gigs, mate? You ain't done none down here? Not for us, sorry.'

Some of them could even be quite funny in how blunt they were with their disdain for open-spot comedians, especially ones with an accent like mine: 'I can't understand you right now, mate. What chance have my audience got?'

I'd even begin leaving messages in a cockney accent, to make it a little more fun and less mundane than it was.

Over the weeks that followed on from my full-on, outbound, cold-call attack on London, the occasional email was replied to and the odd answer-machine message had caught someone in a good mood.

The gigs I could get were all five-minute, open-mic spots, all in different parts of London and all on different dates, which would have been okay if I lived in London, but I needed the trip to work logistically.

I couldn't go all that way for just one five-minute gig and then return a couple of months later and do the same.

I managed to get a spot at a club called Downstairs at the King's Head, which was said to be a well-respected gig amongst comedians.

I used this as my main date to work around and I found gigs on the two nights before, which would give me enough of a run to justify travelling to London.

The gigs were booked and April 2005 was to be my London debut.

I looked into travel and accommodation and worked out

that if I went for three nights I'd need around £100, to get the train or the bus down and then money for accommodation.

I didn't know anyone in London, so I had to look online at hostels and B&Bs, and even these were much more expensive than I'd budgeted for.

The cost of the trip, including travelling across the city and food, was escalating rapidly. I was grossly over budget.

My mum had found out that I hadn't been going to college, as my bursary money had been stopped. She wasn't best pleased about this, so she'd be reluctant to lend me any money.

I knew she was fully supportive and wanted, as much as me, for comedy to be my job, but right now that was a long way away, and if I was a dreamer, then she had to be the realist, watching out for me.

My dad had been somewhere in the middle, but he was now beginning to defend me and asking my mum to cut me some slack.

I'd go out looking for full-time work.

I'd go to the Job Centre and to careers fairs and I'd listen to the careers advisors.

I would look on the job-search machines, at all the jobs I was under-qualified and under-experienced for.

I was messing around one morning in the Job Centre, bored and looking at the 'entertainment' section of the job-search machine and laughing at the thought of me making £20 an hour as a 'webcam performer'.

As I was about to leave, feeling I'd done enough to keep my mum off my case for another day, an army recruitment officer approached me and invited me over to their desk, to discuss a potential career in the armed forces.

He was friendly enough and enthusiastic but I wasn't

listening to what he was saying; in my head, I was imagining myself on stage.

'*I don't have enough qualifications to sell phones, I don't have enough qualifications to sell phones, and you want to let me loose with a fucking machine gun?*'

He handed me a leaflet with more information and I made my way over to a desk, grabbed a pen and wrote this joke on the back of it.

I applied for jobs but with nowhere near the level of passion as I'd apply for a five-minute spot at Uncle Chuckle's Fun Club or somewhere of a similar ilk.

I tried to go about signing on, but the amount of paperwork blew my mind and the money from the dole, at the time around £60 every two weeks, I was probably already making from comedy.

If the government deemed this enough for someone to live on, then I was making a living from comedy.

I was a full-time comedian in Tony Blair's New Labour government's eyes, but, unfortunately, not yet in my mum's.

I didn't know how I'd find the money for my London trip and my mum told me I was getting ahead of myself, and whilst everything had been going well, it would be crazy to travel to London, on my own, for three days, staying in a hostel and just to perform a total of fifteen minutes of comedy.

My dad agreed. He'd listened to Raymond as well, so he knew how important trying to get on to the comedy scene in London was, but he knew it was too soon, that I was too young and that I hadn't been away, as far as London, on my own before.

I knew I could present a strong enough case against every argument my mum and dad put forward and, if it came to it,

I was an adult and they couldn't stop me, but I didn't have any way of financing the operation.

As I priced the trip I had about £30 in my bank account and I didn't have a paid gig for a couple of weeks, but by then it'd be too late. I had to book everything soon before the prices rose further.

I spoke to John about it. John had a couple of mates who'd moved to London and he said he'd been meaning to go down and see them, to catch up.

If John came with me to London, that would relax my mum and dad and it would make the thought of going to London a lot less daunting to me as well.

John told me he'd check with his work and see if he could get the days off. The following night he told me he could and to go ahead and book the trip. It was then I had to explain that I didn't have the money to book the trip.

We looked online and the trains were more expensive than the flights. If we flew at around 6 a.m. from Glasgow airport to Stansted and back at a similar time from Stansted to Glasgow then it'd be just over £100 in total for both our return flights.

John gave me his bankcard to go ahead and book the flights.

If I didn't tell him that I had no money until after it was booked, he wouldn't cancel, surely? I'd promise I'd pay him my share of the flying costs as soon as I got my cash from a £50 gig I had coming up in Fort William in two weeks' time.

Before I booked accommodation, I went in and told John that even the worst-looking bed and breakfast places were still around £50 per night for a twin room, £150 in total for the three nights, and I didn't know if the location was great for where my gigs were.

John phoned his mates and asked for some advice on

Presenting Billy Connolly with a lifetime achievement award.
A pleasure and an honour to meet the man for the first time.

FRANK
SKINNER

---

by Frank Skinner

To Kevin
My comedy Son.
Love + respect

The book that started it all, signed by the man himself.

John, me and my pal and fellow comedian Gary Little in New York, 2013.

Myself and Tony at the Champions League final in Wembley Stadium, 2013.

My dad still going on about 'the good write up in the paper', in the Shish Mahal Indian restaurant, at last, after a show at the Stand.

John, me and my dog, Annie, cruising Loch Lomond, July 2014.

some of the places I'd found to stay, most of them in Paddington. John's mates told him that Paddington was a safe enough area and a well-connected place for us to base ourselves.

Before we booked the digs, I had to come clean and tell John that I had only £30 to contribute to the trip.

John laughed and summarized the situation from his point of view: we were going down to London to try to further my comedy career, but would it be okay if he paid for everything.

I explained passionately that it wasn't like that and as soon as I'd entertained the locals in a pub in Fort William he'd receive his first instalment.

John laughed in an Italian-American, 'I'm only breaking your balls, kid' way and told me it was fine. I could pay him back in my own time.

The trip was confirmed.

I told my mum and dad. They were both relieved that a compromise had been found and thanked John for stepping in.

They both told me again that they would never stand in my way, but that they had to think practically and as my parents.

I knew this and I totally understood.

A couple of days after the trip was booked I remember my dad pulling me aside and telling me he had a plan. He'd seen a newspaper advert for the Scottish Arts Council, who were giving grants to 'young Scottish artists' to support them in their chosen fields.

He'd sent away for the form and filled it in on my behalf, enclosing cuttings of my newspaper articles and reviews, which my mum had kept.

He explained in the application that if I wanted to pursue

my comedy career then I'd have to get to London to perform 'try out' spots in clubs down there. He explained that this wasn't a begging letter, but that he was sure I had potential and that I'd remember to thank them one day.

The maximum grant was £200 and it arrived in the post a couple of weeks after I'd told my dad he'd embarrassed me, that comedy wasn't art and that it was unlikely they'd give me money to go and do gigs in pubs in London.

I was wrong. My dad was right and John was paid back.

My mum explained that they'd only got freaked out because all of this was so new to them. They'd never been to London, but they'd heard about how busy and lonely it can be, and they thought 'the youngest son heading off to the big city to try to make his name' was something that only happened in the movies.

59

John and I arrived in Paddington far too early to check into our B&B.

The B&B didn't look great, so it was probably wise to give the house-keeping staff as long as they needed to 'prepare' our room.

We left our bags and went out to have a look around.

We got back on the Tube, on the 'brown' line, and we headed towards the first place we'd heard of: Piccadilly Circus.

I'd put the song 'Think About the Way' by Ice MC on my iPod in anticipation of walking through the centre of London, taking it all in, in montage form, like the scene from *Trainspotting*.

It was as good a feeling as I'd imagined, looking at all the red double-decker buses, the black taxis, the buildings, the pace of life, the people, so many fucking people, from everywhere. It was like being in the centre of the world. Life was just whizzing by, but I felt like I could relax and watch it all.

I was passing John my iPod and telling him to listen and look around. He laughed, but he wasn't interested; he didn't care for any of my motivational exercises and meditational escapes. He let me have my moment, though, as he looked around for himself.

Just as I was going to ask him what he was thinking, and freak him out, as though I'd really gone transcendental and London had changed me, in under an hour, John announced, 'Right, I'm fucking starving.'

This snapped me back into reality, and we headed to a Subway that was behind us.

I'd gone from a pensive state of pondering our purpose here, in this world, or if there even was a purpose, to talking to an Italian student 'sandwich artist', who'd asked where I was from, commenting that he found it funny the way I said 'meatball marinara'.

I said it again and we both laughed.

I then remembered why I was in London and I felt like telling my new Italian buddy that if he liked the way I said 'meatball marinara' then he should come to my gig tonight.

My first London gig was on a Tuesday night, in Soho, in the upstairs room of the Queen's Head pub, near Piccadilly Circus and not far from where we'd been during the day.

Upstairs at the Queen's Head was a gig compered by a guy called Mike Manera.

Mike introduced himself and said he'd heard a lot about me.

I didn't see how he could have heard anything about me, as this was my first London gig.

I was on quite near the beginning of the night, which was handy, as there were about fifteen performers in total and there wouldn't be much left in the audience at the end of the night.

The audience, from what I could gather, listening to Mike speak to them, were from all over the world.

English, Scottish, Irish, Welsh, Canadian, American, South African, Portuguese and a few more.

There were around forty people in total in the room, a more than healthy turnout, and by far my most universal audience to date.

I got to the mic and said, 'Good evening,' as clearly enun-
ciated and as deliberate as I'd planned to say it on that very
first night.

I was introduced as being from Glasgow so this gave the
audience time to prepare for my accent. I tried to speak better and I'm sure they tried to listen better, but I don't think
they quite knew what I was on about.

*'It's great to be here, upstairs at the Queen's Head! Hopefully it'll be
better than my last gig, which was downstairs, at the Queen's Fanny.'*

This line maybe reads a little funnier than it was, but I
knew as soon as I'd said it that it was a cheap joke, crude and
lazy.

It was a thought I'd had when I arrived at the venue and
which hadn't so much as merited me saying it to John, even
if only for a little laugh, between us.

It was a weak opening line and it sounded like a joke someone on a stag do had probably made, in this same spot, drunk
and boisterous, on his first night in London.

It was funny for him, but I wanted to be a professional
comedian.

I should have opened my first ever London gig with something stronger than that.

The audience laughed, a little, but it wasn't the big opening
line I'd needed, the one that would release me into the gig,
the way my opening lines had done so many times now in
Scotland.

I didn't have time to dwell on this. It was done now and I
still had five minutes to win the audience back. I was learning
not to panic so much if I wasn't getting big reactions. It was
early on in the show, and I could bring the crowd round to
me, gradually.

I used my routine about the London tour bus, compared

to the Glasgow tour bus, changing the Edinburgh landmarks to London landmarks and the word 'rammy' to 'riot', which sounded nowhere near as funny.

I had re-worked a few ideas I had about taking the bus and it was now one long bus routine, featuring an old guy threatening a young guy for 'accusing' him of being less able, and a character I called the 'resident back-seat arsehole'.

'The resident back-seat arsehole is there, talking too loudly, unaware that the whole bus is listening in. "I was up the dancing on Friday, it was hoaching with fanny."

'Hoaching with fanny? Do women talk about nightclubs in the same way? "I was up the dancing on Friday, it was rammed with cock, wall to wall with big, sweaty, boaby."

'Then he's showing off his new phone: "It's got a video camera, games, Internet, polyphonic ringtones," and then his mate asks if he can borrow it to make a phone call. "I don't have any credit on it, sorry."

'A phone that doesn't make phone calls?'

I tried to change the Glasgow terms, as best I could. Words like 'hoaching', which means full of, or consisting of, and the word 'boaby', which is a Scottish word for a penis.

Anyway, I hope it isn't fucking exhausting to take all of this in and maybe there should be a Rosetta Stone-type translation disc available with this book.

I realized it was better if I just dropped these routines when I went outside of Glasgow, rather than edit them to the point where the essence of what was originally funny about the joke had been removed.

I was at a stage where every gig was a learning experience but some would feel like advanced lessons, as though I'd jumped ahead of myself and learned the equivalent of ten gigs in one.

I wasn't yet ready to perform to an audience as cosmopolitan as a central London audience. I'd maybe got away with the gig going okay, as I wasn't on with professionals and the audience's expectations weren't all that high.

The performance skills I'd picked up had maybe carried my lightweight material and, to be brutally harsh on myself, I felt like I was the slick, polished, open-mic comedian who looked sharp but had nothing meaningful to say.

I was glad I'd followed Raymond's advice and got down there quickly, to see how much work had to be done.

I didn't want to be a 'Glasgow comedian' in that you had to be from Glasgow to enjoy my stuff. I was too young to limit myself like that.

I knew I could always talk about Scotland and Glasgow; people would want to hear about that, but it had to be done in an accessible way and with more subtlety and better writing.

I had to write a new set for outside of Glasgow, but that didn't mean binning any routines. Instead I could keep the Glasgow material for my home-town gigs, and I could write more and more of it, without being concerned about how it would go down further afield. It wouldn't be going further afield.

We got to the venue for the gig the following night and met with John's mates, who had come down to watch. Eight o'clock came, the scheduled start time, and John's mates ended up being the only people who had come to watch. The gig was cancelled.

It felt like a wasted night, but we decided to have a few pints and go to see some more of London.

I felt bad that I didn't get to do my gig, but what could I do? I was here now.

I forgot about it and had a night out in London with John.

It was our first night being drunk together, so that was another landmark moment, and it was our first drunken heart-to-heart.

I let John know that I appreciated every lift he'd given me, every bit of cash he'd subbed me and every time he'd let me run my material past him.

He was full of praise and told me he was convinced that I could go all the way, reminding me of how far I'd come already by pointing up at the London sky.

We arrived at Paddington and staggered back towards our B&B, past another Aberdeen Angus Steakhouse, with both of us commenting on how many fucking Aberdeen Angus Steakhouses there were in London.

Waking up in a twin room of a claustrophobic B&B after a good night's drinking wasn't great and the age gap between John and me was closing as we both lay in our beds, unable to move and accusing each other of responsibility for the wide range of foul smells circling the room.

We argued like brothers: 'That was you.' 'For fuck's sake, what is wrong with you? You need to get to a doctor and get yourself checked out.' 'That is putrid, PUTRID!'

The room was uninhabitable and I hope the hotel's house-keeping staff won any damages claims they filed against their employers for the toxic fumes they must have inhaled upon entering our room.

We spent the day walking around London. We'd planned to go and see all of the city's football grounds but we weren't in a fit state of mind, and I had to eat something and then get my head back on the reason we were here.

The Thursday night show at the King's Head was packed.

The atmosphere was almost like the Stand. The ceiling was low, the sound was great, the audience sat up close, rammed in, there was smoke blowing all over the room, and when someone got a laugh, they knew all about it.

418

As was a London open-mic-night tradition, there were about fifteen comedians on. My spot was to be in the final section.

I had a long wait, about two hours, of standing at the back of the room, in the acts' corner, desperate to get on whilst there was so much energy from the crowd.

There were people who didn't seem to have a clue what they wanted to do; they'd freeze and start mentioning how warm it was on stage and how they'd forgotten what they wanted to say. I felt for them and I knew exactly how easy it was for that to happen, but it was frustrating, feeling lulls descend on what had felt like one of the best audiences you could hope for.

By the time I went on there was still enough energy and goodwill in the room to have a great set. I opened up and got straight into my material.

It wasn't too different a set from the Tuesday night, but I felt more alert. I was over the fact that I was in London. It was a gig. A gig was a gig and funny was funny.

I knew I had flaws in my act, but it was all I had, for now, so I needed to perform the life out of it. It was my last night, and when I returned I'd have better material and more gigs behind me, more experience.

The audience laughed at me and at my material. They didn't seem to have too much of a problem with my accent and there had been other London-based Scottish acts on before me, so they had tuned in a little.

They applauded when I finished my final bit of material and it led me to the end of my set. It was the same five minutes from Tuesday, but I'd slowed down, relaxed and let the audience, and myself, laugh.

The manager of the club, Peter, was very generous with

his praise, both about my performance and then about my determination, when he found out I'd travelled down from Glasgow just for two open spots.

He told me that he'd worked with all the best comedians in the business and that every one of them worked and worked and did everything it took to get better.

He told me to phone him the next week and he'd have me back for a paid, Saturday night gig, in five months' time.

I was delighted and it meant everything had been worthwhile.

Whilst the Tuesday had been a learning experience, it was pretty common-sense stuff and probably hadn't merited the expense and the time, but now I had something more tangible to show for the three-night trip.

I thanked Peter sincerely and told him I'd call him the following week, like he'd said.

I didn't want to call first thing on Monday morning as I knew I had to relax a bit and not look desperate. I tried to wait until Tuesday, or at least Monday afternoon, but I couldn't help myself and at just after 9 a.m. on the Monday morning I put my first paid London gig in the diary.

I didn't know how much I was to be paid and I didn't ask.

I knew it wouldn't be much, but it was the progress that mattered, the move from being another name on the waiting list to play at the open-mic night to being a name on the listings for their showpiece Saturday night show.

For the foreseeable future, I'd still make a substantial loss on every trip to London, but if I got in at new clubs after every visit, I could start planning trips down and putting runs of gigs together.

60

My Social Sciences college course officially finished in May, and I'd now used up all of my options with regards to studying.

I'd failed to complete two separate courses now, and if I wanted to study again, I'd need to pay the full tuition fees and wouldn't be entitled to any student bursary.

I was now unemployed, but unofficially, as I still hadn't got round to registering for Jobseekers' Allowance.

Most of my days were spent going to job interviews and on the phone chasing gigs in London and the rest of the UK.

I'd told my mum how well London had gone, but that I didn't want to be borrowing money from anyone again, and the Scottish Arts Council grant was a one-off bonus.

I wouldn't be handed £200 every time I wanted to go to London.

Stupidly, I was gambling more frequently. I had maybe too much free time during the days, and I'd stand in the bookie's, on the roulette machine, thinking that I could double my £40 and £50 fees from gigs, thus enabling me to book travel and accommodation for London.

I found that William Hill and Ladbrokes weren't as supportive of my dreams as the Scottish Arts Council and I ended up skint.

Everything I made I was betting. I wasn't making much money thankfully, but it was becoming a bit of a problem.

There were days I'd make a few hundred quid from as little as a fiver, but I wouldn't take it home and book travel. I was lying to myself. I would keep it and return to the bookie's the next day, and lose it all.

I'd then be back to using my own money, determined to win back the money I'd lost. A horribly grim way to spend time. One of the best things I ever did, a few years later, after several relapses, was giving up betting entirely.

I knew I had the personality to develop compulsive habits and it's a reason I'm glad I've never been tempted to try hard drugs.

I don't know if I was a gambling addict, by Gamblers Anonymous standards, and I'm sure there are far darker case studies than mine, but I realized that the delusion and denial in not viewing something as a problem could lead to the pits. I realized this, crucially, before any real damage was done.

I was travelling more for gigs and it was all I cared about. My search for work was becoming half-hearted and more farcical with every application form I filled in and with every job interview I put a shirt and tie on for and attended.

My hit rate at interviews wasn't great, and I'd only once made it back for a second interview, a 'group' interview where we had to do a teamwork exercise.

'Okay, guys! We're stranded on a desert island. We can only have two of these five items. Which two? Discuss!'

Who gives a fuck, mate? When are we ever going to be stranded on a desert island? We're cold-calling confused pensioners and the unemployed and lying to them about money they may be entitled to.

I sat there thinking and wondering what kind of person the manager was in his own time, amongst his mates, what he was really like?

What was he like at school?

'What about you, Kev?' the manager asked, bringing

me back into the room, acknowledging my lack of contribution.

'The gun, mate, I'd take the gun,' I said, bluntly, like I was a psycho, trying to raise a laugh, but the manager didn't snap out of character, no one did.

'Okay, great, any particular reason?'

Not even a smile from any of the budding candidates as they looked at me, waiting for an explanation, like we really were stranded on a desert island.

'I don't know. In case anyone steps out of line?'

This got a few smiles, out of relief, probably, as there was now less competition for the job.

I'd wiped myself off their radar.

I'd leave these places and it would motivate me to get on the phone, hunting more gigs.

This could be me next year: I'd be back there, in that office block, on that desert island, stranded.

I eventually spoke to my mum and told her that I understood her concerns about me not having another job, a proper job, to fall back on. It could be years before I'd be a professional comedian, if at all.

I asked her to give me until the end of 2005 to focus solely on comedy, and if I hadn't progressed to the point when I could support myself and pay her dig money from my income from gigs, then I'd make it my priority to find a full-time job, and travelling across the UK would have to be specifically for weekends or worked around my nine to five, Monday to Friday, working week.

My mum agreed to this, telling me, again, how I had her total support and that she'd love nothing more than to see me make a living out of something which meant so much to me and that I put so much into, but she had a responsibility, as a parent.

Every morning I'd check my emails, to see if anyone had got in touch regarding gigs.

Most of the bookings came through the phone, but I'd sent off so many emails to comedy clubs now that replies would trickle in, even weeks and months after the original correspondence.

I'd sent an email to Jongleurs Comedy Clubs, having got a contact for their central London booking office, after accepting that the cleaner or the security guard, or whoever found my letter on the floor of their Glasgow venue, wasn't getting back to me.

One of the chief bookers, Julia Chamberlain, replied, telling me that Jongleurs booked only professional comedians, whom they had seen successfully perform a short spot at one of their clubs, and to be even considered for a short spot you had to send a video of yourself.

Instead, Julia suggested that I enter a new-comedian competition called So You Think You're Funny?, which she was in charge of.

I looked up the competition and read that it was sponsored by Channel 4 and had been running since 1988.

The final was one of the comedy industry's biggest nights of the year, at the Edinburgh Fringe Festival.

So You Think You're Funny? had helped to start the careers of Peter Kay, Dylan Moran, Tommy Tiernan, Johnny Vegas and a load of other respected names in comedy. It was well-regarded as the number one new-comedy competition, and if I wanted my emails replied to, my phone calls returned and my diary filled, then this was a huge opportunity.

There were usually hundreds of applications to the heats, which took place in all of the major cities in the UK and Ireland. Every heat had around ten entries and the comedians who impressed Julia and the other judges went through to the semi-finals, and the winners of the semi-finals went on to the grand final.

The prize was £2,000 in cash and a trip to the Montreal Just for Laughs Festival, to perform in a showcase show.

These were the immediate prizes, but there was also the chance to impress in front of agents, bookers, promoters and other influential industry figures.

There were two Glasgow heats, both of them at Billy Bonkers' club in the State Bar. I knew the club well now.

My heat went well. I'd managed to get laughs on a night that felt like a struggle for everyone.

Comedy competitions could be fairly joyless affairs and it was difficult not to view the gig as an audition and feel like you were performing to impress the judges rather than to entertain the audience.

They are, however, undoubtedly influential for new comedians starting out and it definitely helps to move on a level. I didn't see it like that at the time but, looking back, writing this ten years later, I know they definitely laid some foundations for my career.

The audiences at the competitions, particularly at the local heat stage, tended to be made up of friends and families of the comedians, the competitors, and some of them were vocal with their support, shouting encouragement when whoever they'd come to see took the stage and sometimes heckling, or not listening to, the other acts.

I didn't take anyone, except John, as the last thing I needed in front of the judges was a squad about twenty-strong from Clydebank showing up and cheering me on, like I was a darts player.

I was on first in my Glasgow heat. I don't remember enjoying myself on stage, but I got big laughs and put on as good a performance as I could.

I was told on the night that I would be going through to the semi-finals, in August, at the Edinburgh Fringe.

I'd done enough. It was a big boost to my confidence, and it gave me something to look forward to.

I'd never won anything before, which was probably a factor in my decision to try stand-up. But I was only funny because I hadn't won anything before. So if I won something for being funny, would that mean that I wasn't funny any more?

I'd sit tormenting myself with thoughts like this before cutting myself a break and taking the overriding positive from it.

I'd won. I was through. I'd advanced.

I found and entered another competition, this one called the Amused Moose Comedy Awards, run by the Amused Moose chain of comedy clubs in London.

The prize was a trip to Australia, to perform at a few festivals over there, but even just getting to the final was a chance to be seen by the people who never replied to my emails or returned my calls.

Their Scottish heat was in Perth and featured about fifteen acts, with one outright winner to be announced on the night. The winner would then go on to a semi-final, which was also in August, at the Edinburgh Fringe Festival.

My Uncle George drove my dad and me to Perth and, again, I didn't particularly enjoy the gig and noticed the significant difference in atmosphere from a regular comedy show.

I got the laughs and I knew I'd done well and got everything I could from the audience.

We hung around until the end. It was close to midnight when the judges came on to the stage and announced my name.

I was through to another semi-final.

We drove home, and I could tell my Uncle George was proud. He'd coached football teams his whole life, so the talk of semi-finals and winning translated to him.

I didn't like the competitive side that these gigs brought to my comedy, watching the other acts and comparing myself to them, thinking how loud their laughs were compared to mine.

It wasn't a healthy way to perform. It wasn't natural, and comedy is too subjective for a judge to simply decide who was the 'funniest'. I'd remind myself that I only had to do each competition once and I'd have moved forward, no matter what happened.

I was sure I'd get something out of it all, either £2,000 and trips to Canada and Australia, or an agent, or even just some new gigs.

It would all be worthwhile.

I was going to be spending a lot of time in Edinburgh in August. I had my two semi-finals and the Stand had booked me for short spots on their 'Best of Scottish' comedy show-case, and loads of other one-off smaller gigs were coming in as well, gigs in pubs which would come close to matching my 'smallest audience played to' record.

In the run-up to the Fringe, I forced myself to try at least one new joke or routine at every gig. I needed better material. I'd seen what a good comedian was and I wasn't a good comedian yet; a good new comedian maybe, but if I didn't move on, I'd plateau and then start regressing.

I had no college and no job interviews to worry about for now, so I'd make sure I bought the papers, watched the news, read books, watched movies, and did anything that would stimulate me and fill up my days, as I knew I could easily end up slipping into a depression of lying around all day, nervous about the night's gig, doing the gig, getting home late, being unable to sleep and then sleeping all of the next day, waking up and repeating the cycle.

I'd need only seven minutes of material for the comedy competitions, and then between ten and fifteen minutes for the rest of the gigs I had booked in.

The longer sets would take care of themselves, but it was the shorter sets I'd need to work on. I had to trim off everything that wasn't solid; time was precious and I had to show everyone what I could do in seven minutes.

Just a month before the Festival started, the London 7 July bombings took place. I watched all of the footage on TV, and I recognized places where I'd been with John.

I recognized Tube stations and streets, and London seemed much closer to me now that I'd visited and felt a connection with the place.

It was a tragic loss of life. As I watched the reaction over the weeks that followed, I started to write down some things I'd noticed. I'd watch the fear and the hysteria being perpetuated by some media sources. Then, two weeks later, the shooting by the Metropolitan Police of the innocent Brazilian Jean Charles de Menezes, in Stockwell station, blew my mind.

The story of what had actually happened was unclear in the immediate aftermath, but it was commonly accepted at the time, although since proven false in court, that Jean Charles de Menezes had been running, was told by police to stop, but kept on running, presumably to catch his train.

There were also tabloid articles reporting that he had been 'acting suspiciously'.

I'd hear people say how they 'sympathized' with the police officers and the stress they were under, how they 'couldn't take any chances', and making other statements like that which wouldn't have been alarming if we were in the Deep South of America.

'*He was acting suspiciously in a train station. Who doesn't act suspiciously in a train station? If you need a piss or have an itchy arse in a train station, you act suspiciously,*' I'd say, and act out edgily looking around, uncomfortable and trying to have a scratch without anyone noticing.

'*You'd maybe expect people to walk away from you, but not seven fucking bullets in your head.*'

Comedy could be social commentary as well, and I'd enjoy it when the audience would laugh and then applaud, recognizing there was more behind the joke. I liked getting into a ranting style and giving what I was saying some conviction.

This was coming with confidence and experience, and if I could keep my writing up to the same level, I'd be on my way to becoming a good comedian and a professional comedian.

London had recently been awarded the 2012 Olympic Games, and it led me to make a joke about an Olympic city where people are shot for running.

I'd never go into a subject as dark as a terrorist attack purposely looking for a humorous angle, but it was through watching comedians like Richard Pryor and Chris Rock that I saw comedy could also make a point, as long as it was funny.

Articles I read about the 'true cost of asylum seekers to the UK taxpayer' also caught my eye, around about the same time, with certain newspapers rinsing everything they could from the racial tensions and anti-Islam feelings that followed on from the 7 July bombings.

I'd listen to people, guys in pubs, guys in the bookie's, guys on the bus, guys on radio phone-ins or being vox popped on current affairs shows – always guys, guys who'd read tabloid newspapers at face value, taking every headline entirely as fact – ranting that the country was being taken over.

I'd never say anything, but I'd listen and wonder what the real reasons were for what they were saying, what their real problems were.

There was no point engaging in a one-on-one debate with someone who had no real weight behind their claims other than that they wanted to believe them. They wanted to believe that every foreigner who arrived in the UK was immediately given a luxury penthouse apartment and a Premiership footballer's wages every week on benefits.

They wanted to believe that 'this country's lost its identity' because it's an easier way of saying, 'I preferred it when it was all white people.'

Challenging or questioning these outlooks would maybe make people consider looking at the issues in a different way, but only until they met someone who agreed with them and reassured them that they were right, that immigration had destroyed everything.

On stage, though, I could make light of these flawed but increasingly popular viewpoints and maybe offer some sort of defence for people unfortunate enough to be born in a war-torn hellhole, who had managed to make it out, to start a new life.

I'd done some research and found that the majority of asylum seekers, at the time, were fleeing from Iraq and Afghanistan and their 'true cost' to the UK taxpayer was a fraction of the cost of the two wars the UK was needlessly involved in, in Iraq and Afghanistan.

We were the ones dropping the bombs on them, so we couldn't complain when they were looking for a place to stay.

'If somebody blew your house up, you'd expect them to at least put you up. If my house was bombed, I'd be asking questions. Did you just fucking bomb my house? I'll be crashing on your couch for a bit, then.'

61

For my semi-final of So You Think You're Funny?, my dad had come to the gig again, this time with my Uncle Kevin, who'd been to see me only once before, about a year earlier, in a pub in Paisley, where I performed as a warm-up for the pub's weekly pool tournament.

The pool tournament wasn't to start until the comedians had finished, but things began to get heated as everyone struggled and the pool players grew impatient.

I had my back to the pool table, and was performing to the bar, sweating and talking rapidly, trying to get anything from them.

I wrapped it up and said good night, to the particularly tragic sound of a coin being carefully placed into its denomination's allocated slot, followed by a short, sharp push and balls falling down.

They'd heard enough. It was pool time.

I always felt strange around people who'd seen me die on my arse.

It was quite an awakening and a humbling experience, standing there with no one laughing, or listening, no instruments to play and no songs to sing, no magic tricks and no jokes to reply to 'tell us a joke' with.

I found it hard to talk to people who'd watched me at gigs like this, as though they'd always be thinking about it when they were in your company; they probably weren't but that was the paranoia that came with dying on stage.

You remembered everyone who was there, everyone who saw it, who saw you in that vulnerable state.

I hoped to have a good night, to show my Uncle Kevin that I was funny and that at the pool-tournament pub gig in Paisley there were external factors affecting my performance.

He probably knew that anyway, but, still, it was for my own peace of mind. I didn't think of the judges; I knew I wouldn't be funny if I went on and performed with them in mind. My material was strong, topical, current and I was on form at all the gigs, so I just had to relax and be funny. Then my Uncle Kevin would see me make a crowd laugh.

I was on first, again.

That wasn't great, but I was at a stage where I was opening almost every gig I played, a sign of trust from promoters that I could get the night up and running and that I'd moved on from the short spot in the middle of the night.

I remember the compere, Alun Cochrane, telling us all before the show that although this seemed like a massive thing right now, in the grand scale of a comedy career, which most of us would go on to, it was nothing, and to relax and enjoy it.

It was excellent advice. I relaxed. There was a buzz in the room and I felt funny, I felt confident.

I went on and everything got laughs and claps, and I finished to a cheer from the crowd. I looked over at my dad and my Uncle Kevin and both of them were giving me thumbs up and pointing at me.

I hated having to wait around and watch everyone else. I couldn't enjoy anyone else's set for thinking about the judges, who they'd prefer and what they were looking for.

It was a far better standard of new act than I'd seen. This was clearly the pick of the new guys; the competition was doing its job of identifying new talent and I don't remember anyone having a bad set.

The judges took about twenty minutes at the end, leaving the room and returning with an envelope, which they handed to Alun Cochrane.

I looked over at my Uncle Kevin, who I knew would be sitting there like an excited American parent at their daughter's beauty pageant or their son's 'little league' hockey game.

I knew my dad would be nervous for me and be a lot quieter.

Alun quickly opened the envelope, acknowledging that he knew how horrible it felt for the performers at the back, waiting to hear who was going to the final.

He asked for a massive round of applause for all of us and the audience showed their appreciation for what had been a great night of comedy.

The applause died down and went to silence as Alun opened the envelope, leaned into the microphone and announced:

'Kevin Bridges.'

There was a loud cheer from the audience, even though it seemed so long since my set, all the way back at the beginning of what had been a long night.

Alun invited me forward and I began to panic, thinking he was going to ask me to say a few words. Fuck that.

He said my name again. I walked on stage and he shook my hand.

I waved at the audience and stood not knowing what to do. I'd never taken a bow before and I would look so awkward taking a bow that it would overshadow my victory.

I left the stage before I ruined the moment.

Walking back I looked over at my dad and my Uncle Kevin, who were up on their feet, clapping, whistling and punching the air. It was nice but I couldn't shake off the feeling that this wasn't why I'd got into comedy, to perform for seven minutes and win competitions.

A few nights later was the other semi-final, in the Amused Moose competition. The format was different; there was no one winner, just a selection from each semi who would go into the final.

I was put through to the final after having a good enough show, under the circumstances, performing to around ten paying punters and a room of casting directors, TV producers and other people with power, and who knew it. I began to feel out of place, more so than ever before.

'Look at these people,' I was thinking. 'They're from a different planet to me. I'll never make it in comedy; this is their world.'

What was 'making it' anyway?

Being on television?

Being on television doing what?

I'd reached the finals of two respected comedy competitions, and it was my first time in an environment like the Fringe.

Everyone was talking to me at the Stand, at the 'Best of Scottish' shows. I was being congratulated by guys like Bruce Morton, Parrot, Fred MacAulay, legends of the Scottish comedy scene.

They'd introduce me on stage as 'the young hope' of Scottish comedy and tell the audience that I'd reached the final of So You Think You're Funny? and that they should watch out for me.

I should have been enjoying myself. I was eighteen and all of this was happening.

I should have been out at the performers' parties, drinking and getting girls, but instead I was feeling like I was now out of my depth, like it had gone too far.

I was talking to another new comedian and being told that no matter how the finals went, I'd be seen by the biggest and best agents, and be signed up by television networks.

Casting directors would want to meet me. It was no longer about getting a few extra gigs. This was the big league now.

Everyone seemed to have some sort of advice for me: maybe I should dress smarter, lose some weight, speak slower, drop this joke and drop that joke, don't swear, get some acne cream, style your hair.

'It's not what you do on the stage, it's what you do off the stage,' I remember hearing one agent say to a comedian, which was probably the most bleakly flawed piece of advice I'd ever heard.

I became a little disillusioned and unsure of what I wanted to do.

I enjoyed most of the gigs at the Fringe, but it was the first time that other stuff mattered, things like networking and meeting the right people.

I'd met guys with 'five-year plans', guys who knew what agent they wanted, what clubs they wanted to play, what venue they wanted to play for their Fringe solo-show debut. They knew journalists and they hung around the artists' bars, talking to anyone who was important, laughing at their jokes, feigning interest in their stories, before looking around to see if anyone even more important had shown up.

Bill Bailey was the compere for the So You Think You're Funny? final, in front of my biggest crowd yet, over five hundred people, in the Gilded Balloon, one of the Fringe's most famous venues.

I was on first, again. I raised a few laughs, but I was too rigid and afraid to try anything different. I'd listened to too many people and I'd talked myself out of the gig.

I was beginning to fear the idea of success, but my fears proved to be unwarranted.

I won fuck all.

The winner was Tom Allan, with the runner-up spot going to Sarah Millican and third place to Joe Wilkinson.

The other five or six of us were simply finalists.

I knew getting to the final had been an achievement but I felt drained and I was looking forward to getting back to enjoying comedy, to enjoying standing up and making people laugh, with nothing else to consider.

I congratulated Tom, Sarah and Joe and went back out to get my dad and my Uncle George.

On the way home the car was silent. My dad and my Uncle George tried to pick me up. I appreciated it, but I preferred the silence.

I thought back to Alun Cochrane's advice, about how, in the grand scale, this was nothing, but it didn't feel like that.

I felt I'd let myself down. Would I have laughed at myself? Would any of my pals have laughed at that performance?

It was polished and slick and I didn't swear a lot.

I looked sharp, but I wasn't funny.

I didn't go to the after-show party as I'd have felt like I was at my own wake, people would be coming up to me, to express their condolences.

I didn't want to meet agents, casting directors or TV people. Fuck them, I thought, defiantly, feeling I could be a rebel and start a new anarchic wave of comedy.

I'd put on a shirt for nothing.

I don't remember too much about the Amused Moose final other than Sarah Millican winning.

I congratulated Sarah before I left, and we both acknowledged that it would be good to work together again, in a friendlier environment than competitions.

Shortly after the festival, I entered my final two competitions. The first one was a new-act competition for Jongleurs

Comedy Clubs. I reached the final, which secured me two paid short spots with Jongleurs for early in 2006.

The other competition was the BBC New Comedy search. I reached the semi-final, which was a paid gig and had a very receptive audience, who seemed to ignore that it was a competition.

I remember having a good set that went out on BBC Radio 4, and although I didn't win the semi-final, it was a break, and a lot of comedy promoters mentioned they'd heard me, and more short spots in clubs all over the UK began to come in.

After the competitions, I realized that I had to seriously think about what I wanted. I'd met all of the next big TV stars, the young hopefuls looking for their short-cut through stand-up and into acting, presenting, or hosting a game show.

There was nothing wrong with that and good luck to them.

It just wasn't what I wanted.

An email had come to Eva, not long after the Fringe, asking if I'd be able to meet, in Glasgow, for a casting, a 'screen test' with a few producers who were looking for new talent to present a weekend magazine show for young people. I went along to the screen test, thinking, 'Who the fuck wants to see a sixteen-stone eighteen-year-old from Clydebank interviewing bands like Busted and the Kaiser Chiefs?' But I knew the job would pay a shit load of money and I could give it all to my mum, until they sacked me, and that way I'd have bought myself some more time to get ahead in comedy.

I'd imagine the ridicule I'd face from my friends every Saturday and Sunday morning, as they lay in bed, hungover, watching me making peace signs and love hearts at the camera and using annoying, exaggerated, facial expressions.

Dressed like a Topman mannequin, talking excitedly about everything, saying things like 'amaze-balls' and addressing the viewers at home as 'guys'.

The 'screen test' audition consisted of two guys, with names like Zac and Max, asking me rapid questions in front of a camera.

Who's your favourite band and why?

What's a quirky fact we might not know about you?

Have you ever met anyone famous?

If you had one special power what would it be and why?

I managed to answer the questions, but only after stalling and mumbling and asking why they wanted to know these things, as though they actually wanted to know and they weren't fodder to get me animated and talking, exuberantly and unnervingly, with all the forced charm of a timeshare salesman.

It was a disaster but so much of a disaster that we all had to laugh about it and I began to think of how I could incorporate the event into my act.

Someone had made a mistake, somewhere. Surely they hadn't seen me in the flesh and just saw my age, read my reviews and heard there was a bit of a buzz about me.

Zac told me I'd been 'awesome', and Max agreed: 'So great. I loved the deadpan approach. It was something different. Different is awesome. We love different.'

I was expecting Max to turn round and say, 'Hey, Zac! Do we like different?' and them both to break into a song and dance routine as I made my way out of the studio.

I left the building and went for a walk through Glasgow again, like during the college days. I listened to music from all of my favourite bands, whose names I couldn't remember under the bright lights of the studio.

I wasn't going to make a fast buck presenting and what would the satisfaction in that be, anyway?

I needed to lose my 'me against the world' mindset, and get over the fact I'd stumbled into stand-up and that every gig could be the gig that finished me. I was here now and the overwhelming majority of my approximately one hundred gigs had gone well.

I had to stop fixating on the negatives. I was headed in the right direction.

62

I performed my first open spot at the London Comedy Store thanks to Rhod Gilbert, who had recently been signed to their management department and recommended me after we performed together for a weekend at the Stand in Edinburgh.

Rhod hadn't been going long, but he was being tipped for the top and I found him to be very open and supportive. He knew how frustrating it could be, chasing gigs, especially in London, and he'd compiled a document on his computer, with contact details for promoters in every city in the UK and Ireland, with their numbers, what gigs they booked and some additional comments, things like 'pays accommodation' or 'only books open spots who can drive'.

It was a great idea, a guide almost, for any new act.

It saved me time and pointless phone calls.

Rhod emailed me the document and I reckon I phoned every number on it, at least once.

My Comedy Store open spot went well. But this was the most famous and prestigious comedy club in the UK and it would need to have gone exceptionally well for me to even think I could get on their books after one shot at it, at eighteen.

The manager of the club, Don Ward, a comedy-circuit legend, always brought the open spots into his office, to discuss how the gig had gone. I told him I felt it went okay, but that I knew I wasn't ready.

Don was positive. He told me I had potential, but that I

had to write more universal material. He mentioned that I was very young and that I needed experience.

However, he'd like to offer me another open spot, in six months' time, and he reckoned that if I came back to him every six months with new material, better each time, I'd be on my way to maybe one day playing his club.

I was disappointed, but aware that I was being impatient.

This was the London Comedy Store. I watched the rest of the comics, Jim Jefferies, Glenn Wool, Ed Byrne, take the roof off the place, with brilliant, solid, twenty-minute sets. Every line was perfect.

It would be easy to think, 'What's the point?' But it was something else to work towards, another target.

The Stand had been my gig to report back to, improved, after months away, and now the Comedy Store was the same.

I'd been booked by the Stand to play their festive shows at the end of 2005, a five-night run starting from Boxing Day, in the Glasgow club.

Jane Mackay hosted it, with me opening and Bruce Morton and Martin 'Bigpig' Mor alternating between headlining and supporting each night.

The run was a great way to finish off a year that had had some low points, but low points that were helping me grow stronger, mentally and as a comedian.

On the very last night of the run, on New Year's Eve, Jane asked if I'd go in the middle and do twenty minutes instead of opening and doing fifteen, as she wanted to give me a fright, to see if I could step up.

I was delighted at the promotion, especially as my mum and dad and a couple of my friends were in the audience.

It was the last night of 2005 and in the new year I'd have to review my situation with my mum, but with a good gig here, in my new role, how could I be expected to get a real job now?

441

The gig went great, and with my promotion and the increase in wages as it was New Year's Eve, I was handed £200, in cash.

There was little time to think about the money, though. Jane was asking my plans for 2006 and suggesting that I do a solo show, at the Glasgow International Comedy Festival, in March. 'You're getting a bit of a following in here,' she told me, noting that they were getting phone calls to the office on the days after my gigs from people asking, 'Who was the young guy?' They'd quote my jokes and ask when I was on again.

I wanted to do a show. I'd need sixty minutes of material, a full hour. I didn't know how much material I had, but it was another challenge and it would keep me moving forward.

I was beginning to put a plan of my own together.

My mum never mentioned anything about finding a job.

The subject never came up again.

It was all on me now. I'd got what I wanted; comedy was my job and I'd have to work at it.

I performed my solo show, upstairs in a pub called Universal, in the city centre of Glasgow.

I sold fifty tickets, through people who'd seen me before, in shorter sets, and word of mouth.

Some friends and family came down as well, and some fellow comedians, to show their support. I'd say there were around seventy people in the audience and I knew only about twenty of them.

I performed for exactly an hour, and it was the highlight, by far, of the two years since my first gig. I wondered who the people were who'd come out of their way to see me, strangers who'd spent £5 to sit and listen to me.

I didn't ever think I'd be able to talk for an hour. I'd been taking driving lessons and not enjoying them, so I knew how long an hour could be.

I had my beginning and my ending sorted and all of the subjects I wanted to talk about, but I realized that I could be funny when I relaxed and let my natural side come out, as opposed to racing to the punchlines, to the checkpoints.

I didn't feel attached to my material, to a script. It was a more honest kind of comedy and I hoped the audience felt like they knew me, like they could relate to me.

I used a lot of Glasgow material. It was local humour, perhaps, but it was funny, and where else could I do it?

The audience that night were fully aware that I wasn't the finished article and that I had a long way to go. The ticket prices were low and I was billed as one to watch. They were receptive and I spoke to them after the show, thanking them for coming.

It felt like the start of the next level. This was my fan base, this crowd of fifty.

If they'd enjoyed my show then they'd come back again, and they might bring their friends. I'd give them a new show and it would continue on from there.

After this debut solo show, generating material became easier and it felt like I'd had a mental block before. I could talk now, on stage, with confidence, and write longer routines rather than jumping from subject to subject, gag to gag.

I knew it would take more than one solo show to really get good at longer sets, but it felt great to have pushed myself to do it, to have faced another fear.

The Stand were now programming tours, the Glasgow International Comedy Festival's Community Tour, which I was booked for, along with Bruce Morton again and Gary Little.

I'd performed with Gary a few times. He'd started only a year before me, so we'd been on a lot of bills together where I'd be the five-minute open spot and he'd be the ten-minute.

443

We were both getting ahead and progressing now, so we'd seen each other more at nicer, better-organized gigs, and we were both beginning to relax and get used to it all.

Gary was a fairly intimidating-looking guy, well over six foot, bald and built like a man who'd done some jail time.

We got on well on the community tour, performing in community centres all over Glasgow, to some pretty wild but warm and receptive crowds, and he quickly became one of my best mates in comedy.

Gary was closer to my dad's age than mine, but he had a young guy's outlook. He'd stayed with it and he was like a cool-as-fuck uncle who'd hold court at family parties and who all the young ones aspired to be like when they were older.

It was important to make friends in an industry as solitary, ruthless and competitive as comedy.

I enjoyed the car journeys when it was with good people, and the gigs where we'd stay overnight.

I'd look forward to the summer tours of the Highlands and Islands of Scotland.

We'd drive up from Glasgow, do the shows, stay over-night, drink in the local pub. The owner would hear we were all the comedians who'd done a show in town and we'd get a lock-in until the morning.

There were girls, girls who I'd presumed would be out of my league, but who'd approach me now after the shows. They'd stand and talk, at least until a drunk guy would pass, shouting something like, 'Funny gets the fanny,' and then they'd go back to join their pals, but, still, there were girls.

I was relaxing now and being my age a bit more.

I was nineteen and I couldn't continue with the weight of the world on my back. Bad gigs would happen. I'd meet pricks, people would have a go at me, I'd be criticized.

I had to let all of this go, be more carefree, and it would come through in my comedy.

This was my life now. I wasn't stranded on that desert island, cold-calling pensioners.

63

It was a good life, especially for a young guy, but it would be easy to become distracted and for the gigs themselves to suffer, as you spend more and more days hungover, lying fucked in B&Bs and in the back of cars. Some guys would justify this to themselves, saying that they needed chaos to be funny, to create.

I found I needed chaos, in bursts, but that in the long run a hedonistic lifestyle would see me burned out and stuck doing the same gigs, doing the same material and becoming jaded and bitter towards whoever was coming up at my back.

I'd look at a lot of guys that this had happened to and it was a warning. I knew the gigs I could have a good time at, the ones where the promoters would pay less but promise a free bar and a free meal. They were good, for the fun and to see new places, but once I'd done them a few times, the only way was backwards.

I was trying to focus on getting more work in England as well now, which meant a lot of travelling on my own, to places I knew only from football coupons.

A promoter called Warren Speed, who ran gigs all over the north-east of England, was booking me regularly and I'd be down there every couple of weeks. Because I didn't drive, I'd have to stay overnight a lot in B&Bs and on other comedians' couches, so I'd usually find other gigs that I could book in around Warren's gigs.

I was starting to spend weeks away, on the road. I'd use the money from the paid gigs to fund the trips to the unpaid, open-spot, try-out gigs.

I'd play every gig at least once, until I felt they'd seen my best, and if they didn't want to book me, then fuck it; I'd tried and I wasn't going to let them take the piss.

I was becoming a travel and tourism expert, and I'd be in Internet cafés in different towns every day, planning my train journeys, finding the ones with the least changes, deliberating over what was the most convenient, a five-hour train journey with three changes or a six-hour train journey with only two changes. What if I fell asleep and missed a change?

Getting in at the big comedy clubs was difficult, and sometimes I'd think it was a pride thing, that they wanted you jumping through all sorts of hoops before they'd accept you.

When you were in, you were in, though. This was good, but it was part of the problem for new acts trying to come in.

The clubs would have their favourites, the guys who came down on the nights that they weren't working, to drink and to sit backstage. Comedy was a social thing to them; they hadn't written a new joke in years but they'd still be guaranteed their bookings.

The regional, independent promoters were always the first ones to re-book open spots for paid work. They weren't as precious, and their gigs were usually in pubs, hotels, student unions, bingo halls and social clubs, so there wasn't a reputation at stake.

The gigs would start and then stop after a few months, and they'd move on and find another venue to start a gig in. I was aware of this and conscious not to chase the money. I'd do enough of them to support me until I could fill up my diary with bookings for the big clubs.

I was offered £150 to headline a pub gig in Middlesbrough

one night, but I already had a ten-minute open spot booked in for the Banana Cabaret comedy club in London, one of the top clubs. The money was tempting, but that's all it was. I had to think longer term.

I went down to the Banana Cabaret and I struggled, doing only just enough to get myself another open spot six months later. If I'd cancelled the gig, then I could have gone to Middlesbrough, rescheduled my ten-minute spot for six months later, and been in the same position, but £150 better off.

That was the nature of the game and you had to laugh and get on with it or you'd go mental.

I'd still be doing the odd bizarre gig, but now I'd be paid for them, which made them slightly easier. In the space of one month, I'd performed in a prison, a bingo hall and a call centre, during office hours, as part of a comedy show rewarding the top sales people.

These gigs were good as they would provide stories and material, but then you were in danger of becoming the comedian who only talks about other gigs and doesn't seem to have anything to say.

A break for me came when my Jongleurs short spots had gone well, and the manager at their Glasgow and Edinburgh clubs, Patrick Spencer, began to phone the London offices telling them that I should be headlining their clubs, despite my age, as the Scottish crowds were going wild for me and heckling the other acts on after me.

Comedy purists wouldn't have a lot of nice things to say about Jongleurs, even if they'd never played them, and it became something of a stigma to be known as a 'Jongleurs act'.

Jongleurs had clubs all over the country and their mission statement was: 'Eat, Drink, Laugh, Dance.'

Laughing was third on the list. The tickets were usually

sold in bulk, to stag and hen parties and to other large groups. Before the shows, the music would be cranked right up, bass heavy, and light displays would get the crowd fired up. Robbie Williams's 'Let Me Entertain You' would play before the show started and the crowd would sing along. The louder they would sing, the drunker they were and the harder the gig could be.

At first I was too young to see it like that, and I started to be booked by them, more and more. The gigs paid well and for their clubs outside of where you lived, except London, they'd pay for your accommodation, always a hotel, which was a break from B&Bs and other comedians' couches, floors and spare rooms.

Julia Chamberlain, who booked Jongleurs and who took an interest in developing new comedians, would invite me along to her house in Brixton, any time I was in London.

She'd enjoyed my set at the So You Think You're Funny? final, and she'd seen me a few times since and was quick to mention how much I'd progressed.

Julia lived with her partner, the brilliant Australian comedian Trevor Cook, so she'd seen comedy from a performer's perspective as well.

She'd stopped her work as an agent representing new comedians, as most of them would leave her when one of the bigger management companies came in.

Meeting someone like Julia, who knew the comedy industry well, but who, above all, was a kind and genuine person, proved to be the best thing that came out of my first Edinburgh Fringe experience.

I didn't have an agent. I didn't know what agents or managers to approach about representation, but Julia would offer advice on all of that.

Not having an agent didn't bother me and, from what I

could gather from comedians I knew who had one, it was a badge of honour rather than anything that could dramatically change your career.

It was someone who could make the phone calls to fill your diary, make sure you were being paid the going rates and maybe find you the odd bit of corporate work or television warm-ups, but nothing that was going to make you an overnight superstar.

I think I quite enjoyed chasing gigs myself and I was gigging constantly, sometimes every night of the week, and now, with regular Jongleurs work, I could pay dig money to my mum and afford to spend more weekends in London.

Everything was going fine without an agent, and Julia maintained that I didn't need one whilst I was on the club circuit. It was only when I wanted to move on a level, into things like television and touring, that an agent would be neccessary, and by that time there would be plenty of offers.

I had been approached by a few people, but I didn't fancy signing contracts and the people interested in me never seemed to have a lot of big-name acts on their books.

Throughout 2006, I'd see more of Frankie Boyle, having been introduced to him one night at the Stand by our mutual friend, Jim Muir, who performed as the Reverend Obadiah Steppenwolfe III and who'd been a long-term writing partner of Frankie's.

Jim and Frankie were the cool guys of Scottish comedy; their material was pretty out there and they were constantly working on some sort of surreal, dark but daft and funny script for a sitcom or a short movie.

They always seemed to be doing mental shit, like taking mind-bending legal highs and then going to a martial arts class, just to see what happened.

I liked hanging around with them. They both seemed to

have a phenomenal intellect and I'd feel a little out of my depth talking to them about some of the weightier issues that would arise in their conversations.

I'd laugh, though, and they'd recommend books for me to read and movies to watch. They were definitely two of the most interesting people I knew and being in their company was educational and pretty fucking funny.

Frankie's profile was rising; he was in demand and well on the way to becoming who he is today. He'd watched me a few times and was full of praise. His praise was more specific than most people's and he'd pick out lines and certain bits from my act. It was interesting to talk comedy with him. It amazed me how technical he was and how much time and dedication he put into comedy.

He'd begun to send me some writing work, for TV appearances that he had coming up, and he'd pay me, even if he didn't use any of it. I'd never written for a TV show before, and I'd feel embarrassed at some of the weak shit I'd send him.

He kept with me, and he'd pick the bits that were funny and explain that it was a discipline in itself, to be able to sit and write jokes, on demand. I felt myself improve, and a few of my jokes started to make it – not many, but enough to give me confidence.

As well as giving me some writing work, Frankie asked me to be the studio warm-up for a TV pilot he was making for the BBC in Glasgow.

The studio warm-up gigs were fine, and the crowd enjoyed my stuff. I could stand up and make most audiences, in most environments, laugh. It was what I'd done every night of the week now, and it was no problem, but I'd still begin to feel out of place amongst TV people and especially being in a TV studio for the first time.

I remember one of the production staff telling me that if I ever wanted to get ahead in TV I should 'try to sound a little less like a Ned'. She laughed and mentioned how I couldn't pronounce the word 'world' properly, in my introduction to the show, *Frankie Boyle's End of the World Show*. It was like being back at school.

I didn't take things like this to heart any more. I was beginning to think that I might never make it on to TV, for loads of reasons, but it wasn't an obsession to me.

I wanted to tour and play my own shows to my own audiences, like Frankie was about to, and TV would have helped me with that, but I still had a lot of work to do on the comedy circuit, to firmly establish myself.

64

Towards the end of 2006 and the beginning of 2007, I was now regularly working with top comedians, the best on the circuit and the people who, along with Frankie, would soon be household names: Michael McIntyre, Micky Flanagan, John Bishop, Sarah Millican, Craig Campbell, Tom Stade, Stewart Francis and loads more.

I was getting in at most of the top venues in the UK, and I knew I wasn't far off being ready to play the London Comedy Store, which was the pinnacle, as good as it got on the circuit.

In Glasgow, for my solo show at the 2007 Comedy Festival, I was offered the Stand as my venue. I knew selling two hundred tickets would be difficult, but not impossible, given how many great gigs I'd had in the place, and as reviews and articles tipping me for the top and as 'the next big thing' were now appearing in newspapers and magazines.

I paid for posters to be designed and printed in a digital printshop, and I went around nearly every pub in the city centre, asking if I could stick one on their wall.

I printed off smaller ones to give to my Uncle Kevin, to hand out to passengers in his taxi, and I got a website up and running, a cheap, basic one. But it was a collection of all my reviews and a gig list, which was now looking impressive as I'd broken through at all but a few of the big clubs in the UK and now Ireland.

The show sold out. Over two hundred people had come out to see me, and in the place where it had all started. I'd been working towards the show for a year, since my debut solo show, upstairs at the Universal.

The solo shows were still very much the exception and the comedy circuit was my life, but it was the thought of doing the full-length solo shows, telling stories and feeling like I was doing what real comedians did, that got me through the long car journeys, the rail-replacement buses, the cancelled gigs, the quiet gigs, the hard gigs, the rough gigs, the sleeping on relative strangers' couches, the eerie and damp-smelling B&Bs with their 9.30 a.m. check-out times and the full days spent trying to occupy yourself in shit-hole towns.

I was travelling, a lot, and I find it pretty difficult to separate years at this point in the story as I sort of disappeared into my own bubble, the bubble of being a jobbing comedian where it's easy to become lazy and presume that, just because you feel permanently exhausted, you're working hard.

I'd be home maybe once or twice a week; my mum would do my washing for me and I'd pack my bag again. I didn't know if I could keep up the intensity but if I couldn't do it in my early twenties then when could I?

The positives outweighed the negatives, by far, and it was a great life but I sensed that I could become like some of the veteran club comics if I didn't keep writing new material and making myself laugh, if I didn't think to the future and outside of my own head.

You can be the most naturally funny person out there but, in stand-up, laziness will kill you eventually.

I knew I had to produce an hour of new material every year, at least, for my annual solo shows in Glasgow, so this meant that even on the nights I was home, I'd pop into the Stand and try out some new ideas at Red Raw. It was a good discipline and having a new joke that I was proud of would always give me a lift and a reason to look forward to the next gig.

I'd started to listen to Billy Connolly when I was on the road.

I'd seen most of his stand-up shows but now I was enjoying listening to his early audio recordings, recorded in pubs in Glasgow when he was starting out.

I loved the story when he talked about the Crucifixion not taking place in Galilee, but in the Gallowgate, in the east end of Glasgow.

I don't know if that routine was funny to anyone not from Glasgow, but I hoped it was. I'd sit on trains and buses and laugh, and listen to this routine again and again.

I listened to how simple he made it all. He used the Galilee/Gallowgate similarity to get him going, but then he took the crowd with him, a crowd who knew where the joke was going, but they'd no idea how good he'd make it.

It wasn't about catching the crowd off-guard, like a magician. It was about connecting with them and being bang in the centre of yourself, talking to them directly and just getting funnier and funnier.

'And the bold yin's there, with his long hair and his casual sandals.'

I'd laugh at this line and I didn't know why I found it so funny.

There was nothing to explain, there was nothing to analyse or deconstruct. It was just funny.

When I looked out at the crowd, at the Stand in 2007 and at my solo show later in the year in the Tron Theatre in Glasgow, I'd see a range of people, young and old. They'd all come along for a laugh and because they had liked what they'd seen of me.

I was by no means well known but I was now familiar to these people.

I had to keep topping each show, and bringing fresh material, to keep them interested. I had to be prolific, as opposed to doing the same routines every weekend, for years, to people who won't remember anything you say.

I was grateful to everyone who came out, my first 'fans', and I owed them consistently good shows. I hoped one day they'd quote my lines and have a laugh to themselves, like I'd done with Connolly.

It was difficult, performing to your own crowd and doing your own show and then going back to a weekend of performing to drunken birthday parties and shouting over stag and hen nights, but this was my livelihood and the solo shows were a luxury.

By now, I was well established in Scotland, and I was headlining gigs in Ireland, at places like the Roisin Dubh and the Cuba Bar in Galway as well as gigs in Cork, Dublin and, of course, one of my favourite places to perform, Belfast.

I'd regularly go to London and make money, even after paying my travel. I could do two gigs a night, rising to three and four as I reached 2008.

I no longer needed to pay for accommodation now that I had Julia and Trevor to stay with, along with another good mate, a London-based Scottish comedian, Dougie Dunlop.

I'd met Dougie at gigs and we'd got on well. I instantly found him hilarious, on stage but also off. He was a Hibernian fan and had a beautifully downbeat, but somehow infectiously cheery, nature.

Spending time with him made going to London less daunting and, again, they were some of the happiest times of my life. We'd arrive back at his old flat in Peckham around the same time from our respective gigs, and we'd sit up, having a few beers and making each other laugh, talking about football and comedy and any old shite that came into our heads.

Dougie would jokingly tell me to slow down, and laugh at how many gigs I'd do. He'd ask how I coped with all of the travelling, and I don't know how I did.

I suppose, like him, like everyone, I was so scared that someone would take everything away from me that I felt I had to be doing a gig every single night or it'd be over.

I was out on the road every night and I was now being booked for a company called Off The Kerb Productions, who ran gigs all around the UK. Off The Kerb were widely regarded as one of the biggest management companies in the UK, representing acts like Jonathan Ross, Jack Dee, Lee Evans, Michael McIntyre and Alan Carr.

My gigs for them had been going well and one of their workers, Damon Pettit, had told me they'd been keeping an eye on me and they were interested in signing me, but that they didn't think there was anything they could do for me just now. All I needed were gigs, to keep on improving, but if I was going to sign with anyone else, I was to let them know.

It was a huge boost.

It was flattering to have interested any agent, let alone the ones who rarely signed anyone and who had some serious firepower on their roster.

65

I took Damon's advice and continued gigging.

I'd attracted the attention of a woman called Kathleen Hutchison, who worked at Paramount Comedy and who was keen to get her boss along to see me, with a view to booking me for the new series of *The World Stands Up* on the Paramount Comedy Channel/Comedy Central.

For the Glasgow International Comedy Festival in 2008, I played the Stand again and this time the tickets sold out in less than a week. Kathleen came to the show, with other people from Paramount, and they told me they would love to have me on their show.

There had been TV people and producers coming to my gigs and I didn't know how to handle it, or what they wanted. I was being brought in for development meetings, which didn't make any sense.

They'd bring in people with ideas on how to get me on TV.

'We need to find the Kevin Bridges vehicle.'

I appreciated their efforts and the recognition but I only wanted to do stand-up. I'd feel like I was frustrating them because I didn't have a plan. Stand-up wasn't a stepping stone for me; it had changed my life and I didn't want to do anything else.

It was getting above my head and I phoned Damon. He began to take the piss out of me about my 'development meetings' and ask if I was a 'media lovey' now. 'The working-class boy from Glasgow – what will your mates say?' Damon laughed.

He told me not to get too hung up on these things, that they'd soon be on to the next guy, the next hot young property.

Damon said he'd look over my *World Stands Up* contract for me, and not take a commission. He'd do it as a favour. I'd rather he said he'd take a commission and be my agent now and handle all this stuff, all these meetings.

He told me that he was going to come to my next London show and bring his boss, Joe Norris, to see me. After Joe had seen me, they'd make a decision on whether or not to sign me.

My next London shows were on the weekend of my *World Stands Up* recording. I was playing at a comedy club in Covent Garden on the Friday and the Saturday nights, along with a comedy club called Up The Creek, which I'd need to shoot off to straight after the Covent Garden shows.

I'd maybe get a chance to meet Joe briefly, but even if I didn't, he was there to watch me perform. It wasn't about what I'd done off stage; it was what I'd done on stage.

Kathleen was excited for me and told me that, in her opinion, they were the best agents. She told me about Addison Cresswell, the man who'd started the agency in the kitchen of his flat thirty years ago, and who'd launched the careers of so many comedians.

I'd heard about Addison from a few comedians and, by their accounts, he was a fucking nutcase, but the most brutally honest, no-nonsense and smartest manager in comedy.

He was a self-styled cockney wide boy, with a bit of Del Boy Trotter in him and a bit of Tony Soprano. He liked to party and there were stories about him being threatened by gangsters and being thrown out of artist and industry bars at the Edinburgh Festival.

As much as he was wild and a full-on personality,

everyone admitted they'd love to have him as a manager as he had a great mind and looked after his acts like they were family.

I couldn't imagine a guy like this would like me. He'd be like all the other agents who didn't understand my accent or who said I was too Scottish or too young or that my face didn't fit. I was beginning to go into my shell again, and let my own insecurities waste another fucking opportunity.

The Covent Garden gig was a disaster. The audience was fairly quiet for the compere who introduced me to open the show. I couldn't get up and running, and I couldn't get the feeling of performing to Joe and Damon out of my head.

I got laughs, but it wasn't the rip-roaring performance I wanted them to see. I wished they'd been at the Comedy Store, the King's Head, or even that they were coming to my show at Up The Creek, one of the liveliest and best clubs on the London circuit.

I'd blown it. I'd walked on and performed to two people, rather than the audience who'd paid their money. I'd played to the judges again. Damon shook my hand and told me not to worry about it. Joe shook my hand as well, briefly introducing himself, and they both made a move.

I felt flat and I sat, miserable, on the Tube and then the DLR line out to Greenwich, for my second gig. I went for a walk around the area, to clear my head and focus on the next gig.

I couldn't afford to fuck this one up as well. Joe would know that you can't judge a comedian on one bad gig – he was too experienced for that – and Damon would explain that I was usually much better.

The Up The Creek gig was brilliant and the crowd went wild, at the same material, but this time I'd delivered to them and enjoyed the moment. It was a gig again and not an audition.

Of all the gigs I'd done, I'd fucked up the one that could have landed me an agent.

I recorded *The World Stands Up* on the Sunday night. It went well, but, again, it wasn't a classic.

I'd been told, by Frankie, who'd done the same show on his way up, that the audience would be well lit up and a little self-conscious, meaning the atmosphere wouldn't be like a comedy club.

It was my TV debut.

I couldn't say I enjoyed it, but I suppose I was still feeling low from the whole weekend.

I went back to Dougie's and told him about my recent run of poor form and how I'd slipped out of the title race after a few dodgy results.

We laughed about it.

Dougie reminded me that I was a twenty-one-year-old from Clydebank, who was making a living out of stand-up comedy. Things were going great; it was a long journey and this was a temporary blip.

He was right. I had it good.

I was now being booked to headline the Stand comedy clubs in Glasgow and Edinburgh, the Glee Clubs in Birmingham and Cardiff, the Laughter Lounge in Dublin, the Hyena Comedy Café in Newcastle and loads of Jongleurs clubs.

I was now headlining almost everywhere I played. There was more positive press than ever, and the reviews were getting even more effusive in their praise. Every time I'd get home, to Clydebank, my mum and dad would have new newspaper cuttings to show me.

Kevin Bridges is currently sweeping aside all before him, with a raft of fresh material every time you see him. Not just a talent to watch, but one to envy, too.

Let's just call his talent frightening.

The reviews would seem a bit over the top, but I knew my mum and dad were proud and they'd been in it, with me, from the very beginning.

66

My set on *The World Stands Up* was broadcast and it was well received. I don't think the ratings figures were ever great, but it was noted by other people in TV and by the channel itself.

I was offered a short spot, a 'half spot', on the Comedy Store's TV show, also on Paramount/Comedy Central.

Every other act was doing fifteen minutes, but I was to do seven and a half, which was strange, but I didn't have an agent to question this and it was better than not being on the show at all.

As it was in the Comedy Store, it felt far more like how a comedy gig should be, as opposed to *The World Stands Up*.

I had a good gig, and before I left I was stopped by Damon, who'd been down at the recording with the rest of the staff from Off The Kerb, everyone except Addison.

Joe was there again and asked if I could meet with them, the following day, at a café near their office in Islington, north London.

I had a train to Cardiff booked in the morning, for a student gig, but I felt it would be wise to take the hit and book another ticket.

The following morning I was signed to Off The Kerb.

There were no contracts but a handshake, and a promise, a mutual promise, that they would work hard for me – but only if I worked hard, gigged constantly and wrote material, would it work.

They couldn't create a superstar, but they could make sure talent was rewarded and given opportunities. Ultimately, it was up to the act what they wanted and how much they wanted it.

Everyone I'd met at Off The Kerb seemed pretty normal. They didn't dress like powerful comedy-industry people, and they didn't talk any different from your average down-to-earth Londoner or, in Damon's case, Brummie.

They always met their acts in the same north London, greasy-spoon café, and the whole company was run from their 'offices', which were the basement floor of Addison's townhouse.

I hadn't imagined that an agency that looked after as high-profile acts as they did would be run from a room so small, in a basement.

They weren't amateurs, though; they knew the comedy industry and every one of them had been there for years. Danny Julian had been working on a fruit and vegetable stall in Peckham when he was nineteen, near where Addison was living at the time, and was asked one morning if he wanted a job answering the phone, for double his wages.

He's been there ever since.

I asked if I'd get to meet Addison, but I was told he'd hear about me and he'd see me soon enough. It was answers like this that added to the aura and the mystery of the man.

For the first year, not a lot different happened.

I continued to gig, averaging around twenty-five gigs per month, and I was venturing further afield now and regularly boarding planes to do shows overseas, playing the Comedy Store's tours of the Middle East and the Far East and then club gigs all over Europe.

Travelling to these places helped me develop better material, material that was universal, and I found that my accent wasn't actually a problem, people even seemed to like it.

I was told that if I were to get ahead, I'd need to perform a solo show at the Edinburgh Fringe.

I'd thought about it before, but I knew guys who'd lose in excess of £10,000 every August, just to perform to a handful of people, every night for a month, in the hope that a TV executive or a casting agent would maybe see their show and hand them some sort of deal.

That seemed insane to me, and even if I had £10,000 to pay for the extortionate venue-hire costs, a publicist, a flyering team, and posters for my face to be on the side of taxis and buses, I doubt I would have wanted to risk it.

Off The Kerb told me that I wouldn't lose anything.

I wouldn't make much, but it was about raising my profile.

I agreed.

My show was booked in for August 2009 at the Pleasance Dome's fifty-seat capacity 'Joker Dome'.

It seemed daunting to me, performing for almost an entire month in the same venue, and I'd seen how the Edinburgh Festival changed people.

Journalists would reign supreme for a month, knowing they had all the power and that every star on a review was precious to the poor bastards who'd thrown £10,000 behind their show.

I loved performing in Edinburgh and I'd done shows there since I was seventeen. I'd performed in *Trainspotting*-type pubs and met the real people.

I liked the city, but in August it became full of artists, performers, publicists, judges; everyone had an opinion, everyone would talk about how exhausted they were and how much pressure they were under.

A new elitist form of comedy would dominate, and simply trying to be funny for an hour was almost frowned upon.

I wasn't looking forward to the run but I knew I'd have a good show and all I could do was try to make whoever came to see me laugh.

Before the Fringe, I had solo shows at the Leicester Comedy Festival in February, where I played to thirty people in total, over two nights, and then, for the fourth consecutive year, the Glasgow International Comedy Festival, where I was offered the King's Theatre but declined, because of its 1,700 capacity, which seemed unrealistic.

I was booked instead for two nights at the 350-seat Òran Mór Theatre. The shows sold out quickly and there was a bit of a buzz about me at the festival.

I'd been interviewed in the run-up to it, about being one of the 'best-kept secrets' in Scottish comedy, and they'd written about how 2009, with my first Fringe show, could be my year.

I'd watched Michael McIntyre on *Friday Night with Jonathan Ross*, on a rare night off at home, and he'd mentioned that he was going to be travelling the country, hosting comedy shows featuring the best new comedy talent.

He specified that by new, he meant new to a TV audience and not total newcomers. I phoned my agent, my main contact at Off The Kerb, Verity, on the Monday, and asked if I was being considered for this.

I was told that my name had been put forward, by Danny Julian, who was now well established as one of the main men at Off The Kerb, and by the producers of the Comedy Store show, Cameron Banks and Anthony Caveney, who were also to be the producers of *Michael McIntyre's Comedy Roadshow*.

There was to be an episode in Edinburgh and, obviously, they'd like a Scottish comedian who wasn't well known but who was ready. I didn't hear anything, for days and then weeks.

I was hosting a midweek show at the Stand in Edinburgh one night, in the run-up to my Òran Mór shows, and another comedian, who was known for his TV work in Scotland, popped in to run through his set for a BBC One show at the Edinburgh Playhouse that he was doing with Michael McIntyre.

That was it. Someone else had got the gig.

I was disappointed, but the man who'd got it had been nothing but a lovely guy to me every time we'd met and I wished him well.

I phoned Verity the next day and she told me she'd tried her best.

It wasn't to be.

Fuck it.

I had my two nights at the Òran Mór to work towards.

I needed to make these the best shows I'd ever done.

I wanted to do the show in two forty-five-minute sections, to do ninety minutes, for the first time, to live up to the hype that was surrounding me in Glasgow, and to give the seven hundred people who'd bought tickets a great night and one that they'd tell their friends about.

I had these shows on the last Friday and Saturday of March 2009, and on the Sunday I was booked with Frankie Boyle for a double-header show at the Stand, to close the comedy festival.

We'd made it a gangster and molls theme and dress code. I can't remember why, but it meant I had to go and buy a suit.

I managed ninety minutes of material on both nights at the Òran Mór. The crowd stood up at the end and began shouting for an encore.

People would come up to me afterwards and they'd tell me they'd been crying with laughter at certain bits and how much they related to everything I'd said.

I felt like I was connecting with people and that even if I didn't ever get my big break, I could carry this on for years.

The show on the Sunday was a good laugh, and after it I ended up falling asleep backstage at the Stand, waking up on the Monday morning to a sea of bodies who'd also passed out during the comedy festival wrap party.

When I got home and charged my phone I had a voicemail from Verity, asking if I'd call her urgently.

There had been a legal problem with getting the other Scottish comedian's musical cues cleared for use on TV and the producers wanted to know if I could get myself to Edinburgh the following night, to do a fifteen-minute set at the Playhouse, that would be cut to eight minutes, for BBC One prime-time television.

I was second choice, and if I was stubborn enough maybe I'd have told them to stick it up their arse, but that would have been an act of lunacy.

Verity asked me what I was planning on wearing and suggested that maybe I should wear the suit I'd worn to the gangster party show.

I took it to the dry-cleaner's, as I'd slept in it the night before, and I asked if they could have it back with me, in a presentable condition, for the following day.

I picked up my suit as arranged and off I went, from Singer train station in Clydebank, to Queen Street station in Glasgow and then on to the train to Edinburgh Waverley.

A route I'd travelled so many times over the past five years, but now it was to the Playhouse, to play in front of over three thousand people and a TV audience of fuck knows how many.

On the train I listened to music and stared out of the window. I was nervous, naturally, but I felt good.

I was in good form and still on a high from my weekend shows.

I'd blown a few potential breaks before but I knew I wouldn't tonight.

I'd played Jongleurs in Edinburgh so many times. It is only a few yards away from the Playhouse, and I'd stood outside Jongleurs, gathering my thoughts before going in to perform, looking at the Playhouse and imagining getting a chance to perform there one day.

My dreamy gazing would usually be interrupted by a woman dressed in a nurse's uniform, with L-plates on her skirt and an inflatable cock and balls in her hands, asking me if I had a light, but not tonight.

I might never play a venue like this again; it was my big moment, and I had to enjoy it and give it my best.

My mum and dad couldn't make it, partly down to the short notice, but I reminded them that they'd get to see the gig when it was on TV.

I don't think I need to write about how the show went, as I'd imagine that this is the point where most of you reading this first heard of me.

It went well, really well. As I walked off the stage a man with a sharp suit, a Rolex watch and expensive-looking glasses was waiting in the wings, talking rapidly to one of the side-of-stage production crew, and then, as he'd seen me go to walk past, he moved and stood in front of me.

'Kevin, finally we meet. Addison.'

I shook his hand just as I heard Michael McIntyre shout my name and the crowd cheering, rapturously.

Addison put his hand around my shoulder, like we were two lifelong buddies about to have a heart-to-heart.

We walked from the side of the stage and down flights of stairs, past the dressing rooms.

I didn't know where I was going, and I don't think Addison did either, but I was too busy trying to answer the questions that were being rapidly fired at me in this comical, south-London-geezer accent.

'Do you want a drink, you having a drink? Come and have a fucking drink. Of course you're having a fucking drink, you're from fucking Glasgow, for fuck's sake ... I know people from Glasgow, the big bloke, what's his fucking name?'

We appeared to be lost backstage at the Playhouse but Addison didn't seem to care and nothing was interrupting his performance.

His conversation was jumping between subjects, and I was struggling to follow the thread and how he'd gone from talking about drinking with Hibernian casuals to meeting Puff Daddy.

'I hadn't fucking heard of him. Poof Daddy? Who the fuck calls themselves Poof Daddy? His bodyguard was ready for fucking killing me ...'

I didn't know where we were headed, and I was still trying to process everything that was happening.

I'd just walked off stage after performing to thousands of people, I was pumping with adrenalin and now I felt like I was on an acid trip, walking through these dark, ancient-looking corridors with a character from a Film 4-style British gangster movie.

Addison finally acknowledged he didn't know where he was going. He looked around, continuing his story and getting more animated. 'So the band are due on stage and this fucking lorry still hasn't arrived ...'

Without any hesitation or concern that an alarm might go off and the building be evacuated, he pushed down this big metal bar and a door swung open.

We were out on the streets and in the alleyway near the Playhouse stage door, where I'd arrived hours before, on my own and in silence. I was now walking out, trying to piece together what was going on.

I began to laugh at Addison's stories when I was finally taking them in and I could tell he was enjoying making me laugh as we walked up the hill, towards the main entrance to the Playhouse.

Addison flashed his Executive Producer pass at a few security guards and we arrived in a private box, full of producers and directors from the BBC, who were watching the rest of the show on monitors and taking notes.

A room full of the same kind of people in whose company I'd always felt out of place and inferior, but now I had back-up.

'Here he is, Kevin Bridges! What about that for a set? Twenty-fucking-two years old!'

Addison didn't stop speaking the whole night, and no one seemed perturbed. Everyone knew him and knew this was nothing out of the ordinary.

He was loud and he was in your face, but there was a charm behind it all. He genuinely loved what he did and the thrill of making big shows and watching his acts get ahead.

The show went on air on 6 June 2009, whilst I was on stage, headlining the Stand, again, in Edinburgh.

I left the Stand and walked towards Waverley Station. I turned my phone on and it felt like it was going to explode.

I had text messages and voicemail messages from everyone, from my mum and dad, from John, from my Uncle George and my Uncle Kevin, from Tony, Jamie, George, Doc, Halpin and the rest of them, and from Dougie, Frankie, Big Gary, Julia, Eva and all of my other friends in comedy.

I knew things were about to go pretty wild and I started to panic, but there was nothing I could do. I didn't know what to do next except continue as normal. I had a solo show in

471

Leith the following night, which hadn't sold all that well, but that changed the following morning. The show felt strange, and I felt like I was being seen differently.

I was 'that guy from the telly' now.

Something I'd have to get used to.

On the Monday Addison phoned me, with the news about the viewing figures. Five million people had seen me and it was a record for a stand-up show.

I began to speak to Addison every day. I'd meet up with him and we'd discuss the next move.

I felt it was right that I honoured all of my club bookings. The clubs had been good to me and I'd worked hard to get in, so I wanted to go out with a bit of class.

Addison agreed, but he wanted to come and see my show at the Edinburgh Festival, to see if I had more material of the same standard, with a view to doing *Live at the Apollo*, as the BBC were keen to see more of me, and then, hopefully, a national tour in 2010.

I had to work and push myself, yet again. I had to write and the demand for material was going to be high.

My Edinburgh Fringe show sold out in under an hour, the entire run.

Extra shows were added in bigger venues and I was doing two shows a night to cope with the demand.

I was nominated for the Edinburgh Comedy Awards Best Newcomer Award.

Addison came to one of the extra shows, in a small Porta-kabin venue at the Pleasance Courtyard.

It wasn't ideal, but I had to forget he was there and not make the mistake I'd made over a year ago, when Joe had come to see me.

I riffed with the crowd in the intimate venue, like I'd done in the clubs. It was a gig, it didn't matter who was in or how much pressure was on me. The guy who'd sold out his entire debut run in under an hour. The critics would write what they wanted; I couldn't control that.

I was a stand-up comedian, a professional stand-up comedian, and I made sure the crowd were entertained.

I could just about make out Addison from the stage, towards the end, and I saw him wiping his eyes, laughing and applauding.

I couldn't imagine, from what I'd seen of him, that he could sit and watch a show for an hour, but then I didn't yet know the man.

We went for dinner after the gig, and there was a much calmer and more laid-back side to him. He asked me if I felt I was ready for *Live at the Apollo* and for a national tour.

The show was almost there; I'd need more material but that would only come if I kept going to new-material nights and forcing it out of myself.

Addison suggested that we finish the UK tour with a home-coming show in Glasgow, to be recorded for DVD, at either the King's Theatre, or at the SECC arena – to ten thousand people.

The idea of playing to ten thousand people was inconceivable to me and I told Addison that the King's Theatre was far less terrifying.

He came to see me a few more times and he became utterly convinced that I could do the SECC arena show and that the DVD would look great.

I was coming round to the idea, but I knew the thought of it would haunt me every night in the lead-up and I didn't think there would be ten thousand people who'd buy tickets.

'You write the show and I'll worry about the rest.'

Addison then jokingly suggested a bet.

'A hundred pounds. If we sell out the SECC, you owe me a hundred, and if we don't, I owe you a hundred.'

I was still gambling at the time. I laughed and then agreed.

Fuck it. The only way I could improve and hit the top was if I frightened myself to this extent.

There were days when, under the pressure, I struggled to get up in the mornings, and times when Addison would ask if I felt I was being pushed too much.

I told him no and that I'd be fine. I thought of all the shite gigs I'd done, all the soul-destroying nights that hurt at the time, but which I'd come through.

I didn't want Addison seeing me as a young comic, as a twenty-two-year-old, as someone to go easy on, as one for the future.

I was ready.

I knew I could do it and I'd write and try new routines every week.

I'd look through all of my notepads, my collections of thoughts from the past six years, which I brought to life on stage at the Stand in Glasgow, in the run-up to the show on 28 May 2010, and which became the routines that people still shout and quote to me in the street to this day.

Addison told me he'd introduced Jonathan Ross, whom he also managed, to my stand-up and that he'd like to have me on his chat show to talk about my career to date and how far I'd come since deciding to give it a shot not long after my seventeenth birthday.

The show was recorded on Thursday nights and the only Thursday night I had free, due to my tour commitments, was the night before the SECC show.

I'd be coming off stage after performing to ten thousand people at the same time that I was making my chat-show debut, to a TV audience of millions.

I felt ill thinking about it and I'd look at myself in the mirror and imagine how much easier it would have been if I'd got stuck in at school or college and landed myself a normal job.

I could still be the funny guy in the pub every weekend and there would be no pressure, no waking up at night unable to get back to sleep after a nightmare about ten thousand people booing and my teeth flying out of my mouth as I tried to speak.

Addison standing at the side of the stage, throwing the towel in for me, his hand round my shoulder, escorting me out of the building, the budding young contender, floored, in the first minute of the first round, blowing his shot at the title.

I had to have these thoughts in order to get rid of them, to drive them out of my head, counteracting them with positivity.

This was my night.

I'd probably done close to a thousand gigs and this was another one.

It was big, but with ten thousand people, somebody was going to laugh.

Five people in a pub didn't offer such guarantees and, even then, I could sometimes do okay.

The show had sold out and tickets were going on eBay for well over the odds. I owed Addison £100.

I stood in the wings, watching the audience arriving, wondering who they were, what their story was.

I watched the pastiche *Sopranos* intro video we'd filmed a few weeks before, from the side of the stage. The stage I'd be walking on to, alone, in under a minute.

I thought of how I'd created all of this, lying alone in my bedroom in our house in Hardgate.

I thought of how disappointed I'd be if I'd got stuck in at school or college and landed myself a job, if I'd never felt fear like this, if I'd been too scared to go for my dreams.

I thought of my mum never working again, after all the years supporting us, all on her own.

I thought of my dad, who had given me everything in his strength to keep me going through the nights that were difficult, the nights I'd phone him from train stations, having had a tough gig and missed my train, when I'd feel exhausted and demoralized by it all, with hours to kill in places I'd never heard of.

I thought of John who had come to so many of my shows and picked me up when they hadn't gone well and celebrated with me when they had. He was out there with his friends and I wanted him to have a brilliant night.

I thought of my grandparents, whom I hardly knew, but who were in my heart.

I began to feel emotional as the video stopped.

I thought of the ten thousand people who'd paid good money to see me and who were here for a laugh.

'Get out there and fucking enjoy it. Do yourself proud,' Addison said, smiling and shuffling outside, to watch the gig.

He gave me a look, acknowledging that these were the nights we lived for.

I felt good, I felt funny.

'Ladies and gentlemen, please welcome Kevin Bridges.'

I don't remember much after the sound of ten thousand people cheering. It was an out-of-body experience, but I knew I had to keep calm and deliver my opening line, like always.

I got my first laugh and I was off.

Ninety minutes later, I walked off the stage. The crowd

were on their feet and Addison was waiting backstage, euphoric and grabbing me, jumping up and down.

'The empties, the empties, what the fuck is an empty! I fucking loved it. The guy trying on the jackets, that's fucking me. You've done it, you've fucking done it!'

Addison began frantically looking around, looking for a production runner to go out into the arena and find my mum and dad and bring them backstage to watch my Jonathan Ross interview, which was about to start.

I watched my dad and Addison, two guys who had more faith in me than I'd sometimes had in myself, standing together, talking and laughing.

I heard Addison promise my dad that he'd look after me, that this was just the start of everything and that he'd treat me like a son.

'This industry is full of cunts, but don't worry, I'm Mr Cunt.'

I'd say it was this night and the months that followed that most of you became aware of me and my comedy so it is here that I'll finish up.

Three days after the euphoria of the SECC and the prestige of appearing on *Friday Night with Jonathan Ross*, I was back on the road, being sick at the side of a motorway somewhere between Dublin and Kilkenny having eaten a dodgy chicken wrap in a service station whilst en route to perform at a comedy festival.

The show goes on and maybe one day I'll be back with more stories.

For now, though, I thank you for your time.

I dedicate this book to the memory and the family of my friend and manager, Addison Cresswell.

Addison passed away suddenly on 23 December 2013.

It breaks my heart to write this and to write this book knowing that he will never read it, or read, in my own words, how much I thought of him.

Addison was a one-off and every minute in his company was an event.

He was a man worthy of several books, devoted to his own life and his own ascendancy into the man he became, a man who instantly sparked life into everyone he met.

Every single morning and every single night I think about the man who changed my life, and I don't think it will ever really sink in that he's gone.

He was true to the promise he made to my dad and he treated me like a son.

I hope to continue and do you and your family proud, big man.

As I write this, I can hear your voice shouting at me:

'Fucking hell, leave it on a fucking cheerier note than that!'

I don't feel skilled enough as a writer to describe a man for whom I had as much admiration as Addison, but there is a Mark Twain quote that I think resonates.

Keep away from people who try to belittle your ambitions. Small people always do that, but the really great make you feel that you, too, can become great.

Thank you for reading, and I'll see you all on the road.
Live forever,
Kevin

Addison, collecting his money upfront,
with my mum, my dad and me, after
the SECC show in 2010.

Acknowledgements

I usually skip this bit of a book, the bit where the author thanks the publisher, the publicist, agents and all these people you don't know, but if you bear with me, I'll keep it brief.

Firstly, I have only written this book up until May 2010, when I walked on stage in front of 10,000 people, at the SECC arena in Glasgow, so I'd like to mention, first of all, those who I didn't get to know until after this point.

Special thanks to my agent Rick Hughes, for all of his continued advice, support and for being an all-round top bloke.

To Joe, Danny, Damon, Flo, Fay, Tom, Andy, Ann, Ashley and everyone else at my management company, Off The Kerb Productions.

To Verity Overs-Morrell, who has since left Off The Kerb but who looked after me for four great years. Thanks Vito, and all the best to you and the family.

To Alex Clarke from Penguin UK, for first approaching me about the possibility of writing this book.

I didn't think I had a book in me until I started writing, so sincerest thanks to Alex for what has been a genuinely enjoyable experience and to everyone else at Penguin UK, who have been a pleasure to work with.

To James Rampton, for his positivity and great feedback all through the writing process.

Special mentions here to my mum & dad and my big brother, John, the only ones who have been there from the very beginning and to whom I hope my love and admiration for comes through in these pages.

To all of my friends who I grew up with and who are still my friends to this day, and to most of the new ones, who are all right as well.

To everyone who has ever made me laugh and to everyone who has inspired me: Billy Connolly, Frank Skinner, Richard Pryor, Noel Gallagher, Irvine Welsh and many more.

A very special mention to my girlfriend, Susan, who doesn't feature in this book but who is lying beside me, watching something on her iPad and growing increasingly frustrated with me interrupting her to ask what she thinks I should write here.

I don't imagine it's easy being in a relationship with a comedian – an insecure clown who spends half his year on the road and the other half at home, struggling to function in the real world and constantly asking 'is this funny?', looking for approval on new ideas for jokes.

So I'd like to thank to Susan for her patience, but above all for her love, constant support, understanding and for being someone who has been there with me and for me through so much.

A special mention here as well to Susan's family: to Maureen, Auntie Susan, Neil, Jacqueline and baby James.

And a mention here, of course, to my dog, Annie, who makes me laugh, every single day.

Finally, thanks to you, for opening this book and giving it a life, and to anyone who has ever laughed at any of my jokes.

There, that's all.
Enjoy.
Kevin